Lulu Rumsey Wiley

The Sources and Influence of
the Novels of

Charles Brockden Brown

by

Lulu Rumsey Wiley

Author of "Bible Music" and
"Children and Youths of the Bible"

Vantage Press, Inc.
Publishers New York

21314

Table of Contents

Preface

Frankly admitting and deprecating the amateurishness of a thesis on the same subject at the University of Southern California, the author has rewritten all parts of the former treatise and amplified the subject to include a very considerable amount of new material.

A complete bibliography of the works of Charles Brockden Brown is appended. It can not be free from errors because of the variations in punctuation, capitalization, spelling and other details, even in the titles of his novels in the several editions, given by different bibliographers. The chief bibliographies of Brown's works consulted are in the Library of Congress Catalogue, the English Catalog, the British Museum Catalog, the Bibliotheca, the Henry E. Huntington Library and by the authors—Wegelin, Loshe, Foley and Dunlap. A second bibliography lists the majority of the works consulted.

In the foot-references, only the authors' names and short titles of books are given; fuller details will be found in the bibliographies. *Ibid.*, the same, is used for additional references to a given work on the same page, and *op. cit., opus citatum,* in place of the extensive title of *The Life of C—B—Brown . . . with Selections* by William Dunlap.

Dunlap makes the statement: "The plan of these volumes, and the proposals for their publication were laid before the public without the knowledge of the writer of the biography."
He does not name the planner of the work; but it is given as Allen by Fred Lewis Pattee in *The First Century of American Literature.* Dunlap's "Life" is the basis for facts about Brown, used by most students and critics of him and his works.

Permission has been granted by the publishers of all copyrighted books, if direct quotations are made. If there occurs an oversight, it is wholly unintentional. Particular thanks are expressed for material "Reprinted from Loshe, *The Early American Novel,*" and from Clark, *Charles Brockden Brown: A Critical Biography,* by permission of Columbia University Press; to The Macmillan Company for permission to quote from the Introduction of *Edgar Huntly* by David Lee Clark and from other works; to Houghton Mifflin Company for permission to quote the essay: "Fanaticism" by Whittier and from Higginson & Boynton's *A Reader's History of American Literature;* and to Harper & Brothers for permission to quote from Matthews, *Aspects of Fiction*.

The author of this book will be glad to have corrections and criticisms made of the material in the body of the work and in the bibliographies. Of course, old spellings and other irregularities, different from modern usage, are retained in all direct quotations.

Lulu Rumsey Wiley
4202 *S. E. 16th Ave.*
Portland 2, Oregon.

Introduction

The literary and political history of what is now the United States of America, up to and including the lifetime of Charles Brockden Brown, is usually divided into two periods, designated as the Colonial (1607-1765) and the Revolutionary (1765-1812). The principal productions of the Colonial period represent mainly English culture, rather than American, and contain chiefly descriptions of the New World, stories of its colonization and erudite discussions of Biblical and theological subjects by the leaders of the religious sects that found an asylum here. In the Revolutionary period, the awakening in the American colonies of a spirit of remonstrance against English misrule, the drift of sentiment towards separation from England, the long, exhausting war for independence and the establishment of a republic found expression in the language and ideals of public liberty.

Literature images the life of a people—its acts, thoughts and emotions. That of the first period reveals American life dominated primarily by religious passion and was expressed in the literary forms inherited from the mother country; the literature of the second period reveals the same life dominated almost completely by political passion—passion for American rights,—and it created for itself new literary types more nearly original and distinctive of American thought and feeling—popular oratory, political pamphlets and official documents. Mingled with the religious and political kinds was that literature, always more or less in evidence, describing the environments of life and humane projects, such as Franklin fostered and which have been an essential part of the national writings, including the novels of the author under consideration.

The writers of both these periods portrayed the customs and standards of their own time, in industry, society and morals, with a realism and a faithfulness which can scarcely be appreciated now. Many of their writings were immature, bigoted and inelegant. Yet within the elaborate metrical compositions are glimpses of the love of nature and romance against a background of native scenery:

within the scholastic, theological treatises and sermons are convictions of religious virtues and freedom of thought; within the discourses on homely subjects are the beginnings of useful science; and within the patriotic productions are principles of national conduct. Later authors took these elements and organized them into an effective, artistic American literature, whose character is determined in each era by the kind of people, the historic happenings and the surroundings.

The life-span of Charles Brockden Brown (1771-1810) was almost co-extensive with the Revolutionary period and he combined in his writings both political literature, such as flourished in this period, and the literature of the ever-present general current. To understand his novels in a complete sense, one must investigate as far as possible the trains of influence that had acted upon the author previous to the time of his writing, the influences that were in effect at that time and the resulting influence of his works. Dunlap, Brown's biographer, quoted a friend who said,

"in the life of a literary man character is biography. . . . The *incidents* of an author are his ideas, and those who look for more than these in the history of an author, must expect to find what they deserve—disappointment. . . . Incident . . . means fairly this, a dispassionate recital of the thoughts which passed in the mind of C. B. B."[1] The present writer would rather agree with Carlyle that the object of biography is

"In one word, what and how produced was the effect of society on him; what and how produced was his effect on society. He who should answer these questions . . . would . . . furnish a model of perfection in Biography."[2]

As interwoven and numerous as are the threads of influence that combine to make up a personality, so interwoven and numerous are the influences that may be seen in the writings of an author. The chief sources of influence acting upon the life of Brown and seen again in his works proceed from personal characteristics (heredity), from environment and his personal response to it and from the literature of his day. To leave out any of these sources would greatly mislead one in the study of his novels.

---

1. Dunlap, *Life of Brown with Selections*, I, 67, 68-9.
2. Carlyle, *Essay on Burns*, par. 5.

The Sources and Influence of the Novels of

CHARLES BROCKDEN BROWN

CHAPTER I

CHARLES BROCKDEN BROWN—THE MAN

Charles Brockden Brown was born, January 17, 1771, in Philadelphia, the seat of government and the literary centre. The name Charles Brockden was inherited from a distant relative who came from England to America, probably about 1677. The story is told that he escaped to avoid the vengeance of certain unsuccessful conspirators against the Crown, whose secret conversation he had accidentally overheard. This

"old family tradition of escape from assassination . . . may have given a more lurid color to the mysterious happenings and counter-happenings in his stories. The dark closets, the movable panels in the wainscot, the trap-doors, the strange noises—might all grow out of the germ of the conspiration, and the deathly peril of an unwitting listener."[1]

A like involuntary concealment was Arthur Mervyn's in a closet of the Thetford house, where he could not help hearing a conversation. And Brown brought into his story of Stephen Calvert the same conspiracy from which his ancestor escaped, in the conspiracy of the grandfather of Stephen.

Of this relative of Brown, Franklin makes respectful mention as a "skilful conveyancer, Mr. Charles Brockden,—the scrivener; . . . I drew up the proposals (for a public library), got them put into form by our great scrivener Brockden."[2]

Brown's father, Elijah, was descended from one of the English immigrants who came to America (Pennsylvania) to find freedom from the persecutions in the mother country under Charles II. His mother was Mary Armit, daughter of Joseph Armit, a merchant of Philadelphia. Their children were Joseph, who died in infancy,

---

1. Mitchell, *American Lands and Letters*, I, 184.
2. Franklin, *Autobiography*, 94, 95.

James, Joseph, Armit, Charles, Elijah and Jane Elizabeth. Charles loved his home and had congenial relations with his brothers, especially James, who resided in England, Joseph, the eldest brother, according to Dunlap, who resided in North Carolina, and Armit. Several of his letters, still extant, were written to them, some of which will be cited hereafter. Brown's ancestors in both lines were members of the Society of Friends of Truth, or Quakers, a class staunch and enobled through persecution abroad and oppression at home, because of having no active part in the Revolution, in whose meetings silence was equal with speech and women equal with men.

Charles was brought up in the Quaker faith. From that influence he received a hatred of war and of slavery, repugnance toward military service, capital punishment and suicide, his peaceful temperament, his firm faith in religion, his gentleness of manners, his meditative disposition and his spirit of benevolence,—perhaps, also, his lack of self-confidence. ". . . his mental constitution exemplified that union of sobriety with mysticism which characterizes the Friend."[1]

Charles was born a precocious child and a genius and inherited a frail constitution. He thus gave little heed to the sports of children, but spent much time over books, maps, prints and architectural designs. Almost from babyhood, his fondness for books supplied an unfailing store of enjoyment and an inexhaustible fund of knowledge to his active, acquisitive mind. When only ten years of age, it is said he was indignant when some visitor called him a boy:

"Why does he call me boy? Does he not know that it is neither size nor age, but understanding that makes a man? I could ask him a hundred questions, none of which he could answer."[2]

In *Arthur Mervyn,* Brown expresses his sense of the value of books:

"What was to be dreaded from them (physical toils) was their tendency . . . to supersede and create indifference or aversion to the only instruments of rational improvement, the pen and the book."[3]

---

1. *Cornhill Magazine* 86:494.
2. Brown, in Dunlap, *op. cit.,* I, 13.
3. *Arthur Mervyn,* II, 95.

And in *Edgar Huntly,* he annexes pleasure to learning:

"Knowledge is of value for its own sake, and pleasure is annexed to the acquisition, without regard to anything beyond. It is precious even when disconnected with moral inducements and heart-felt sympathies."[1]

Between the ages of eleven and sixteen, Brown attended the Friends' Latin School, which was conducted by Robert Proud, author of the *History of Pennsylvania,* a remarkable teacher, loved and revered by all his students. He imbued Brown and his particular friends with a love of literature and science and an enthusiasm for disinterested service to mankind. Letters in Brown's private Journal and Proud's letters in the Library of the Pennsylvania Historical Society testify to the intimate relationship between the master and these young men, in Brown's case until his death. The problems of life and speculations in science, philosophy and poetry, which interested Mr. Proud, are the ones present in Brown's early thinking and writings, for he wrote even in his school days. These five years at school leave no uncertainty as to the effectiveness of the environment there.

Often in his novels, Brown makes comments which seem to be autobiographical, interpreting his character, his person, his habits and his mode of thinking, as creative writers would naturally do. The first words of Carwin, the biloquist, may characterize the author:

"My thirst of knowledge was augmented in proportion as it was supplied with gratification. . . . My senses were perpetually alive to novelty; my fancy teemed with visions of the future, and my attention fastened upon everything mysterious or unknown."[2]

By the words of Arthur Mervyn, Brown may reveal a habit and show his acceptance of a precept of a fellow townsman, Benjamin Franklin:

"It is not my custom to defer till to-morrow what can be done to-day. The destiny of man frequently hangs upon the lapse of a minute."[3]

---

1. *Edgar Huntly,* 13.
2. Brown, *Memoirs of Carwin, the Biloquist,* bound with *Wieland,* 275.
3. *Arthur Mervyn,* II, 118.

One of the maxims prefixed to *Poor Richard's Almanac,* 1757, reads: "Never leave that till to-morrow which you can do to-day."

The statements following tell of the assiduity with which young Wieland pursued the study of a book containing the doctrine of the Camisards during his apprenticeship to a London merchant in years of "mercantile servitude": "He now supplied himself with candles, and employed his nocturnal and Sunday hours in studying this book," together with the Bible; and, of her brother at this period, Clara says, "My brother was an indefatigable student."[1] This may have been Brown's method of study, which led to the undermining of his health.

His health being endangered by a too continuous application to study, his instructor advised him to abstain from study and take long rambling excursions into the country. This species of recreation became a source of great delight to him and he continued the practice throughout his life. His habit of walking much alone gave an impulse toward idealistic musing and abstract thinking, which greatly increased the natural meditativeness of his mind. This exposition may well apply to the author of it:

"The activity of muscles is no obstacle to thought. So far from being inconsistent with intense musing, it is, in my own case, propitious to that state of mind. . . . If men be chiefly distinguished from each other by the modes in which attention is employed, either on external and sensible objects, or merely on abstract ideas and the creatures of reflection, I may justly claim to be enrolled in the second class. My existence is a series of thoughts rather than of motions. Ratiocination and deduction leave my senses unemployed. The fulness of my fancy renders my eye vacant and inactive. Sensations do not precede and suggest, but follow and are secondary to, the acts of my mind."[2]

Although to the boy the walks often proved a time for lonely, somber fancies, yet he gained impressions of fine scenery, which were used afterward in his writings.

"Thou knowest my devotion to the spirit that breathes its inspiration in the gloom of forests and on the verge of streams. I love to immerse myself in shades and dells, and hold converse with the

---

1. *Wieland,* 28, 44.
2. *Arthur Mervyn,* **II,** 49.

solemnities and secrecies of nature."[1] "I . . . weigh . . . the benefits of mental exercise, the pleasures of the woods and streams, healthful sensations, and the luxury of musing."[2]

The description of young Colvill, the teacher, fits Brown closely: "His demeanour was gentle and modest; his habits, as to sleep, food, and exercise, abstemious and regular. Meditation in the forest, or reading in his closet, seemed to constitute, together with attention to his scholars, his sole amusement and employment. He estranged himself from company, not because society afforded no pleasure, but because studious seclusion afforded him chief satisfaction. . . . His character seemed open to boundless inspection, and his conduct was pronounced by all to be faultless."[3]

One commentator said that Brown was listed as teacher one year in a certain school.

Before the age of sixteen, Brown had made verse versions of parts of The Book of Job, The Book of Psalms, and Ossian. Having learned to love the epics of Homer and Vergil, he sketched plans for three epic poems,—on Columbus' discovery of America, on Pizarro's conquest of Peru and on Cortez's expedition to Mexico, subjects which Cooper, Irving, and Parkman so successfully handled afterward in story form. His ambition began to soar early,— perhaps inspired at this time by the poem, *The Vision of Columbus,* published by Joel Barlow in Brown's sixteenth year (1787), or by the poem, *Columbus to Ferdinand* (1786), by Philip Freneau, who had contemplated an epic poem on the life and discoveries of Columbus. Brown got off to a bad start in his writing of poetry. He had written a *Poetical Address* to Dr. Franklin, his friend, and the printer substituted Washington's name for Franklin's, making it ridiculous. A curious incident happened a few years later when Brown was publishing his first magazine (1799-1800). He criticized his future brother-in-law's Ossianic poem, *The Death of Washington.* The poet was John Blair Linn. During the same period Brown was occupied in drawing practical architectural plans, in inventing a species of shorthand writing for his own use and in the study of French, unassisted except by books, that he might gain a first-hand knowledge of French literature.

---

1. *Edgar Huntly,* 97-8.
2. *Arthur Mervyn,* II, 126.
3. *Ibid.,* I, 187.

Much of Brown's learning may be discovered from the sources insinuated into his novels, classical largely, which he takes for granted as authoritative. One cannot study them without being reminded again and again of their literary background.

Clara Wieland says of her brother: "In his studies he pursued an austerer and more arduous path . . . the son was enriched by science and embellished with literature . . . (for the temple) from an Italian adventurer . . . my brother had purchased a bust of Cicero . . . dug up . . . at Modena. . . . The authors whom he read were numerous; but the chief object of his veneration was Cicero. . . . He was never tired of conning and rehearsing his productions. . . . He was very scrupulous in selecting a true scheme of pronunciation for the Latin tongue . . . he was diligent in setting and restoring the purity of the text. . . . For this end, he collected all the editions and commentaries that could be procured . . . his passion for Roman eloquence was countenanced and fostered by his friend Pleyel. . . . He was much conversant with the history of religious opinions,"

the Camisards, the Albigenses, or French Protestants, the disciples of Zinzendorf, the Calvinistic inspiration, the Quakers and the Catholics, being mentioned. "My brother's skill in Greek and Roman learning was exceeded by that of few,"—Cluentius, the Daemon of Socrates, the dramas of Apostolo Zeno and extracts from Latin and Greek poets, being named.
"To this was to be ascribed a design in which his pen was at this period engaged, of collecting and investigating the facts which relate to the mysterious personage, the Daemon of Socrates," referring, one would think, to Brown's having studied the same "stages" to get at the principles underlying them.

Doubtless Brown was familiar with the Daemon of Socrates in his investigation of psychology and science. The daemon, or genius, is a relic of the Dark Ages and
"is akin to those immediate stages of psychical life which we know under the names, somnambulism, dreaming, premonition, hypnotism, and is a return of the conscious to instinct—the transplanting, as it were, of the augury from external appearance to internal impression" (Universal Encyclopedia).

Another source which may have influenced Brown in his predeliction for scientific phenomena and in his final choices was the book of his Puritan countryman, Cotton Mather.

"The Wonders of the Invisible World: Observations as well Historical as Theological, upon the Nature, the Number, and the Operations of Devils. Some Accounts of the Grievous Molestations, by Daemons, and Witchcrafts which have lately annoyed the Country. . . . Some Councils Directing a due Improvement of the terrible things, lately done, by the Universal, Unusual and Amazing Range of Evil Spirits," and so on, the title taking a whole page (1693).

Brown shows familiarity with various national works and travels, from which might be assembled many facts for his uncompleted *System of General Geography*:—of Germany, "A new book from Germany, exploits of Zisca, the Bohemian hero," Mettingen, Saxony, Lusatia, Prussian Wars, Leipsic, Hamburg, a German Cavalier who fell at the siege of Nice under Godfrey of Bouillon;—of Italy, the Alps of Glarus, the stone of Carrara from Italian quarries, Tuscan columns, the Della Crusca dictionary, Veneroni's grammar, "The ancient language of Italy possessed a strong affinity with the modern";—of France, "He apologized for the liberty of addressing me . . . and inquired if I understood the French language. Being answered in the affirmative," the description of the Boa in La Cepide;— of Spain, an excursion from Valencia to Murviedro, work of the deacon Marti, Catholics, "Britains . . . and Spaniards are votaries of the same Deity";—of Britain, "nations have arisen in arms, as in the case of the Stuarts"; Mrs. Fielding calls Arthur Mervyn the "penseroso" and then sings a few lines from *L'Allegro;* Arthur, when giving a sample of his penmanship, wrote a line from Shakespeare: "My poverty, but not my will, consents"; Carwin's method to halt any endeavor was to cry, "Hold! Hold!", the mode by which heaven is said by the same poet to interfere for the prevention of crimes: "Peeps through the blanket of the dark, and cries, Hold! Hold!"; Arthur says, "I shall be ranked with the story tellers of Shiraz and Bagdad"; Brown often refers to warring, living and travelling in many of the Old World countries—England, France, Spain, Italy, Germany, Prussia, Austria, Egypt, Greece, Syria and Turkey; "Travellers tell us much; Volney and Mariti would have told you nearly all I have told"; acquaintance is shown with Haller (Swiss), Linnaeus (Swedish), Petrarcha, Racine, Tacitus, Milton, Newton, Hartley.

That Brown was not given the benefit of a college training at

the University of Pennsylvania not far from his home is a matter
of regret. The prejudices of the Quakers against a higher education must have prevailed; Brown himself may have been in favor
of advanced study, though with tutors instead of in college, for
his mind was set in the paths of scientific investigation and explora-
tion in every field that would yield knowledge and curious information. He wrote continuously before his ideals were fixed. A sys-
temizing of his learning by further schooling would have caused
him automatically to have thought through the materials of his
writings and finished each work as it was begun, like the plans
of his novels, instead of trying to compose five at one time, meanwhile publishing his first magazines.

However, the boy was nearly sixteen now and, from following
one avocation after another and from that almost perfect freedom
in the pursuit of knowledge with which his unguided spirit busied
itself, it became imperative that he make choice of a profession.
Law was chosen because it promised to his zealous and generous
nature an unlimited field of usefulness, as well as a source of
income; and he was apprenticed (1787) to Alexander Wilcox, Esq.,
an eminent lawyer of Philadelphia. Although law became his
ostensible occupation, yet in reality he was indulging every whim
suggested by his love of literature, by contributing to the magazines
and writing on miscellaneous subjects. The following comment
was written by a local historian after the novelist's death:

"Mr. Brown had received an education which qualified him for the
profession which secured wealth free from the risks of commerce,—
the profession from which proceeded our statesmen, legislators, and
rulers;—yet he preferred the toilsome occupation of book-making,
from the pure love of literature, and a benevolent desire to benefit
his fellow creatures."[1]

One might apply to Brown himself the words concerning young
Wilmot:

"He was smitten with the charms of literature, and . . . refused
to engage in any of those professions which lead to riches and
honour. . . . The desk, bar, and pulpit, had no attractions for
him."[2].   Dunlap said: "Society was to him solitude, and
in solitude he found delightful converse. It was this shrinking

---

1. Simpson, *Eminent Philadelphians,* 150.
2. *Clara Howard,* 318-9.

from society; this solitude; this wrong estimate of the views, motives, and characters of mankind, which wrought so powerfully upon the mind of Brown, as to make him turn aside from the obvious path which led to competence, honour, and self-approbation."[1]

R. H. Dana the elder, a contemporary of Brown, said:

"To the speculative mind, it is a curious fact, that a man like Brown should of a sudden make his appearance in a new country, in which almost every individual was taken up in the eager pursuit of riches, or the hot and noisy contests of party politics; when every man of talents, who sought out distinction, went into one of the professions; when to make literature one's main employment was held little better than being a drone; when almost the only men who wrote with force and simplicity were some of the leader* amongst our active politicians; when a man might look over our wide and busy territory and see only here and there some self-deluded creature seated, harping on some weedy knoll, and fancying it the efflorescent mount of all the Muses.

"Did not the fact of Brown's having produced such works at such a time clearly show the power of genius over circumstances, we might be inclined to attribute to his loneliness of situation something of that solitariness, mysteriousness, and gloom, which surround all he wrote."[2]

In the first number of the *Nineteenth Century*, January, 1848, was an article entitled "The Heart Broken," a story of Brown's life, death and burial, contributed by George Lippard, who, a Pennsylvanian like Brown, born twelve years after Brown's death, no doubt having read his novels as a boy and commiserated his untimely end, ridiculed him:

"He became an—author! Yes, a miserable penster, a scribbler, a fellow who spills ink for bread! For a career like this he forsook the brilliant prospects of the bar. Yes, he set himself down in the prime of his young manhood to make his bread by his pen. At that time the cow with seven horns, or the calf with two heads and five legs, exhibited in some mountebank's show, was not half so rare a curiosity as—an American author!"[3]

---

1. Dunlap, *op. cit.*, I., 40-1.
2. Dana Sr., *Poems and Prose Writings*, II, 327.
3. Lippard, "The Heart Broken," in the Nineteenth Century 1:1, 1848, quoted by Smyth, in *Philadelphia Magazines and Their Contributors*, 236.

Possibly Lippard titled his article from a story in Irving's *Sketch Book,* "The Broken Heart." Of his typical woman who dies of a broken heart he says he fancies he can trace the symptoms of declension—disappointed love, melancholy, languor, debility, cold, consumption, death. Certainly Brown passed through all these stages. His first love, the beautiful Connecticut girl Henrietta G., while visiting in Philadelphia was betrothed and associated with him in study, she to teach him Italian and play the harpsichord to his lute and he to teach her the classics. His uncongenial law study and indecision as to his life work produced melancholy; and a predisposition toward consumption (frailty from childhood) and other contributing factors aided in the debilitating, final, fatal outcome.

Brown's self-education had been desultory; he pursued the studies that pleased him most. Painting may have been one of these, in that he contributed liberally to Isham's *History of American Painting* a few years later. Charles and two brothers, James and Armit, kept a store together until it began to fail. Charles then operated alone a mercantile store until his death, showing that he hardly depended on his literary labors to make a living. One is assured that, in the passage from *Ormond* quoted below, Brown was expressing his own opinions about the law and storekeeping in thus describing Constantia's father. After Mr. Dudley had been educated in the profession of a painter, though rather for pleasure than for profit, his father's death

"introduced an important change in his situation. It henceforth became necessary to strike into some new path, to deny himself the indulgence of his inclinations and regulate his future exertions by a view to nothing but gain. . . . The drudgery of a shop . . . was too incongenial to his disposition not to be a source of discontent. . . . The longer he endured it the less tolerable it became. . . . (Mr. Dudley then turned to law.) The task assigned him was technical and formal. He was perpetually encumbered with the rubbish of the law, and waded with laborious steps through its endless tautologies, its impertinent circuities, its lying assertions and hateful artifices. Nothing occurred to relieve or diversify the scene. It was one tedious round of scrawling and jargon; a tissue made up of the shreds and remnants of barbarous antiquity, polluted with the rust of ages, and patched, by the stupidity of modern workmen, into new deformity."[1]

The decision of Brown not to practice law (1793) grievously disappointed the members of his own family, by whom he was much beloved and who were constantly solicitous about his welfare. His going contrary to their wishes caused him to pass through the bitterest experience of his whole life. Unsatisfied in his own mind whether to follow the strong tendencies of his genius or the profession which at times seemed to be his duty and opposed by the opinion and pained silence of those whom he loved, he became harassed and dejected. He argued with his friends and made excuses to himself, to justify his course. His habitual contemplativeness was changed for the time being into the most profound melancholy and direst despair. He wrote:

"I seize any thing however weak and dubious, by which I can hope to raise myself from that profound abyss of ignominy and debasement into which I am sunk by my own reflections."[2]

"He still doubted," said Dana, "and when at last he did resolve, he felt not the relief and vigor of a resolved man; for he feared it might be the yielding of weakness, not the resolution of strength. . . . Instead of living as only one of a multitude of keen and clever men at the bar, and then dying, and being forgotten, he is going down with the history of our country as the earliest author of genius in our literature. Already this distinction is something; but it is yet to be greater, we trust. The writers of genius who have and may come up among us, instead of taking from his good name, will but bring to it fresh honor and reverence, for he will be called the father of them all."[3]

During the interval of five years from the close of his legal studies till the time of his becoming professedly an author, Brown's pen was never idle. He wrote on a variety of subjects of political and speculative interest, in both prose and verse, maintained an extensive correspondence with several of his friends and kept a minute, copious journal, not merely of the incidents and occurrences of the day, but of his thoughts, feelings and reflections. He was accustomed, also, according to Dunlap, to copy in his journal letters written and received as well as other papers. He did this

1. *Ormond,* 5-6, 16.
2. Dunlap, *op. cit.,* I, 53.
3. Dana Sr., *Poems and Prose Writings,* II, 341.

for improvement in thinking and composition and for acquiring facility in writing a correct, graceful style. He associated with a Law Society, a set of young men of excellent talents, amiable dispositions and ardent minds, for debating questions of law, over whose deliberations he presided with credit and ability. The recorded decisions, still preserved, which his office as president required him to make, bear testimony to his sagacity, sound judgment, and power of research. In such pursuits, he gained subtlety in reasoning and the plainness and gravity of style of his composition. In *Alcuin,* he thus expressed his ideal:

"I hate a lecture. I find little or no benefit in listening to a man who does not occasionally call upon me for my opinion, and allow me to canvass every step in his argument. . . . A single proof, or question, or hint, may be all that the state of the controversy, or the reflections of the speaker, suggest; but this must be amplified and iterated, till the sense, perhaps, is lost or enfeebled, that he may not fall below the dignity of an orator. Conversation, careless, and unfettered, that is sometimes abrupt and sententious, sometimes fugitive and brilliant, and sometimes copious and declamatory is a scene for which . . . I entertain great affection."[1]

During his law-study period, at the invitation of Davidson, Brown became one of the founders of a literary society, whose object was two-fold: improvement in composition and eloquence; "and in both, there is good reason to believe that Brown excelled his companions" (Dunlap). The society consisted of nine members. Brown was chosen first president and asked to read a paper setting forth the aims of the society and he did it with thoroughness and comprehension, for a sixteen-seventeen-year-old youth. Two characteristic sentences from the address follow:

"Reason is the authority which exacts our obedience; and emulation the principle that promotes our improvement. . . . to ornament the mind as well as to improve the understanding is, I think, the business of this society. With this view we have entitled it the society of Belle Lettres (sic) . . . it even comprehends science and art, within the same circle."[2]

In *The Rhapsodist,* a series of essays, contributed to the *Colum-*

---

1. Brown, "Alcuin," in Dunlap, *op. cit.,* I, 72-3.
2. Brown, Address before the Belles-Lettres Society, in Dunlap, *op. cit.,* I, 24, 26.

bian Magazine, 1789, by Brown, he betrays himself. Dunlap said:

"He presented himself to the world . . . in the character of a rhapsodist. Although the title was assumed, the character was not. . . . We behold a young and ardent mind straining after unattainable perfection, always dissatisfied with and struggling to surpass, its most successful efforts. He tells the world with what rapture he has held communion with his own thoughts amidst the gloom of surrounding woods, where his fancy has peopled every object with ideal beings, and the barrier between himself and the world of spirits, seemed burst by the force of meditation. In this solitude he feels himself surrounded by a delightful society; but when he is transported thence, and compelled to listen to the frivolous chat of his fellow beings, he then suffers all the miseries of solitude. He acknowledges, however, that his intercourse and conversation with mankind had wrought a salutary change; that he can now mingle in the concerns of life, perform his appropriate duties, and reserve that high species of discourse for the solitude and silence of his study."[1]   Similarly, Brown wrote in *Alcuin*: "When I want company, it is always at hand. My solitude is populous, whenever my fancy thinks proper to people it, and with the very beings that best suit my taste."[2]

By 1795, Brown had changed his discipleship of the Sentimentalists to the guidance of the Rationalists. Social and political speculations were rampant. In letters of 1795-6 to Dunlap, Brown wrote that he was engaged upon a didactic work of some magnitude. It was *Alcuin: A Dialogue on the Rights of Women* (1797).

It seems a strange contradiction in Brown to find that in writing to his lately freed American countrymen he should be indifferent to their new-found freedom and to their everyday life and interests. He thought that it was society that was wrong and not that there was in himself any fault or narrowness of interest. Like all high-minded youth at that time, he would free society of its defects and adapt it to the needs of human nature, which he believed could attain perfection in the right environment. Dunlap, his friend, said concerning him:

"In common with many others, he imputed to wrong causes the defects which are but too apparent in existing systems. He saw

---

1. Brown, "The Rhapsodist," in Dunlap, *op. cit.,* I, 16-7.
2. Brown, "Alcuin," in Dunlap, *op. cit.,* I, 74.

the wrong and injustice and evil which exist, and instead of attributing them to the ignorance and selfishness of individuals, he assigned as the cause the errors or inefficiency of those codes which are intended to enlighten or to restrain."[1]

Undoubtedly his theories were derived from his reading of history partly and partly from his philosophical thinking and in part from his own uneasiness under the restraint of social conventions.

Unquestionably Brown was familiar with More's *Utopia* (1516), Sidney's *Arcadia* (1580) and Bacon's *The New Atlantis* (1627). Mary Wollstonecraft in *Rights of Woman* (1792) and William Godwin in *Caleb Williams* (1794) and in *An Enquiry Concerning Political Justice,* published in America in 1796, endeavored by discussion and reasoning to improve the members of society until there would be no need of shackling laws. A curious book was discussed by a historian of the English novel—*Hermsprong* (1796) by Robert Bage. The author gives a picture of an earthly paradise among the American Indians, who spend very agreeable and innocent lives playing and singing and sleeping in the sun. This view of Indian life is quite fanciful and seems not to have influenced Brown at all, unless in subject, for he gives some wholly different views of Indians.

Several "Eutopian" plans for the relief of society, such as had been, and still were, fashionable abroad were begun by Brown, among them *Sketches of a History of Carsol,* an ideal island state, Carsol (Sardinia), continued as *Sketches of the History of the Carrils and Ormes,* in England and Italy, in which the author manifested his delight in architectural study, spending a whole day with pencil and compasses planning a castle or cathedral (Dunlap). Brown gives a wilderness of dates and personages, purporting to correlate them to real European history, and names hereafter or heretofore used—Norwalk, Huntly (Huntley), Henry, Eliza, Louisa, Mary, Catharine, Francis, Elizabeth and twins. *Memoirs of Carwin, the Biloquist* contains a utopian plan, also. The author had a liberal faith in human nature, which obtrudes itself into his novels, even after he had given up writing of such visionary projects, as in *Ormond*:

---

1. Dunlap, *op. cit.,* I, 70.

"Others, more wisely, had devoted their secret efforts, not to over-turn, but to build; that, for this end, they embraced an exploring and colonizing project. . . . What were the moral or political maxims which this adventurous and visionary sect had adopted, and what was the seat of their new-born empire,—whether on the shores of an *austral* continent, or in the heart of desert America—he carefully concealed."[1]   The "visionary sect" was probably the Illuminati.

Brown came into intimate knowledge of three literary periods: the first was classic, consisting of the classic school studies and the law, a trip through Puritanic New England and writing essays on diverse subjects and some poetry; the second (1798-1801) was in New York in the creative atmosphere among his friends, where fiction was not proscribed and where he wrote on five novels and published three of them; the third period took him back to his home, Philadelphia, where he completed his novels and continued as magazine editor and literary critic. For a few years during the first period Brown had no definite occupation, barring two years spent in a small Connecticut town practising law, except study and writing to perfect himself for a literary career and visiting and travelling about the country. From his New England trip he arrived in New York. On this temporary visit, he met Dr. Elihu Hubbard Smith, whom he had known in Philadelphia, who was now living in New York. He introduced Brown to William Dunlap and to William Samuel Johnson and later to the members of the Friendly Club after Brown had taken up his residence there (1798), just three years after his first visit. The U. S. capital had been removed from Philadelphia to Washington in 1800 and New York was becoming the centre of political society, commerce and literature. Writings were more abundant, especially poetry, society novels, many written by women, and journalism, but was probably less refined and likewise less provincial than that of Philadelphia during its pre-eminence.

During this time Brown first ventured into fiction writing, con-tributing to the *Weekly Magazine of Original Essays, Fugitive Pieces, and Interesting Intelligence,* conducted by James Watters and Company (1798-9), "The Man at Home," which ran through

---

1. *Ormond,* 209.

thirteen numbers (Feb. 3-Apr. 28, 1799), "Rights of Women," the beginnings of "Sky-Walk" and "Arthur Mervyn." *Alcuin,* published in book form earlier, now revised, was printed as the *Rights of Women* (Mar. 17-Apr. 7, 1798) in the magazine. *Arthur Mervyn* and *Sky-Walk, or, the Man Unknown to Himself* were completed to book length. An unfortunate occurrence prevented the latter from being printed. It was in type when the printer, who had undertaken to publish it at his own risk, died of the fever. The title of the romance, as explained by Brown, is a "popular corruption of Ski-Wahkee, or Big Spring, the name given by the Lenni-Lennaffee or Delawares to the district where the principal scenes of the novel are transacted."

In the prospectus of *Sky-Walk,* issued Mar. 17, 1798, Brown set forth the principles that were to animate not only this forthcoming work but all his novels:

"To the story-telling moralist the United States is a new untrodden field. He who shall examine objects with his own eyes, who shall employ the European models merely for the improvement of his taste, and adapt his fiction to all that is genuine and peculiar in the scene before him, will be entitled at least to the praise of originality. . . . He, therefore, who paints not from books, but from nature, who introduces those lines and hues in which we differ, rather than those in which we resemble our kindred nations beyond the ocean, may lay some claim to the patronage of his countrymen. The value of such works lies without doubt in their moral tendency. The popular tales have their merit, but there is one thing in which they are deficient. They are generally adapted to one class of readers only. . . . The world is governed not by the simpleton, but by the men of soaring passions and intellectual energy. By the display of such only can we hope to enchain the attention and ravish the souls of those who study and reflect. . . . A contexture of facts capable of suspending the faculties of every soul in curiosity may be joined with depths of views into human nature and all the subtleties of reasoning."[1]

The Man at Home contains fiction and essays on many subjects: yellow fever, labor, wealth, debtors, prisons, criminals, ungovernable curiosity, mysterious chests, Indians, prominent personages

---

1. Pattee, *The First Century of American Literature,* 1770-1870, 100-1.

and so on. This work is not a novel, but a series of short stories. Brown just missed being the originator of the modern short story, perfected by Poe, who benefited from Brown in certain materials and in psychological investigations, which Brown had evolved.

The members of the Friendly Club were distinguished for literature and science—writers, physicians, ministers and lawyers—the most important men in the intellectual and professional life of New York, and included "William Johnson, esq.; Doctor Edward Miller; the Rev. Doctor Samuel Miller; Doctor S(amuel) L. Mitchill; James Kent, esq. Anthony Bleecker, esq. Doctor E. H. Smith; Charles Adams, esq. John Wells, esq. W. W. Woolsey, esq. C. B. Brown, and the writer (Dunlap)."[1]

Dunlap, in whose home at Perth Amboy Brown was at times an inmate, has since celebrated the talents and virtues of his friend in a biography. Dunlap (1766-1839) was an American painter, dramatist and writer. Besides dramas, he wrote several works on art and the theatre in America and was one of the founders of the National Academy of Design.

Johnson, afterward an eminent lawyer, and Dr. Smith were the friends with whom Brown lived during his residence in New York. Smith had had a college training, which enabled him to prosecute his undertakings, first law and then medicine, in unswerving loyalty. He must have had a wholesome influence on Brown. He had a saner outlook on life; Brown had a morbid and self-condemnatory tendency toward life while adjusting himself after giving up law for literature. Both were desirous of alleviating the sufferings of mankind: Brown was to rid diseased minds of errors, fears and superstitions, which he thought would relieve bodily ailments, and Dr. Smith, to eradicate physical ills. Brown honors his friend by making him the original of the good physician in *Arthur Mervyn*, who finds Arthur ill of the fever, invites him to his home and heals him. Dr. Smith lost his life during Brown's residence with him, at twenty-seven years, the same age as Brown, by a similar benevolent act. He attempted to save the life of a stricken foreigner, an Italian physician, Scandella by name, by administering to him in his own home. The

---

1. Dunlap, *op. cit.,* I, 57.

malady that bereft Dr. Smith of his life almost proved fatal to Brown, who remained in New York out of sympathy for his friend and in the hope of giving assistance to the fever sufferers. He wrote:

"If when this fever attacks our neighbourhood I run away, I am not sure that I shall do right. . . . I must not forget that others may require to be nursed by me, in a disease where personal attentions are *all in all*."[1]   "In the autumn of *ninety-seven,* and when death had spent his shafts in my own family, I went to see how a family fared. . . . I hoped they had left the city; yet Mrs. Henning had told me that her husband, who was a devout man, held it criminal to fly on such occasions, and that she, having passed safely through the pestilence of former years, had no apprehensions from staying,"[2] additional words of Brown.

In Doctor Miller's home to which Brown and Dr. Smith had been taken, Brown's symptoms yielded to medicine, his friend's did not. Dr. Smith "saw the last symptom of the disease, black vomit, pronounced the word 'decomposition' and died." His friends, the Miller brothers, said:

"As a physician his loss is irreparable. . . . The love of science and the impulse of philanthropy, directed his whole professional career, and left little room for the calculations of emolument. He had formed vast designs of medical improvement, which embraced the whole family of mankind."[3]

Samuel Miller was a divine of New York. He helped in his brother's work and wrote his biography. Dr. Edward Miller (1760-1812) was appointed resident physician in New York, after having served as a surgeon in the U. S. Army. He lectured for the New York *Clinical Hospital* and wrote several medical works, most of which may be found in the *Medical Repository.* With his brother, he prepared a *Brief Retrospect of the XVIII Century.*

Dr. Mitchill (1764-1831), with Dr. Smith and Dr. Miller, founded the *Medical Repository,* the first scientific periodical in the United States. He was U. S. Representative and

---

1. Brown, Letter to his brother James, New York, September 4th, 1798, in Dunlap, *op. cit.,* II, 4, 5.
2. *Jane Talbot,* 112.
3. Miller and Mitchill, in the Medical Repository, in Dunlap, *op. cit.,* II, 9.

U. S. Senator in 1801 and 1804 respectively, vice-president of Rutger's Medical School and author of several medical works and of a work entitled *Life, Exploits, and Precepts of Tammany.*

Kent (1763-1847) was an eminent jurist, serving as Chief Justice and Chancellor from 1814 to 1823, since known as "the great Chancellor." He was a Federal member of Congress (1790-2) and a friend of Hamilton and Jay. Among his written works are his *Chancery Reports* and *Commentaries on American Law* (1826-30), which embody his lectures as Professor of Law in Columbia College, 1796. Wells (1770-1823) was a lawyer, who revised *The Federalist* for publication.

W. W. Woolsey is probably the "W" mentioned by Dunlap as a friend of Brown. He was a young man of singular beauty, animation, talents and wit, and his eloquence was ready, persuasive and fascinating, but was used sometimes to embellish a subject which he was too careless or too indolent to investigate, it was said. He belonged to the Law Society of which Brown was a member. Their acquaintance in the meetings of the Society soon ripened into a permanent friendship, which existed till the death of Woolsey. They were inseparable companions and, when absent from each other, kept up a punctual correspondence. Bleecher (Bleeker) was a young lawyer, who was a lover of literature and an occasional writer of verse. A copy of a letter to him from Brown is included in Dunlap's *Life of Brown.*

No one had truer friends than Brown and no one loved them more than he. Like many persons of reserved habits he took intense delight in the society of these intimate friends, whose tastes were wholly congenial with his own. During an excursion into Connecticut (1799) he thus writes in his journal at Middleton:

"What a wretched possession is solitude. Intelligence and sympathy beaming from eye to eye, constitute all the happiness of man. Nature owes all her charms to her alliance with images flowing from society."[1] "I like society; I believe all persons who have any talent (who are in good health) do. . . . Books do much; but the living intercourse is the vital heat. Debarred from that, how have I pined and died,"[2] spoke Mrs. Shelley later in the manner

---

1. Brown, His Journal, in Dunlap, *op. cit.,* II, 49.
2. Shelley, Mrs. P. B., *Shelley Memorials,* 250.

of Brown.

In the fellowship of the Friendly Club, during the three years spent in New York, Brown regained his cheerfulness and obtained a broader prospect and a certain interest in common things. Under somewhat similar conditions, Brown's hero, Arthur Mervyn, says,

"My curiosity and thirst of knowledge had likewise received a new direction. Books and inanimate nature were cold and lifeless instructors. Men, and the works of men, were the objects of rational study, and our own eyes only could communicate just conceptions of human performances. The influence of manners, professions, and social institutions, could be thoroughly known only by direct inspection."[1]

A statement of like import may be found in one of Brown's letters:

"I am a lover and admirer of all that is good and fair in the physical and moral universe. No man gazes at genius with more enthusiastic delight and admiration, or at virtue with greater love and reverence."[2]

The companionship and sympathy of his friends re-awakened in Brown his literary and scientific tastes, gave him confidence in his own resources and made him choose once for all literature as his life work. Not to have done so would have proved him traitor to the irresistible instinct of literary genius that he knew to be in his own heart and mind. Said his biographer:

"This (the planning of a magazine, 1798) was one of the many literary schemes, which now occupied the attention of Mr. B.; for he at this time carried into effect the plan which had long been forming in his mind of becoming an author by profession; of devoting his life to book-making, and trusting his future fortunes, as well as fame, to the labours of his pen. To become exclusively an author was at that time a novelty in the United States, and if we except the editors of news-papers, no one had relied solely upon the support of his talents as a writer, and deliberately chosen this station in society. Mr. Brown was so far successful, that he never relinquished his plan, and, if health and life had been continued to him, would have supported in competence and reared to usefulness, a numerous and amiable family."[3]

---

1. *Arthur Mervyn*, II, 77.
2. Brown, Letter to W., in Dunlap, *op. cit.*, I, 53.
3. Dunlap, *op. cit.*, II, 12.

Journals and magazines up to the Revolution were imitative of those of England; during the Revolution they were suspended; from the Revolution to 1800 were numerous ambitious attempts in most large cities and many failures. Nevertheless, the members of the New York Friendly Club wanted a literary magazine and suggested Brown for the editorship and the other members, eight in number, as contributors. In the first number was an article signed "Candidus," promising

"to extract the quintessence of European wisdom; to review and estimate the labours of all writers, domestic and foreign; and to speculate on the manners and morals in the style of Addison and Johnson."

The Club magazine: *The Monthly Magazine and American Review* (1799-1800) contains the customary, conventional departments. The Review, which was Brown's idea, became the most characteristic and important department. The project's newness soon wore off and the other contributors left much of the contributing to Brown, which he did unsparing of himself. He published in the first number the part of *Edgar Huntly* which deals with the Indian adventures (Chapters 16-19), *Thessalonica, A Roman Story* and *Memoirs of Stephen Calvert,* among fiction pieces.

The Review critic showed keen insight into the literary problems of the day and, by masterful, fearless, patient, wise criticism, according to the broad and sympathetic standards determined upon by him, endeavored to create and promote a native literature. He desired to elevate American criticism to the same high level of excellence to which he thought British criticism had reached. Brown was abundantly equipped by training in Latin and Greek, by knowledge of the French and German literatures, by his upbringing in honesty, seriousness and fairness, and by his own work as a writer, to be a competent critic. He put his whole soul into the editing, not as the convivial and unenergetic Dennie. He was the greatest critic before Poe and had but one rival, his friend Dennie of the *Port Folio,* to which he had contributed. One can only surmise what Brown might have become if he had chosen that field only and lived a normal length of life. As it was, his influence was felt by poets, essayists, sermonizers and novelists, in America, and by writers in Europe, during his journalistic career of over ten years. He won the title—"father of American literary criticism."

Finding that the magazine did not do any too well, partly because of the Friendly Club's lack of collaboration, Brown changed the magazine to a quarterly, which existed for only a short time. Learning by starving experience that New York was no proper place at that time for a literary magazine, he transferred his interests to Philadelphia and established his own magazine.

"More irksome, more deadening to my fancy is this city, on its *own* account, than ever. . . . Social and intellectual pleasures (of New York) being everything,"[1] wrote Brown to a friend after nine months' absence.

During the last eleven years of his life with little interruption, Brown was a hard-working, aspiring journalist, undaunted in spirit and in the determination to increase the knowledge and widen the tastes of the American public. He thus states his views and purposes as editor of *The Literary Magazine and American Register*: "he cannot but be desirous of an ample subscription, not merely because pecuniary profit is acceptable, but because this is the best proof which he can receive that his endeavours to amuse and instruct have not been unsuccessful. Useful information and rational amusement being his objects, he will not scruple to collect materials from all quarters. He will ransack the newest foreign publications. . . . As to domestic publications, . . . (he will) collect in one focal point the rays of a great number of luminaries. He will give a critical account of them, and in this respect, make his work an American Review, in which the history of our native literature shall be carefully detailed . . . and he will give from time to time some account of selected works which he deems above the common level."[2]

After concluding that novels—his novels all having been written by this time—were not highly acceptable for his purpose, Brown published magazines only and thus expressed his faith in their future:

"Those have a much more extensive circulation than any other kind of works; they are cheaper in proportion to their bulk, and, besides a good deal of original matter, they contain, under various forms diurnal, weekly, monthly, quarterly and annual, the essence of all other publications, together with the whole contemporary history of the world. . . . Other works would be in some measure useless and unread without their assistance."[3]

---

1. Brown, Letter to R. P., in Dunlap, *op. cit.,* II, 101.
2. Brown, Literary Magazine and American Register, Philadelphia, Saturday, Oct. 1, 1803, No. 1, P. 1-3, in Dunlap, *op. cit.,* II, 58, 60-1.
3. Pattee, *The First Century of American Literature,* 1770-1870, 191-2.

It is doubtful if Brown ever wrote anything without the welfare of men, and especially of his fellow citizens, in mind, of which a few years later (1825) Neal said: "It is now the fashion to be philanthropical." He followed the spirit of the times and had generous and impulsive notions of social betterment. The new truths that he acquired from foreign culture and readily absorbed for himself, he seemed anxious to impart to others and tried to remold them to suit conditions in this country. He was a constant contributor to the periodical literature of Philadelphia and New York for many years before he himself became an editor of magazines. He published—1799-1800, *The Monthly Magazine and American Review;* 1801-1802, *The American Review and Literary Journal;* 1803-1807, *The Literary Magazine and American Register;* and from 1806 until his death in 1810, *The Annual Register, or General Repository of History, Politics, and Science.* His magazines won a moderate patronage and exerted among an extremely provincial people a far-reaching influence for culture and for the appreciation of world-literature in all its forms.

It can truthfully be said that his magazines were distinctive with discriminatingly selected poetry and articles, that they are a survey of his time, both historical and of literary output. "They are replete with the effusions of erudition, taste and genius" (Dunlap). It would be of service to the people of the United States today to gather out and republish some of his criticisms and his literary choices.

Brown's magazines continued until his death in 1810, almost paralleling the efforts of Joseph Dennie, who had established a literary magazine in Philadelphia, the *Port Folio* (1801), which he edited until his death in 1812.

Among many contributors to the *Port Folio* were Brown; Royall Tyler, social and political prose and verse; John Davis, Travels; Dr. Richard Rush, who had served mightily in the yellow fever epidemics; Joseph Hopkinson, author of "Hail, Columbia," Shakespeare articles; John Blair Linn, poet; Charles Jared Ingersoll, dramatist; Alexander Wilson, ornithologist; Gouverneur Morris, political satires; also, John Dickenson, Philip Freneau, Hugh Henry Brackenridge, Francis Hopkinson and Thomas Paine. Franklin's influence was most felt then. Brown published his last three novels and his own magazines. It was the Golden Age of Philadelphia, the centre of culture, with its fine arts—music, painting, printing, publishing books, magazines and newspapers—and with political and scientific discussions. Brown's career was in a sense symbolic of the fate of his native city, as Mr. Parrington said, "a few brilliant years and then a swift decline. Death cut him down before he fulfilled his promise."

That Brown was elected in 1809 an honorary member of the New York Historical Society was reported by one critic. In those days it was considered a high honor to be enrolled with such notables as Timothy Dwight, Noah Webster, Josiah Quincey and George Clinton.

According to Dunlap, "Ever fond of analysis, Charles, even in very early life, would take no opinion upon trust. He found in his own mind abundant reason to reject many of the received opinions of mankind. . . . Much of his reading at this time tended to bewilder rather than enlighten and to confirm his predisposition to scepticism."[1]

This finds some support in descriptions of his characters:

"Waldegrave, like other men early devoted to meditation and books, had adopted, at different periods, different systems of opinion on topics connected with religion and morals. His earliest creeds tended to efface the impressions of his education; to deify necessity and universalize matter; to destroy the popular distinctions between soul and body, and to dissolve the supposed connection between the moral condition of man anterior and subsequent to death. . . . Thou art acquainted with the revolution that afterward took place in his mind, . . . and the subtle and laborious argumentations, which he had formerly produced against religion, and which were contained in a permanent form (letters), were combated in transient conversation."[2]   Jane Talbot thus speaks to Colden: "In order to benefit you, I was obliged to scrutinize the foundation of my own principles. I found nothing but a void. I was astonished and alarmed; and instantly set myself to the business of inquiry. Had I never extorted from you your doubts, and the occasion of those doubts; had I never known the most powerful objections to religion from your lips, I should have been no less ignorant of the topics and arguments favorable to it. . . . My belief is stronger than it ever was, but I no longer

---

1. Dunlap, *op. cit.*, I, 69-70.
2. *Edgar Huntly*, 136-7.

hold in scorn or abhorrence those who differ from me. . . . I find it possible for men to disbelieve and yet retain their claims to our reverence, our affection, and especially our good offices . . ."[1]

In speaking of Sophia Westwyn's mother, the author makes a specific reference to religion:

"With this accession of wealth, she returned to her ancient abode. The mask lately worn seemed preparing to be thrown aside, and her profligate habits to be resumed with more eagerness than ever; but an unexpected and total revolution was effected, by the exhortations of a Methodist divine. Her heart seemed, on a sudden, to be remolded, her vices and the abettors of them were abjured, she . . . prepared to expiate, by the rigors of abstinence and the bitterness of tears, the offences of her past life."[2]

Clara Wieland thus contrasts her brother and Pleyel, his brother-in-law:

"Pleyel was not behind his friend in his knowledge of the history and metaphysics of religion. Their creeds, however, were in many respects opposite. Where one discovered only confirmations of his faith, the other could find nothing but reasons for doubt. Moral necessity and Calvinistic inspiration were the props on which my brother thought proper to repose. Pleyel was the champion of intellectual liberty, and rejected all guidance but that of his reason."[3]

The tide of rationalism and free thought that spread from Europe to America affected Brown, and he was carried away by it for a time. "The truth is," he said, "I am no better than an outcast of that unwarlike sect (Quakers)."[4] But there is very clear evidence of the fact that he could never get away wholly from his early religious training and of his return fully to a firm faith in God. In his prospectus to the *Literary Magazine and American Register* (1803), setting forth its purposes, he says:

"In an age like this, when the foundations of religion and morality have been so boldly attacked, it seems necessary in announcing a work of this nature, to be particularly explicit as to the path which the editor means to pursue. He, therefore, avows himself to be, without equivocation or reserve, the ardent friend and the willing champion of the Christian religion. Christian piety he reveres as the

---

1. *Jane Talbot*, 135-6.
2. *Ormond*, 187.
3. *Wieland*, 45.
4 Smith, in *Fortnightly Review*, XXX, 339-421, 1878.

highest excellence of human beings, and the amplest reward he can seek, for his labour, is the consciousness of having, in some degree, however inconsiderable, contributed to recommend the practice of religious duties. As, in the conduct of this work, a supreme regard will be paid to the interests of religion and morality, he will scrupulously guard against all that dishonours or impairs that principle."[1]

A sidelight on Brown's deflection from faith, if so be he did deflect from it, and from the church may have resulted partly from the fact that after his marriage he was dismissed from the Society of Friends,
"having accomplished his marriage by the assistance of an hireling minister—to a person not in profession with us."

Religion was without doubt one of the topics up frequently for discussion among the associates of the Friendly Club, for Methodism and various other sects were striving to get a foothold in many localities. Enthusiasts, or jerkers, animated with the jerks, burst out in all religious groups. Brown, with his habit of assaying every subject, pro and con, expressed his views, as intimated in the quotation from *Jane Talbot* above.

This may point to Brown's recovery of his early faith. Of youthful Wieland, he says:
"He enjoyed leisure, and was visited afresh by devotional con-templation. The reading of the Scriptures, and other religious books, became once more his favourite employment. . . . He allied himself with no sect, because he perfectly agreed with none. Social worship is that by which they are all distinguished; but this article found no place in his creed. He rigidly interpreted that precept which enjoins us, when we worship, to retire into solitude, and shut out every species of society. According to him, devotion was not only a silent office, but must be performed alone. An hour at noon and an hour at midnight were thus appropriated."[2]

Brown the outcast could not ally himself to any other sect. It is told of him that on his death-bed he often expressed his confidence in God and was granted a vision of the glory beyond. "I had the most transporting and sublime feelings I ever experi-

---

1. Brown, Literary Magazine and American Register, Philadelphia, Saturday, Oct. 1, 1803, No. 1, P. 1-3, in Albert H. Smyth, *Philadelphia Magazines and Their Contributors*, 154-63.
2. *Wieland*, 30, 31.

enced."

A deep and pervasive loyalty to his country and faith in her political supremacy and intellectual awakening were cherished in the heart of America's first novelist. The French and Indian War, with the conquest of Canada by England, had ended in 1763; the Revolutionary War and triumph of the Colonists over England soon followed; then came the French Revolution, 1789-1794, making France free. The inspiring conviction that America had taken her place among the nations of the world put new and patriotic life into her people, which new life expressed itself in her literature.

Besides American writers, arguing for and against the Revolution and the making of the Constitution, were some influential foreigners. Thomas Paine, advised by Franklin to come to America, arrived in 1774, wrote *Common Sense* and *The Crisis* in 1776 and the *Rights of Man* (1791-2), in reply to Burke, to vindicate the French Revolution. He lived here thereafter and died in New York in 1809. Joseph Priestley, physicist and writer on theology, who had written *Letters to Burke* (1791), giving his reflections on the French Revolution, came to America in 1794 and died in Pennsylvania in 1804. During the last decade of the century, America became the asylum for the refugees from England and France and the forum for radicals of every persuasion. Writers here and abroad stirred up American thinking: on political reform,—Paine, Price, Priestley, Holcroft, Godwin, Pitt, Burke; on education and the rights of women,—Defoe, Alexander, Swift, Gregory, Bennett, Hannah Moore, Mary Wollstonecraft; on religion,—Priestley, the Wesleys, Cowper; on atheism,—Rosseau, Voltaire, Paine; on humanitarian effort,—Goldsmith.

Brown heard everything, read everything, and took toll of everything. Several of the above names are mentioned in his early writings. He had access to the best libraries of the nation, begun as Subscription Libraries by Franklin in 1731, with the document drawn up by Charles Brockden. He probably sympathized with that staunch, liberal-minded co-patriot and, perhaps, frequented his home. When facts like these are known, it does not surprise one to find that Brown, devoted to all kinds of learning, developed a philosophy on the subjects of the day and declared his opinions.

His pride as an American citizen revolted against English manners and customs, controlled largely through the prestige of rank and wealth. He longed for the time when, just as America had thrown off English tyranny, she would throw off the prejudices derived from England. The following passage is indicative of his conscious devotion to his country and to her democracy, in thus discriminating between Europe and America:

"I found that the difference between Europe and America lay chiefly in this: that, in the former, all things tended to extremes, whereas, in the latter, all things tended to the same level. Genius, and virtue, and happiness, on these shores, were distinguished by a sort of mediocrity. Conditions were less unequal, and men were strangers to the heights of enjoyment and the depths of misery to which the inhabitants of Europe are accustomed."[1]

Although Brown gives inklings of his love of country and of his countrymen in his novels, he discloses his views more specifically and forcefully in his pamphlets and magazine contributions. From 1803 is to be dated his career as a political writer. In that year, he published *An Address to the Government of the United States on the cession of Louisiana to the French,* urging her to retain the territory. He exclaims:

"no man can look upon these evils with indifference. Yet no wise man will think a renewal of all the devastations of our last war (Revolutionary), too great a price to give for the expulsion of foreigners from this land; for securing to our own posterity the possession of this continent."[2]

In these words Brown appears to suggest war with France, having in mind the French and Indian War, 1754-63, by which France yielded to England the territory east of the Mississippi. The territory west of the Mississippi was bought by President Jefferson from France in 1803, the Louisiana Purchase. Public attention was firmly and frankly directed by Brown to the importance of its acquisition, at all hazards. He thus anticipated the views of most of the eminent statesmen of the period and attempted to destroy opposition to the measure. He may, therefore, claim the honor of having, in a degree, contributed to the subsequent annexation of that valuable and extensive country to the American Union.

Every governmental measure and problem that Brown discussed

---

1. *Ormond,* 195-6.
2. Brown, An Address to the Government of the United States on the cession of Louisiana to the French, in Dunlap, *op. cit.,* II, 66.

he stated the arguments for and against. This facility proceeded from the acuteness of his perceptions and the freedom of his mind from all foreign or party bias (Dunlap). He touched upon many subjects of interest to the American public, among them, besides the cession address above: *The British Treaty* (1808), *An Address to the Congress of the United States on the utility and justice of restrictions upon Foreign Commerce* (1809), which was his last publication, *Dialogues* on music and painting, "American Painting" as a contribution to the *History of American Painting* by Samuel Isham and a translation from the French of Volney's *A View of the Soil and Climate of the United States of America.* These writings are the work of a clear, sagacious, original and comprehending thinker.

Notwithstanding the fact that Brown was at heart a political writer and journalist, he is usually thought of as a novelist. He discovered the possibilities of romance in America and used in all his novels scenes and characters recorded from actual observations and experiences. His romances were temporary makeshifts to inculcate the social theories and moral beliefs he had arrived at as "instruction" to his countrymen. Nearly a century later, an American, Sidney Lanier, said: "In short, as a people the novel is educating us." To bring this idea down to date, it would be true to say that the novel and the novel through the movies are educating us.

It was the success of *Arthur Mervyn,* begun in the Friendly Club magazine, that encouraged Brown to prepare to issue his own first literary magazine. *Arthur Mervyn* was written to instil into the minds of Americans "lessons of justice and humanity." To do this, the author gives, in striking contrast, examples of men who are sordidly selfish and of men who are benevolent and thoughtful of others. He summarizes his ideas of duty and happiness in the following sentence:

"The accumulation of knowledge, and the diffusion of happiness, in which riches may be rendered eminently instrumental, were the only precepts of duty, and the only avenues to genuine felicity."[1]

This statement almost echoes something the author had read before:

---

1. *Arthur Mervyn,* I, 128-9.

"What a pity that the wealthy, who can command such sunshine, should ever pass their days in gloom—in the cold shade of selfishness."[1]

In *Edgar Huntly*, Brown planned to show his appreciation of American scenery. He thought that American scenery would be as effective for the setting of stories as foreign scenery and that American Indians would satisfy the reader's craving for excitement better than Gothic ghosts and chimeras. He proved the correctness of his belief by making the scenery fascinating and the Indians blood-curdling. He enticed future writers to employ American scenery and started the Indians on trails through many subsequent novels.

Beyond all else Brown was a student of human passions and a psycho-analyst, and his method was that of the scientist. In his letter concerning his visit to Rockaway, he writes:
"An accurate history of the thoughts and feelings of any man, for one hour, is more valuable to some minds, than a system of geography. . . . I confess, mere mental vacuity gives me neither health nor pleasure."[2]   And of himself he says: "I have not been deficient in the pursuit of that necessary branch of knowledge; the study of myself."[3]   It seems to be Brown, the student of human nature, speaking, when he says of Constantia: "She delighted to investigate the human countenance, and treasured up numberless conclusions as to the co-incidence between mental and external qualities."[4]

Brown's habit of roaming, usually without a companion, led him, in the solitude of nature, to communicate deeply with his own heart, indulge in fanciful reveries and accustom himself to watch the action of the outward world upon his consciousness. "My fancy outstripped my footsteps, and was busy in picturing faces and rehearsing dialogues."[5] He understood much of himself, his inner life, and thus much of the inner lives of those about him. This makes Brown a truly imaginative artist of the mind and heart, one who was able to appreciate and interpret the minds and

---

1. Radcliffe, *The Mysteries of Udolpho*, I, 29.
2. Brown, Letter concerning his visit to Rockaway, Aug. 25, 1798, in Dunlap, *op. cit.*, I, 59, 67.
3. Dunlap, *op. cit.*, I, 51.
4. *Ormond*, 63.
5. *Arthur Mervyn*, II, 98.

hearts of others. So later he portrays his characters as self-conscious, self-revealing individuals. All of his novels rest upon an idea, the development of human character or the exhibition of the soul under pressure of unusual circumstances. They must be read, not as descriptions of persons, but as studies of individuals being transformed by incitements from without and from within. He makes his characters dissect their passions and analyze their motives.

In *Jane Talbot*, the letters that form the greater part of the book are intended as analyses of the heart. The method fits well, also, with Brown's gift for debate and discussion. The reader feels that it is the author speaking, when Jane declares,
"It has always been so. I have always found an unaccountable pleasure in dissecting, as it were, my heart; uncovering, one by one, its many folds, and laying it before you, as a country is shown in a map."[1]   "I have long accustomed myself to the study of my own heart, and have sought and found in its recesses that which cannot embody itself in words—hardly in feelings. . . . I am much of a self-examiner."[2]
The sentiment and words sound like a repetition of Brown's thought. *Recesses* instead of folds, Mrs. Shelley has used.

To furnish opportunities for dissection and analysis, Brown devised striking and perilous situations and arranged conditions of strong moral excitement—a troubled conscience, foregleams of insanity and premonitions of evil, which haunt the soul and drive it into the agonies of terror and despair. Reliving the events of fearful strife, the reader is obliged to investigate its causes and all the various phenomena that attend it. Every contingency, every probability, every possibility even, however remote, is pondered over and its results considered. This method fits well with Brown's gift for debate. One is sometimes struck with the strange contrast of over-passion and over-reason; yet it is known that Brown had experienced such deep conflicting emotions and understood these intricate mental processes. "I compared the cause with the effect, and they seemed disproportioned to each other."[3]

---

1. *Jane Talbot,* 91.
2. Shelley, Mrs. P. B., *Shelley Memorials,* 244, 247.
3. *Wieland,* 89.

After the completion of his novels and during his residence in Philadelphia, Brown married, in 1804, Miss Elizabeth Linn, the eldest daughter of the Rev. William Linn, pastor of the Presbyterian church of New York. In the following year he wrote to his friend Dunlap:

"As to myself, my friend, you judge rightly when you think me situated happily; my present way of life is in every respect, to my mind. There is nothing to disturb my felicity but the sense of the uncertainty and instability that sticks to every thing human. I cannot be happier than I am. . . . My business . . . is altogether pleasurable. . . . I have nothing to wish but that it may last."[1]

A year later he wrote to another friend: "You will find it the abode of content, and may enjoy the spectacle, not very common, of a happy family."[2]

However, Brown was not always at home to share the enjoyments of his family. In a letter to his wife he assents: "You confirm my prognostics that the lovely babes (twins) will scamper about the house, by the time of my return."[3] The writer must have loved babies, for he has included several of them among the characters in his novels.

A fellow-Philadelphian, Henry Simpson, said of Brown's home life:

"No situation more calculated for happiness—contentment. His wife, his children, his parents, his brothers, and their children, were his riches and his world; but like all worldly riches, they were soon to pass from him. Ever delicate, he became a victim to that cruel disease, consumption."[4]

John Blair Linn, the poet, had been settled in Philadelphia as pastor of the Presbyterian Church from 1799 until his death, August, 1804. Between him and Brown, who had returned permanently to Philadelphia in 1801, an intimate and warm friendship grew up, partly owing to Brown's love for his sister Elizabeth. In 1805, Brown published in the *Literary Magazine and American*

---

1. Brown, Letter to Dunlap, Philadelphia, 1805, in Dunlap, *op. cit.,* II, 113.
2. Brown, Letter to John H. Payne, Philadelphia, August 25, 1806, in Dunlap, *op. cit.,* II, 117.
3. Brown, *Manuscript letter,* June 17, 1806, written from Albany in Library of the Historical Society of Pennsylvania.
4. Simpson, *The Lives of Eminent Philadelphians,* 152.

Register a biographical sketch of his friend, "most elegant and interesting," "the facts judiciously arranged and the character . . . developed with singular correctness and felicity" (Introduction to Wieland, 1889).

The activity of mind necessary to the continued prosecution of his literary labors and the affection experienced in his home life alleviated the self-distrust Brown felt after the writing of his novels and caused him to forget at times the sickness of his body. In a letter to his friend Mary, he writes sadly:

"When have I known that lightness and vivacity of mind which the divine flow of health, even in calamity, produces in some men?—never: scarcely ever: not longer than an half hour at a time, since I have called myself man. . . . Till here, I could not find books, which have, with me, great efficacy in beguiling body of its pains, and thoughts of their melancholy, in relieving heads and hearts of their aches."[1]

Nevertheless, Brown deemed it proper, except in pursuance of some rational motive, to cover from the eyes of others with an impenetrable mask whatever fears and anxieties agitated him. If at any time he complained, "he severely censures himself in his journal; taxes himself with pusillanimity" (Dunlap). Thus, often his letters and general deportment before friends furnished a noticeable contrast to his private journal, which sometimes divulges the fact that his heart was secretly oppressed with foreboding and dejection.

"All the anxiety that he testified was, that he should become burthensome to his friends; a reflection which seemed to give him much more uneasiness than the pains with which he was afflicted."[2] His friend Mary says of him: "He always felt for others more than for himself, and the evidences of sorrow in those around him, which could not at all times be suppressed, appeared to affect him more than his own sufferings."[3]

As a commentary on this trait of his character are quoted the words of Jane Talbot to Colden:

"Every mournful secret must be wrung from you. You hoard up

---

1. Brown, Letter to Mary, from Hobocken, on the Hudson, 1809, in Dunlap, *op. cit.,* II, 86.
2. Dunlap, *op. cit.,* I, 55.
3. Letter of Mary, 1809, in Dunlap, *op. cit.,* II. 88.

all your evil thoughts, and brood over them alone. Nothing but earnest importunity ever got from you any of your griefs."[1]

In a letter to "W", Brown departs from his usual reticence as to his feelings: "I sincerely lament that I ever gave you reason to imagine that I was not so happy, as a gay indifference with regard to the present, stubborn forgetfulness with respect to the uneasy past, and excursions into lightsome futurity could make me: for what end, what useful purposes were promoted by the discovery? . . . forget that any latent anguish or corroding sorrow, is concealed under that aspect of indifference which has become habitual. For shame, thou idiot or thou madman! cease thy lamentable croakings. . . . Had I never had friends and relations, I am convinced that before this time I had ceased either to exist, or to exist as an inhabitant of America. I know from experience the strength of that obstacle to the direful schemes of despair, which results from possessing friends who would be, at least for a time, inconsolably afflicted by the loss of the sufferer. It is indeed my interest perhaps to add to the number of my friends, because in proportion to their number, will be the obstacles to my rash design."[2]

Suicide came often to the mind of Brown, if it may be judged from the frequent reference to it in his Journal and through the mouths of his characters. In Arthur Mervyn's words to Welbeck, there is expressed the choice between drudgery and death, the former probably suggested by Brown's own distaste for the law:

"If his tasks should enable him to live, but, at the same time, bereave him of all satisfaction, they inflicted injury, and were to be shunned as worse evils than death."[3]   "To such as I," Clithero says, "annihilation is the supreme good. To shake off the ills that fasten on us by shaking off existence, is a lot which the system of nature has denied to man. . . . Death is but a shifting of the scene; and the endless progress of eternity, which to the good is merely the perfection of felicity, is to the wicked an accumulation of woe. The self-destroyer is his own enemy: this has ever been my opinion. Hitherto it has influenced my actions."[4]

On February 22, 1810, in Philadelphia, his native city, Brown died at the age of thirty-nine, of consumption, due to the under-

---

1. *Jane Talbot*, 94.
2. Brown, Letter to W., in Dunlap, *op. cit.*, I, 51, 52.
3. *Arthur Mervyn*, I, 10.
4. *Edgar Huntly*, 88, 89-90.

mining of his fragile health in youth by overstudy and aggravated later by the intensity of his disposition and the laboriousness of his work. He left his wife Elizabeth, of whom he said, "My companion is all that an husband can wish for," and four young children, two of whom died young, but the two eldest, twins, Charles Brockden Jr. and William Linn, lived to old age and were influential in the business life of Philadelphia. Whether or not Brown knew early of his predisposition to consumption is unknown, but it is, at least, pathetic to read his own horror of the disease, as implied in *Arthur Mervyn*:

"The seeds of an early and lingering death are sown in my constitution. . . . We are exposed, in common with the rest of mankind, to innumerable casualties; but, if these be shunned, we are unalterably fated to perish by *consumption*. . . . Starving was a disease preferable to consumption. . . . My frame was delicate and feeble. Exposure to wet blasts and vertical suns was sure to make me sick. . . My constitution was predisposed to diseases of the lungs."[1]

A word portrait of Brown at the last is given by Thomas Sully, the painter. The writer has chosen the "prose poem" version by Pattee.

"I saw him a little before his death. I had never known him, never read any of his works. He was in a deep decline. It was in the month of November. . . . Passing a window one day I was caught by the sight of a man, with a remarkable physiognomy, writing at a table in a dark room. The sun shone directly upon his head. I never shall forget it. The dead leaves were falling then. It was Charles Brockden Brown."[2]

Whenever Dunlap's name is mentioned, to him must be accorded the supreme authority with regard to Brown and his works, for he was one friend with whom Brown lived and who became his biographer, writing his *Life of Brown: together with Selections . . .*, in 1815, five years after Brown's death. He wrote with sympathy and discernment. Other sources are Brown's own works, those of Neal, and one or two others who knew him and the magazines and newspapers of his time. Dunlap's "Life" is the foundation used by most critics.

---

1. *Arthur Mervyn*, I, 136, 10; II, 126; I, 51. (See I, 17.)
2. Sully, Introduction by Fred Lewis Pattee, in *Wieland*, XXV.

Speaking of Brown's death, Dunlap said:
"Thus at the age of thirty-nine, died Charles Brockden Brown, taken from the world at a time when the mass of knowledge which he had acquired by unwearied but desultory reading, and by acute and accurate observation, being preserved by a strong memory and marshalled by an uncommonly vigorous understanding, was fitted with the aid of his perseverance and zeal in the cause of virtue, to have conferred the most important benefits upon his fellow men.

"Though not imposing in personal appearance and with great simplicity of manners, he was winning in his address and made friends of both sexes wherever he felt the object was worthy. . . . If the impression of his character made by the foregoing pages, is not that of a man of uncommon acquirements, superior talents, amiable manners, and exalted virtue, it is owing to want of skill in his biographer."[1]

One hopes that the full fruition of his labors may be attained from the influence he exerted upon his contemporaries and in the continuing influence from his writings and mayhap in the life hereafter, expressed in the following words:
"Enough of this! The great work of life goes on. Death draws near. To be better after death than in life, is one's hope and endeavour—to be so through self-schooling."[2]
With a slight improvisation, Coleridge's epitaph for himself applies well to Brown. Here lies Brown the novelist: Pray that he who scant two-score years,
"with toil of breath,
Found death in life, may here find life in death."

As a boy, Brown was sensitive, restless, imaginative, and devoted to books, architectural designing and maps; as a man, he was of alert, masterful mind and "congratulates himself upon this infirmity" that destined him to meditative pursuits (Dunlap), introspective to a morbid degree, an idealist, impelled by high ideals and self-depreciatory because he failed to attain them. His refinement and gentleness of manners kept him free from the vices of young men of his time. He used no liquors and was abstemious in his eating. He was careless of appearance; yet he says, "Appear-

---

1. Dunlap, *op. cit.,* II, 89, 90.
2. Shelley, Mrs. P. B., "Extracts from her Private Journal," in *Shelley Memorials,* 251.

ances are wonderfully influenced by dress." He was unmethodical in affairs, modest and unobstrusive in behavior, long-suffering, self-sacrificing and enduring.

John Neal, an American contemporary of Brown, provides a camera-like description of his person. His general appearance was remarkable. He was a tall man, with a powerful frame, with little or no flesh, which gave the impression of much more strength than he had. It was impossible to pass him in the street, without stopping to look at him. He had straight, black hair, "black as death," and a pale, sallow, strange complexion; and "the melancholy, broken-hearted look of his eyes," and his altogether extraordinary face,—"if seen once were never to be forgotten." Those who saw him were impressed by his remarkable personality, apparent at a glance.[1] His acquaintances bear testimony to the charm of his conversations and the goodness of his heart. In conclusion, one would mention the strong impression he made upon his contemporaries, both English and American, as a man of genius.

As has been said, Brown lived within the Revolutionary period, the time when American nationality was evolved and established, and the aims of the new nation were gradually dissociated from those of England. The chief writings of the first half of the period were political and make up the most important, interesting, forceful, genuine and profound assemblage of literature on the fundamental principles of government and the natural rights of man ever written. This kind of writings leaped to maturity, shaped American thought, crossed the Atlantic and helped mold European thought. The general literature of the under current is insignificant, both in quantity and quality. The authors were often provincial in outlook and biased in judgment, yet inspired by the one purpose of proclaiming liberty, which distinguishes their output from that of the Colonial period. The dominant quality of all the writings was that "rugged sincerity," which, as Carlyle declared, is "the essence of originality." Those who felt the literary impulse from imported writings were few during this period and they wrought, not servilely, but rather from suggestion. Satirical poetry and

---

1. Neal in *Blackwood's Magazine*, XVI, 421-6, Oct., 1824. (Signed X. Y. Z.)

essays flourished,—in subject matter, American; in form and style, British.

Although the strife between England and her Colonies had been crushed, yet the writings of the second part of the period continued largely controversial, as before, bent now on repressing internal, sectional dissensions and establishing a prosperous, unified nation. Fervid emotion, vigorous argumentation, and a style, sometimes bombastic, characterized these writings. Theology was not neglected; however, the power of the clergy in public affairs was declining. Not one of the great orators of the Revolutionary era was a clergyman. The legal profession was becoming more and more influential. That may be the reason Brown chose it as a way of making a living. Both these classes, statesmen and the clergy, used straightforward, persuasive, positive language, usually prose, only as a carriage for asserting their convictions. Scant attention was given to the fine arts and aesthetic culture. There was little associative life among authors and no centre for publishers, as in England, no interest in letters, no place for a man of letters, no market for letters among the people. They had writings in abundance dealing with moral and political ideals and they felt no need for anything else.

The nation was industrious and fully employed in material tasks—subduing the soil, advancing the border, building towns and cities, producing mechanical inventions, founding institutions, establishing trade, manufacture and commerce, mastering self-government and organizing a social order on the rights of human equality and personal freedom. Letters could not flourish in such an environment. Imported books were becoming plentiful. There was no inducement to adopt the literary profession on the part of those possessing indisputable talent.

A more diversified life was developing. There were avenues other than politics and theology attractive to the educated man. Brown opened one more avenue to eminence—the literary profession. He was the first man who saw that men, in a new and better political state than that of Europe, should free themselves from her opinions and writings. There were writers who, though they acknowledged the value of English, French and German literatures, "saw the necessity of establishing a literature for their own country; who saw the advantages of publications suited to a new state of manners and political economy, and which should not only produce original instruction, but point out and sever the good from the bad in the literature and institutions of Europe. . . . On this ground, as well as on that of uncommon talents and exemplary virtues, Brown is entitled to a large portion of public attention and will be esteemed, not merely in proportion to that which he performed, but to the effects of his efforts upon those who followed in the path he opened."[1]

Writing to his brother James, Brown wrote, after publishing *Edgar Huntly,* his fourth novel:

"Book-making, as you observe, is the dullest of all trades, and the utmost that any American can look for, in his native country, is to be re-imbursed his unavoidable expenses."[2]

In a letter to his publisher Conrad, Brown wrote that he "expected little subsistence, but some success to amuse and instruct." Brown's career is touching. No wonder that his stories are tinged with the seriousness and despondency of his own nature. The appearance of a native novel was an exceptional literary event. The generation born after the Revolution profited from the foundation laid by Colonial and Revolutionary literature, which was largely religious, political and historical, and were able to develop a literature free and unhampered.

Brown is one of the most tragic instances of genius arrested in its orderly development, due to adverse circumstances, ill-health and an early death. The keenness of his natural powers and his inventiveness are recognizable on nearly every page of his novels; yet he followed the prevalent usages in methods of the schools of novelists in England. Few writers, particularly the young, invent new literary forms. They envision success along the old paths that please the public and that have brought fame and fortune. Had Brown been a little surer of his genius, he would have discarded the practices that bound the art of literature and would have stood forth alone as the single representative, up to his time, of a new, independent American literature. His novels display his originality in the choice of American and scientific subjects, in the succession of enthralling events narrated and in the clear-cut, vivid style of

1. Dunlap, *op. cit.,* I, 10.
2. Brown, Letter to his brother James, New York, April, 1800, in Dunlap, *op. cit.,* II, 100.

his language.

The fact that American writers did not give any adequate expression of American life and ideals or build up American culture and literature was deprecated by Brown. He thought it was the part of an American writer to use American themes and said in To the Public of *Edgar Huntly*:

"America has opened new views to the naturalist and politician, but has seldom furnished themes to the moral painter. That new springs of action and new motives to curiosity should operate, . . . may be readily conceived. The sources of amusement to the fancy and instruction to the heart, that are peculiar to ourselves, are equally numerous and inexhaustible. . . . for a native of America to overlook these would admit of no apology."

In pursuance of this intention, he purposed to use American material and adapt his adventures to American conditions. He describes American settings and events against a background of speculation upon moral and religious problems, thus fulfilling in part that prophecy of Goethe, who expressed in this verse his disgust at the extravagance of the European romanticists:

"America, thy happy lot   Above old Europe's I exalt:
Thou hast no castle ruin hoar   No giant column of basalt.
Thy soul is not troubled   In living light of day
By useless tradition,   Vain strife and affray.
Grasp but the present that is thine,
And when thy children take to writing,
May kindly Fate preserve their tales
From robbers, knights, and ghosts affrighting."[1]

Goethe asserted: "The classical is health; and the romantic, disease."

Prescott said: "Great doubts were long entertained of our capabilities for immediate success in this department. We had none of the buoyant, stirring associations of a romantic age, none of the chivalrous pageantry, the feudal or border story or Robin-Hood adventure, none of the dim, shadowy superstitions and the traditional legends, which had gathered like moss, round every stone, hill, and valley of the olden country. Every thing here wore a spick-and-span new aspect, and lay in the broad, garish sunshine of everyday life. We had none of the picturesque varieties of situation or cos-

---

1. Boyesen, "The Progressive Realism in American Fiction," in *Literary and Social Silhouettes,* 58.

tume; every thing lay on the same dull, prosaic level, in short, we had none of the most obvious elements of poetry, at least so it appeared to the vulgar eye."[1]   "We have no old established faith, no hereditary romance, no such stuff as Catholicism, Chivalry afforded. . . . Without such ideas ("fresh and original forms") all attempts to construct a national literature must end in abortions like the monster of Frankenstein. . . . We cannot have expression till there is something to be expressed,"[2] said Mrs. Ossoli. Hawthorne had the same idea in mind in his lament, copied in the discussion of Brown and Hawthorne, in Chapter V.

The American romance grew as a result of natural occurrences or causes. The first generation of Americans were young men, full of the vigor, the imagination and the daring of youth. Post-war and physical conditions tended to produce an emotional temperament as revealed in the histories written in those days. The passion for discovery, the pioneering urge, the fascination of forest and sea, an adventurous sense of danger and mystery aroused by the depredations of Indians, and pietistic, scientific and humanitarian enthusiasm,—all aided to develop the romantic spirit. The belief in miracles and marvellous happenings naturally throve in this exciting environment and kept the American mind in unrest. Contemporary with the new interest in the sciences—chemistry, mineralogy, botany, birds, bees and butterflies—among the educated classes were the feverish speculations among the ignorant about clairvoyance, somnambulism, ventriloquism, intercourse with spirits, dreams, visions, insanity, hallucinations and other mysteries on the borderland between notion and knowledge.

"To his (Brown's) active imagination and fertile mind, they suggested the materials for erecting a superstructure of the greatest magnitude and of the most awful importance. Man, frail, ignorant and dependant (sic), is prone to superstition. In all ages the natural phenomena which are beyond the reach of our knowledge have been deemed supernatural."[3]

Quacks were common and credulity reigned. Evidence of such distracting inquiries is found in the dramas, novels, magazines and newspapers of that time. Such a statement as the following might

---

1. Prescott, "C. B. Brown," in *Miscellaneous Essays*, 51.
2. Ossoli, *Papers on Literature and Art*, Part II, 110, 124.
3. Dunlap, *op. cit.*, II, 13.

be read: "The unrivalled necromancer and ventriloquist" held the audience spellbound. An author, therefore, should be judged according to the place that he occupies in his own generation. Writings usually take themes from the arresting events among which they are produced. The readers partly make an author what he is. They demand a certain kind of literature and it is provided. Brown sought to "amuse" as well as to "instruct," though instruction came first. So judged he will reflect in his novels the unsolved, worrisome thoughts that disturbed the minds of his countrymen. The most graphic disclosure of his genius was his conscious employment of disconcerting scientific truths as the unprecedented, unfamiliar agencies or motives for the excitement of curiosity and information. Wherefore he chose his material from the most haunting and agitating occurrences: mental disorders and ills of the body. Sleepwalking was common, but unexplained; accounts of ventriloquism and spontaneous combustion had been reported in the magazines and newspapers; the existence and power of demons and good and evil spirits provoked controversy.

For two-score years, perhaps, there has been progress by physicians and philosophers in what is called today "abnormal psychology," a subject treated by Brown nearly a century earlier. His first four novels may be called studies in abnormal psychology,— aberrations of the mind,—especially in the analyses of the mental states of his villains. Abnormal states are what makes them villains. Brown loved mystery and he realized how mystified many of his countrymen were over the natural powers that were beyond their mental grasp. Natural causes with seemingly unnatural effects fascinated him. In trying to explain the truth, he chose his agents from the unexplained, dismaying and perturbing events among the people and then finally explained them rationally by natural causes, his mind being unwilling to countenance anything which he himself did not believe. A neat statement is made by the translator of Wieland's . . . *Don Sylvio* . . . (406):

"I am firmly persuaded that many things are held impossible, only because they are incomprehensible to our ignorance."

Preceding Clara Reeve by nearly thirty years and Mrs. Radcliffe and Brown by nearly fifty, Fielding in *Tom Jones* sets forth his judgment:

"I think it may very reasonably be required of every writer, that he keeps within the bounds of possibility; . . . nor is possibility alone sufficient to justify us; we must keep likewise within the rules of probability."[1]

In *Wieland,* Brown introduced spontaneous combustion, biloquium, the debated question of good and evil spirits—whether they exist and have power over human life,—religious fanaticism and insanity; in *Ormond,* the education of women, yellow fever, virtue and seduction, poverty and wealth; in *Arthur Mervyn,* yellow fever, which caused fear, excitement and the wildest excesses, greed for riches and philanthropy; in *Edgar Huntly,* sleep-walking, a common and confusing malady, Indians, with frequent rumors of their savagery or actual forays, panthers, occasional and unwelcome visitors in those early days in the woods and mountains of Pennsylvania, heredity and insanity; in *Clara Howard* and *Jane Talbot,* the intellectual and moral emancipation of women. These are the realities behind his fiction.

"Some of them (these agents), perhaps, approach as nearly to the nature of miracles as can be done by that which is not truly miraculous. It is hoped that intelligent readers will not disapprove of the manner in which appearances are solved, but that the solution will be found to correspond with the known principles of human nature" (Brown's Advertisement of *Wieland*).

Walter Just proclaimed Brown the first to make a study of the night-side of Nature:

"Die Nachtseite der Natur zu studieren, über die dunkeln, noch nicht erklärten Erscheinungen im Naturleben, wie sie sich im tierischen Magnetismus, in dem Treiben der Somnambulen, im Wahnsinn und überhaupt in allen psychischen Störungen zeigen, nachzugrübeln und sie auch in der Literatur zu verwerten, findet sich bei den Amerikanischen Romantikern im höchsten Masse ausgeprägt. . . . Dagegen scheint Brown ganz selbständig erkannt zu haben, welche Wirkung er erzielen könne, wenn er diese Erscheinungen in seiner Dichtung verwerte. Browns Roman, die sich mit dem Krankhaften und Pathologischen beschäftigen, sind ungefähr die ersten Werke dieser Art in der Literatur."[2]

That Brown understood himself to be an innovator is clear from his frank assertion in To the Public of *Edgar Huntly*:

---

1. Fielding, *Tom Jones,* I, 375, 377.
2. Just, *Die Romantische Bewegung in der Amerikanischen Literatur—Brown, Poe, Hawthorne,* 48-51.

"One merit, the writer may at least claim: that of calling forth the passions and engaging the sympathy of the reader by means hitherto unemployed by preceding authors."

Brown was going to deal with facts. One cannot doubt that this would-be realistic reformer took himself and these matters seriously; though the realist of today will peruse his novels with amusement other than that which the author intended, if he judges their old-fashioned style and content with present-day manners in life and in fiction. The main events discussed by Brown were unusual, but not impossible. Romanticism, or Gothecism, was never indigenous in America, so the departure from it to the side of the Revolutionists was simple. Almost without exception the tendency of American authors is to deal frankly and honestly with American life, as they know it and see it. Each aims to chronicle the particular phases of American life with which he is most intimately acquainted. Readers are of many types. Those who take pride in their culture and criticism repudiate that which is merely imaginative, entertaining, popular and sensational, for facts, exacting mental processes, inevitable conclusions and the problems of American society. Realistic fiction in America was first written by way of direct imitation of truthful records. Brown aimed at this ideal of reality in his own way.

Considering the ways that Brown's character has been assayed above, he might be called a psychological idealist in the realm of morals and a psychological realist because he views objects of the world in general—scenes, peoples, facts—not independent of psychical concepts.

Not only was Brown the first American who chose literature as a profession, but he was the first American fiction writer who founded his fiction upon American facts and localized his stories on American soil. Just so far as he relegated Gothic trappings and the supernatural to the discard and substituted for them actual events and the strange in nature, so far he represents the change from romanticism to realism. He dwelt upon the romantic side of familiar things.

The novel was one of the latest forms to develop for three reasons. First, the importation and reprinting of British fiction sufficed. Second, a realization of the true relation of man to his neighbors and his surroundings must precede the creation of the novel. Conditions in America were not favorable,—indeed, could not be,—until the nation became stabilized after independence had been won. Literature took the forms of argumentation and satire to secure national harmony. Fiction was delayed, also, by a spirit of opposition in religious groups, who objected to anything that was not true. In his *Travels in New England and New York* (London, 1823, I, 477), Timothy Dwight expressed the Puritan attitude when he said,

"Between the Bible and novels there is a gulf fixed, which few novel readers are willing to pass over."   "The consciousness of virtue, the dignified pleasure of having performed one's duty, the serene remembrance of a useful life, the hope of an interest in the Redeemer, and the promise of a glorious inheritance in the favor of God are never found in novels,"[1] is a summation of the same spirit by Charles Angoff.

The legitimacy of imaginative narration or fiction was questioned by many, as is suggested by Brown in a letter to Thomas Jefferson, on the presentation of a copy of *Wieland,* published shortly before:

"I am conscious, however, that this form of composition may be regarded by you with indifference or contempt, that social & intellectual theories, that the history of facts in the processes of nature & the operations of government may appear to you the only laudable pursuits; that fictitious narratives, in their own nature, or, in the manner in which they have been hitherto conducted, may be thought not to deserve notice, & that, consequently, whatever may be the merit of my book as a fiction, yet it is to be condemned because it is a fiction."[2]

Jefferson was away from home, so his reply was delayed for more than a year. He wrote:

"I received on my arrival here some days ago the copy of the book you were so kind as to send me together with your letter, for which be pleased to accept my thanks. as soon as I am in a situation to admit it (which is hardly the case here) I shall read it, & I doubt not with great pleasure. some of the most agreeable moments of my life have been spent in reading works of imagination which have this advantage over history that the incidents of the former may be dressed in the most interesting form, while those of the

---

1. Angoff, *A Literary History of the American People,* 315.
2. Brown, Letter to Thomas Jefferson, Dec. 25, 1798, New York, in *Jefferson Papers,* Volume 104. Library of Congress.

latter must be confined to fact. they cannot therefore present virtue in the best & vice in the worst forms possible, as the former may. I have the honor to be with great consideration (Sir)

your most obed.t serv.t

Th: Jefferson."[1]

Fifteen years after Brown's first novel, when Scott was contemplating writing *Waverley* (1814), he said:

"In truth, I am not sure it would be considered quite decorous for me, as a Clerk of Session, to write novels."[2]

Brown probably gave up the writing of fiction after six novels in four short years, partly from the insecure place that such composition held among his puritanical countrymen and partly from the discouragement of the English critics. Young literary geniuses, both English and American, were criticized severely. John Blair Linn, in his *Powers of Genius,* said:

"I shall not attempt to conceal the enthusiasm which I feel for meritorious performances of native Americans, nor can I repress my indignation at the unjust manner in which they are treated by the reviewers of England. America, notwithstanding their aspersions, has attained an eminence in literature, which is, at least, respectable. A national literature was never altogether absent from their thoughts, however the fear of English censure and ridicule may have checked the aspiration."[3]

In A. H. Smyth's words are found the following statements:

"Sydney Smith waved American literature contemptuously aside in the *Edinburgh Review. The Quarterly* was brutal in its attacks upon transatlantic books. William Godwin reproached American ignorance, and proceeded to locate Philadelphia on Chesapeake Bay. No wonder that the *Port Folio* exclaimed in 1810 'The fastidious arrogance with which the reviewers and magazine makers of Great Britain treat the genius and intellect of this country is equalled by nothing but their profound ignorance of the situation.' . . . American writers, after the Revolution which lost England her colonies, felt themselves to be under the opprobrium of the literary world. They felt keenly the sneers of the English men-of-letters,

---

1. Jefferson, Letter to Brown, Jan. 15, 1800, Philadelphia, in *Jefferson Papers*, Volume 106. Library of Congress.

2. Lockhart, *Life of Sir Walter Scott*, I. 238.

3. Linn, "Powers of Genius," quoted by Smyth, in *Philadelphia Magazines and Their Contributors*, 15, 19.

and winced under the injustice and invective that they were not strong enough to resent . . . The insolence of British travelers was especially provoking."[1]

Yet Dennie, the *Port Folio* editor, gave Brown "scant praise, saying that the Pennsylvanian novelist wrote 'uncommonly' well for an American," according to Blake, who also said:

"a contributor to the *North American Review,* as late as June, 1815, said Brown was 'very far from being a popular author' and that there was no demand for a second edition of his novels,— this after many of them had been re-issued in New York and in London."[2]

However, Dennie, in the issue of the *Port Folio* following Brown's death, discussed his attitude toward the Gothic situation:

"Disgusted with the dull, insipid tales of the German school, the ghosts, the castles and the hobgoblins of the modern romance, he (Brown) searched the mysterious volume of nature and found prodigies more to his liking. Somnambulism and ventriloquism furnished fields equally large and commodious for fancy to expatiate and capable of the same embellishment of incident."[3]

The contemptuous remark of Sydney Smith was: "Who reads an American book?" John (O'Cataract) Neal dashed pell-mell over to Europe (1824) to answer the challenging criticism (1820); but when he arrived he not so much tried to vindicate American writers as to do some writing for himself. In *Blackwood's Magazine* is the statement:

"With two exceptions, or at the most three, there is no American writer, who would not pass just as readily for an English writer, as for an American, whatever were the subject upon which he was writing; and these three are Paulding, Neal and Charles Brockden Brown."[4]

This critic praised Brown and tore him to shreds in his general criticism, having read Brown's novels years before and writing from memory, thus making numerous errors and using outlandish figures of speech and language and giving a sort of slap-dash estimate.

---

1. Smyth, *Philadelphia Magazines and Their Contributors,* 13, 12.
2. Blake, "Brockden Brown and the Novel," in *The Sewanee Review,* XVIII, 433, October, 1910.
3. Pattee, *The First Century of American Literature,* 1770-1870, 106.
4. Neal, in *Blackwood's Magazine,* XVI, 305, Sept., 1824. (Signed X. Y. Z.)

Later, having read Dunlap's *Life of Brown,* he said:

"Yet, our conclusion respecting Charles Brockden Brown, is this. He was the Godwin of America. Had he lived here—or anywhere, but in America,—he would have been one of the most capital story-tellers—in a serious way, that ever lived. . . . It would be well for his countrymen to profit by—not imitate—we despise imitation even of what is excellent—it would be well for them to profit by his example."[1]

It is worthy of note that the critic was John Neal, who was in England from 1824-1827; and his offer to write a series of sketches about American authors in *Blackwood's* was accepted. Several of the articles are signed "X. Y. Z." Neal (1793-1876) was a callow critic at this time, but thirty-one years of age, aspiring to write fiction. Within seven years of Brown's death he published his first romance, *Keep Cool* (1817). Many more romances and other works followed until 1870. He had plenty of time to remedy his criticisms of Brown. If he had put into practice the opposite of those criticisms, he ought to have pleased himself well and his romances might have remained readable to this day. Neal wrote, pretending to be an Englishman, so his viewpoint was wrong and warped every criticism. He condemned most American writers, while urging better relations between England and America and a more just criticism by English critics. Of American critics he said:

"Few of our literary men have read him (Brown). . . . Any praise which Brown may receive in America is due, not to admiration of his work, but to the commendation which it received in England."

Of the English critics he said: "If you would be severe on the Americans, in a better way—a way more worthy of yourself, if you are a man,—speak the truth of them. Nothing cuts like the truth. . . . We venture to say that another revolution will soon take place in the New World . . . an escape from the worst of bondage—that of the soul; the true bondage of death—literary, not political bondage."[2]

Brown's importance in early American fiction may be known from the fact that he was the first American novelist who won a reputa-

1. Neal, in *Blackwood's Magazine,* XVI, c. 425, October, 1824.
2. *Ibid.,* XVI, 415-28, Oct., 1824; XVII, 186-207, Feb., 1825.

tion and exerted an influence outside his own country, his novels all having been republished in England after publication here.

Three years after Neal's first criticism, a complete edition of Brown's novels was published in America (1827), by S. G. Goodrich, who said:

"It will be sufficient to say, that among other works I published an edition of the novels of Charles Brockden Brown, with a life of the author, furnished by the widow, she having a share of the edition."[1]

Goodrich was an author as well as a publisher and remarked about this same time:

"As an amusement to a man of fortune, who is also a man of genius, authorship is a glorious pastime; to men of other and more active and profitable professions, it is often an inspiring episode; but to one who has no resources but his brains, it is too often the coining of his heart's blood to feed his family. One thing should never be forgotten by those who are tempted to follow a literary career that not one author in a hundred attains success in life by his profession alone."[2]

Magnificent Brown! The one per cent, who succeeded over a quarter of a century before.

"But, Mr. Smith, you would today not be remembered at all in America, if you had not once said, 'In the four quarters of the globe, who reads an American book?'"

This was the conclusion of a pretended interview with Sydney Smith by E. P. P. (probably Elizabeth Palmer Peabody, sister-in-law of Hawthorne and Horace Mann), entitled *Oliver Wendell Holmes,* published in the St. Louis *Globe-Democrat,* which the writer said, "will be read all over England." Mr. Smith (1771-1845) was an English divine, essayist and wit, one among several energetic young men who started *The Edinburgh Review* in 1802. Smith acted as the original editor and contributed seven articles to the first number. E. P. P. reminds Smith of Emerson, John Fiske, Bryant, Agassiz, Hawthorne, Longfellow, Lowell, Whittier and Swinburne, read in England and translated into other langauges. The writer was reading the book catalogue of Houghton and Mifflin.

---

1. Goodrich, *Recollections of a Lifetime,* I, 255.
2. *Ibid.,* I, 279, note.

"Why did I start this picture of Oliver Wendell Holmes, Mr. Smith? Because all England has of late done its best to put its arms around our American favorite, and show that all the world not only reads but enjoys his writings."

In justice to Mr. Smith, this answer to him was made quite a number of years after his remark. However, other writers had made earlier replies and confutations.

Almost one hundred years later an American critic, scarcely familiar with Brown's novels, it is feared, gave this derogatory personal estimate:

"Charles Brockden Brown was a man of keen sensibilities—excellently well-intentioned—with humanities large and active, but with curiously fantastic notions about the construction of fiction. I could never bring myself into a state of enjoyment in reading one of his books—not even for a dozen consecutive pages; one wonders; one is piqued; one admires bits of description; one acquiesces solemnly in some solemn bit of excellent philosophical remark; again you are astounded by some sudden piece of clap-trap."[1]

This writer is pleased to quote a portion of Fielding's view of true criticism given some fifty to seventy-five years previous to the critics of American fiction.

"If a person who pries into the characters of others, with no other design, but to discover their faults to publish them to the world, deserves the title of a slanderer of the reputations of men, why should not a critic, who reads with the same malevolent view, be as properly styled the slanderer of the reputation of books? . . . Nor shall we conclude the injury done this way to be very slight, when we consider a book as the author's offspring, and indeed as the child of his brain. . . . In reality, to depreciate a book maliciously, or even wantonly, is at least a very ill-natured office; and a morose, snarling critic may, I believe, be suspected to be a bad man. . . . But without ascertaining all the proper qualifications of a critic . . . I may very boldly object to the censures of any one past upon works which he hath not himself read. . . . Such may likewise be deserving this character, who, without assigning any particular faults, condemns the whole in general, defamatory terms; such as vile, dull, d—d stuff, etc., and particularly by the use of the monosyllable *low*. . . . Again, though there may be some faults justly assigned

---

1. Mitchell, *American Lands and Letters*, I, 179-80.

to a work, yet, if those are not in the most essential parts, or if they are compensated by greater beauties, it will savour rather of the malice of the slanderer than of the judgment of a true critic to pass a severe sentence upon the whole, merely on account of some vicious part."[1]

In the Preface: "A Plea for Fiction" of his picaresque tale, *The Algerine Captive, or the Life and Adventures of Dr. Updike Underhill* (1797), Royall Tyler, speaking from the standpoint of his hero and introducing for the first time that shrewd, fictitious Yankee character, Brother Jonathan, makes some remarks concerning affairs during his absence.

"One of the first observations the author of the following sheets made upon his return to his native country, after an absence of seven years, was the extreme avidity with which books of mere amusement were purchased and perused by all ranks of his countrymen. When he left New England, books of biography, travels, novels, and modern romances, were confined to our seaports; or, if known in the country, were read only in the families of clergymen, physicians and lawyers; while certain funeral discourses, the last words and dying speeches . . and some dreary somebody's Day of Doom, formed the most diverting part of the farmer's library. On his return from captivity, he found a surprising alteration in the public taste. In our inland towns of consequence, social libraries had been instituted, composed of books designed to amuse rather than to instruct; and country booksellers, fostering the new-born taste of the people, had filled the whole land with modern travels, and novels almost as incredible. . . . Yet there are two things to be deplored in it. The first is, that, while so many books are vended, they are not of our own manufacture. . . . The second misfortune is, that novels, being the picture of the times, the New England reader is insensibly taught to admire the levity and often the vices, of the parent country. While the fancy is enchanted, the heart is corrupted. . . . There are two things wanted . . . that we write our own books of amusement, and that they exhibit our own manners, . . . hitherto unattempted."[2]

Facts and figures were given by John Neal to show how publishers here could make such simple copyright arrangements for the

---

1. Fielding, *Tom Jones*, II, 47-9.
2. Tyler, "The Algerine Captive," in F. C. Prescott and J. H. Nelson, *Prose and Poetry of the Revolution*, 253-4.

reprint of popular English novels that they could enjoy all the profits; whereas American authors were scarcely given a hearing because their works must needs be paid for.

That revolution spoken of by Neal had been begun by Brown. The literary bonds of the Old World were being broken by him. He is called "the first American man of letters," "the first American novelist," "the Father of American fiction," "the father of them all."

"That the field of investigation, opened to us by our country, should differ essentially from those which exist in Europe, may be readily conceived," said Brown in To the Public of *Edgar Huntly*.

"He wished to become a teacher of truth, and he adopted the vehicle of novel writing as most likely to produce the effect he desired upon the greater number of his fellow creatures."[1]

European fiction, mostly of the didactic class, had been imported and imitated by Brown's predecessors and influenced his contemporaries. The Gothic novel and the historical tale were running their course abroad and were just being introduced into America. Brown wrote with a new viewpoint—that of creating an American literature separate from England's. He could not break away at once from the form and method of handling his material, but he surely sought new material from the manners and thoughts of the people and from the events and nature of the country. He became America's first imaginative, as well as realistic, writer. He opened up the national field of romance in which American literature won its most notable successes a few years later,—in Cooper, Poe and Hawthorne.

As a romancer, Brown was idealistic, rather than imaginative; he employed picturesque strangeness or variety, suggestive of adventure. As a realist, he was objective and scientific; he employed natural backgrounds, facts and development in mental and moral faculties. His novels combine romance and realism.

Brown belonged to the experimental period of American fiction and suffered the fate that attends all who try to bridge over from the old to the new. If he had lived in a later period, perhaps, or in a more hospitable time and if he had lived the length of a

---

1. Simpson, *Lives of Eminent Philadelphians*, 151.

normal life and in health, he would have produced works of a superior class, have won a secure place in fiction and have had a large following.

". . . as it is, his importance historically in the evolution of American novel making is great, for he may be pointed to as the founder of serious fiction in this country,"[1] according to Richard Burton.

---

1. Burton, *Literary Leaders of America*, 11.

CHAPTER II

INFLUENCES OPERATIVE UPON BROWN AS NOVELIST

"This was a good fellow; a sound, hearty specimen of Trans-Atlantic stuff. Brown was an American to the backbone—without knowing it. He was a novelist, an imitator of Godwin, whose *Caleb Williams* made him."[1]

Although this statement by Neal is not wholly true, yet it is a fact that Brown, like all early American writers, gained much inspiration from the literary influences that came from the mother country. *Caleb Williams* is a fictional demonstration of some of the doctrines of the author's *Political Justice*. Many of these doctrines, as Preston pointed out, have their sources in the works of previous writers. Shakespeare has been such a source of supply that it is interesting to quote the words of Herman Melville in *Pierre* (p. 151) regarding Hamlet as

"the Hamletism of 3000 years ago. . . . And the English tragedy is but Egyptian Memnon, Montaignized and modernized; for being but a mortal man Shakespeare had his fathers too."

The same thought was succinctly axiomized by Lowell thus: "The pedigrees of books are as interesting and instructive as those of men." The pedigrees of Brown's novels will be traced in this chapter and in a later chapter the pedigrees of novels stemming from his novels.

Certain writers began to show revolt against the Classicists, or the didactic school,—the age of Dryden, Pope and Johnson. The general tendency of literature was to look at life critically, to emphasize intellect rather than imagination and form rather than content. Writers strove to suppress all emotion and to use only

---

1. Neal, in *Blackwood's Magazine*, XVI, 421, Oct., 1824. (Signed X. Y. Z.)

elegant, precise methods of expression. Literature was critical, intellectual, polished. The transition from the dominating didactic writings, much of it poetry, and the imported French heroic romances and their English imitators, to natural prose, was of slow growth. The works of the lesser writers for a century showed the rise of a new spirit—a spirit of observation, attention to detail, stress upon factual material, bold analysis of feeling and argument upon institutions—and included character writings, satires on romance, the works of Bunyan, Addison, Steele, Defoe, Swift, Congreve, whose novel, *Incognita,* he said, was the first to observe dramatic laws.

The literature of England, especially the novel, showed many variations during the last half of the eighteenth century and the literature of this country reflected more or less closely most of its phases. Five types of revolt literature as they developed in fiction will be discussed, showing how they influenced Brown.

A beginning of sentimentalism is found in Richardson (1740), its full flowering in Fielding and Sterne and its climax in Mackenzie. Richardson sought to investigate the emotions of the heart and to interpret them in a sympathetic manner. His use of the epistolary form and his portrayal of sentiment gained an immediate popularity and resulted in founding the School of Sentiment, which settled the trend of fiction in England and on the Continent for several decades and found followers, besides those named, in Goldsmith, Fannie Burney, Jane Austen, Thackeray and a multitude of others, including the early American novelists. The best of these writers gave a refined view of society, a true insight into the psychological nature and incidents of a commonplace kind. Of all the persons to criticize the cultivation of sentiment, the last would be Mrs. Radcliffe, one would think. She said, it is
"a dangerous quality which is continually extracting the excess of misery or delight from every surrounding object."

The autobiographical novel was an outgrowth of the Richardson novel, which was itself autobiographical to a certain extent. Richardson captured the idea from Defoe, who, copying somewhat the Spanish picaresque type of story, developed in England a sort of realistic autobiographical adventure narrative which was largely fictitious. He made a fabric of invention, a fabulous story, or a pretended argument appear absolutely real and true, for he went to recorders of facts, biographers, writers of voyages and travels, historians and annalists, for much of his source material. But he did not subordinate incident to the depiction of life and character. Fielding, Smollett, Sterne, Godwin and Dickens were followers of Defoe in this line of development.

Another important type of novel of the same period was the so-called historical novel. In 1762, Thomas Leland published *Longsword,* in which he tried to provide a story of adventure against a background of history. The historical novel, presenting characters, manners and customs, was attempted by many writers with mediocre success, of whom were Clara Reeve, Jane Porter and Maria Edgeworth. It reached its fullest development when perfected in the first third of the nineteenth century by the incomparable Sir Walter Scott, who said in his General Preface to the Waverly Novels (1829):

"Without being so presumptuous, as to hope to emulate the rich humour, pathetic tenderness, and admirable tact, which pervade the works of my accomplished friend, I felt that something might be attempted for my own country, of the same kind with that which Miss Edgeworth so fortunately achieved for Ireland."

A fourth variation in fiction was the romance. A new school arose called the Romantic or Gothic School or the School of Terror. The term Gothic came from Germany after the English romances, embodying the extravagant and grotesque details of mediaeval material, had been taken to Germany and brought back again. The Romanticists used imaginative, improbable and abnormal circumstances in place of the intellectual, satiric, practical and conventional, of the didacticians. They maintained that a reality of the imagination might be as satisfying and as important as a reality of the reason, since the human mind has the power of imagining as well as of thinking. The Gothic School, almost from its beginning, was noted for its lavish use of the unusual, the mysterious, the terrible. Improbabilities and the supernatural were employed at will. Overwrought joys and sorrows, abductions, seductions, murders, imprisonments and a gloomy or morose environment enveloping the whole were habitual. This school was pre-Romantic to Romanticism in the best sense. Romantic manifestations were evident in the Orientalism of Johnson and Beckford and in the works of Smollett and many others. Horace Walpole wrote the first truly Gothic romance, *The Castle of Otranto,* and awakened supernatural terrors that, half a century or more later, reached its height in *Frankenstein* by Mrs. Shelley and *Melmoth the Wanderer* by Maturin. He declared his intention to unite the marvellous and the real. In three particulars, at least, he created innovations which were to become commonplace in early romantic literature. He made the ancient ruined Gothic castle with all its accessories and mediaeval machinery, such as under-ground vaults, pictures, panels, trap-doors and so forth, the centre of interest. To the scene of the castle, he suited physical and climatic conditions—the moonlight, the blasts of wind, the dark and awesome woods, storms and the like, which were used to such good effect by Clara Reeve, Mrs. Radcliffe, Lewis, Godwin, Maturin, Scott, the Shelleys and others. And, finally, he gave the earliest prototype of the Byronic hero, a mysterious man, dark, handsome, melancholy, passionate, "with large black eyes, a smooth white forehead, and manly curling locks like jet."[1] If one comes to think of it, John Neal's description of Brown's appearance makes him Byronic.

Fifteen years before "Otranto" and many years preceding the sentimentalists and romanticists, Fielding predicted that "a swarm of foolish novels and monstrous romances will be produced, to impoverishment of booksellers, or to the great loss of time and depravation of morals in the reader . . . even to the spreading of scandal and calumny."[2]

The variations of the Gothic type, which may be said to consist in the addition of strangeness to terror, have been grouped into three classes: "the supernatural Gothic of Walpole and Lewis, the mechanical or architectural Gothic of Mrs. Radcliffe, and the psychological or Revolutionary Gothic of William Godwin."[3]

The novel of purpose in England grew out of the political unrest occasioned by the French Revolution, which immeasurably affected the whole civilized world. After the turmoil was over, literature began her resolute work of reform, in behalf of the natural rights of man and the abolition of class distinctions. It came to be the fashion, almost the necessity, one might say, that fiction to be

1. Walpole, *The Castle of Otranto*, Preface, **XX**.
2. Fielding, *Tom Jones*, I, 461.
3. Loshe, *The Early American Novel*, 30.

acceptable must be written as an educational story, an illustration
of some truth, a novel of theory or, at least, a historical tale.
Numerous authors put purpose into their stories, but Godwin and
Mary Wollstonecraft out-ranked the rest and became the typical
writers of this class of novel. Nearly all novelists of the period
were reformers. Their theme was the history of persons, regarded
as moral beings and treated in relation to each other and to society.
In this manner Brown treated his characters. Social, political and
educational reforms, ordinarily expressed in didactic prose, were
now introduced into fiction.

The School of Terror and the School of Reform or Theory ran
neck and neck. The latter said, appropriating the words of Johnson
regarding Gray's poem, "The Bard" (1780):

"he that forsakes the probable may always find the marvelous. And
it has little use; we are affected only as we believe; we are improved only as we find something to be imitated or declined."
By Walpole's recognition of the age-old truth that "we are affected
also as we imagine," he is entitled to a high place among the
builders of modern Romanticism, which founded the School of
Terror. Edith Birkhead in *The Tale of Terror* remarked:

"The dictum that we are affected only as we believe is open to grave
doubt. We are often thrown into a state of trepidation simply
through the power of imagination. We are wise after the event."

The two schools were by no means exhaustive of the prose fiction
of the modern Romantic Revival—"the renascence of wonder,"
Theodore Watts-Dunton called it. They brought forth a renewed
feeling for Nature, an interest in the supernatural through Gothic
mediaevalism and a love for poetic effects. The historical romance,
largely pseudo-historic, came to its completeness in Scott, who
revived Scottish legendary lore. Early in life he

"nourished the ambitious desire of composing a tale of chivalry,
which was to be in the style of the castle of Otranto, with plenty
of Border characters and supernatural incidents."
He did just that with his discursive, imaginative, humorous, historical tales.

Thus were blended currents from the School of Sentiment, the
Autobiographical Story, the Historical Tale, the School of Terror
and the Rationalistic School of Theory. From these sources Brown
drew inspiration; and mingled strains from them appear in his

novels. These influences together with the American environment and his own mind, the impelling quality of which was its ingenuity, both imaginative and psychological, determined the nature of his novels. His work as novelist ended when he was thirty; it is the immature product of a born writer with a well-stored, creative brain, eager to express original conceptions, yet hampered by the influence of English models.

That Brown fully appreciated the influence of English writers on the thought of the American public may be noted in the following quotation, designed chiefly as a discussion of the question of class in England:
"There is somewhat in the advantages of birth and rank, in the habit of viewing objects through the medium of books, that gives a sacred obscurity, a mysterious elevation, to human beings. I had been familiar with the names nobility and royalty, but the things themselves had ever been shrouded in an awe-creating darkness. . . . The ideas annexed to the term *peasant* are wholly inapplicable to the tillers of the ground in America; but our notions are the offspring more of the books we read, than of any other of our external circumstances. Our books are almost wholly the productions of Europe, and the prejudices which infect us are derived chiefly from this source. . . . In me they possessed an unusual degree of strength. My words were selected and defined according to foreign usages and my notions of dignity were modelled on a scale which the *Revolution* has completely taken away. I could never forget that my condition was that of a *peasant;* and, in spite of reflection, I was the slave of those sentiments of self-contempt and humiliation which pertain to that condition elsewhere, though chimerical and visionary on the western side of the Atlantic."[1]

To obviate repeating Brown's name each time one of his novels is mentioned, the titles are listed here: *Wieland, Ormond, Arthur Mervyn, Edgar Huntly, Clara Howard* and *Jane Talbot,* published between 1798 and 1801. The novels will be treated individually in Chapter III. In this chapter, illustrations from these six novels and from novels of the five classes will be given to suggest their relationship.

The epistolary form of Brown's novels unquestionably follows the precedent of Richardson, Fielding and Sterne, the three out-

---

1. *Clara Howard,* 329.

standing sentimentalists. From acting as a letter-writer for working girls and receiving a commission to write a series of Familiar Letters as models, Samuel Richardson first wrote *Pamela, or Virtue Rewarded* (1740-1), a four-volumed publication of a series of letters telling of the trials, tribulations and happy marriage of a young maiden. By this method, the girl reveals her inner life, among her English neighbors, from within. *Clarissa, or the History of a Young Lady* (1747-8) followed, was popular and is more human, giving the young lady's doubts and scruples of conscience, her grief and her humiliation. Constantia Dudley in *Ormond,* like Clarissa, is long-suffering and her virtue is maintained steadfast against Ormond's pursuit of her. The word *closet,* applied to one of Clara Wieland's rooms and used a few times elsewhere may stem from Richardson's reading the parts of *Pamela* to his wife and a young lady living with them. They used to come into his little *closet* every night with, "Have you any more of Pamela, Mr. R.?"

Of *Wieland,* Brown says in the Advertisement, September 3, 1798:
"It will be necessary to add, that this narrative is addressed, in an epistolary form, by the lady whose story it contains, to a small number of friends, whose curiosity, with regard to it, had been greatly awakened."
All Brown's novels are epistolary, but *Clara Howard* and *Jane Talbot* follow the pattern more closely and are stories of sentiment and self-revelation of maidens.

The letter method provides information that seems to be natural and plausible; and the writer is enabled to give minute analyses of mood, temper and motive. Whether the letter is written by one person, as *Wieland,* or whether the letters are written by different characters, who provide information from several viewpoints, the result is a continuous soliloquy. The soliloquy is the greatest device for self-revelation and self-analysis and serves the author well in his revelation of sentiment.

Two works are of interest before conceding credit to Richardson. More than fifty years before *Pamela,* Madame de la Fayette had written her last story and masterpiece, *La Princesse de Cleves* (1678), no doubt well known in England. Her stories manifested interest in the study of passions and the analysis of conduct; and their brevity, directness and simplicity are a great contrast to the long and involved novels of this period. Richardson wrote long stories, but cut them up by the form of letters. Both he and his English followers and Brown studied passions and reasons for conduct. This method of analysis and sentiment and the name Pamela (shortened) Richardson inherited, the former from La Fayette and the name from Sidney's *Arcadia,* published fifty years earlier yet. The epistolary style may have come to Richardson from his countrywoman, Margaret, Duchess of Newcastle, who wrote *CCXI Sociable Letters* (1664). She anticipated him in the discovery that letters, to be entertaining, need not be really exchanged by living correspondents and explained that they are, "rather scenes than letters, for I have endeavoured under cover of letters to express the humours of mankind."[1]

Richardson is credited with having fathered the epistolary vogue which
"in a manner produced Henry Fielding and all the fair herd of his successors down to the present day," said George Saintsbury.
He also receives the credit of having written the first modern novel. A true novel must subordinate incidents to the faithful description of characters and actions. Before completing *Pamela,* Richardson perceived that he was introducing "a new species of writing." His hope was that it
"might possibly turn young people into a course of reading different from the pomp and parade of romance writing, and dismissing the improbable and marvellous, with which novels generally abound, might tend to promote the cause of religion and virtue . . . All my stories carried with them, I am bold to say, an useful moral."[2]
Brown expressed a similar thought in the Advertisement of *Wieland*:
"The following work is delivered to the world as the first of a series of performances. . . . His purpose is neither selfish nor temporary, but aims at the illustration of some important branches of the moral constitution of man."

Fielding's first novel, *Joseph Andrews,* was inspired by the success of *Pamela* and was begun as a burlesque upon the false senti-

---

1. Raleigh, *The English Novel,* 118.
2. *Ibid.,* 143-4.

mentality and the conventional virtues of the heroine. His hero is the alleged brother of Pamela, who was exposed to the same kind of temptations, but who, instead of being rewarded, was turned out of doors by his mistress. Fielding used humor and direct, vigorous, harsh, coarse language; whereas Richardson used no humor and sentimental words and morals. Fielding laid most stress on native impulse, goodness of heart and the individual's conformity to his better self; Richardson built his morality on conformity to social standards—good form. Brown, especially in *Arthur Mervyn,* based all the actions of the hero on his right intentions and habitual benevolence of heart, after the manner of Fielding.

With the foibles and feminine emotions of women of middle class society, who move in a narrow circle, Richardson was acquainted; Fielding knew all classes, from the aristocratic to which he and his cousin, Lady Montagu, also a writer, belonged, to those of sponging-houses, which he frequented, and dens of vice, courts, prisons and other places, which he as an officer of the law investigated. He was a dramatist; and, although the plots of *Tom Jones* (1749) (which Coleridge called one of the three perfect ones of the world) and *Joseph Andrews* contain innumerable adventures, yet they lead to inevitable conclusions. Unity of action is achieved partly, at least, by his introducing minor plots rather than mere episodes or digressions. In *Tom Jones,* the relation of the by-plots and even the book introductions to the principal theme is everywhere established. Brown maintained this same kind of unity,—for example, in *Wieland* and *Arthur Mervyn,* by means of confessions, though not smoothly entered in every case. Wieland's and Carwin's are introduced rather abruptly; Welbeck's confessions of his crimes and Arthur's explanations of his many enterprises and the story of the yellow fever seem less forced into position, having preliminary introductions.

It is to Fielding to go for models of conversation. He enlivens it by making single sentences do for the purpose. Brown makes use of conversation, often in short sentences and questions and suits the words to his characters, perceptibly where Arthur's many visits to persons of many sorts occasion varied conversations. Fielding satirizes false conventions of conduct and false ideas of greatness. Brown may not employ real satire often, but he denounces false ideas,—for instance, superstitions about good and evil spirits, religious fanaticism, imposture and gullibility, in *Wieland.*

Variety of incident, scenery and character with little pictures of action and behavior show the moralistic progress in Fielding's stories and probably influenced Brown to a limited degree. That he recognized Fielding, aside from incidentally, is his choice of names: Sophia Westwyn in *Ormond* from Sophia Western, the heroine of *Tom Jones,* Field and Fielding in *Arthur Mervyn,* Fielder in *Edgar Huntly,* Fields in *Jane Talbot.* It may be that the name Sophia, used by Fielding, Brown and Scott, is a reflection from the novelist, "Sophia, a Person of Quality," writer of a work on women (1739), or, perhaps, from Sophia Lee, author of *Recess* (1783-5).

The third of the great sentimentalists, Laurence Sterne, may have influenced Brown specifically, in his two dissimilar stories, *Tristram Shandy* and *A Sentimental Journey Through France and Italy,* never completed. The former records the experiences of the eccentric Shandy family. Clara Wieland writes the story of the susceptible, harassed Wieland family that it may benefit mankind by inculcating the duty of avoiding deceit. At the opening and a few more times within the narrative she stops to express her feelings about writing such a story:

"You are a stranger to the depth of my distresses. . . . The experience of no human being can furnish a parallel: that I, beyond the rest of mankind, should be reserved for a destiny without alleviation and without example! . . . A few more words and I lay aside the pen forever. . . . Every sentiment has perished in my bosom. Even friendship is extinct. Your love for me has prompted me to this task; but I would not have complied if it had not been a luxury thus to feast upon my woes. . . . Why not terminate at once this series of horrors? . . . I will die, but then only when my task is at an end."[1]

She continues agitating herself sentimentally and adds an extra chapter to make the story "turn out."

A *Sentimental Journey* is a miscellany of essays of fiction, travel and descriptions of odd characters. Part II of *Arthur Mervyn,* detailing Arthur's journeys hither and thither, reminds one of

---

1. *Wieland,* 25, 26, 240, 247.

Sterne's work in form, but not in purpose. Arthur interviews people to do them good; Sterne seeks for sentiment in himself with relation to the characters he meets. *Arthur Mervyn,* being written in the first person, follows the autobiographical method as Sterne does, which gives a chance for intimate, personal soliloquy and minute details of experience. It makes for individuality and exception to the general concepts of the novel.

As an example of Sterne's epistles is this excerpt from his mawkish letter to Eliza:

"He heard me talk of thee, Eliza, with uncommon satisfaction—as I talked of thee an hour without intermission. . . . But thou, Eliza, wert the star that conducted and livened the discourse (till past nine o'clock)! And when I talked not of thee, still didst thou fill my mind, and warm every thought I uttered, for I am not ashamed to acknowledge I greatly miss thee. Best of all good girls! . . . Grateful and good girl! . . . You could least dispense with what is contrary to your own nature, which is soft and gentle, Eliza; it would civilize savages. . . . Write to me, my child, thy delicious letters. Let them speak the easy carelessness of a heart that opens itself anyhow, everyhow. Such, Eliza, I write to thee!"[1]

Thus wrote Sterne at 54 to Eliza at 25. He was tired of his wife of 25 years. Before he had married her, he wrote:

"As I take up my pen, my poor pulse quickens, my pale face glows, and my tears are trickling down on my paper as I trace the word L."[2]

Did Brown know of Sterne's Eliza when he gave that name to the Hadwin girl in whom Arthur became interested?

"The images that haunted me at home and abroad, in her absence and her presence, gradually coalesced into one shape, and gave birth to an incessant train of latent palpitations and indefinable hopes. My days were little else than uninterrupted reveries, and night only called up phantoms more vivid and equally enchanting."[3]

Arthur thought matters over. Eliza was fifteen and a Quaker, which "sect forbade marriage of its votaries with those of a different communion." He provided for her care and education after the deaths of the others of her family. They kept up a corre-

---

1. Thackeray, The English Humorists: Sterne, in John Matthews Manly, *English Prose and Poetry,* 574-5.
2. *Ibid.,* 574.
3. *Arthur Mervyn,* I, 125.

spondence; and one of Eliza's letters has all the flutterings of accusation over his forgetfulness, upbraidings, pleadings and imaginings as to what he is doing. In spite of long letters to her, she complains:

"but my soul droops when I call to mind your voice and your looks. . . . I am at a loss for words; I am bewildered and bemazed. . . . With your arm about me, and your sweet face close to mine, I can prattle forever. . . . I don't read somehow so earnestly and understand so well as . . . when my mind was all at ease, always frolicksome, and ever upon *tiptoe,* as I may say. . . . I, that was ever light of heart, the very soul of gayety, brimfull of glee, am now demure as our old *tabby.*"[1]

Arthur decided he would tire of her endless prattle and married Mrs. Fielding, who knew and loved books.

Betty Lawrence, the stepmother of Arthur, may have been surnamed from Laurence Sterne, with a different spelling. Certainly Brown's "inevitability of death," several ways expressed, reminds one of the tale, "This Is the House That Jack Built." In *Tom Jones* (1749), Fielding says, "Death is certainly unavoidable and is the common lot in which alone the fortunes of all men agree."[2] Sterne says in *Tristram Shandy* (1760-7): " 'Tis an inevitable chance—the first statute in Magna Charta." He copied from Robert Burton who wrote the very same words in his *Anatomy of Melancholy* (1621) about one hundred fifty years earlier. The American author denationalized the saying thus: "Death is the inevitable and universal lot. When or how it comes is of little moment."[3] "Death being the universal lot, he considered the time and manner as indifferent circumstances."[4]

Continuing the discussion of the novels of sentiment, or society novels as they are called, three other authors will be mentioned and their possible influence over Brown.

To connect the influence of Oliver Goldsmith upon Brown to any appreciable extent may be supposing. His knowledge of human nature is comparable with Brown's in *Arthur Mervyn,* whose hero this writer thinks means the author himself in his attitude toward

---

1. *Arthur Mervyn,* II, 182, 183.
2. Fielding, *Tom Jones,* I, 218.
3. *Arthur Mervyn,* I, 193.
4. Brown, "Sketches of the Carrils and Ormes," in Dunlap, *op. cit.,* I, 387.

life. Goldsmith, in his only novel, *The Vicar of Wakefield* (1766), exhibits a good man unmoved by adversity and multiplies misfortunes upon the head of his hero until he lands in prison. This experience in prison shows discipleship in Brown, perhaps. Goldsmith's simplicity of diction and power to create real and ordinary life among the Vicar's family and acquaintances, his loosely-constructed plot, indifference to the temporal destiny of his characters and huddled conclusions of incidents at the end may have had an unconscious, rather than a definite, influence upon Brown.

The year of Brown's birth (1771), a young man of twenty-six, about the age of Brown when he wrote his first novel, Henry Mackenzie, sprang into sentimental fame with his book, *The Man of Feeling.*
" 'The illustration of the nicer and finer sensibilities of the human breast,' his single theme, is entirely unrelieved by any touch of humour or satire, and the Man of Feeling—all feeling and nothing but feeling, becomes merely maudlin . . . a mere succession of scenes designed to awake tender or compassionate sensibilities,"[1] commented Raleigh.

If people take color from all whom they have met and from all the books they have read, Frances (Fannie) Burney may claim a contribution to Brown. Miss Burney, at the English Court as Madame D'Arblay, wrote the novel *Evelina* (1778), describing the speech, manners and characters of the ordinary life of middle-class society, amid a life of fashion. She introduces Evelina into the ways of the world and to her unknown father. In this latter respect, Brown seems to have modeled the life of Louisa in *Wieland.* One of the children murdered by Wieland was Louisa Conway, whom the Wielands had reared from the age of four. It is interesting to connect the discovery of her relationship to Major Stuart, with the father-daughter revelation in *Evelina,* written twenty years before *Wieland.* The child's mother had left England for America and changed her name. When Stuart is incidentally introduced to Miss Conway, he exclaims in an eager and faltering tone,
" 'Who is she? whence does she come? what is her name?' . . . Having heard the tale, he melted into tears, eagerly clasped the young lady in his arms, and called himself her father. . . . Major

---

1. Raleigh, *The English Novel,* 201, 202.

Stuart proved himself a man of most amiable character. His attachment to Louisa appeared hourly to increase."[1]

In *Evelina,* Mrs. Selwyn calls: "Come forth and see your father!" Evelina gave an involuntary scream and sank to the floor.

Her father says: "My God! does Caroline Evelyn still live! (meaning the injured wife whom he had destroyed)."

Mrs. Selwyn urges him to do his wife justice by acknowledging her child. He says, "Yes, yes . . . I see, I see thou art her child! she lives—she breathes,—she is present to my view! . . . Go, child, go (added he, wildly starting and pushing her from him), take her away, Madam,—I cannot bear to look at her!"[2] Then with a violence almost fanatic, he ran upstairs.

Perhaps, Brown's Louisa was named from Lady Louisa in *Evelina.* Brown may have read of such a situation closer to his own time. Mrs. Inchbald in *A Simple Story* (1791) has a meeting of a father with a daughter who, though not exactly casting her off, has persistently refused to see her, in revenge for her mother's unfaithfulness,—adopting the attitude of the father of Evelina. They are similar incidents, but oppositely carried out,—carried out by Brown with all the tenderness of his heart for the orphan Louisa.

Two renowned English writers of autobiographical or adventure stories surely affected Brown,—Smollett and Defoe. Of Tobias Smollett, Thackeray remarked: "I fancy he did not invent much." In *Roderick Random* (1748) and *Humphrey Clinker* (1771) he kept very close to experience and sometimes reported only his family history,—which makes them largely autobiographical. It can be said of Brown that he kept close to his personal experience and knowledge of the yellow fever in *Ormond* and *Arthur Mervyn.* Contrary to the reported general inability to invention by Smollett, Brown was not without constant surprises of invention and description of scenes and events purely American and unheard of heretofore in fiction, unless incidentally. Smollett is credited with supplying his characters and scenes with accessories. Brown does it often, as where Clara Wieland is provided a house suitable in all respects to her activities and to the machinations of her opponents, Carwin and Judith,—also, convenient for her brother and Pleyel. Of course, Brown's love of architecture from his early years gave

---

1. *Wieland,* 47-9.
2. Burney, *Evelina,* 344, 345.

him an advantage in house-planning and in interior furnishings, of which he makes frequent mention and particularizes.

No doubt, Smollett suffered as Brown did in the rush of producing stories. He published three picaresque novels in five years. Brown was working on five stories at once, which with his sixth were published within three or four years. In *Roderick Random* (1748) and *Peregrine Pickle* (1751), Smollett surrounded some of his ocean scenes and fights with such gloom and tragedy, such imaginary terrors of darkness and solitude, that he may be said to have fathered the Gothic as far as sea stories are concerned and may have given Brown the same tincture of gloom, maybe even his fear of the ocean. In *Ferdinand, Count Fathom* (1753), the author furthered, "The clock struck twelve, the owl screeched from the ruined battlement," on their peregrinage. These and most other typical accessories—witchcraft, spirits, ghosts, and howling dogs—Shakespeare, two centures earlier, started on their way to full fruition in the Gothic romance. Smollett preceded both Walpole and Mrs. Radcliffe in the effects of natural scenery, nerve-jitters, suspicions and forebodings.

"A novel," Smollett defined, "is a large diffused picture, comprehending the characters of life, disposed in different groups and exhibited in various attitudes, for the purposes of an uniform plan. . . . this plan cannot be executed with propriety, probability, or success, without a principal personage to attract the attention, unite the incidents, unwind the clue of the labyrinth, and at last close the scene, by virtue of his own importance."[1]
Such unity as his novels have is due entirely to this device of the "principal personage." Every one of Brown's novels has the name of the hero or heroine for its title; so he followed Smollett's definition in that respect. Notwithstanding the principal personage suggested as a unifier, it is not the person as actor so much as acted upon by circumstances, which transform his character. With Brown the theme is the means of unity of characters and incidents.

Long before Smollett gave his definition of the novel, Defoe adopted the method of dramatizing and unifying the events narrated from their bearing on the fortunes of one person. Nobody can doubt that Defoe was read eagerly by Brown as a youth and

---

1. Raleigh, *The English Novel*, 185.

colored his writings. *Robinson Crusoe* (1719-20) is often placed first in the list of modern novels, vying with the same claim for Richardson. The story is undeniably based upon fact, is realistic in that and in the bold, convincing style of the telling of thoughts, feelings and incidents, which every reader recognizes as being true to life, and withal exhibits the human will in its patience, fortitude and indomitable spirit of overcoming all obstacles. Defoe purports to give an allegoric version of his own history—
"of one whole scene of real life of eight and twenty years, spent in the most wandering, desolate and afflicting circumstances that ever a man went through."

He discovered that biography loses none of its interest when the life it records has never been lived.

The autobiographical form is typical in *Arthur Mervyn*. In Part I, Arthur relates his experiences during the yellow fever epidemic; in Part II, he carries out his beneficent undertakings. He insinuates himself into all kinds of predicaments, some foolhardy enough; but through his good intentions and will to persevere he accomplishes his purposes in the end. He divulges his hopes and feelings as he goes from one adventure to another as Brown might have done, were it his life story.

Defoe's novel is one of memory and research, not of imagination: he pictures the splendors and terrors of nature, but does not show how they affect man in his solitude. In both these respects Brown wrote quite contrarywise. He is imaginative in his choice of wonders and in the incidents to support them; and his familiarity with nature in all its variety led him to employ scenes to reflect the moods of his characters.

In studying the unusual scientific phenomena, about which people were superstitious, Brown had, without doubt, read Defoe's *Essay on the History and Reality of Apparitions* (1727). Disbelieving in the supernatural himself, he explains the only supposed apparition, when Clara Wieland, one evening in her home, gets a glimpse of Carwin,—"a form ordinarily invisible had been unshrouded."

When considering Defoe's influence, recognition must be made of his *Journal of the Plague Year* (1722), in which the horrors of the plague in London, 1665, are minutely recorded. In *Arthur Mervyn*, by means of the yellow fever, Brown tests the benevolence and selfishness of people as they are respectively exhibited by many individuals in the face of such calamity. The alternate title of the book, *Memoirs of the Year 1793,* refers to but one year, as does Defoe's, from which the title may have been suggested; yet the fever he describes may have been of both Philadelphia (1793) and New York (1798).

To go back a little farther, one might ally Brown through Defoe to Thomas Nash, if not directly, who in his *The Unfortunate Traveller, or the Life of Jacke Wilton* (1594), gave the earliest English example of the picaresque romance, which contains a historical element in that Jacke Wilton is page to the Earl of Surrey, of the time of Henry VIII., and describes the desolate condition of Rome during the plague, as does also another work, *Christ's Teares. The Unfortunate Traveller* stands alone in its era as the first realistic novel, as does Defoe's *Robinson Crusoe* in his time, a century later, the author of which in going back to nature may also have gone back to Nash, for there are many parallelisms in the books of the two, it is reported.

Brown was also a political writer and a journalist. He may have admired Defoe in this kind of writing and followed somewhat his method. For Defoe was an occasional writer,
"pouring from the press a profusion of satires, political pamphlets, verses, and moral treatises, to the number of more than two hundred, inspired by the moment and writing under a pressure that sometimes contorts his syntax."[1]
"Defoe was a journalist and pamphleteer. . . . This long journalistic career, lasting half a century, accounts for his direct, simple, narrative style."[2]
Brown's published works are the equivalent of twenty-four volumes, all of which were crowded within about half of his thirty-nine years of life. He never had a chance at mature writing. *Robinson Crusoe* was written when Defoe was fifty-eight years of age.

In the course of time, the purely supernatural and romantic were supplemented by the historical, or purportedly historical, element. Perhaps, taking a hint from Smollett's grim horrors, Thomas Leland produced *Longsword, Earl of Salisbury,* in which he introduced the graveyard scene, the clock striking twelve, and the

---

1.   Raleigh, *The English Novel,* 127.
2.   Long, *English Literature,* 347.

owl's screech, thus becoming a forerunner of the standard-type Gothic romance a few years later, according to a commentator. He was among the first to use history as the background. This historical tale is based upon the character of the Norman nobleman, William Longespee (surnamed Longsword), the third earl of Salisbury, natural son of Henry II., who died in 1226.

Clara Reeve, from whom Brown partook, as evidenced from the name Clara Wieland, it may be, and from the quotation about the baby in the discussion of *Arthur Mervyn,* which she may have borrowed from Fielding's foundling baby Tom Jones, added another link in the chain of the Gothic romance. *The Old English Baron,* formerly titled *Champion of Virtue* (1777), was "the literary offspring" of Walpole's *The Castle of Otranto,* the author asserted. "Had the story been kept within the utmost *verge* of possibility the effect had been preserved." So Miss Reeve planned to keep her story within the realm of probability by revising it. The supernatural element is the ghost of the murdered baron. However, it was a forward movement, anticipating Mrs. Radcliffe's romances in certain particulars—atmosphere, music, logical explanations and secret closed rooms, believed haunted.

One of the earliest of these modern historical tales was that of Sophia Lee: *Recess, or a Tale of Other Times,* dealing with intrigue in the days of Elizabeth.

"The heroine is one of twin sisters, the offspring of a secret marriage, unknown to history, between Mary Queen of Scots and the Duke of Norfolk; the events of her life are represented, with almost incredible effrontery, as interwoven with the lives and fates of" Queen Elizabeth and the lords of her time.[1]
Twins! May not Sophia Lee's twins have prompted Brown to enter twins in *Edgar Huntly* and in his earlier *Sophia—Jessy Romance* and in *Memoirs of Stephen Calvert?* May not the name of Clara Wieland's room, the recess, have come from the title of this book? Her swooning, lute-playing heroine, thunderstorms and banditti may have been given to Mrs. Radcliffe.

The historical element appears in numerous details in Brown's novels, but at length in his introduction of yellow fever in *Ormond* and *Arthur Mervyn.* The division of historical fiction would lack

---

1. Raleigh, *The English Novel,* 279.

much without the naming of Scott. The influence in his case is reversed. He wrote after Brown and partook of the heritage of novels that Brown left,—as shall be explained in due time.

Brown was the first American who transferred the Gothic type of romance from the Old World to the New. Although he was influenced by the Gothic School in England, he struck out for himself in certain essentials. He abandoned the highly improbable methods of the extreme Gothicists and attempted to attain the two characteristics which are now aimed at by every literary artist— truth in local color and truth to the facts of science. He tried to make his backgrounds American and to use incidents which had happened or might happen in America, instead of in the haunted castles of his English predecessors. It has been charged against Brown that he too freely made use of improbabilities and that he was un-American in many particulars. In general, romance gathers materials from wherever it can find them, and on the whole the novels of Brown are far more American than *The Castle of Otranto, The Mysteries of Udolpho* and *The Monk* are English.

Without realizing it, Horace Walpole, the most brilliant writer of his time, by his *The Castle of Otranto* (1764), fathered the Gothic School. He opened the whole untouched mediaeval source of historical, social and literary material, which a flock of writers used subsequently in their romances. These centered round old castles with hidden doors, haunted chambers, secret corridors and subterranean dungeons. A few pages farther on will be garnered from Brown's novels similar furnishings and nerve-wracking fears, such as Walpole Pandora-like let loose.

From 1789-97, Mrs. Ann Radcliffe wrote several weird romances of haunted castles and distressed heroines, ridding them of ghosts and unexplainable phenomena and substituting fears and hallucinations brought about by hair-raising circumstances and events that worked on the victim's nerves.

In *The Monk* (1795), written by Matthew Lewis when he was twenty, the author reached the height, or the depth, of atrocity and indecency, which Walpole was "far too much of a gentleman and a true man of letters to attempt or to tolerate," remarked a critic. Lewis' "imagination is gross, boyish, vulgar, and his horrors rest mainly on a physical basis. He was foolish enough to throw over all the restraints that Mrs. Radcliffe had observed, and to attempt explicit climax," said Raleigh. In this and in other works he showed himself a clever youth with a lively fancy and grasped in advance and even anticipated popular tendencies in literature. In his *Tales of Terror* he set fashions that novelists revelled in and dwelt upon long and painfully, by relating stories of crime and supernatural agencies and giving the most loathsome details too revolting to recall.

The Orientalism that was so exotic a feature of the later French romantic movement invaded England. An Oriental novel, if novel it can be called, because of its strong moral and didactic purpose, *Rasselas, Prince of Abyssinia* (1759) by Samuel Johnson, may have had something to do with the general gloom and sadness of those who followed in writing novels of moral purpose, including Brown. It is called one of the most powerful of modern fables. *Vathek, an Arabian Tale* (1784) appeared anonymously. It was written by William Beckford in French, translated and published by his friend, Samuel Henley. The hero, a haughty, effeminate Mohammedan calif, influenced by a giaour (infidel) and his evil mother, commits crimes, abjures his faith and offers allegiance to Eblis, the Mohammedan Satan, hoping to regain the throne of the ancient sultans. He is doomed to eternal torment and remorse. About ten years later, Lewis has his monk sell himself to the Devil. Beckford, to vivify to himself his contrivances and gloom, had a castle, Fonthill Abbey, built in Wiltshire, England.

To appreciate Brown's use of the Gothic style, one can do no better than compare in a general way his characteristics with those of Mrs. Radcliffe, considered the most noteworthy writer of that type of fiction in England. None of her imitators approach her in scenic effects, fabrication of plot, creating expedients and skill in devising apparently supernatural occurrences, capable of explanation by human agency and natural co-incidence. She composed her stories of sensational incidents grouped about distinctively romantic characters, especially mysterious heroes stained with unknown vices and crimes, who inspire fear by something unusual or profoundly somber or foreign in their appearance, and young, chaste, beautiful weeping heroines, over whom there hang unsolved mysteries and whose lovers are frank, generous, wild and heroic. She sought to provide for every tragic situation a suitable natural setting of the larger aspects of nature—the gloom of impenetrable forests, wild sunsets, melancholy dawns, the terror and magnificence of tempests. Finally, like a true disciple of the Rationalistic School, she explained with predetermined and satisfying exactness her mysterious machinery. Her machinery, as well as her chief characters, became models for later romanticists.

Although Brown repudiated the employment of such "excesses," to quote his own phrase, as Mrs. Radcliffe used, yet, perhaps, unconsciously, he benefited by suggestion. He did not use Gothic castles, banditti or ghosts, but he followed her example in the use of scenic backgrounds and rational explanation of seemingly impossible events and to some extent in the use of sentiment, type-characters and rush of incident with reality of setting. In Brown's own words, concerning *Arthur Mervyn,*
"to excite and baffle curiosity, without shocking belief, is the end to be contemplated. I have endeavoured to wind up the reader's passions to the highest pitch, and to make the catastrophe, in the highest degree, unexpected and momentous."[1]

The relationship of Brown's novels to Mrs. Radcliffe's, especially to *The Mysteries of Udolpho,* her most famous story, published in 1794, four years before *Wieland,* will now be considered. The major part of her romance in number of words is description of landscapes, seashores, the waters of Italy, mountain masses and passes, rivers, storms, sunshine and shadow,—suiting each picture to the moods and adventures of her characters. At times it seems as if the author forced upon the reader her elaborateness of scenery by repetition of details,—for instance, the many times she repeats the names of the kinds of trees and flowers in different localities. The author had never visited the Apennines, so her revels in mountain vistas, stately forests, glorious skies and splendid sunshine, names of flowers in this region, are gained from reading, from pictures and from tours with her husband to English abbeys, castles, landscapes and lakes. Her wordy descriptions of scenes are almost too poetic and romantic to be emphatic.

Brown describes his scenes more minutely, giving details with nicety, showing that he pictured them as he had actually seen them intimately in his walks—precipitous peaks, limestone caves, narrow

---

1. Brown, Letter to his brother James, New York, Feb. 15th, 1799, in Dunlap, *op. cit.,* II, 97.

gorges, swift mountain torrents. Does this generalized picture sound like Brown's?

"It (walking) was one of Emily's earliest pleasures to ramble among the scenes of nature—soft and glowing landscape—wild wood walks that skirted the mountain—the mountain's stupendous recesses."[1]

Almost competing with her prolificacy in the uses of scenery are her allusions to music, sung by her characters, played on their instruments, heard eerily at midnight in groves and under windows, creating dismay or palpitations of hope. If Brown had not written a treatise on music and had not loved it enough to play an instrument himself and to introduce it in his letters and stories for his own sake, one might consider that Mrs. Radcliffe had inspired him to adopt it.

The plot of her story is somewhat involved, following the St. Aubert family, including Emily the heroine, for a hundred pages of Book I, referring to the castle Udolpho once or twice and dropping it out of Book II at page sixty-four except to tell of the death of Montoni, the owner. The fact that the author carries unexplained superstitions, apparitions, ghostly sounds and voices, a terrible figure in a picture frame behind a veil, secreted or imprisoned persons, supposed ghosts, for long periods or until almost the end of the story, with occasional references to them, unsatisfies the reader, unless he knows beforehand that all will be explained normally. Her stories are romances of suspense.

The readers of Brown's novels are delivered from too long periods of suspense by his giving, at intervals, confessions,—as those of Wieland for his murders and Carwin for his offenses through his power of biloquium. Mrs. Radcliffe's plots have a similarity in that they revolve round beautiful virtuous women tempted almost to their destruction, like Richardson's heroines, as Emily beset by the machinations of Montoni. Brown has that type of story also, as in *Ormond,* Constantia versus Ormond.

The story of Udolpho is not without its scientific interest. It is incidental, however, not such scientific phenomena as Brown made the mainstay of his stories—the bursting of Montoni's glass

---

1. Radcliffe, *The Mysteries of Udolpho,* I, 7.

of liquor as he was about to drink, later explained as caused by the chemical action of liquor poured over poison, and the points of flame seen on the tips of the spears of the guards of the castle, creating wild excitement and dreadful omens, partially explained as electricity drawn to the metal during the gathering of the storm. St. Foix discourses on the natural history of the mountains—mineral and fossil substances—veins of marble and granite—strata of shells near the mountain tops—chasms and caverns. Brown describes, first-hand, mountains, caves and masses of white marble.

A typical scene of Mrs. Radcliffe's handed down to Brown and others is the following: In the haunted wing of Udolpho, Emily is shut up by night and occupies herself variously. If the night is clear, she throws open the casement and lets the moonlight stream into her room. She sits and thinks of her distant lover; and hears the soft tones of a lute. She searches and finds in an old chest a dusty manuscript. She reads and suspects a horrible crime committed in this very room. The candle goes out. She goes to bed. A door, hitherto unnoticed, the bolt drawn, is opened; a man enters and draws near with uplifted sword. She screams. On a rainy night,

"Emily opened her casement, listened with a gloomy pleasure to the distant thunder that began to murmur among the mountains, and watched the arrowy lightnings which broke over the remote scene . . . (she) remained at her casement till the vivid lightning, that now every instant revealed the wide horizon and the landscape below, made it no longer safe to do so, and she went to her couch."[1]

Having seen Carwin, Clara Wieland drew his portrait and says:

"I placed it at all distances and in all lights. . . . Half the night passed away in wakefulness and in contemplation of this picture. . . . Next day arose in darkness and storm. Torrents of rain fell during the whole day, attended with incessant thunder. . . . I had, indeed, no inclination to leave my apartment. . . . I laid aside my usual occupations, and, seating myself at a window, consumed the day in alternately looking out upon the storm and gazing at the picture. . . . I can account for my devotion to this image no otherwise than by supposing that its properties were rare and prodigious."[2]

---

1. Radcliffe, *The Mysteries of Udolpho*, II, 23.
2. *Wieland*, 73-4.

Clara occupied herself with the portrait; Emily, with a manuscript. Clithero in *Edgar Huntly* approached the bed of Mrs. Lorimer with uplifted sword to kill her. The character of Carwin, the "double-tongued deceiver," would have delighted Mrs. Radcliffe, as well as to have done her honor, considering her Montoni who heard voices.

Mrs. Radcliffe presents an atmosphere of terror by association, suggestion, vacuity, darkness, solitude and silence, persuading the reader that something very terrible is going to happen. Brown prepares situations with sights and sounds and unaccountable voices, as in *Wieland* often, that cause Clara to fall in a fit, not a faint or swoon as in older novels; and, like Mrs. Radcliffe, he never permits anything apparently supernatural that cannot be and is not eventually explained, like the facts of ventriloquism and sleep-walking.

Now will follow a discussion of *The Monk,* an estimate of the terror romance, including Brown's novels, a list of some of his Gothecisms and a linking of *Wieland* with the German romance, *Der Geisterseher.*

In the Introduction to his edition of Matthew G. Lewis's *The Monk* (1907), Ernest A. Baker ranked it as
"the most notorious exemplar of the Gothic school of romance, the novel that summarized most concisely the idiosyncracies of its kind and gave so forcible a stimulus to the manufacture of tales of terror."
"Manufacture" is a true epithet in this case, for the author borrowed his effects as he candidly states in his Preface—Santos Barsisa, the Bleeding Nun, the Water King, the Wandering Jew, the Inquisition, and German and Spanish tales,—in whose countries the action of the story takes place.

Incited by the perusal of *The Mysteries of Udolpho,* Lewis wrote *The Monk,* the following year, within ten weeks, before he was twenty. He said, taking the part of a character:
"Authorship is a mania, to conquer which no reasons are sufficiently strong; and you might as easily persuade me not to love, as I persuade you not to write."[1]

---

1. Lewis, *The Monk,* 157.

The book had a large sale and made a great sensation, greeted by both praise and denunciation. Attacks upon its immorality and a reprimand by his father caused Lewis half-heartedly to produce an expurgated edition. He prided himself upon his nickname *Monk.* The story pleased Byron, Shelley and Mrs. Shelley, who hoped to write one book that "would frighten my readers as I have been frightened."

Lewis employed real ghosts, horrendous graveyard, burial and charnel scenes, displayals of gruesome disease and mortality, deaths by starvation, fire and mob violence, abductions and seductions, whose acquaintance he made by the study of German models,— revivals of feudalism, monasticism, ghosts and hobgoblins. His hero is the irreproachable monk, of whom the author says, "What he wanted in purity of heart, he supplied by exterior sanctity," being stained with the most loathed and monstrous crimes—rape, murder and sorcery. His accomplice is in league with demons, and both finally sell their souls to the Devil. All of these things Lewis imaged before the reader with no mincing of words and shocks his nerves through the senses of sight, hearing, smelling and feeling.

The methods of Mrs. Radcliffe and Lewis are given thus explicitly to contrast the two methods used by the School of Terror writers: realistic and poetic. It is the real difference between horror and terror, as Mr. Baker explained.
"By the first, the writer tries to make a semblance of fact, either by apparent truth of description or by the pretense of logical reasoning; or he aims, not at convincing us, but merely by poetic faith—that is, he stimulates the imagination of the reader by means of the suggestive power of language. . . . Whichever method is adopted, the writer may re-inforce his effects to a vast extent by agitating the feelings skilfully and powerfully; and the portrayal of mental states, emotions especially, not only enlarges the field to be exploited, but it is an invaluable aid to both realist and poet, helping to make more credible by awakening sympathy, and adding depth and harmony to the narrative. Mrs. Radcliffe wielded it with masterly skill, by suggestions instead of description, vague hints in lieu of plain statements. Lewis overlooked it. He had no sense of the unnerving power that stalks unseen: a corpse, or at least a skeleton was as efficient a bogey as a ghost."

Another point of contrast is atmosphere:

"one thing of unique importance, the value of atmosphere: land-scapes, ruins, characters, costumes, light and shade, Mrs. Radcliffe subdued by delicate touches to the right key of emotion; everything lulls the reader into the state of mind most harmonious with the incidents to be enacted. Her novels were of the nature of complete symphonies, with the feelings of awe and fear among the dominant motives . . . they certainly abound in passages of real beauty, which leave an indelible impression on the mind, and have not been without their influence on later literature." Lewis "showed no appreciation of what was best in Mrs. Radcliffe. Atmosphere was a thing too supersensual for his blunt perceptions. Violent blows upon the reader's nerves seemed to him the most straightforward way to secure his effects. . . . He found that horror is an easy thing to produce; he never learned that terror requires more skill and subtlety," said Mr. Baker.

"One of the most superlative gifts of the literary mind is the faculty of *reticence,* the instinct that tells what to omit," said Mr. Baker. "Lewis's peculiar gift was the negative of reticence; he is most forcible and emphatic where other men are silent. To write in complete defiance of the literary canons requires cleverness of a sort; and this is how *The Monk* is such a curiosity in the literary annals of that period."

The conclusion of this discussion weighs Brown's material and methods. Brown shunned the blatant exposures of nauseating horrors, such as delighted Lewis. He tried to be true to the scientific results of spontaneous combustion and the yellow fever and told in a very few words some details disgusting to sensitive souls, but not for the sake of the revolting details themselves. The same holds for attempts at seduction, burials and murders; Brown almost always stopped short of painting a painful scene in verisimili-tude. He had the restraint of a gentleman before gentlemen and gentlewomen.

Mr. Baker gave so discriminating an estimate and appraisal of Lewis, Brown and others, and of the novels of that period that one is tempted to quote much exactly.
"It is interesting to observe how original and how strikingly successful transatlantic authors have always been in this byway of letters. Charles Brockden Brown was the first American novelist and like Lewis began to write under the influence of Mrs. Rad-cliffe. He was an intelligent imitator, and, while he copied her better features, he adapted them with success to a totally new class

of subject, and developed them according to his own conceptions. He, too, aimed at the effects of supernaturalism without the reality. But, instead of seeking to explain incredible incidents by means of an extraordinary concatenation of ordinary events, he based the whole structure on the durable foundation of certain strange, but not impossible circumstances; the erratic behaviour of a somnambulist (E-H-, 1799-1801), the mysterious conduct of a concealed criminal (A-M-, 1798-1800), or the utterances of a ventriloquist in Wieland (1798). Although things of this kind are in themselves exceptional and contrary to ordinary experience, Brown managed to keep them in the background so as not to offend the reader's sense of probability too much. They were inconspicuous, though essential parts of the machinery. It was in conjunction with less abnormal circumstances that they had their full effect. One may forget the actual incidents of the novel, E. H.; but the sense of abject and incomprehensible fear that pervades the book, the formless dread with which we accompany the adventures into the panther-haunted caves of the Alleghanies, and flee with him through the midnight woods infested with murdering Indian braves, will remain as an indestructible impression of the book. B. excelled in evoking the nightmare atmosphere, in making the reader's hair stand on end for no definable reason whatever. He was also peculiarly skilful in giving, by means of a few touches, the idea of a fearful personality, of a human being more to be dreaded than a fiend from the pit. Welbeck in A. M., the scoundrel who exercises such a deadly fascination over the hero, is a striking illustration of this terrible glamour; and there is another figure in the same book, who does not even appear on the scene and is merely alluded to by the hero in his fevered cogitations, yet gives one the same mental shock as ,A. M. felt when he thought he heard his menacing footsteps at his chamber-door. The secret is, of course, that B. does not relate incidents, but records impressions, sets down the thoughts and feelings of the actors directly, and so arouses in us thoughts and feelings only a little less powerful.''

This is why readers are captivated by many passages in Brown's novels; and it goes a long way in testifying to the author's genius.

Gothecisms, such as Brown's predecessors used, are easily discoverable in his novels, chiefly in *Wieland,* his earliest tale. Some of these are recorded in the discussions of his novels.

The biloquistic power of Carwin, though a scientific possibility, is so related to events and contraptions, as to lend it a Gothic flavor.

The victims of the voices immediately ally them to the existence of spirits.

"As to alliance with evil genii, the power and the malice of demons have been a thousand times exemplified in human beings. . . . My brother was a much more sanguine reasoner than our guest. . . . he maintained the probability of celestial interference."[1]

Evidently Brown had read of such mysterious voices, as he says: "Mysterious voices had always a share in producing the catastrophe; but they were always to be explained on some known principles, either as reflected into a focus or communicated through a tube."[2]

Clara is confronted in her dreams by a deep pit, or gulf, into which her brother seemed to beckon her:

"one step more would have plunged me into this abyss. . . . I remembered the gulf to which my brother's invitation had conducted me."[3]

Brown had seen such pits or gulfs in his woodland wanderings, but he makes it here an "omen of destiny."

Closets are found regularly in houses, but the author puts them to unusual uses, like Carwin's being concealed in Clara's closet with his night-time whisperings at one time and his speeches through the closet window, to which he had climbed up a ladder to do it, at another time. He frequently prowls Clara's room and closet, being admitted "by a trap-door which led into the cellar," by aid of Judith, Clara's maid. The ladder at the window by which the accomplice of the sorcerer might direct the magic lantern, in Schiller's *Der Geisterseher,* may have given a precedent to Brown. Arthur Mervyn finds himself locked in a bedroom and hides in a closet at the sound of talk at the door:

"Smiling cherub! safe and sound, I see. Would to God my experiment may succeed, and that thou mayest find a mother where I have found a wife."[4]

Previously, Arthur had seen a babe sleeping. He rattles armor in the closet, yet makes his exit by unlocking the door without being heard by the sleeping couple, leaving his shoes, and escapes through a first-story window. He says: "I put up prayers to my Deity that

---

1. *Wieland,* 151, 94.
2. *Ibid.,* 93.
3. *Ibid.,* 82, 208.
4. *Arthur Mervyn,* I, 38.

he would deliver me from these toils."

Not long after this, Arthur, fever-stricken, enters Welbeck's house. Fearful of fever-patient hunters, he ascends by a ladder and enters by a trap-door into a third-story nook, which he remembers having once seen in an angle of the roof. He hears some one in Welbeck's study, from which he had earlier purloined a certain manuscript, believing Welbeck drowned. Welbeck mimics the voice of Arthur's former acquaintance Colvill. When induced to come out, Arthur is confronted by Welbeck, who tells of the loss of the Lodi manuscript. It had contained bills to the amount of $20,000, which, after some colloquy, Arthur burns, being told by Welbeck that they were forged. This reminds one of the papers which St. Aubert demanded a promise of Emily to destroy without reading them, hidden under a sliding panel in the floor of a closet in their home.

The death of Susan Hadwin calls for a midnight burial by Arthur alone secretly. He assisted at another night interment. In a duel, Welbeck had shot Watson, and Arthur gained entrance. Welbeck then tells of their dealings to justify the duel and asks Arthur to help bury Watson. They go to a dark basement vault, shovel a shallow grave by the light of candles, bury the body and make their escape across the river, in which Welbeck stages a fake drowning. Welbeck, reading an advertisement concerning Watson's money, subsequently disinters the body and discovers his belt containing the gold. These midnight burials recall the burial scenes of Emily's aunt in Udolpho's subterranean vaults and of her father, whose grave in an abbey his daughter visited alone.

Some things are not Gothic in themselves until Brown makes them so; he writes in To the Public of *Edgar Huntly*, that he is eschewing "puerile superstition and exploded manners, Gothic castles, and chimeras."

One might go on and on picking out what the term Gothic fits; yet in one week in a large city as many and as morbid events are reported in the daily papers—the barefoot burglar, the auger-boring, window-opening thief, drownings from leaping from the river bridges or deaths from dropping from "suicide trestle," deaths by murder, gas, hanging, auto exhaust, poisoning, auto, train and airplane wrecks and so on. These are newspaper items, but, if introduced into a story, they would partake of the Gothic.

Inquiry might be made as to whether Brown was influenced in any degree by the German Gothic or Kotzebue school. Tourists and writers were beginning to travel in Germany in the last years of the eighteenth century. Mrs. Radcliffe made a tour of the Rhine after her book, *The Mysteries of Udolpho,* came out. Lewis went to Germany in 1792, and his story, *The Monk,* appeared in 1795. That and other works show his serious depredations on German literature. He studied German and translated between the years 1797 and 1801 German plays and poems and from 1804 to 1808 German prose tales. A society was started in England in 1788 for the study of German, and some interest was roused in German in America, as German translations came to America almost as soon as they were made in England. Dunlap was a dramatist and did much to bring the German drama into America, translating and producing sensational German dramas, many of those of Kotzebue. Most of his works were written to acquaint the people with the state of the theatre, of actors and dramas, both at home and abroad. From 1799-1800, Brown published at New York the *Monthly Magazine and American Review,* at the time when the influence of German literature had reached the highwater mark in England; and it devoted more attention to German literature than did any other periodical in America. Doubtless, through his friendship with Dunlap, Brown assumed a sympathetic attitude toward German literature and promoted it. The Philadelphia magazine, *Port Folio,* established by Dennie a year later, opposed it, saying,

"The rage for German literature is one of the foolish and uncouth whims of the time and deserves all the acrimony of the lampooners. We are sick, heartsick, of the rambling bombast, infamous sentiments, and distempered sensibility of the Teutonic tribe."[1]

Measured by modern standards, Brown's magazine seems an amateur attempt, but in comparison with former American magazines it shows an advance that is most creditable to its editor. Dunlap and other literary characters of New York were contribu-

---

1. Higginson & Boynton, *A Reader's History of American Literature,* 66-7.

tors. Among the reviews were those of Dunlap's and Smith's translations from Kotzebue, the life of Bürger, anecdotes of Kotzebue and Schiller, an account of the state of the German stage, remarks on the literary labor of the Germans, and, most interesting of all, an article on the study of German.

In *Wieland* (1798), the author intended to give a German atmosphere, as that influence was just then new in America. It is conceded that Brown ushered the German element into American fiction. He gives his chief characters very renowned German names and frequently mentions their friends and estates in Germany. The grandfather of the hero, Theodore, and of his sister Clara is Wieland. Brown chose that name to introduce to the American public the poet, dramatist, romancer and journalist, Christoph Martin Wieland, whose writings span a period of over sixty-five years, his last romance being written after Brown's first three novels, at about the time of his last three. To Wieland can be traced Germany's love for Shakespeare's plays, which he translated, and for the works of the Middle Ages. He made German fiction attractive to the upper classes and sponsored an important element— naturalness. Without question, his important works came to America and influenced Brown. From his *The Adventures of Don Sylvio de Rosalva,* may have come the summer-house, the name Gabriel, and the relation of the marvellous to the natural. Wieland says,

"Particular and extraordinary experiences, whenever they contradict the general experience, are always to be suspected . . . possibly imagination was the only and real mother of the marvellous, which hitherto from a want of experience, he (Don Sylvio) had taken for a part of nature itself" (p. 410, 419).

The strangenesses in nature in Brown's novels bereft of the experience of their readers, under his guidance, become acquaintances.

Brown's Wieland was a native of Saxony, educated at a German college and married to the daughter of Leonard Weise—another famous German name. Of the elder Wieland, it was said:

"His youth had been eagerly devoted to literature and music. . . . My ancestor may be considered as the founder of the German Theatre. . . . His life was spent in the composition of sonatas and dramatic pieces. . . . The modern poet of the same name is sprung from the same family, and, perhaps, surpasses but little, in the fruitfulness of his invention, or the soundness of his taste, the elder Wieland."[1]

Brown through Clara mentions a German play, as it appeared in America:

"My brother had received a new book from Germany. It was a tragedy, and the first attempt of a Saxon poet. . . . The exploits of Zisca, the Bohemian hero, were woven into a dramatic series and connection. According to German custom, it was minute and diffuse, and dictated by an adventurous and lawless fancy. It was a chain of audacious acts and unheard-of disasters. The moated fortress and the thicket, the ambush and the battle, and the conflict of headlong passions, were portrayed in wild numbers and with terrific energy. . . . Yesterday had been selected for the rehearsal of the newly-imported tragedy."[2]

German material may have been taken by Brown from an early drama by Schiller, *Der Geisterseher,* first published between 1785 and 1789 and translated into English in 1795, as *The Ghost-Seer; or, Apparitionist.* It appeared in America in 1796. Certain details in *Wieland* follow the German. Like Wieland, the Prince was of an intense, thoughtful nature, his contemplativeness growing into a settled gravity and possessive melancholy.

"Tiefer Ernst und eine schwärmerische Melancholie herrschten in seiner Gemüthsart." An incident somewhat paralleling the announcement by the voice of the ventriloquist in *Wieland* of the death of Pleyel's betrothed in Germany is found in this drama in the disclosure made by the Mask to the Prince.   "Neun Uhr vorbei. . . . Wir vergessen, das man uns im Louvre erwartet," sagte der Prinz.   "Neun Uhr," wiederholte sie (die Maske) in eben der Sprache nachdrücklich und langsam. "Wünchen Sie sich Glück, Prinz. . . . Um neun Uhr ist er gestorben."   "Wer is gestorben?" sagte endlich der Prinz;—die Maske war nicht mehr zufinden." Later it was found that the favorite cousin of the Prince had died at that hour.

The Prince had ever a curiosity and fondness for the mysterious and supernatural, as had Wieland:

---

1. *Wieland,* 26, 27.
2. *Ibid.,* 97, 147.

"Die Neugierde des Prinzen war bereits auf den höchsten Grad gespannt. Mit der Geisterwelt in Verbindung zu stehen, war ehedem seine Lieblings-schwärmerei gewesen, und seit jener ersten Erscheinung des Armeniers (die Maske) hatten sich alle Ideen wieder bei ihm gemeldet, die seine reifere Vernunft so lange abgewiesen hatte."

The peculiar stroke that bereft the elder Wieland of life in his temple on the rock has a suggestive precedent in the stroke of lightning seen and heard by the Prince and the company who were watching the ghostly demonstration of the conjurer:

"Hier erzitterte das Haus von Neuem. Die Thüre sprang freiwillig unter einem heftigen Donnerschlag auf, ein Blitz erleuchtete das Zimmer, und eine anders körperliche Gestalt, blutig und blass wie die erste, aber schrecklicher, erschien an der Schwelle. Der Spiritus fing von selbst an zu brennen, und der Saal wurde helle wie zuvor."[1]

The Prince says:
"A superior power attends us. Omniscience surrounds us. An invisible Being, whom I cannot escape, watches over my steps."
      His friend the Count speaks: "Religious melancholy was a hereditary disorder of the family. . . . To stifle all the sprightliness of the boy by a gloomy restraint of his mental faculties, was the only method of securing to themselves the highest approbation of his royal parents. . . . All his ideas of religion were accompanied by some frightful image. . . . His God was an object of terror, a being whose object is to chastise; . . . a silent indignation was gradually kindled against it . . . an abhorrence of a ruler before whom he trembled. I began to observe an extraordinary alteration in the disposition of the Prince. . . . Hitherto he had avoided every severe trial of his faith. . . . The Prince already began . . . to lose the pure and charming simplicity of his character, and the delicacy of his moral feelings. The influence of this new philosophy soon showed itself in the Prince's conduct. . . . He had launched out into the torrent of the great world. . . . Amusements, banquets, and galas followed each other in rapid succession. . . . Strange that there should be something . . . that yet on a sudden, one should seem to live and breathe for that alone! Can one single moment so completely metamorphose a human being? His whole being seems metamorphosed. He goes about as if wrapped in a dream (after seeing a beautiful girl), and nothing

---

1. Schiller, *Werke,* "Der Geisterseher," 398, 399, 408, 413. (Cf. Wieland, 42-3, 64-5, 55, 36-7.)

that formerly interested him has now power to arrest his attention for a moment."[1]
"The whole story is visibly nothing but a series of impostures," might apply to Schiller's story as well as to the digression about the Marquis, which is likewise true of *Wieland*.

As one first sees the Prince, he is superstitious and taken in by the deceptions practiced upon him by the Mask, like the Wielands by the voices of Carwin. In the Prince's metamorphoses, from a reticent man to a spendthrift among the gayest of gay crowds, and from an interest in society to the enthrallment by seeing this maiden, who dies, and to his entering a convent, is conveyed an influence that may have led Brown to the transformation of Wieland in his romance. (See Chapters III and VI.)

There remains to attest the influence of the novelists of the School of Theory and of the American novelists preceding Brown. Mary Wollstonecraft and William Godwin really summarized the theories of two long lines of ancestors. The former in . . . *The Rights of Woman* shows chiefly how women should be educated. She and other writers of this class—Defoe, Rosseau, Elizabeth Inchbald and Day—will be recalled later. The procession of purpose writers, who speculated about government and morals, of whom Godwin was head, was a long one, including Locke, Hume, Mackenzie, Charlotte Smith and others.

Among the latter was Bage, whose *Hermsprong, or Man As He Is Not* was mentioned heretofore as portraying a Utopian paradise among American Indians, of which sort of scheme Brown wrote several,—perhaps, *Sky-Walk*, with its seemingly imitative alternate title, *the Man Unknown to Himself*. Hermsprong represents a "natural man," living an ideal kind of life, such as Mrs. Behn's Oroonoko (negro), to be touched upon in a later chapter, and Shebbeare's Cannassatego (Annassatego) (Indian), imported from savage lands, that attracted authors of this period. It was a new and singular type of hero in fiction, that shared popularity with the pre-Byronic type of Mrs. Radcliffe and other writers. The problem was how primitive virtues might be regained and how they might

---

1. Schiller, "The Ghost-Seer," in *Early Dramas and Romances,* **386,** 429-430, 433, 434, 458, 480.

be retained unsullied. The former was a question of morals; the latter, of education.

In the first chapter of Dr. John Shebbeare's novel *Lydia, or Filial Piety* (1755), he enters "patriotism, heroism, fainting, dying, loving, sentiment, generosity, all amongst Indians in America." Cannassatego, the noble Indian warrior who is brought in as a foil for the vices of English characters, gains the love of Yarico, a dove-like Indian maiden, a very exceptional squaw because

"She conceived it the most unnatural idea . . . that rage and the destruction of mankind should prevail over the softer passions of love and friendship, and fame be obtained by what ought to be the horror of humanity." The "natural man," imported from savage lands, soon "became a naturalized Englishman."[1]

Writing of Smollett's *Peregrine Pickle,* Taine, quoted, said:
"He flings together personages the most revolting with the most grotesque—a Lieutenant Lismahago half-roasted by Red Indians . . . had been married once to an Indian squaw; Miss Tabitha's curiosity was aroused by his hints about this wild damsel . . . discovering . . . that his princess had neither shoes, stockings, shift, nor any kind of linen; that her bridal dress consisted of a petticoat of red baise and a blanket fastened about her shoulders with a copper skewer . . . her arms and legs were adorned with bracelets of wampum . . . about her neck was hung the fresh scalp of a Mohawk Warrior."

The works reviewed show that the name Indian had been bandied about in literature at least forty years before Brown's *Edgar Huntly.* Early American historians, poets and story writers described the Indians as they knew them first-hand or from local reports, as cunning, crafty, scalping killers. In course of time, with the impetus given by Cooper later, European writers enhaloed American Indians as types of the noble super-savage. Brown knew the Indian too well to make him the idealistic "natural man"; he chose a green country lad as his ideal of proper young manhood, as Parrington thus describes him:
"But it is in Arthur Mervyn that he gives his fullest pronouncement of what he conceives must be done in America. He takes his hero fresh from the plow-tail, one of nature's noblemen, and traces his triumphant course through the thick of sordid intrigue to a happy end. Generous in instincts, impulsive in sociability,

---

1. Raleigh, *The English Novel,* 241-2.

responsive to suffering, hating injustice, loving the pure and disinterested, Arthur Mervyn is a Godwinian figure drawn to captivate the imagination with the social ideal. It is not so much the plot of the story that reveals the enormous influence of Godwin— patent as the likeness is to *Caleb Williams*; but rather the expansive nature of the title hero, whose instincts bid him espouse justice, and whose life is an implied criticism of all that is sordid and mean."[1]

Nature and Art (1796) by Mrs. Inchbald is a story whose principal characters, William and Henry, cousins, are contrasted, the one educated in a deanery and the other among savages of Zocotora Island. Henry returned to civilization, called compliments, lies,—reserve, pride,—stateliness, affectation,—and war, massacre,— to the disparagement of William.[2]

Henry Brooke in his famous novel, *The Fool of Quality* (1766-70), sets up in the history of Henry, Earl of Moreland, a pattern of natural education and simple virtue. The author has so many interests, political and social reforms, that his story is completely overlaid by moral digressions; the definition of a gentleman, the honor due to commerce, the British constitution, the position of women, imprisonment for debt, and statutes at large—all have his attention and train Godwin for his place in literature later.[3].

Thomas Holcroft wrote this sort of novel, representing his political principles. Of government he said, "Everything in which government interferes is spoiled." Frank Henley in his *Anna St. Ives* is a "natural." In that novel (1792) and in other works are to be found almost all the doctrines which received consecutive, logical exposition in Godwin's *Political Justice* (1793). As Godwin admitted his obligations to Holcroft, so will the outcome of these doctrines be discussed in Brown's novels,—in *Wieland* particularly, from the older, more distinguished writer; and Mrs. Wollstonecraft's views will be correlated with Brown's in *Ormond* especially.

Caleb Williams (1794), Godwin's outstanding work, has for its inspiration a definite purpose, as he himself discloses in the alternate title:

---

1. Parrington, *The Romantic Revolution in America,* 190.
2. Raleigh, *The English Novel,* 248.
3. *Ibid.,* 213.

"The question now afloat in the world respecting *Things as They Are* is the most interesting that can be presented to the human mind. . . . What is now presented to the public is no refined and abstract speculation; it is a study and delineation of things passing in the moral world. . . . It is now known to philosophers that the spirit and character of the government intrudes itself into every rank of society. But this is a truth highly worthy to be communicated to persons whom books of philosophy and science are never likely to reach. Accordingly, it was proposed, in the invention of the following work, to comprehend, as far as the progressive nature of a single story would allow, a general review of the modes of domestic and unrecorded despotism, by which man becomes the destroyer of man."[1]   "I said to myself a thousand times, 'I will write a tale that shall constitute an epoch in the mind of the reader, that no one, after he has read it, shall ever be exactly the same man that he was before'."[2]

Godwin bestowed infinite pains on the composition of *Caleb Williams*.

To his theme, despotism in society and government, with his motivated characters, Godwin followed the methods of the Gothic romance, but subordinated its romanticism to its didactic purpose. The story embodies the spirit of the French Revolution. It was intended as a protest against the existing social order and concerns itself with how man should be governed.

Attention will be directed to Mrs. Ann Maria Bleecker again in the discussion of *Wieland*. She wrote *The History of Maria Kittle* (1779), published posthumously in 1793, and writes in a letter to her sister Susan:

"However fond of novels and romances you may be, the unfortunate adventures of one of my neighbors, who died yesterday, will make you despise that fiction, in which, knowing the subject to be fabulous, we can never be so truly interested. . . . her dear kinswoman related to me her unhappy history."

This is a tale of actual depredations and brutalities of the Indians,—facts not fictionized. If Brown was influenced, other than by the atrocity related to the tragedy in *Wieland,* it must have been in minor, unconscious ways. Mrs. Bleecker uses words such as

---

1. Godwin, *Caleb Williams,* Preface, May 12, 1794.
2. *Ibid.,* Author's Last Preface, November 20, 1832.

Brown used, which may have been current in most writings: asperities, assiduities, ruminating, mellifluous, transition, mutable, corrode, corrosive (care), indefatigable, sylvan recess, appellative, the closet, the hut. These sentences sound slightly like Brown's: "I see no sunshine but in the face of a friend" and "I love to expose my whole heart to my artless Susan." Eliza and Susan were sisters, which may have led Brown to so name the Hadwin sisters in *Arthur Mervyn*. Apparently the most important Indian tale before Brown was this of Mrs. Bleecker, a true occurrence during the French and Indian War. After years of friendly intercourse with the Kittle family and their neighbors, the blood-thirsty Indian wretches fell upon them treacherously and slaughtered all but Mrs. Kittle, who escaped and finally reached Canada.

Many early stories were little more than common facts; for instance, Mathew Carey, author, publisher and bookseller, wrote "A Short Account of the Malignant Fever," for his magazine, *The American Museum* (1787-1793). This is the most faithful history of the yellow fever epidemic in Philadelphia in 1793.

Brown's choice of fiction as a means to teach moral lessons and his originating the true American novel should also be preceded by the listing of these other examples of early fiction. His compatriot Benjamin Franklin, who wrote no novel, anticipated fictional characters in his Poor Richard, Bridget and Father Abraham— typical Americans and lifelike characters. Such forms as allegories and analogues are fiction, but not novels.

The first true example of American fiction, perhaps, was *A Pretty Story* (1774) by Francis Hopkinson, in the guise of an allegory, after the manner of Swift's *Tale of a Tub*. He satirizes the relationship between England, the "Old Farm," and America, the "New Farm." The nobleman, his wife and steward are the king, parliament and the ministry; and their sons are the colonies and their sons' wives are the colonial legislatures. After having given certain privileges by the Great Paper to the children and they have become prosperous, the parent Farm imposes taxes, demands that trials be held in England and finally sends a liar-general to carry out its demands. A strange device, described in his story, may have confirmed or inspired Brown's plan to use ventriloquism, or biloquium, as he calls it, twenty-five years later.

"I have heard of a man in England, some years ago, called a *ventriloquist,* who had the extraordinary faculty of making his voice seem to come from where he pleased. The man kept a great dog, and for the entertainment of visitors, would throw his voice into the dog's belly; and then wagging the poor beast's jaws with his hands, make him seem to say anything he pleased."[1]

In Brown's unfinished story, *Carwin, the Biloquist,* Carwin uses his biloquistic power to speak through his dog's mouth. He had trained his dog very carefully to obey many signals to correspond to his words, thus making the dog seem to understand human conversation. The liar-general is the man with the wonderful voice and they (the Tories, Humphreys and Town) are only his dogs, whom he causes to utter what he thinks proper. In consequence of these lying pronouncements, the Colonists advertise for a liar-general and three associates to offset their influence.

Of that "fair herd" of Richardson successors were American novelists, whose novels had been written and printed in America before those of Brown. They were either English immigrants or authors who wrote as a pastime, not as a profession, and imitated British models and methods. In his *Rachel Dyer,* Neal remarked:

"Our best writers are English writers. They are English in everything they do, and in everything they say, as authors, in the structure and moral of their stories; in their dialogue, speech, and pronunciation; yea, in the very characters they draw."

Long before, Brown made a like statement in *Clara Howard,* quoted earlier in this chapter.

Most of these novels, the majority of them written by women, show the influence of Richardson in aiming to teach a lesson. Puritanical opposition and the flood of English reprints held back American fiction. In fact, American novels had "to climb up some other way," under subterfuge, as it were, disguised as the history of something or other, as a sermon or as instruction. Another characteristic is a flat or exaggerated sentimentality or a "plaintive and melancholy wail," as one critic voiced it. These novels are of interest only to the antiquary or to the investigator or student of early American literature. If they made any impression on Brown, it is indistinguishable, except incidentally, unless in the general

---

1. Hopkinson, in Prescott & Nelson, *Prose and Poetry,* 125.

tone of his last two society novels.

The first novel written by an American was probably *The Power of Sympathy* (1789), dedicated to young ladies, whose purpose was "to expose the dangerous Consequences of Seduction and to set forth the Advantages of female Education." This makes novel writing in America just as old as the Republic. The novel, published anonymously, is generally attributed to Mrs. Sarah Wentworth Morton, now attributed to William Hill Brown (Pattee). This novel was the first of twenty-two novels thought to have been published between 1789 and 1798, when Brown's first novel appeared; and between that time and the date of his death (1810) thirty-six novels appeared, according to the bibliography in Loshe's *The Early American Novel*.

Charlotte Temple (1790), published in England and popular there before it came to America (1793), a novel of Mrs. Susannah Haswell Rowson, may have given Brown the name Stanly from that of her heroine, Charlotte Temple or Stanly (real name); and his Lucy Villars may have come from *Lucy Temple*, a novel sequel, and from the anonymous novels, *The Fortunate Discovery: or, The History of Henry Villars* (New York, 1798) and *Plain Sense: or, The History of Henry Villars and Ellen Mordaunt* (Philadelphia, 1799). The influence of *Charlotte Temple* was immediate and is lasting to this day, the novel being never out of print. It started the flood of feminine fiction; and its seduction motif out-rivaled in popularity the horror motif of Mrs. Radcliffe and others of the terror school. Such a novel was *The Coquette: or, The History of Eliza Wharton* (1797), . . . Founded on Facts, by Hannah Foster. All novels purported to be based on true events. Brown's novels feature seduction, as one of the entangling themes, or the chief one, in *Ormond*. Against this theme, the pulpit, press and polemics wreaked their wrath when they awoke to the baleful effects of the reading and writing matter of women. Dennie in the *Port Folio* denounced American female writings, but he praised the works of the English feminists: Madame D'Arblay (Fannie Burney), Mrs. Radcliffe, Mrs. Hamilton, Charlotte Smith, Hannah Moore and Maria Edgeworth. Mrs. Rowson was a dramatist and the first prominent writer to use the American Revolution as a background and even the Indian as a character in fiction.

Among the favorite names so pleasing to feminine writers, such as Eliza, Emeline, Ellen, Maria, Catherine, Sarah and Julia, a few suggestions may have come to Brown. From Mrs. Morton's name above he may have chosen the name Wentworth and for the orphaned Eliza Hadwin the name Eliza from the heroine of *The Hapless Orphan, or Innocent Victim of Revenge* (1793), "By an American Lady." Some of these early writers dared to say, "By an American" or "An American Tale"; but fiction writing and writing by females was too unpopular for them to risk signing their own names.

There is no conclusive evidence that these novels directly influenced Brown. His novels are more philosophical and show a deeper common sense than those of his lady predecessors, but without humor, as theirs were. Some of his characters, like Constantia Dudley, Miss Carlton, Jane Talbot, Sophia Westwyn and Clara Howard are examples of constancy in friendship and fortitude in trials, in contrast to many in these other stories who solicit the sympathy of their readers.

"Our fiction began well with Hugh Henry Brackenridge's picaresque and satiric 'Modern Chivalry' . . . a sharp, realistic record of the rude, turbulent life of the early Republic. . . . But the romantic movement was too imminent for either the picaresque or the eighteenth century sentimental (like the Richardson imitators mentioned above) to prevail."[1]

The author of *Modern Chivalry, or Adventures of Captain Farrago* (1792+) was a man of a single book, not a classic, not a novel. It is a

"mass of lay-sermons chiefly political and satirical which grew by accretions year by year, infinitely varied like a newspaper column and having as its theme 'all created things and certain others.' . . . A hodgepodge undoubtedly, this chaotic book. All America is in it: prose and poetry, philosophy and horse-play, dialect and Addisonian diction, humor and pathos. A dozen frontier characters stand clean-cut, and a dozen characteristics. But never lost in the miscellany is the author's central thesis: democratic power unbalanced is the despotism of the many instead of one. . . . (The author comments): I shall have accomplished something by this book,

---

1. Lewisohn, *Expression in America,* 54.

if it shall keep some honest man from lessening his respectability by pushing himself into public trusts for which he is not qualified; or when pushed forward into public station, it shall contribute to keep him honest by teaching him the folly of ambition, and farther advancement; when in fact, the shade is more to be coveted, and the mind, on reflection, will be better satisfied with itself, for having chosen it. This is in great part, the moral of this book; if it should be at all necessary to give a hint of it."[1]

In Quixotic fashion, Captain Farrago and his uneducated Irish servant travel from Pittsburgh to the Capital. Two ideals are contrasted: the conservative East with its caution and experience is embodied in Captain Farrago and the New West with its freedom, exuberance and democratic ideas is embodied in the uncultured servant, Teague O'Regan. Farrago makes shrewd, humorous observations on elections, finance, commerce, manners and customs of the country. He counsels prudence, common sense and wisdom, as Franklin does. The work is not a true novel any more than the allegories of Franklin and Hopkinson, but it does furnish materials such as novels could use.

Here closes this division of the book, tracing the influence of the chief writers acting upon Brown as displayed by their novels in his novels.

---

1. Pattee, *The First Century of American Literature,* 1770-1870, 154-65.

CHAPTER III

DISCUSSION OF BROWN'S NOVELS IN DETAIL

Wieland; or the Transformation. An American Tale (1798) was written when the influence of the writers of the School of Terror and of the School of Theory came most powerfully to America, when their works were imported, reprinted here and read with enjoyment. From a temperament, studious and refined, but dispirited, in which the intellectual forces overbalanced the physical forces, sprang Brown's first book. In a manuscript letter to Dunlap, written from Philadelphia, a year after his winter in New York, Brown alludes to his first attempt at novel-writing and gives strong evidence of the morose moods which sometimes overwhelmed him:

"I think upon the life of last winter with self-loathing, almost insupportable. Alas! My friend, few consolations of a self-approving mind have fallen to my lot. . . . I am sometimes apt to think that few human beings have drunk so deeply of the cup of self-abhorrence as I have. . . . Whether it will end but with my life I know not. . . . As I am, you despise me. I *shall* die, as I have lived, a victim to perverse and incurable habits. My progress in knowledge has enlightened my judgement, without adding to my power."
    "So at certain moments could think and write one of the purest and best of men,"[1]

commented his biographer in a note below this letter. This depressed and extravagant tone of self-depreciation was characteristic of the writer.

In imitation of the English School of Terror, Brown planned to invoke the incomprehensible and marvellous in order to stimulate

---

1. Brown, Letter to Dunlap, Care of Dunlap and Judah, Pearl St., New York, January 1, 1798, in manuscript in the collection of the Historical Society of Pennsylvania, quoted by Marble, in *Heralds of American Literature*, 289-90.

interest. He used mystifying scientific forces that were original and would in his estimation arouse the emotions in the most sensational manner. His early novels are not unimpressive in the portrayal of terrifying, thrilling scenes and in their appeal to the sentiments of curiosity and fear. They compare very favorably with the romances of the Terrorists in most of the best qualities essential to the Gothic romance. He had a more intuitive sense of the sources of terror and could therefore more effectively lead his readers to share his emotions.

The story of Wieland, though not wholly a tale of disasters, is overshadowed with the tragic element. A relentless fate pursues and overhangs the hero and his associates. They have forebodings of some awful calamity. Brown is a true imitator of his English predecessors in exciting in a high degree a feeling of alarm and fearful expectation. The events of this story take place between the conclusion of the French and Indian War and the beginning of the Revolutionary War. The scene is laid in Pennsylvania, near the Schuylkill, among the Wielands, an educated and estimable family.

The elder Wieland, a devout man, had died in a dreadful manner, by spontaneous combustion, an awful and mysterious phenomenon of nature. His son, the hero, with a mind constitutionally grave, considerate, thoughtful and imaginative, is being changed by a credulous and superstitious contemplation of his father's death and by habitual reading, into a man disquieted with doubts and religious previsions, which steadily deepen into a fixed and deadly fanaticism. This temper, predisposed to insane images, is nourished by peculiar voices, which are referred to supernatural agency. Two of the main supports of his belief are moral necessity and Calvinistic inspiration. Thus Brown makes a direct protest against the dogmatic narrowness of such a belief,—much as he did also in criticizing his future father-in-law, Rev. William Linn, for the same beliefs, in his first magazine.

Clara Wieland, who relates the story, lives alone in a house near her brother's, the combined estates being given the German name, Mettingen; and Pleyel, the brother of Wieland's wife and suitor of Clara, spends much time in the neighborhood. Unaccountable voices are heard at various times by different members of the family, warning, commanding, foretelling. Wieland, in particular, is disturbed by these occurrences as indications of divine power. In the meantime, a middle-aged man, named Carwin, comes to Clara's home and asks for a drink. The music of his voice and the striking appearance of his face greatly affect her. His delightful conversation and unlimited knowledge admit him to the home of Wieland, where he participates in the family gatherings. The strange voices are heard more frequently. The perplexity and apprehension of the family daily increase and all seem anxiously to wait the outcome. Finally, Wieland, at the bidding of the voice of God, as he thinks, sacrifices his wife, "Wieland's angel," and five children and tries to take the life of his sister. The wretched fanatic is arrested, brought to trial, deemed a murderer, acquitted on the ground of insanity and confined in a dungeon as a lunatic. As a "minister" of God, he bears all calmly, confident of having fulfilled the will of the Almighty. During an escape in which he again threatens the life of his sister, he is persuaded, by the voice, in a moment of weakness, to believe that he has been misguided by a disorder of his mind. He cannot sustain the shock and, in frenzy over the discovery, kills himself. Thus ends the career of one whose mind, devoted to morbid and religious illusions, was already prepared for the operations and impositions of Carwin, the biloquist. The story concludes with the marriage of Clara Wieland to Henry Pleyel.

For this novel, Brown chose the abnormal forces of spontaneous combustion, biloquium, hallucinations resulting in mania, and visions and dreams as minor factors. "Knowledge is the irreconcilable foe of delusion," said Godwin; and Brown purposefully planned to supply that knowledge. These agencies may have been suggested to him by his medical friends, among whom he lived in New York, and from his study of Socrates, Defoe and Mather.

In support of the theory of spontaneous or self-combustion, the author reports (Footnote, Wieland, 39):
"A case in its symptoms exactly parallel to this is published in one of the Journals of Florence. See, likewise, similar cases reported by Messrs. Merrille and Muraire in the 'Journal de Medicine' for February and May, 1783. The researches of Maffei and Fontana have thrown some light upon this subject."
Supposed cases of spontaneous combustion were reported in the reviews of the day of superficial observation, commented one critic.

In justification of the use of biloquium, Brown gives the following explanation in his Advertisement of *Wieland*:

"The incidents related are extraordinary and rare. . . . The power (ventriloquism) which the principal person is said to possess can scarcely be denied to be real. It must be acknowledged to be extremely rare; but no fact, equally uncommon, is supported by the same strength of historical evidence."   *"Biloquium,* or ventrilocution. Sound is varied according to the variations of direction and distance. The art of the ventriloquist consists in modifying his voice according to all these variations, without changing his place. See the work of Abbe' de la Chappelle, in which are accurately recorded the performances of one of these artists. . . . This power is difficult to explain, but the fact is undeniable. Experience shows that the human voice can imitate the voice of all men and of all inferior animals. The sound of musical instruments, and even noises from the contact of inanimate substances, have been accurately imitated. The mimicry of animals is notorious; and Dr. Burney ("Musical Travels") mentions one who imitated a flute and violin, so as to deceive even his ears" (Footnote, Wieland, 217).

"Some readers may think the conduct of the younger Wieland impossible," Brown continues in his Advertisement:

"It will not be objected that the instances of similar delusion are rare, because it is the business of moral painters to exhibit their subject in its most instructive and memorable forms. If history furnishes one parallel fact, it is a sufficient vindication of the writer; but most readers will probably recollect an authentic case, remarkably similar to that of Wieland."

The fact of hallucinations such as Wieland's was known before the tale was written and is affirmed in two reviews of Brown's novels. *The American Review and Literary Journal,* edited partly by C. B. Brown, says of *Wieland*:

"The incidents, however incredible and shocking, are founded on well authenticated facts, sublime and tragical in the highest degree. (See New York Weekly Magazine, July 20, 1796, II, 20-28, and July 27, 1796, II, 28, for the actual facts of such tragedy. Title: "An account of a murder committed by Mr. J— — Y — —, upon his family, in December, A. D. 1781").[1]

This article contains a summary of the murder. A farmer living near Tomhanick, New York, a man of great gentleness and nobility

---

1. *American Review and Literary Journal,* I, 335, July-Sept., 1801.

and piety, on a Sunday afternoon became suddenly the victim of religious mania and killed his wife and their four children.

As late as 1819, in a survey of Brown's work in the *North American Review,* the critic commended the novelist's choice of American scenes and added:

"Sometimes the author takes advantage of a recent event amongst ourselves, as in *Wieland,* which is too shocking to receive any aid from exaggeration or to lose any interest from its notoriety."[1]

The recital, Brown's own acknowledgment in the *American Review,* is the original of *Wieland,* according to Van Doren in the *Nation* 99: 577-588, Nov. 12, 1914.

Notwithstanding Van Doren's conclusion that Brown used the report in the *New York Weekly Magazine* (1796) as his source of *Wieland,* he probably had also the account of December, A. D. 1781, from other hints in his novel from the same source. *Title* infers that it had been printed previously to that time. About ten years after her death, *The Posthumous Works of Ann Eliza Bleecker, in Prose and Verse* was published (1793) by T. and J. Swords with the help of Mrs. Bleecker's daughter, Margaretta V. Faugeres. In the "To the Public" is the explanation: "Writings of Mrs. Bleecker which had appeared in the New York Magazine." Among her letters, which were written with the expectation of their being put in the magazine was this one (p. 151) to her beloved half-sister: To Miss T (en) E (yck), December, 1781:

"My dearest Susan, The most tragical affair has happened here that I ever remember to have heard of. James Yates (a son of him at Pitt's-Town) a few nights ago murdered his wife, four children, his horses and cow, with circumstances of cruelty too horrid to mention: by all appearance he is a religious lunatic. . . . poor Mrs. F— — was lately delivered of a child who is a terror to every one that sees it. It seems she was struck with so much horror at the sight of James Yates's murdered family, that it made too fatal an impression."

It may be far-fetched; yet, perhaps, Brown used this last detail in making the impression upon Theodore Wieland of his father's tragic death by spontaneous combustion fatal to his mentality. Doubtless, the Mr. J— — Y— — of the later-written account is

---

1. *North American Review,* IX, 69, June, 1819.

the same James Yates of Mrs. Bleecker's letter and she the author of the original 1781 "Account."

The action of the story in *Wieland* is much refined and superior, not mere facts. The actual murders of the children are not given; and the birth and growth of Wieland's insanity resulting from unwholesome ideas planted in his mind in childhood, Brown's own creation in accordance with his theme of transformation, are related with understanding and sympathy. The accounts are similar in many details: Clara Wieland and Mrs. J— — N— —, sister of Mr. J— — Y— —, remain to tell the story. Both stricken families had four children, two boys and two girls, the youngest a girl; but Wieland included in his slaughter a fifth child, Louisa.

Because Brown was not specifically concerned with the terrible *per se,* he did not always fully develop and emphasize these phases of his story. One can conceive of *Wieland's* being improved as a novel by excluding the agencies of spontaneous combustion and ventriloquism, leaving the death of Wieland's father to occur in some disagreeable way and making only an increasing religious fanaticism responsible for the deeds of Wieland.

Although the intention of the author was to use new and distinctly American means of excitement, yet Old World elements are not lacking in the various expedients devised. Twice daily, at noon and midnight, for his devotions, Wieland visited a summer-house, which his father had built "three hundred yards from his house, on the top of a rock, . . . the temple of his Deity."[1] The summer-house had an ancestry and descendants. It appears in Day's *Sandford and Merton,* Johnson's *Rasselas,* Wieland's *Don Sylvio* and Schiller's *Der Geisterseher* before Brown and in Brown's *Wieland, Romance of Sophia and Jessy, Adini,* and *Memoirs of Stephen Calvert* and will be discussed in connection with Shelley. Clara says:

"near the southern verge of my little demesne, was placed a slight building, with seats and lattices." . . . (Here she had dreamed and heard the voice warning her.) "I leagued to murder you. I repent. Mark by bidding, and be safe. Avoid this spot. The snares of death encompass it."[2]

---

1. *Wieland,* 31, 43-5.
2. *Ibid.,* 82, 83.

Here, too, Pleyel overheard the conversation injurious to his lady's honor. In place of highway robberies and abductions, Brown freely employed murders and suicides, which latter methods were also commonly used by the European romancers. Carwin, the man with a past ("for he had not been free from the guilt of murder," before coming to Mettingen), frequented the summer-house at will nights and, having the ability to throw his voice, is a tributary cause of the murders and the suicide in the Wieland family.

As a particular admirer of Godwin, who was didactic as well as Gothic, Brown put a definite purpose in each of his novels. In his Advertisement, he gives notice of his purpose:

"The following work is delivered to the world as the first of a series of performances, which the favourable reception of this will induce the writer to publish. His purpose is neither selfish nor temporary, but aims at the illustration of some important branches of the moral constitution of man. Whether this tale will be classed with the ordinary or frivolous sources of amusement, or be ranked with the few productions whose usefulness secures to them a lasting reputation, the reader must be permitted to decide."

Like the great English fictionists, Brown was in his time a reforming novelist. The more one investigates his novels and almost all of his other writings, the more one feels the distinct purpose behind the unusual realism of the descriptions and events. His novels should be read and studied with a thought of their purposes and themes in mind.

"He creates for a purpose, and in each romance he subdues to this purpose the background, the incidents, the plot, the characters, and even the imagery and phrasing,"[1] said of Hawthorne, but applicable to Brown.

In this respect, Brown emulates Godwin and thus falls into some of the same inartistic errors, such as lack of free will in some characters, plot incidents loosely connected with each other and extravagance in style and language. To the moral purpose the author joined an additional theme, usually scientific and intended to arouse astonishment and curiosity. He is like the School of Theory in his purpose and like the Romanticists in his wonder-inspiring themes.

---

1. Gates, *Studies and Appreciations*, 95, 96.

In *Wieland,* the purpose is to expose the direful consequences resulting from the life of a man dominated to an inordinate degree by pious enthusiasm and some kind of superstition or self-delusion. A disputable subject among Brown's countrymen was the existence of good and evil spirits and of their possible intervention in human affairs; so that is made one of the underlying causes of Wieland's illusions. A few words of the hero himself, in his defense at his trial, reveal the state of mind of the religious fanatic:

"It is needless to say that God is the object of my supreme passion. . . . I have burnt with ardour to approve my faith and my obedience. My days have been spent in searching for the revelation of that will; but my days have been mournful, because my search failed. . . . Dissatisfaction has insinuated itself into all my thoughts. My purposes have been pure, my wishes indefatigable; but not till lately were these purposes thoroughly accomplished and these wishes fully gratified. . . . The Author of my being was likewise the dispenser of every gift with which that being was embellished. The service to which a benefactor like this was entitled could not be circumscribed."[1]

Wieland is Brown's masterpiece in the history of a human soul. If one reads this novel, keeping the transformation of Wieland in mind, he will see how consistently and how gradually the hero is changed from the kind, loving, rational husband and father, full of tenderest affection for the family, into the most inhuman of murderous maniacs. There is scarcely a page of digression from the main thesis in the whole work, unless the supplementary chapter be counted such.

Several critics, among whom was William Prescott, made the statement that ventriloquism, upon which the plot of *Wieland* turns, is not adequate to explain the terrible happenings in the book. Henry A. Beers said, "Brown frequently raised a superstructure of mystery on a basis ludicrously weak."[2] It is true that it does not explain, but the present writer believes that it should not. Ventriloquism is employed only as one of the instruments that tend to produce a superstitious insanity in Wieland and could be omitted altogether and yet not interfere materially with the unfold-

---

1. *Wieland,* 184, 185. (See also 183-96.)
2. Beers, *Initial Studies in American Letters,* 65.

ment of his soul. It is but an external mechanical device, extraneous to Brown's real purpose. Preferable is John Erskine's view that these

"outward circumstances of the novel, the spontaneous combustion and ventriloquism,—are but slightly related to the author's main interest. Wieland's progress to insanity, step by step, is the real story."[1]   Thomas Love Peacock said: "There are many stories in which the supernatural is only apparent, and is finally explained. But some of these, especially the novels of Brockden Brown, carry the principle of terror to its utmost limits. What can be more appalling than his Wieland? It is one of the few tales in which the final explanation of the apparently supernatural does not destroy or diminish the original effect."[2]

This illusion of the senses was gradual, proceeding from a naturally thoughtful, virtuous disposition, which was accustomed to ruminate:

"The future, either as anterior or subsequent to death, was a scene that required some preparation and provision to be made for it,"[3] to a determined series of speculations. His father's death was a source of meditation, whose traces were gloomy and permanent. The result of the first voice upon Wieland causes Clara to say,

"The worst effect that could flow was not indeed very formidable. Yet I could not bear to think that his senses should be the victims of such delusion. It argued a diseased condition of his frame, which might show itself hereafter in more dangerous symptoms."[4]

Brown recognizes the effects of ventriloquism as promotive of delusion, but hints here of the growing trend toward insanity in Wieland. His method involves a rather comprehensive treatment of the subject of good and evil spirits. He questions whether the elder Wieland died by the stroke of some agent, whom the Divine Ruler had selected and commissioned.

After the second visitation of the voice, Clara affirms:
"Here were proofs of a sensible and intelligent existence, which could not be denied. Here was information obtained and imparted by means unquestionably superhuman. That there are conscious

1. Erskine, *Leading American Novelists*, 20.
2. Peacock, "The Tale of a Shadow," in *Gryll Grange*.
3. *Wieland*, 42.
4. *Ibid.*, 55. (See 38-9.)

beings besides ourselves in existence, whose modes of activity and information surpass our own, can scarcely be denied."[1]

She was disposed to believe that the vocal warning against her brother given her in the summer-house was of divine origin and that the cry—"Hold"—given from her closet was a propitious power acting in her behalf, as the natural protector of virtue against vice. Pleyel, in speaking of the deportment of Carwin, thus concludes:

"As to alliance with evil genii, the power and the malice of demons have been a thousand times exemplified in human beings. There are no devils but those which are begotten upon selfishness and reared by cunning."[2]

When Wieland was commanded to sacrifice his wife, he thus relates it:

"As it spoke, the accents thrilled to my heart:—'Thy prayers are heard. In proof of thy faith, render me thy wife. This is the victim I choose!' . . . (Then turning to Catharine) Catharine, . . . I pity thee, but must not spare. Thy life is claimed from my hands; thou must die. . . . It is forbidden to describe what I saw. . . . The lineaments of that being whose veil was now lifted and whose visage beamed upon my sight, no hues of pencil or of language can portray."[3]

Clara's uncle, Dr. Cambridge, says, "Neither angel nor devil had any part in this affair" and explained to her that Wieland's murders were caused by illusions; that her own grandfather had grieved for the loss of a brother and had believed that his own death was connected with it in some unforeseeable way; that often in the German army he had met similar illusions, and that they were all maniacal and "reducible to one class (Mania mutabilis. See Darwin's Zoonomia, Vol. II, Class III. 1, 2, where similar cases are stated.)"[4] Clara still doubts:

"I could not deny faith to the evidence of my religion; the testimony of men was loud and unanimous; both these concurred to persuade me that evil spirits existed, and that their energy was frequently exerted in the system of the world. . . . The dreams of superstition are worthy of contempt. Witchcraft, its instruments and miracles

1. *Wieland,* 65.
2. *Ibid.,* 151.
3. *Ibid.,* 186-7, 190, 186.
4. *Ibid.,* 196-8 and Footnote.

. . . are monstrous and chimerical. . . . That conscious beings, dissimilar from human, but moral and voluntary agents as we are, somewhere exist, can scarcely be denied. That their aid may be employed to benign or malignant purposes cannot be disproved." Speaking of her brother, Clara continues, "None but a command from heaven could have swayed his will; and nothing but unerring proof of divine approbation could sustain his mind in its present elevation."[1]   When Wieland attempted the life of his sister, a voice "commanded him—*to hold!* . . . Man of errors! cease to cherish thy delusion; not heaven or hell, but thy senses, have misled thee to commit these acts. Shake off thy frenzy, and ascend into rational and human. Be lunatic no longer."[2]

As far as the Wieland family are concerned, the moral of the story is found stated by Clara in the last sentence of the book:

"If Wieland had framed juster notions of moral duty and of the divine attributes, or if I had been gifted with ordinary equanimity or foresight, the double-tongued deceiver would have been baffled and repelled."[3]

Instead of putting this essay, "Fanaticism" (1848), by John Greenleaf Whittier, among the writings which show Brown's influence, in Chapter V, it seems appropriate to follow the transformation of Wieland by Whittier's assaying of his character, by the kind permission of Houghton Mifflin Company. Whittier says:

"There are occasionally deeds committed almost too horrible and revolting for publication. The tongue falters in giving them utterance; the pen trembles that records them. . . .

"Alas for man when he turns from the light of reason and from the simple and clearly defined duties of the present life, and undertakes to pry into the mysteries of the future, bewildering himself with uncertain and vague prophecies, Oriental imagery, and obscure Hebrew texts! Simple, cheerful faith in God as our great and good Father, and love of His children as our brethren, acted out in all relations and duties, is certainly best for this world, and we believe also the best preparation for that to come. Once possessed by the falsity that God's design is that man should be wretched and gloomy here in order to obtain rest and happiness hereafter; that the mental agonies and bodily tortures of His creatures are

---

1. *Wieland,* 199-200.
2. *Ibid.,* 248, 249.
3. *Ibid.,* 263.

pleasant to Him; that, after bestowing upon us reason for our guidance, He makes it of no avail by interposing contradictory revelations and arbitrary commands,—there is nothing to prevent one of a melancholic and excitable temperament from excesses so horrible as almost to justify the old belief of demonic obsession.

"Charles Brockden Brown, a writer whose merits have not yet been sufficiently acknowledged, has given a powerful and philosophical analysis of this morbid state of mind—this diseased conscientiousness, obeying the mad suggestions of a disordered brain as the injunctions of Divinity—in his remarkable story of *Wieland*. The hero of this strange and solemn romance, inheriting a melancholy and superstitious mental constitution, becomes in middle age the victim of a deep, and tranquil because deep, fanaticism. A demon in human form, perceiving his state of mind, wantonly experiments upon it, deepening and intensifying it by a fearful series of illusions of sight and sound. Tricks of jugglery and ventriloquism seem to his feverish fancies miracles and omens—the eye and the voice of the Almighty piercing the atmosphere of supernatural mystery in which he has long dwelt. He believes that he is called upon to sacrifice the beloved wife of his bosom as a testimony of the entire subjugation of his carnal reason and earthly affections to the Divine will. In the entire range of English literature there is no more thrilling passage than that which describes the execution of this baleful suggestion. The coloring of the picture is an intermingling of the lights of heaven and hell,—soft shades of tenderest pity and warm tints of unextinguishable love contrasting with the terrible outlines of an insane and cruel purpose, traced with the blood of murder. The masters of the old Greek tragedy have scarcely exceeded the sublime horror of this scene from the American novelist. The murderer confronted with his gentle and loving victim in her chamber; her anxious solicitude for his health and quiet; her affectionate caress of welcome; his own relentings and natural shrinking from his dreadful purpose; and the terrible strength which he supposes is lent him of Heaven, by which he puts down the promptings and yearnings of his human heart, and is enabled to execute the mandate of an inexorable Being,—are described with an intensity which almost stops the heart of the reader. When the deed is done a frightful conflict of passions takes place, which can only be told in the words of the author:—'I lifted the corpse in my arms and laid it on the bed. . . . I have sacrificed, O my God! thy last and best gift, my wife!' . . . 'the sacrifice is incomplete—thy children must be offered—they must perish with their mother!' " (Wieland, 191-2, part copied also in Chapter V, in discussing Dana's Paul Felton).

"The misguided man obeys the voice; his children are destroyed in their bloom and innocent beauty. He is arrested, tried for murder, and acquitted as insane. The light breaks in upon him at last; he discovers the imposture which has controlled him; and, made desperate by the full consciousness of his folly and crime, ends the terrible drama by suicide.

"Wieland is not a pleasant book. In one respect it resembles the modern tale of *Wuthering Heights*: it has great strength and power, but no beauty. Unlike that, however, it has an important and salutary moral. It is a warning to all who tamper with the mind and rashly experiment upon its religious element. As such, its perusal by the sectarian Zealots of all classes would perhaps be quite as profitable as much of their present studies."[1]

Thirty-seven years before this discourse by Whittier, the reviewer of new publications in the *Gentleman's Magazine* (1811) said:
"Wieland, or, The Transformation; an American tale (1798) . . . 'A most improbable and horrid tale; and evidently written by one whose talents might have been better employed'."
Neither the reviewer nor Whittier seemed to know the source of Brown's story.

The character of Carwin is quite erratic as he is revealed. Pleyel had met him in Spain, an Englishman who had transformed himself into a Spaniard and embraced Catholicism. A newspaper that came into the hands of Pleyel stated that he was a convict lately escaped from Newgate Prison in Dublin. Carwin, in his defense, excuses his offenses on the ground of a "passion for mystery, and a species of imposture," enhanced by the possession of the potent and stupendous endowment of biloquial power. He definitely states what was his only purpose in regard to Clara:

"It is you whom I have injured, . . . I have deceived you; I have sported with your terrors; . . . This is the amount of my guilt, and this the fruit of my remorse."[2]
Carwin knew nothing of the murders till Clara told him.

The author wrote a sequel to the book to elucidate further Carwin's singular mental traits and left an incomplete narrative, *Mem-*

---

1. Whittier, *The Conflict with Slavery, Politics and Reform, The Inner Life Criticism*: "Fanaticism", 391-5.
2. *Wieland*, 216.

oirs of *Carwin, the Biloquist,* which gives his early life and should
be read before *Wieland* can be fully appreciated. The deceptions
that he practiced on mankind grew, not out of a fatal necessity,
but from circumstances connected with his youth, as he reveals:

"My thirst of knowledge was augmented in proportion as it was
supplied with gratification. . . . My senses were perpetually alive to
novelty, my fancy teemed with visions of the future, and my attention fastened upon every thing mysterious or unknown. . . . My
father . . . conceived that all (knowledge) beyond the mere capacity
to write and read was useless or pernicious. He took . . . much
pains to keep me within these limits. . . . The most vigilant and
jealous scrutiny was exerted in vain: reproaches and blows, painful
privations and ignominious penances had no power to slacken my
zeal, and abate my perseverance. . . . I exerted all my powers to
elude his watchfulness. . . . I was incessantly employed in the invention of stratagems and the execution of expedients. . . . This contention lasted from the sixth to the fourteenth year of my age."[1]

In the person of Carwin, Brown seems clearly to develop the
theme that too much curiosity in the search for knowledge, especially when combined with an inborn aptitude in any direction, is
morally dangerous and would be fatal to the life and happiness of
the possessor. In *Edgar Huntly,* he says, "Curiosity is vicious, if
undisciplined by reason, and inconducive to benefit."[2] His purpose
with regard to Carwin, as related to the Wieland family and expressed through Clara's lips, is to expose the calamitous results
attendant upon the folly of deceit and imposture:

"I do not disdain to contribute what little I can to the benefit of
mankind. . . . If it be communicated to the world, it will inculcate
the duty of avoiding deceit. It will exemplify the force of early
impressions, and show the immeasurable evils that flow from an
erroneous or imperfect discipline."[3]

These words that Brown several times repeats have a Fielding
sound. In the Preface of his play, *The Historical Register* (1737),
the author promised to continue exerting his talents "in ridiculing
vice and imposture." Donald Grant Mitchell described Carwin
as a

---

1. *Memoirs of Carwin, the Biloquist,* bound with *Wieland,* 275-6.
2. *Edgar Huntly,* 13.
3. *Wieland,* 25.

"loathsome, scoundrelly tramp, who has not the sensibilities to measure or to pity the griefs that flow from his diabolism."[1]

Rufus W. Griswold said of him, on his return after an absence from Mettingen:

"He (Carwin) . . . learned with undissembled horror the last scenes in the family of Wieland. He was unwise, unfortunate, wicked, but not a 'fiend,' nor actuated by 'diabolical malice'."[2]

In concluding the character-exposition of Carwin, Brown permits him to make a complete confession to Dr. Cambridge, who exonerates him from all malicious intent concerning the fates of the Wielands, according to the words of Clara:

"Talk not to me, O my reverend friend! of Carwin. He has told thee his tale, and thou exculpatest him from all direct concern in the fate of Wieland. This scene of havoc was produced by an illusion of the senses. . . . though he conceived the previous and unseen agency of Carwin to have indirectly but powerfully predisposed to this deplorable perversion of mind. . . . He saw, when too late, the danger of imposture."[3]

The double purpose in the conduct of Wieland and Carwin may be seen in the way Carwin speaks of his confession:

"I designed it as my vindication from the aspersions that had rested on my character, and as a lesson to mankind on the evils of credulity on the one hand, and of imposture on the other."[4]

Wieland was the victim of both superstition and imposture.

Writing to his countrymen on American subjects, Brown was led to use unexplained scientific phenomena as the features of greatest interest. Some of his critics objected to the employment of exceptional manifestations of nature and of the extraordinary phases of human character as the legitimate groundwork for a novel, but Brown has used these things and practically conveyed a memorable lesson against all superstition and imposture. Man is rebuked for proneness to believe in supernatural powers which, when brooded over, inevitably lead to the dethronement of reason. The author has transformed the materials of *Wieland* into a portentous and awful warning.

---

1. Mitchell, *American Lands and Letters*, I, 179-80.
2. Griswold, *Prose Writers of America*, 108.
3. *Wieland*, 252, 258.
4. *Ibid.*, 231. (See 213-31.)

The creativity of Brown is seen in the skill with which he trans-
fers the spirit of Romanticism and the German and didactic elements to American life and scenes, in the astuteness with which
he reveals and analyzes strange sensations, in the ingenuity with
which he invents incidents and depicts individual catastrophic situations and in the subtlety with which he transforms the human mind
and character. The reader is carried along by the interest of the
story until he does not notice or forgets the incredibility of some
incidents and the improbability of some situations.

This romance contains little of the new freedom experienced by
Americans or of the social activities with which Brown was familiar
in Philadelphia and New York. There is a paucity of description
of American scenery which the author knew so well and displayed
in his later novels, except snatches of intimate details of the beauties about Mettingen—its rugged heights, cliffs, streams, trees and
waterfalls.

The period of Brown's life-time was one of considerable excitement, in both Europe and America. Revolutionary forces were
vigorously alive. New theories, affecting political and social relations, were promulgated daily and often disappeared as quickly as
they had come. Brown's mind was earnestly active and speculated
over every new development of public opinion. He had written
copiously on nearly every subject—social, political, moral, educational and literary,—before his first novel appeared in 1798.

That Brown wrote novels is due to the fact that he needed a
medium of expression for his views about life; and he readily chose
the novel form because Godwin had used it effectively for a like
reason. Surely if Brown chose any author as his model in fiction
writing, he would choose the one who was the most conspicuous,
the most typical, of the times, the one who summed up the theories
that had become current property by the close of the eighteenth
century. Godwin was this man; and he wrote the best novel of
purpose. Brown wished to transplant the philosophy of the Old
World to the New and spread his expositions of social and psychological beliefs among the people.

Critics generally agreed that Brown's early novels resemble *Caleb
Williams,* in style and plot construction. He did imitate somewhat
faithfully his autobiographical style and accept some Godwin

theories almost undigested. In support of this statement are the words of Brown himself, written after the completion of *Wieland*: "What is the nature or merit of my performance? This question is not for me to answer. My decision is favourable or otherwise, according to the views which I take of the subject. When a mental comparison is made between this and the mass of novels, I am inclined to be pleased with my own production. But when the objects of comparison are changed, and I revolve the transcendant merits of Caleb Williams, my pleasure is diminished, and is preserved from a total extinction only by the reflection that this performance is the first. That every new attempt will be better than the last, and that considered in the light of a prelude or first link, it may merit that praise to which it may possess no claim, considered as a last best creation."[1]

"Yet historically, he (Brown) is curiously interesting. His pages reflect both a state of mind and a mood of imagination in which he shared only as a member of a larger world of men (Romanticists and Rationalists), some of whom were destined to a better fortune: It is not only the literary reformer who is found in the gallery of forgotten things; the portrait of the *social innovator* is as commonly to be met with there; and in Brown we find the stamp and impress of one of the most noted in his day and most obscure in ours—the philosopher William Godwin."[2]

In the strictest definition of the meaning and construction of the novel, *Wieland* can scarcely be called other than a romance, a term fitting *Caleb Williams*. Neither author tells a real, convincing story or gives a true representation of everyday life. Both force facts to fit a predetermined purpose, which may lead at times to a distortion of the facts. Brown makes frequent assertions of his purpose,—at the beginning, within the story and in the added chapter,—instead of letting the purpose take care of itself. He seemingly arranged situations arbitrarily to further the desired effect. Long after having written the above statement, the author read a similar one by Raleigh:

"Fielding conducts his narrative under the dominant influence of one prevailing purpose, in the service of which he employs all his irony, never suffering the reader for one moment to forget the main thesis, which is stated at the beginning of the story, restated

1. Brown, Journal, in Dunlap, *op. cit.*, I, 107.
2. *Atlantic Monthly* 61: 710-14, May, 1888.

at the close and illustrated with matchless skill throughout."[1] Perhaps, in *Wieland* Brown deliberately planned to employ Fielding's method in this respect.

To assume likenesses in form and thought between Godwin's novel and the novels of Brown, when no absolute imitation was meant, would be a simple matter. Brown had read and assimilated so much of European philosophy and of current works of fiction that unconsciously he garnered from that material without once reflecting that it was not originally his own. His views and sentiments about life and his dissections and discussions of motives and states of mind appear often on the pages of his novels.

However, it is Godwin to whom Brown is more indebted than to any other and he represented the whole school of radical thought. Among the books that came to America and were reprinted here were those of Godwin, Mary Wollstonecraft and Thomas Paine. English radicalism was early welcomed and affected contemporary writers. Brown connects the new literature of America with the fashions of thought prevalent in his time abroad. On both sides of the water were revolutions in society in the interest of democracy. The thinkers of the period were free-thinkers. Infidelity and rationalism were the outcome in philosophy.

As a result of his investigations of European theories, Brown was affected; but a certain conservatism present in the New World and his Quaker up-bringing constrained him from going to the extremes that Godwin and others did. In passing, one might say that Godwin's theories were modified and somewhat softened from the reading of Brown's novels; perhaps, all England was influenced by his novels in like manner. Brown's reasonings in youth were made in a sort of abstract way, detached from real experience. His acceptance of standardized morals prevented his mind from discerning them always in their right relations with his observations; for instance, the fallacies regarding government, property, justice, religion, marriage and suicide, as evidenced from the following quotations from his novels. Later his ideas were modified and personalized. One must be on guard against assuming that Brown accepted as his own beliefs all that he put into the mouths of his

---

1. Raleigh, *The English Novel*, 168.

characters. Too radical ideas and those subversive of religion and the morals of society he almost invariably has his villains assert. Some of his characters who proclaim beliefs at first change and repent or recant those beliefs later, as Colden in the ensuing pages and Waldegrave in *Edgar Huntly* quoted in the first chapter of this work, of whom his friend Huntly says, "His piety was rapturous." Brown believed in the value of remorse: "Remorse is an ample and proper expiation for all offenses" and commends Huntly's aged friend Inglefield for "inculcating the lessons of penitence and duty."

People usually think of Brown as a romancer of the School of Terror and that he aimed only at arousing the excitement of terror and wonder. That is but partially true. He was essentially a philosopher, interested in moral problems, and a psychologist, greatly attracted to abnormal mental states. To this latter fact may be attributed the unfailingly grave and unwholesome tone in his first romance. He had made a careful study of the mind, but had never understood its healthy workings.

"To do this one must himself possess a mind that has for considerable periods of time felt the delight of living in that state of semiunconsciousness to our physical being which we call health. So only will he be able to feel as other men have felt and usually feel, to come in contact with and measure himself by the common standard. This great pleasure and power we are assured Brown never possessed; accordingly, he was given constantly to introspection and self-contemplation."[1]

The ghastliness and worries of the contemplations of Wieland, Brown must have experienced in a measure in his mind, as when abandoning his law practice, presaging the fatal result of consumption and being expelled from the Quaker sect, or he could never have written so sentiently of them. In his treatment of yellow fever, of Indian depredations and of mountain lions, one knows that these things had been close to his own experience.

It is revealing to compare in detail some of Brown's theories with those of his great English contemporary, chiefly from his *Political Justice*, a philosophy of social anarchism. In the main, Godwin's philosophy is calculating, unpracticable, uncompromising,

---

1. Vilas, *Charles Brockden Brown*, 22-3.

fatalistic; while Brown's is calm, unemotional, considerate, but not unsympathetic. The following passage from *Ormond* seems like a quotation from *Political Justice,* Godwin's theory of society and man's relation to it:

"He carefully distinguished between men in the abstract, and men as they are. The former were beings to be impelled, by the breath of accident, in a right or a wrong road; but whatever direction they should receive, it was the property of their nature to persist in it. . . . A mortal poison pervaded the whole system, by means of which every thing received was converted into bane and purulence. Efforts designed to ameliorate the condition of an individual were sure of answering a contrary purpose. The principles of the social machine must be rectified, before men can be beneficially active. Our motives may be neutral or beneficent, but our actions tend merely to the production of evil. . . . He was part of a machine, . . . A wise man will relinquish the pursuit of general benefit, but not the desire of that benefit, or the perception of that in which this benefit consists, because these are among the ingredients of virtue and the sources of his happiness. Principles, in the looser sense of the term, have little influence on practice. Ormond was, for the most part, governed, like others, by the influences of education and present circumstances."[1]

It is plain that Brown did not swallow that belief in entirety. His remarks about "a wise man" and "little influence on practice" and his own known character preclude his whole-hearted acceptance.

Of property, Godwin says:

"Possessions are in equity a common stock, from which all shall draw according to their need. . . . Nothing can be more iniquitous than for one man to possess superfluities, while there is a human being in existence that is not adequately supplied with these"; and of inheritance: "The present system of property confers on one man immense wealth in consideration of the accident of his birth."[2]   "It makes one's heart ache to think that one man is born to the inheritance of every superfluity, while the whole share of another, without any demerit of his, is drudgery and starving; and that all this is indispensable."[3]

Brown shows plainly his discipleship: "Wealth has ever been

---

1. *Ormond,* 92, 93.
2. Godwin, *Political Justice,* "Of Property," II, Book VIII; I, 228.
3. Godwin, *Caleb Williams,* 104-5.

capriciously distributed. The mere physical relation of birth is all that entitles us to manors and thrones. . . . It ascertains our portion of felicity and usefulness, and fixes our lot among peasants or princes."[1]   "I (Philip Stanley) reflected on the futility of titular distinction; on the capriciousness of wealth, and its independence of all real merit in the possessor."[2]

"Power and riches were chiefly to be dreaded on account of their tendency to deprave the possessor. He held them in abhorrence, not only as instruments of misery to others, but to him on whom they were conferred. . . . The evil flowing from this power, in malignant hands, was proportioned to the good that would arise from the virtuous use of it."[3]

Fate, necessitarianism and justice predominate in Godwin's philosophy. So through the lips of Constantia's friend Sophia, Brown expresses like pessimistic ideas:

"I pondered on the condition of my friend. I reviewed the incidents of her life. I compared her lot with that of others. I could not but discover a sort of incurable malignity in her fate. I felt as if it were denied to her to enjoy a long life or permanent tranquillity. I asked myself what she had done, entitling her to this incessant persecution";[4] and, of Constantia, he says: "She had learned to square her conduct, in a considerable degree, not by the hasty impulses of inclination, but by the dictates of truth. She yielded nothing to caprice or passion";[5] and of Mrs. Lorimer: "But she was not to be forever deceived. Her tenderness was subservient to justice. And when his vices had led him from the gaming-table to the highway, when seized at length by the ministers of law, when convicted and sentenced to transportation . . . her justice was inflexible. . . . The sentence was executed";[6] and of Edgar Huntly: "My life was suspended, as it were, by a spider's thread. . . . Surely my fate has never been paralleled!"[7]

Punishment for crime is wrong, thought Godwin. He precluded the idea of retribution, except only as a temporary expedient for purposes of restraint where personal liberty interferes with the

---

1. *Arthur Mervyn*, I, 58-9.
2. *Clara Howard*, 330.
3. *Ibid.*, 70.
4. *Ormond*, 219.
5. *Ibid.*, 17.
6. *Edgar Huntly*, 46-7.
7. *Ibid.*, 185, 234.

liberty of others.
"All vice is nothing more than error and mistake reduced into practice and adopted as the principle of conduct. It may reasonably be doubted whether error could ever be formidable or long-lived if government did not lend it support"; e.g., the doctrine of transubstantiation, advocated by the church and re-inforced by civil authority (the State Church). "The reason has unlimited power over the emotions; hence, arguments, not an appeal to the emotions, and not force, are the most effective motives."[1]

By similar reasoning, Arthur Mervyn prevents himself from contracting a secret marriage with Eliza:
"It was only requisite for my understanding clearly to discern, to be convinced of the insuperability of this obstacle."[2]
Of Craig, Constantia meditates thus: "he was liable to prosecution; but her heart rejected the thought of being the author of injury to any man. The dread of punishment, however, might induce him to refund, uncoersively, the whole or some part of the stolen property. . . . Menaces of legal prosecution she meant not to use. . . . She confided in the efficacy of her pleadings to awaken his justice. . . . Her mind was unnerved, and recoiled with loathing from considerations of abstract justice, or political utility, when they prompted to the prosecution of the murderer."[3]

Carwin, responsible for the tragedies in the Wieland family to a certain extent, after his complete confession to Clara, is permitted to go free. Clara's maid, Judith, despite her disloyalty and irregular behavior, is not even reasoned with and is unheard of more. Yet Brown, in a later novel showing the unsettled state of his judgment says:
"Methought that to ascertain the hand who killed my friend was not impossible, but to punish the crime was just. That to forbear inquiry or withhold punishment was to violate my duty to my God and to mankind."[4]

Godwin believed that religion and many other things should be taught the pupil not directly, in a compulsory manner, as in school, but indirectly and insensibly, by means of conversation, as restraint of any kind tended to destroy the chance of perfectibility in the

---

1. Godwin, *Political Justice*, I, 2.
2. *Arthur Mervyn*, I, 126.
3. *Ormond*, 75, 76, 179.
4. *Edgar Huntly*, 4.

individual. Thus the murderous villain, Tyrrel, in *Caleb Williams,* was brought up without the rod and without learning:

"Force she (his mother) absolutely forbade; and of the intrinsic allurements of literature and knowledge she had no conception."[1]   Pleyel says to Clara Wieland: "I know that mankind are more easily enticed to virtue by example than by precept. I know that the absoluteness of a model, when supplied by invention, diminishes its salutary influence, since it is useless, we think, to strive after that which we know to be beyond our reach";[2] and Clara writes, "We were left to the guidance of our own understanding and the casual impressions which society might make upon us."[3]   Of Constantia and Ormond, it is said: "She was unacquainted with religion. She was unhabituated to conform herself to any standard but that connected with the present life. Matrimonial as well as every other human duty was disconnected in her mind with any awful or divine sanction. . . . It was otherwise with Ormond. His disbelief was at once unchangeable and strenuous. The universe was to him a series of events connected by an undesigning and inscrutable necessity, and an assemblage of forms to which no beginning or end can be conceived. . . . Enthusiasm was added to disbelief, and he not only dissented but abhorred."[4]

So saturated was Brown with radical theories that, on the question of marriage, he argued about the rejection of the marriage tie, as Godwin in *Political Justice.* In that work, he promulged the fallacy that

"Marriage checks the independent progress of mind. . . . It is absurd to expect that the inclinations and wishes of two human beings should co-incide through any long period of time."

In his own life, at first, Godwin carried out with Mary Wollstonecraft the idea of man and wife living in separate houses that each might be as free as possible. Brown has Colden say to Jane Talbot:

"There is one difficulty I know not how to surmount. Giving to the wife will be only giving to the husband. . . . The wedded pair must live together, she will think. . . . A low roof, a narrow chamber, and an obscure avenue. . . . (are) all thou must look

1. Godwin, *Caleb Williams,* 51.
2. *Wieland,* 141.
3. *Ibid.,* 42.
4. *Ormond,* 148, 149.

for as *my* wife. . . . I must not live with thee; only an occasional visitor. . . . Thy pittance will do no more than support thyself. *I must house myself and feed elsewhere.*"[1] Of Helena and Ormond, Brown says: "Helena was unable to participate in his graver occupations. . . . In her were assembled an exquisite and delicious variety. As it was he was daily in her company. He should scarcely be more so if marriage should take place. . . . There was no need of dwelling under the same roof. His revenue was equal to the support of many household establishments";[2] and of Constantia's father: "His morality, besides, was of a much more flexible kind; and the marriage vows were, in his opinion, formal and unmeaning, and neither in themselves, nor in the apprehension of the world, accompanied with any rigorous obligation,"[3] which expressed the current radical doctrine in regard to marriage. Brown's equivocal thoughts are also stated by Arthur Mervyn: "But marriage was a contract awful and irrevocable. Was this the woman with whom my reason enjoined me to blend my fate, without the power of dissolution?"[4]

In *Alcuin* (1797), Brown says: "Marriage is an union founded on free and mutual consent. It cannot exist without friendship. It cannot exist without personal fidelity. As soon as the union ceases to be spontaneous it ceases to be just. This is the sum. If I were to talk for months, I could add nothing to the completeness of this definition."[5]

Though Carwin, in *Wieland* (1798), is blamed as the misguided biloquist and is not censured at all over his relations with Wieland's sister Clara and his intrigues with Judith, her servant and companion, yet Brown in his novels generally has no patience with the seducer or the disregard of the marriage-bond. Even Godwin, later in life, abandoned his anti-marriage views. Brown seems convinced of the sophistry of his arguments when he envisioned the alternate of marriage with its resulting miseries, injustice and oppression, criticizing Welbeck (Arthur Mervyn, 1799) because of his mistress, Clemenza, and loose conduct generally. All such

---

1. *Jane Talbot,* 105-106. (Cf. Ormond, 127.)
2. *Ormond,* 108.
3. *Ibid.,* 70.
4. *Arthur Mervyn,* II, 81.
5. Brown, "Alcuin," in Dunlap, *op. cit.,* I, 105.

vacillation is reminiscent of the philosophizing manner of the times and of Brown's youthful theorizing.

Brown always spoke hopefully and interestedly of home life and family ties, as found in his own words:
"My conceptions of the delights and benefits connected with love and marriage, are exquisite. They have swayed most of my thoughts, and many of my actions since I arrived at the age of reflection and maturity";[1] and he writes to a friend: "This goes by M. who is preparing to carry home with him a *wife*. . . . That is a destiny which, I hope, will come to us all. I shall be very sorry to be left farthest behind in the race towards the matrimonial goal, but my sorrow will, I believe, be unmixed with envy. There is no event, I think, if happening under tolerably auspicious circumstances, on which we may more reasonably congratulate our friends."[2]

To Godwin, one must go for the theory relating to suicide. He taught in *Political Justice* that suicide is not a crime, the only difficulty being to decide in each individual case whether the social advantage of thirty supplementary years of life forbids recourse to a voluntary death. Brown often suggests this course:
"Grief carries its own antidote along with it. When thought becomes merely a vehicle of pain, its progress must be stopped. Death is a cure which nature or ourselves must administer. To this cure I now looked forward with gloomy satisfaction."[3]
"The pressure of grief is sometimes such as to prompt us to seek a refuge in voluntary death. We must lay aside the burden which we cannot sustain. If thought degenerate into a vehicle of pain, what remains but to destroy that vehicle? For this end death is the obvious, but not the only, or, morally speaking, the worst means. There is one method of obtaining the bliss of forgetfulness (drunkenness), in comparison with which suicide is innocent."[4]   Clithero says at the end of his confession: "I am not fearful of the use that you may be disposed to make of it. I shall quickly set myself beyond the reach of human tribunals. I shall relieve the ministers of law from the trouble of punishing."[5]   It is said of Welbeck: "His own gratification

1. Brown, in Dunlap, *op. cit.*, II, 50.
2. Brown, Letter to Anthony Bleeker, Esq., Philadelphia, Oct. 31, 1801, in Dunlap, *op. cit.*, II, 104.
3. *Wieland*, 199.
4. *Ormond*, 21-2.
5. *Edgar Huntly*, 91.

was the supreme law of his actions. To be subjected to the necessity of honest labour was the heaviest of all evils, and one from which he was willing to escape by the commission of suicide. . . . Suicide was familiar to his thoughts. He had consented to live but on one condition; that of regaining possession of this money."[1]

In his confession, he asks: "whither could I fly, where I should not be pursued, by the phantoms of remorse, by the dread of hourly detection, and by the necessities of hunger and thirst? . . . To rush into the stream before me, and put an end at once to my life and the miseries inseparably linked with it, was the only proceeding which fate had left to my choice. . . . To free myself from self-upbraiding and to shun the persecutions of my fortune was possible only by shaking off life itself. . . . An interview with this man (Watson, whose sister he had betrayed and to recover certain monies) was less to be endured than to look upon the face of an avenging deity. I was determined to avoid this interview, and, for this end, to execute my fatal purpose within the hour."[2]

"For a time she (Constantia) was deserted of her admirable equanimity. . . . she would, perhaps, have adopted any scheme, however dismal and atrocious, which her father's despair might suggest. She would not refuse to terminate her own and her father's unfortunate existence by poison or the cord."[3]

When Constantia urged Ormond to marry Helena, he lies: "Marriage is impossible. You are merely prompting me to suicide; . . . I should, with unspeakably more willingness, assail my own life,"[4] in which he was bluffing, and, by his last brutal denouncing of Helena, drove her to suicide.

"Few novels or romances have been written, which seize so strongly upon the imagination and feelings of the reader, hurry him from the realities which surround him, bury in oblivion his joys and sorrows and fix his whole attention on the images which the author presents before him, as Wieland. . . . The writer (Dunlap) is disposed to class Wieland among novels of the highest order. It has a well conducted fable, the incidents of which all tend to its progress and development, and the style is pure, strong and eloquent."[5]

---

1. *Arthur Mervyn*, I, 200, 207.
2. *Ibid.*, I, 104, 91.
3. *Ormond*, 85.
4. *Ibid.*, 137, 139.
5. Dunlap, *op. cit.*, II, 12, 14-5.

Ormond; or the Secret Witness (1799), Brown's second novel, published the year after *Wieland*, shows the influence of European writers, not of the political romanticists so much, including Godwin, whose influence over Brown has just been set forth, as of the would-be educational reformers, of whom Mary Wollstonecraft was chief. The purpose in *Ormond* is to contrast the supreme value of an intellectual education of women as a foundation for virtue over the sensual or polite accomplishments of the finished lady of that day, in opposing the seducer Ormond.

In his Preface, Marchand says of *Ormond*:

"It is an old-fashioned tale, presenting an ideal heroine of the Age of the Enlightenment, whose rays warmed not France, Britain, and Germany alone, but the young American Republic as well. It is a tale of struggle against poverty and pestilence, the persecutions of grasping and unscrupulous men, and, most fearful of all, the devilish arts of the seducer."

The plot structure of *Ormond* follows the two-part division of *Caleb Williams,* as do *Arthur Mervyn* and *Edgar Huntly.* The first part of Godwin's novel is the narrative of Mr. Collins of the main events of the life of Falkland, previous to the service of Caleb Williams with him; the remainder gives the story of Caleb and evolves the author's purpose. The first part of *Ormond* concludes Ormond's relations with Helena Cleves and the second part relates his dealings with Constantia Dudley.

The story revolves about the association of Ormond with these two girls brought up in such radically different ways. The cities of New York and Philadelphia are the scene of the story and the time includes a visitation of the yellow fever to the latter city. An artist of some skill, but of little business ability, named Stephen Dudley, brought up in ease, is forced by circumstances to engage in his father's occupation of pharmacy to support his family. He later becomes bankrupt through the frauds practised upon him by a young man, Thomas Craig, whom he had befriended and finally made his partner. The Dudleys remove from New York to Philadelphia after their misfortune, where the wife and mother soon dies. Constantia, an only child and one of the heroines of the story, meets each new misfortune bravely. When her discouraged father becomes

"enslaved by a depraved appetite, to be enamored of low debauchery, and to grasp at the happiness that intoxication had to bestow . . . (and then grows blind, she becomes the family's support). The only intellectual amusement which this lady allowed herself was writing. She enjoyed one distant friend, with whom she maintained an uninterrupted correspondence, and to whom she confided a circumstantial and copious relation of all these particulars. That friend is the writer of these memoirs,"[1] Sophia Westwyn Courtland. The scourge of yellow fever added to the discomfort of the already overburdened family and Mr. Dudley endeavored

"to undermine her fortitude and disconcert her schemes. . . . 'This malady is pestilential. Havoc and despair will accompany its progress, and its progress will be rapid. . . . I have been at Messina, and talked with many who witnessed the state of that city in 1743. . . . Anticipation has a tendency to lessen or prevent some evils, but pestilence is not of that number'."[2]

Constantia discovers Craig and seeks his aid and another deception follows.

Now, by a chance meeting with Constantia, Ormond is introduced into the story. Like Carwin, he appears upon the scene with many things unknown about him, though he pretends great cordiality and openness.

"That in which he chiefly placed his boast was his sincerity. . . . He affected to conceal nothing. . . . His aversion to duplicity had flowed from experience of its evils. He had frequently been made its victim."[3]

He combines in himself a keen mind and a passionate disposition. He is naturally generous, but made selfish by society and an unscrupulous killer from participation in revolutions and wars. Ormond had lived on terms of intimacy with the enchanting Helena Cleves, but his meetings with Constantia in friendship cause him basely to desert Helena.

May not Helena Cleves have been named by Brown from the heroine of the classic story *La Princesse de Cleves* (1679) of the highly-educated Madame de la Fayette? That story was in the epistolary style and may have influenced both Richardson and Brown.

---

1. *Ormond*, 22.
2. *Ibid.*, 30.
3. *Ibid.*, 94, 95.

Through an operation, paid for by Ormond, Dudley's sight is restored and through the bequest of Helena the Dudley fortunes are mended and the Dudley home, which Ormond had purchased and given to her, was returned.

"In her (Constantia's) mind, gratitude was no perverse or ignoble principle. She viewed this man as the author of extensive benefits. . . . She had always been solicitous for mental improvement. Any means subservient to this end were valuable. The conversation of Ormond was an inexhaustible fund."[1]

Ormond inspires Constantia with positive, but enigmatical, forebodings as to the future. She is about to sail to Europe with her friend Sophia, when, in a final meeting with Ormond, she kills him in self-defence. Before his death, in a fit of malice and jealousy, he had killed Craig, the despoiler of the Dudley fortunes and the assassin of Dudley at the instigation of himself. Thus Ormond exemplifies both the seducer and the murderer. The tale ends with Constantia living in quiet with her friend in Europe.

There is a strong resemblance between Ormond and Falkland, whom Saintsbury called "not human except in his crime." These men seem admirable in the earlier parts of their careers, because of their noble acts and apparent disinterestedness. Under the guise of friendship, both seek by honorable means to attain their separate objects, but, when they discover their endeavors are vain, they suddenly change into unrestrained monsters and strive to obtain by force and disreputable acts what, otherwise, they cannot accomplish. They put off their assumed characters; and hidden passions blaze forth now where before was an appearance of only courtesy and kindness. The object of the two character delineations is to demonstrate the fatal tendency of a master passion; and what seems to be an unnatural change in the character is but the true character and purpose of life being revealed, according to the principles laid down by their authors. *Specious* is descriptive of the two men. Falkland in a rage had killed his rival Tyrrel. Two innocent men were executed for the crime. More from fear of disgrace, in accordance with his guiding principle, than from fear of death, Falkland, "the fool of fame," remained silent; and henceforth

1. *Ormond*, 146.

every thought is given to guarding the secret. Ormond, baffled in his efforts to win Constantia by systematically loading her with favors and raising her gratitude to the greatest magnitude by his liberality, changes his calculating method and tries to carry out his purpose by open violence. Despite all these assaults, her virtue remains steadfast.

Typically Gothic elements are not difficult to find in *Ormond*. The hero has secret chambers leading to the Dudley home and to Helena's apartments, somewhat similar to the secret stairs to Emily's rooms in "Udolpho," that he may have access to the privacy of others, to gratify his curiosity. He also disguises himself as a chimney-sweep that he may gain access to numerous homes. "It flattered him with the possession of something like omniscience."[1] In these arrangements is explained Brown's intended meaning of the alternate title of the novel—*the Secret Witness*. A Gothic leave-over is perceived in Constantia's determination to revisit alone, before sailing for Europe, the secluded, "artistic" dwelling of her childhood, of which she is now owner, some miles distant from the city. Here she was visited by Ormond and here occurred the deaths of Craig and of Ormond by her hand.

The specific scientific American interest in this novel is the introduction of the frightful horrors of yellow fever, which the author had experienced in Philadelphia, his native city, and more recently in New York. The subject will be expanded in connection with the next novel, *Arthur Mervyn*. Brown may have wished to stress chess-playing as a science, with which many hours were consumed by Ormond and Helena. "He who had acquired skill in this *science* could not be infirm in mind."[2]

Many of Brown's ideas bear testimony to his acquaintance with Mary Wollstonecraft's *A Vindication of the Rights of Woman* (1792), specifically in his differentiation of Helena and Constantia. Rosseau, quoted, taught that
"the education of the women should be always relative to the men. To please, to be useful to us, to make us love and esteem them, to educate us when young, and take care of us when grown up,

---

1. *Ormond*, 96.
2. *Ibid.*, 107-8.

to advise, to console us, to render our lives easy and agreeable: these are the duties of women at all times, and what they should be taught in their infancy," on which Mrs. Wollstonecraft commented: Rosseau "avowed his reason for belittling women from the cradle to the grave to be that otherwise they would be less subservient to men."[1]

"All beauty of personal devotion and self-abnegation, which count for so much in the happiness of family life, disappear and wither when they are selfishly claimed by one member of the family as due to him from the others. . . . The woman who has only been taught to please will soon find her charms are oblique sunbeams, and that they cannot have much effect on her husband's heart when they are seen every day, when the summer is past and gone. . . . Yet only taught to please, women are always on the watch to please, and with true heroic ardour endeavour to gain hearts merely to resign or spurn them. . . . Novels, music, poetry, and gallantry, all tend to make women the creatures ("the weathercock") of sensation. . . . Fragile in every sense of the word, they are obliged to look up to man for every comfort. . . . and their natural protector extends his arm, or lifts up his voice, to guard the lovely trembler—from what? Perhaps the frown of an old cow, or the jump of a mouse; a rat would be a serious danger,"[2] ridiculed Mrs. Wollstonecraft.

The woman educated to please is described thus by Brown:

"Helena Cleves was endowed with every feminine and fascinating quality. Her features were modified by the most transient sentiments and were the seat of a softness at all times blushful and bewitching. All those graces of symmetry, smoothness, and luster, . . . blended their perfection in the shape, complexion, and hair of this lady. Her voice was naturally thrilling and melodious, and her utterance clear and distinct. A musical education had added to all these advantages the improvements of art. . . . Her presence produced a trance of the senses rather than an illumination of the soul. . . . Her understanding bore no disadvantageous comparison with that of the majority of her sex, but, when placed in competition with that of some eminent females or of Ormond, it was exposed to the risk of contempt. . . . To make her wise it would be requisite to change her sex. . . . Her attainments, indeed, were suitable to the imbecility of her sex; but did she not surpass, in those attainments, the ordin-

---

1. Wollstonecraft, *A Vindication of the Rights of Woman*, 131, 15.
2. *Ibid.*, 16, 60, 99, 105, 107.

ary rate of women? They must not be condemned because they are outshone by qualities that are necessarily male births."[1]

In particular are mentioned her proficiency in dancing and dramatic characterization, her study of painting and her exquisite skill in music, especially her playing the harp and clavichord.

The views of Mrs. Wollstonecraft, assembled from her advocacy of the rights of women, may be summarized under five freedoms: uncontrolled freedom of reason . . . "which makes us independent of everything"; political freedom—"women ought to have representatives, instead of being arbitrarily governed without having any direct share allowed them in the deliberations of government"; the author advocated enfranchisement nearly seventy years before women's suffrage was heard of in the House of Commons; educational freedom—"without knowledge there can be no morality! . . . Ignorance is a frail base for virtue! . . . When the mind has been stored with useful knowledge, and strengthened by being employed, the regulation of the behaviour may safely be left to its guidance"; economic freedom—"If marriage be the cement of society, mankind should all be educated after the same model, or the intercourse of the sexes will never deserve the name of fellowship, nor will women ever fulfil the peculiar duties of their sex, till they become enlightened citizens, till they become free by being enabled to earn their own subsistence, independent of men"; marriage freedom—"I principally wish to enforce the necessity of educating the sexes together to perfect both. . . . Besides, this would be a sure way to promote early (voluntary) marriages, and from early marriages the most salutary physical and moral effects naturally flow."[2]

These are such freedoms, contended for one hundred fifty to two hundred years ago, as women take for granted as their rights in present days. How radical the ideas seemed one can never conceive.

In the following excerpts is a resumé of Mrs. Wollstonecraft's opinions:

"I wish to show that elegance is inferior to virtue, that the first object of laudable ambition is to obtain a character as a human being, regardless of the distinction of sex; and that secondary views should be brought to this simple touchstone" (Introduction

---

1. *Ormond*, 98, 106.
2. Wollstonecraft, *A Vindication of the Rights of Woman*, 180, 184, 220, 107, 108, 54, 247, 255, 253.

to First Edition). "Contending for the rights of woman, my main argument is built on this simple principle, that if she be not prepared by education to become the companion of man, she will stop the progress of knowledge and virtue. . . . the more understanding women acquire, the more they will be attached to their duty—comprehending it—for unless they comprehend it, unless their morals be fixed on the same immutable principle as those of men, no authority can make them discharge it in a virtuous manner" (Dedication, VIII, X). . . . "it is a farce to call any being virtuous whose virtues do not result from the exercise of its own reason. . . . Strengthen the female mind by enlarging it, and there will be an end to blind obedience; . . . I do not know of what use is an improved taste, if the individual be not rendered more independent of the casualties of life; . . . as sound politics diffuse liberty, mankind, including woman, will become more wise and virtuous. . . . till women are more rationally educated, the progress of human virtue and improvement in knowledge must receive continual checks. . . . trifling employments have rendered woman a trifler. . . . Educate women as men to gain power over *themselves,* not over men. . . . I do not wish them to have power over men; but over themselves. . . . Let woman share the rights, and she will emulate the virtues of man. . . . (If men) be content with rational fellowship instead of slavish obedience . . . they would find us more observant daughters, more affectionate sisters, more faithful wives, more reasonable mothers—in a word, better citizens. . . . I mean explicitly to say that they (women) must only bow to the authority of reason, instead of being the *modest* slaves of opinion."[1]

The aim of Mrs. Wollstonecraft's book is to demonstrate the falsity, the immorality and the miserable consequences, of acting upon the opinion that

"she (woman) must always strive to make it appear that her physical and mental weakness had caused her to yield to force, . . . that women must never openly acknowledge that they wish to marry while secretly making marriage the one object of their existence."[2]

She said this led to dissimulation and the appearance of wantonness and immorality.

Clara Wieland, in contemplating her love for Pleyel and her

---

1. Wollstonecraft, *A Vindication of the Rights of Woman,* 52, 56, 67, 73, 77, 126, 287, 107, 287, 17, 92.
2. *Ibid.,* 5, 6.

desire that he should reveal his love for her, thus speaks of this erroneous training of women:

"Time was, when these emotions would be hidden with immeasurable solicitude from every human eye. Alas! these airy and fleeting impulses of shame are gone. My scruples were preposterous and criminal. They are bred in all hearts by a perverse and vicious education. . . . My errors have taught me thus much wisdom:— that those sentiments which we ought not to disclose it is criminal to harbour."[1]

Clara exhibits a feminine transition from the old school for maidens to the new. She and her brother and Catharine and Henry Pleyel had been children together and educated in the same ways. Wieland married Catharine; and Pleyel, having spent some years in Europe, became affianced to a German woman. On his return, Clara falls in love with him and her chief anxiety is to keep him from knowing it. He is really interested in her, but circumstances bring it about for him to marry the other woman, who soon dies, leaving him free for their subsequent marriage.

The musings of Clara run on as follows:

"though this object of his love be snatched away, is there not another who is able and willing to console him for her loss? . . . That the belief of my having bestowed my heart upon another (Carwin) produced in my friend (Pleyel) none but ludicrous sensations was the true cause of my distress; but if this had been discovered by him my distress would have been unspeakably aggravated. . . . A nameless ecstasy thrilled through my frame when any new proof occurred that the ambiguousness of my behaviour was the cause (of his distress). . . . I must not speak. Neither eyes nor lips must impart the information. He must not be assured that my heart is his, previous to the tender of his own; . . . he must be supplied with space whereon to build a doubt as to the true state of my affections; he must be prompted to avow himself. The line of delicate propriety,—how hard it is not to fall short, and not to over-leap it! . . . (Disappointed once by his not coming to a drama rehearsal by the Wieland families): Thus had my golden vision melted into air! . . . Why should I prolong by hypocrisy or silence, his misery as well as my own? . . . Wrapt up in the consciousness of innocence (when accused of duplicity), . . .

---

1. *Wieland*, 98-9.

I strove in vain to believe in the assuaging influence of time, to look forward to the birthday of new hopes, and the re-exaltation of that luminary of whose effulgencies I had so long and so liberally partaken."[1]

The single quotation preceding these excerpts was spoken before most of them, which shows the unsettled thought of Brown on the subject of women and marriage, but Clara, being the narrator, probably had come to her fixed decision before writing at all or writing her musings.

In contrast to Helena Cleves, Brown presents the well-educated woman, in Constantia Dudley.

"Women are generally limited to what is sensual and ornamental. Music and painting, and the Italian and French languages, are bounds which they seldom pass, . . . The education of Constantia had been regulated by the peculiar views of her father, who sought to make her, not alluring and voluptuous, but eloquent and wise. He therefore limited her studies to Latin and English. Instead of familiarizing her with the amorous effusions of Petrarcha and Racine, he made her thoroughly conversant with Tacitus and Milton. Instead of making her a practical musician or pencilist, he conducted her to the school of Newton and Hartley, unveiled to her the mathematical properties of light and sound, taught her, as a metaphysician and anatomist, the structure and power of the senses, and discussed with her the principles and progress of human society. . . . Her knowledge of the Latin tongue and of grammatical principles rendered easy the acquisition of Italian and French."[2]

Apparently Brown is advocating something other than the usual pursuits of women, by suggesting natural sciences, metaphysics and physiology.

A few words of Mrs. Radcliffe regarding the bringing up of Emily may have helped set Brown aright: St. Aubert (her father) gave Emily a general view of the sciences and an exact acquaintance with every part of elegant literature, including Latin and English.

"A well-informed mind, he would say, is the best security against the contagion of folly and of vice. The vacant mind is ever on the watch for relief, and ready to plunge into error to escape from the languor of idleness. Store it with ideas, teach it the pleasure of

---

1. *Wieland*, 66, 89, 96, 97-8, 100, 101, 125, 159-60.
2. *Ormond*, 27-8.

thinking, and the temptations of the world without will be counteracted by the gratifications from the world within."[1]

That women should have the power of making a living, if necessary, was advocated by Brown. Both Helena and Constantia suffered reverse of fortune.

"Helena was destined to experience the vicissitudes of fortune. Her father died suddenly and left her without provision. . . . She was not qualified to sustain this reverse of fortune in a graceful manner. . . . She is ignorant and helpless as a child, on every topic that relates to the procuring of subsistance. Her education has disabled her from standing alone"; and of Constantia, Ormond says: "The manner in which this lady had sustained so cruel a reverse of fortune, the cheerfulness with which she appeared to forego all the gratifications of affluence, the skill with which she selected her path of humble industry, and the steadiness with which she pursued it, were proofs of a moral constitution from which he supposed the female sex to be debarred. The comparison was obvious between Constantia and Helena, and the result was by no means advantageous to the latter. . . . There is no disgrace in earning your subsistence by your own industry. . . . A consciousness of her own worth, and disdain of the malevolence of fortune, perpetually shone forth in her behavior. . . . She did not soothe our vanity nor fascinate our pity by diffident reserves and flutterings." [2] These words sustain the author's views: "What is it makes one calling more lucrative than another? Not superior strength of shoulders or sleight of hand; not the greater quantity of brute matter that is reduced into form or set in motion. No. The difference lies in the mental powers of the artist, and the direction accidentally given to these powers. What should hinder a girl like this from growing rich by her diligence and ingenuity?"[3]

It will be recalled that Brown wrote *Alcuin; or, The Rights of Women* (1797), a dialogue arrangement of his findings from his study of the works of Continental writers, before the writing of his novels, the first in America to express his belief in the intellectual equality of the sexes and to advise for men and women similar instruction, equal industrial opportunities and a more rational system of education. A reflection from Brown's Quaker

---

1. Radcliffe, *The Mysteries of Udolpho,* I, 7.
2. *Ormond,* 99, 117, 112, 89, 90.
3. *Jane Talbot,* 118.

training may possibly be seen here, regarding the equality of men and women. Brown and this work of his were carefully discussed by David Lee Clark. One sentence is of interest here:

"He (Brown) courageously maintained that there should be no distinction in the form or content of the education of men and women; women should be allowed to study the natural sciences."[1]

Eliza complains to Arthur Mervyn:

"You desire to obtain knowledge by travelling and conversing with many persons, and studying many sciences; but you desire it for yourself alone"; and Arthur says, "In my previous reasonings I had certainly considered her sex utterly unfitting her for those scenes and pursuits to which I had destined myself. . . . I could not deny that human ignorance was curable by the same means in one sex as in the other; that fortitude and skill were of no less value to one than to the other."[2]

Mrs. Wollstonecraft advocated a national education, for girls and boys together, preferably in day schools, at home, in political and moral subjects, in lessons of politeness and fortitude, in exercises of the body—a public school system. She condemned colleges and boarding schools for young children; and Brown says of the Wielands,

"Our social pleasures were subject to no unreasonable restraints. We were instructed in most branches of useful knowledge, and were saved from the corruption and tyranny of colleges and boarding schools."[3]

Toward the close of the century there was a general criticism of boarding schools, which did not adopt the new enlightening program,—that they made young women weak, vain, indolent and sly. In place of them were advocated nationalized day schools, where boys and girls should receive the same training. Brown was familiar also, no doubt, with Elizabeth Inchbald's *A Simple Story,* published a year before Mrs. Wollstonecraft's famous book. She denounced boarding schools, because as she said, they fostered ignorance, indolence, and vanity. "The character of Miss Milner entitles Mrs. Inchbald to a very high place among the novelists of her day," Raleigh said.

---

1. Clark, *Brockden Brown and the Rights of Women,* 23.
2. *Arthur Mervyn,* II, 80-1.
3. *Wieland,* 40.

In contrast to Godwin and the rationalistic school, Mary Woll-stonecraft respected "marriage as the foundation of every social virtue," but demanded that "man and wife should be equally well-educated and responsible." This opinion is re-iterated by Brown in his description of Constantia:

"Marriage could be justified in her eyes only by community of affections and opinions. She might love without the sanction of her judgment, but while destitute of that sanction, she would never suffer it to sway her conduct."   And Ormond says of marriage with the uneducated wife: "Marriage is absurd. This flows from the general and incurable imperfection of the female character. No woman can possess that worth which would induce me to enter into this contract, and bind myself, without power of revoking the decree, to her society. . . . The terms of this contract were, in his eyes, iniquitous and absurd. . . . To forego the liberty of choosing his companion, and bind himself to associate with one whom he despised; to raise to his own level one whom nature had irretrievably degraded; to avow, and persist in his adherence to, a falsehood, palpable and loathsome to his understanding . . . was a height of infatuation that he could never attain. . . . A wife is generally nothing more than a household superintendent. . . .

Helena's intellectual deficiencies could not be concealed. She was a proficient in the elements of no science. The doctrine of lines and surfaces was as disproportionate with her intellects as with those of a mock-bird. She had not reasoned on the principle of human action, nor examined the structure of society. She was ignorant of the past or present condition of mankind. . . . The heights of eloquence and poetry were shut out from her view. . . . The constitution of nature, the attributes of its Author, the arrangement of the parts of the external universe, and the substance, modes of operation, and ultimate destiny of human intelligence, were enigmas unsolved and insoluble by her. . . . He did nothing but lay the conditions before her. . . . No doubt, the irksomeness of her present situation, the allurements of luxury and ease which Ormond had to bestow, and the revival of her ancient independence and security, had some share in dictating her assent. . . . She did so because assent was more eligible than refusal."[1]

Doubtless, too much credit has been accorded Mrs. Wollstone-craft as an influence over Brown's thinking concerning the studies

---

1. *Ormond,* 150, 100, 104-5, 101, 100.

and teaching of women. Fifty years before *A Vindication of the Rights of Woman* was published (1792), there died in England the prolific writer Daniel Defoe. It was said by Rousseau, contradicting in large measure his own teaching on the subject, that *Robinson Crusoe* is a better treatise on education than anything which Aristotle or the moderns have written. Defoe's hero represents the whole of human society, doing with his hands all the things which, by the division of labor and the demands of modern civilization, are now done by many different workers. One is not limited to that romance of Defoe as a survey of the needs and accomplishments for young ladies.

Among the author's numerous works is one entitled *An Essay upon Projects* (1697), a part of which gives the plan of an academy for women and their studies which these excerpts suggest: "I am confidant, had they the advantages of education equal to us, they would be guilty of less than ourselves. . . . The capacities of women are supposed to be greater and their senses quicker than those of men; and what they might be capable of being bred to is plain from some instances of female wit (intelligence), which this age is not without."   After sketching the kind of buildings and grounds, he proposes "music and dancing, which it would be cruelty to bar the sex of, because they are their darlings; . . . they should be taught languages; . . . and I would venture the injury of giving a woman more tongues than one. . . . They should . . . be taught all the graces of speech and all the necessary air of conversation. . . . They should be brought to read books, and especially history. . . . Women, in my observation, have little or no difference in them, but as they are or are not distinguished by education. . . . A woman well bred and well taught, furnished with the additional accomplishments of knowledge and behavior, is a creature without comparison; her society is the emblem of sublimer enjoyments; her person is angelic and her conversation heavenly; she is all softness and sweetness, peace, love, wit, and delight. She is every way suitable to the sublimest wish, and the man that has such a one to his portion has nothing to do but to rejoice in her and be thankful. . . . The great distinguishing difference which is seen in the world between men and women is in their education, . . . for I cannot think that God Almighty ever made them so delicate, so glorious creatures, and furnished them with such charms, so agreeable and so delightful to mankind, with souls capable of the same accomplishments with men, and all to be

only stewards of our houses, cooks, and slaves."
Brown, in contrasting Helena and Constantia says: "So great
is the difference between forms animated by different degrees of
intelligence."[1]

Many of the proposals made by Defoe are but repeated and expanded by Mrs. Wollstonecraft and others. There is one sure
proof that Brown had read this essay before he wrote his letter
about Rockaway and *Arthur Mervyn,* for Defoe uses an erroneous
spelling of a certain rather uncommon word, and Brown misspells
it likewise twice—*conversible* for *conversable.* Poe, following in
Brown's footsteps, misspells it. Before Brown, Mrs. Bleecker and
Lewis spell it correctly, as do Cowper and Jane Austen, after him.

A story earlier than the "Vindication" forecasts the new woman
and a revised education for men and women—*The History of
Sandford and Merton* (1783-89) by Thomas Day. Harry Sandford,
the son of plain, honest farmer folk, is studious, truthful and a
favorite of everybody. Tommy Merton, born in Jamaica of very
wealthy parents, is waited on hand and foot, by negro slaves, is
selfish, very much spoiled and despises those who work, as if they
were a lower order of beings. The theme of the book is the contrast between rich and poor, those working and those living off the
labor of others, and correct discipline as the leveler. Mr. Barlow,
a clergyman, accepts the boys as pupils. He instructs them, by means
of short tales and dialogues, history, the natural sciences, geography
and so on. He teaches the dignity of labor, explains the wrongs of
slavery, exalts the virtues and condemns boarding schools. Like
Sandford, Arthur Mervyn is an honest, kind-spirited country lad,
is brought to the city and self-reliantly pursues his course, heedless
of money.

From this time, said Raleigh, there were never lacking tales
for the young, many having a strong flavor of the theories of
the Revolution.

"Rank and wealth are almost always denuded in these stories, of
their fair share of the trappings lent by the imagination. ' 'Tis only
noble to be good'—a definition of nobility . . . permitted to those
of maturer years to supplement by a study of *Burke's Peerage.*"[2]

---

1. *Ormond,* 131.
2. Raleigh, *The English Novel,* 249-50.

Miss Sukey Simmons, Day's heroine, may be conceded to be the first modern woman, in knowing mathematics and scientific subjects, besides a feminine smattering of literature, language and handicrafts. Sukey is the prototype of the informed woman, whom Brown portrayed and set forward on her way. The teaching of the Wieland and Pleyel children was modernized; and of that group Clara foreshadows Constantia.

In 1749, in *Tom Jones* (I, 300), Fielding clinched the subject for his successors:
"English women, brother, I thank Heaven, are no slaves. We have as good a right to liberty as yourselves. We are to be convinced by reason and persuasion only; and not governed by force."

The most significant triumph of the author's ingenuity in *Ormond* is the clear delineation of his characters. They are drawn with boldness and great distinction. Constantia is the best, most natural and most original among his women, quite different from the females of the romancers. She became the admiration and type character of several of Brown's successors. Though prone to over-meditation, perhaps, weighing the good and the bad and the possible plans she might follow, she is a model of womanly virtue and independence, one who can rise above disappointments and adversity. She is sympathetic, wise, patient, thrifty, self-poised usually, self-reliant and capable of earning a living, under all kinds of discouraging conditions, a positive character and representative of an ideal,—Brown's ideal of woman. She seems a sort of being, set apart, a little self-righteous. She was adored by her father, who
"never reflected on his relation to her without rapture. Her qualities were the objects of his adoration. He resigned himself with pleasure to her guidance."[1]   In closing her narrative, Sophia concludes: "I have only to add my wishes that the perusal of this tale may afford you as much instruction as the contemplation of the sufferings and vicissitudes of Constantia Dudley has afforded to me. Farewell."[2]

In Helena and Constantia, Brown is contrasting two kinds of education. The weak, sentimental, yielding Helena represents all

---

1. *Ormond,* 144.
2. *Ibid.,* 242.

that the typical education of that period would make a young girl become. In Constantia, the author embodies all that he would have woman's education do for her. She displays the superiority of reason over sentimentality and condemns the falsity of the theory of the Rationalists in regard to marriage. As Brown's Constantia may have given the title *Constantia Neville* to Helena Wells' novel (1800), so may he have borrowed from a novel written two years before his *Ormond,* entitled *History of Constantius and Pulchera, or Constancy Rewarded,* with no author signed, or from an earlier book by Langhorne: *The Letters that passed between Theodosius and Constantia* (1763).

The merits of Constantia are enhanced by comparison of her with her companions. The narrator, Sophia Westwyn Courtland, is a friend of Constantia, reared with her to her seventeenth year, which "connection," she says, "has constituted the joy and misery of my existence," to which charge, Constantia counters: "Sophia Courtland has never been wise. Her affections disdain the cold dictates of discretion, and spurn at every limit that contending duties and mixed obligations prescribe. And yet, O precious inebriation of the heart! O pre-eminent love! What pleasure of reason or of sense can stand in competition with those attendant upon thee?"[1] To her, Constantia had written all the years she had spent in Europe with her ailing mother; and the substance of the letters make the story *Ormond.*

An altogether unique character among Brown's women is Madame Martinette de Beauvais, of Greek-Sclavonian parents, who died of the plague, leaving Martinette and a brother a year older. She loses trace of him until Brown acquaints the reader that Ormond is the lost brother. Martinette had lived in most of the southern European countries, learning several languages, of which "Latin is the mother of them all," with "versatile curiosity and flexible organs." She tells much of modern European history; while Constantia knows little but of ancient times and personages.

In Vienna she married an Englishman, Wentworth. She says, "My soul was engrossed by two passions—a wild spirit of adventure, and a boundless devotion to him," and of him, "He was a

---

1. *Ormond,* 185, 207.

political enthusiast, who esteemed nothing more graceful or glorious than to die for the liberties of mankind."

The husband and wife fought side by side in the French Revolution.

"I delighted to assume the male dress, to acquire skill at the sword, and dexterity in every boisterous exercise. . . . My hand never faltered when liberty demanded the victim,"

she exulted and bragged that she saved her husband from death more than once, killing thirteen officers at Jemappe, at one time. When Constantia asks if she intends to return to Europe and so much danger, she replies,

"Danger, my girl? It is my element. I am an adorer of liberty, and liberty without peril can never exist. . . . Have I not been three years in a camp? What are bleeding wounds and mangled corpses, when accustomed to the daily sight of them for years?"

The two warriors come to America and fight for the Colonies in the Revolution for four years, before Wentworth is wounded at Germantown, captured by the English, taken to England and dies. Martinette has again come to America. Constantia says of her animated, vivacious Amazon-like friend,

"They (her peculiarities and deportment) merely denoted large experience, vigorous faculties, and masculine attainments."[1]

This sketch of Madame Beauvais gave Brown an opportunity to disclose his love of liberty and of country. It also reveals to the reader Brown's knowledge of a Mr. Roseveldt of Philadelphia, the musical shopman, to whom Constantia sold her father's lute during yellow fever hard times and from whom Madame Beauvais bought it, in consequence of which she called upon Constantia.

"I know no task more arduous than a just delineation of the character of Ormond. . . . Ormond was, of all mankind, the being most difficult and most deserving to be studied. . . . No one could entertain loftier conceptions of human capacity than Ormond. . . . His income was large, and he managed it nearly on the same principles as other men. . . . He was without the attractions of candor, because he regarded not the happiness of others. . . . His asperities wounded, and his sternness chilled. . . . He had fashioned his treatment of Helena on sullen and ferocious principles. Yet he was able, it seemed, to mold her, by means of them nearly into the creature that he wished. . . . Ormond was a stranger to her (Con-

---

1. *Ormond*, 159, 167, 171, 170, 171, 157.

stantia). His manners were repulsive and austere. She was a mere girl. . . . A blunt and irregular character like Ormond's might throw an air of ridicule over the scene. She shrunk from the encounter of a boisterous and manlike spirit. . . . Such a man is incurable and obdurate. . . . He knew what was due to his guest. He loved to mortify, by his negligence, the pride of his equals and superiors." . . . "I know the sternness of your probity. . . . Am I deceived, or is it an incontrollable destiny that unites us?"

And Constania replies, "I cannot love but when my understanding points out to me the propriety of love." . . . "Ormond aspired to nothing more ardently than to hold the reins of opinion—to exercise absolute power over the conduct of others. . . . She was unaware, that if he were unable to effect a change in her creed, he was determined to adopt a system of imposture. . . . He had embraced a multitude of opinions which appeared to her erroneous." . . . "He (Mr. Dudley) expatiated on the dubious character of this man, the wildness of his schemes, and the magnitude of his errors. But what could be expected from a man, half of whose life had been spent at the head of a band of Cossacks, spreading devastation in the regions of the Danube, and supporting by flagitious intrigues the tyranny of Catharine, and the other half in traversing inhospitable countries, and extinguishing what remained of clemency and justice by intercourse with savages."[1]

The relationship between Constantia and Ormond shows clearly that it was a contest between idealisms and in Constantia a conflict of ideas, a modern departure in fiction. The conflict in her mind is between faith and practice, between love and misgivings, between a desire to be loved by the attractive Ormond and apprehension inspired by his subtleties of expression and irregular personality.

The belief of Ormond may be summarized in this excerpt:

"In his intercourse with women he deemed himself superior to the allurements of what is called love. . . . In his scale of enjoyments the gratifications which belonged to these ("the physical propensities of a human being") were placed at the bottom. . . . He had not hitherto met with a female worthy of his confidence. . . . He found in them no intellectual energy, . . . and the uniformity of his experience at length instilled into him a belief that the intellectual constitution of females was essentially defective. He denied the reality of that passion which claimed a similitude or sympathy of

---

1. *Ormond*, 92, 93-4, 115, 120, 121, 122, 138, 147, 148, 150, 174.

minds as one of its ingredients."[1]

Sophia persuaded Constantia to go to Europe, having estimated justly Ormond's ignominious character. When he meets Constantia as for the last visit, he reveals their plan, Sophia's accusations and threatens her:

"thou wilt feed upon sighs; thy tears will flow without remission; thou wilt grow enamored of death, and perhaps wilt anticipate the stroke of disease."   Constantia cogitates: "All human precautions had been used to baffle the attempts of any secret witness. . . . In what ambiguous terms had he couched his prognostics of some mighty evil that awaited her! . . . capable of urging her to suicide." . . . "Human life is momentous or trivial in our eyes, according to the course which our habits and opinions have taken. Passion greedily accepts, and habit readily offers, the sacrifice of another's life, and reason obeys the impulse of education and desire."   Ormond says, "I am come to witness the fulfilment of my words and the completion of your destiny."[2]

Ormond is Brown's most consummate villain, the most detailed portrait of the heroic criminal. The conception of his character is one of mingled benevolence and crime with a strange superhuman force commanding awe and attention. It is due to his misconceptions of the principles of uprightness and virtue that he thinks he can buy friendship and love by means of material gifts and benefits. Hardened to war and bloodshed and director and fellow-worker in schemes of intrigue, he holds the death of opponents as legitimate. He disregards the conventions of society, because he is confident of his superiority and thinks that all others should bow to the force of his personality. He gives the results of a false home-training when he tells Constantia of the death of the impostor Craig:

"What scruples can be expected from a man inured from infancy to cunning and pillage? Will he abstain from murder when urged by excruciating poverty, by menaces of persecution, by terror of expiring on the gallows? . . . His death was a due and disinterested offering on the altar of your felicity and mine."[3]

The conception of Ormond as a man of dark passions is Byronic,

---

1. *Ormond*, 97.
2. *Ibid.*, 215-6, 218, 226-7.
3. *Ibid.*, 230, 231.

as it would have been designated a score of years later. Brown did not invent Byronism, but he may be said,

"to clothe this type of passion with a power and lift it to the height that made it his own creation in literature; and it happened fortunately for his own fame that he in his own person embodied it for the imagination of his contemporaries."[1]

In a letter "To I. E. Rosenberg" (given in the American Fiction Series edition of Ormond), Brown wrote:

"You are anxious to obtain some knowledge of the history of Constantia Dudley. . . . Constantia, like all the beings made known to us, not by fancy, but experience, has numerous defects. . . .

"Ormond will, perhaps, appear to you a contradictory or unintelligible being. I pretend not to the infallibility of inspiration. He is not a creature of fancy. It was not prudent to unfold *all* the means by which I gained a knowledge of his actions; but these means, though singularly fortunate and accurate, could not be unerring and complete. I have shown him to you as he appeared, on different occasions and at successive periods, to me. This is all that you will demand from a faithful biographer. . . .

"The modes of life, the influence of public events upon the character and happiness of individuals, in America, are new to you. The distinctions of birth, the artificial degrees of esteem or contempt which connect themselves with different professions and ranks in your native country (Germany, footnote), are but little known among us."

Arthur Mervyn; or, Memoirs of the Year 1793, Brown's third novel, grew directly out of his knowledge of the plague of yellow fever, in New York (1798), at the time of the death of his friend Dr. Smith, in whose household he himself had been stricken, and, also, from the ravages of a like epidemic, which he had withstood in his native city, Philadelphia, in 1793.

Although Brown consciously used real yellow fever happenings as the framework and the exciting theme of his story, his chief motives were psychological, ethical and scientific. Under the stress of a common national disaster, he aimed to rouse sentiment that would lead the rich to aid the poor and his countrymen to use general preventive measures in controlling the disease and to see the

---

1. *Atlantic Monthly* 61: 710-14, May, 1888.

need of hospital reform.

In his Preface, Brown says,

"The evils of pestilence . . . have already supplied new and copious
materials for reflection to the physician and the political economist.
They have not been less fertile of instruction to the moral ob-
server, to whom they have furnished new displays of the influence
of human passions and motives. . . . It is every one's duty to
profit by all opportunities of inculcating on mankind the lessons of
justice and humanity. The influences of hope and fear, the trials of
fortitude and constancy . . . have, perhaps, never been exceeded
in any age. . . . Men only require to be made acquainted with
distress for their compassion and their charity to be awakened.
He that depicts, in lively colours, the evils of disease and poverty,
performs an eminent service to the sufferers, by calling forth
benevolence in those who are able to afford relief; and he who
portrays examples of disinterestedness and intrepidity confers on
virtue the notoriety and homage that are due to it, and rouses in
the spectators the spirit of salutary emulation."

The plot of *Arthur Mervyn* is divided into two parts. Brown
continues in his Preface:

"In the following tale a particular series of adventures is brought
to a close; but these are necessarily connected with the events which
happened subsequent to the period here described. These events
are not less memorable than those which form the subject of the
present volume, and may hereafter be published, either separately
or in addition to this." (See *Ormond*, 203.)

The story was completed. Part One, published in 1799, corresponds
to Volume I, in which Arthur recites his own story in the first
person to Dr. Stevens and his wife after the doctor tells of his
finding Arthur sick. He includes the history of the pestilence
and his relations with Welbeck. Part Two corresponds to Volume
II, published in 1800, and recounts the philanthropical adventures
of Arthur.

"Here ended the narrative of Mervyn," the doctor says. "Surely
its incidents were of no common kind. During this season of
pestilence, my opportunities of observation had been numerous. . . .
The occurrences which fell within my own experience bore a general
resemblance to those which has just been related, but . . . striking
on my mind with all the force of novelty. They served no end,
but as vouchers for the truth of the tale. Surely the youth had
displayed inimitable and heroic qualities. His courage was the

growth of benevolence and reason, . . . He had been qualified for the encounter of gigantic dangers by no laborious education. He stepped forth upon the stage, unfurnished, by anticipation or experience, with the means of security against fraud; and yet, by the aid of pure intentions, had frustrated the wiles of an accomplished and veteran deceiver. . . . The foresight of man is in proportion to his knowledge."[1]

Arthur is an ingenuous youth of unrobust physique, indulged by his mother, an intellectual woman, who died when he was a young man. His father, a man of slight education, soon marries an ignorant servant girl and consequently Arthur leaves home. He goes to Philadelphia with almost no money, without friends, utterly unacquainted with the world, and contracts the dread disease.

In the introductory episode of the story, Brown registered an event similar to one he had witnessed and expressed his appreciation of Dr. Smith. (See Chapter I.) Dr. Stevens sees near his home "the figure of a man reclining against the wall," whom he addresses:
"Rise, I pray you, and come into the house. . . . We will find you a physician and a nurse, and all we ask in return is good spirits and compliance."[2]

Before his illness, on arriving in Philadelphia, Arthur had had several strange adventures, one of which may have been suggested to Brown by an incident in the *The Old English Baron* by Clara Reeve. Arthur had been befriended in the city by a young man, who took him to his home and locked him in a chamber. Arthur heard breathing. "The sleeper was a babe." He took to the closet when he heard the door being unlocked. Now entered a man and wife, she weeping and he trying to comfort her for the loss of their infant child. Finally, she discovers the babe, and her husband, pretending to be equally astonished,
"artfully insinuated the propriety of bestowing care upon the little foundling. . . . She . . . at length was persuaded to take the babe to her bosom and give it nourishment."[3]   Clara Reeve's account is similar: "Just one and twenty years ago, on that very day, I lost my first-born son; . . . And so as I was sitting all alone,

1. *Arthur Mervyn*, II, 3; I, 23.
2. *Ibid.*, I, 5, 7.
3. *Ibid.*, I, 40.

and very melancholy, Andrew came home from work; 'See, Margery,' said he, 'I have brought you a child instead of that you have lost.' . . . The poor infant was cold and it cried, and looked up at me so pitifully that I loved it; . . . as if it were my own: and so I do still, if I dared to own it."[1]

Thus Andrew and Margery Styles had brought up Edmund, heir to the baron. Perhaps, Brown called the babe a foundling after Tom Jones, and both he and Miss Reeve based their baby incidents on Fielding's.

Arthur, wholly destitute, is soon engaged as secretary by Thomas Welbeck, a cruder villain than Ormond, who inspires Arthur with veneration and unease, an unscrupulous man of the world, who appears to his friends to be very wealthy. Arthur is treated with the consideration due to a son, but is required to keep secret all his previous history. On the morning after his arrival, he is introduced to a beautiful woman whom Welbeck calls his daughter, but who is really his mistress, Clemenza, by name. Welbeck's career as a rich man is ended when he kills Watson, a man whose sister he had wronged. Discovered by Arthur, after the very act of murder, he confesses to Arthur all the crimes and misdeeds of his life. They decide to leave Philadelphia and separate. The next that is heard of Arthur is as servant in the home of the Hadwins. To rescue a nephew of Mr. Hadwin, named Wallace, Arthur goes into the pest-plagued city. On his return he finds the Hadwin family destroyed except Susan dying, Eliza, whom he takes to a neighbor's, and Caleb, an old servant, whom he leaves in charge of the Hadwin estate. One notes here a borrowing from *Caleb Williams* in the servant's name. Arthur returns to Welbeck's home to secure a certain manuscript, written by Lodi, the deceased brother of Clemenza. He discovers twenty thousand dollars in it. A little later, stricken with the fever, he re-enters the house to die. He encounters Welbeck, who had searched for the manuscript and now menaces him to regain it and the notes, which through a deception of Welbeck Arthur burns. It is soon after this that Dr. Stevens finds Arthur.

Dr. Stevens' invitation to Arthur to study medicine Arthur

---

1. Reeve, *The Old English Baron*, 65.

gratefully accepts, but, before he can begin work upon that study, he wishes to execute certain projects he has in mind. Brown shows his appreciation of the profession followed by his medical friends by the way the doctor addresses Arthur:

"I dwelt upon the benefits that adhered to the medical profession, the power which it confers of lightening the distresses of our neighbours, the dignity which popular opinion annexes to it, the avenue which it opens to the acquisition of competence, the freedom from servile cares which attends it, and the means of intellectual gratification with which it supplies us."[1]

In Arthur, Brown embodies the spirit of beneficence. He completes his search for Wallace,[2] cares for Eliza Hadwin,[3] finds his old father in the debtors' prison,[4] procures a home for Clemenza Lodi, now abandoned by Welbeck, whose fortune had been burned,[5] visits Welbeck on his death-bed in prison,[6] and restores to Mrs. Watson and the Maurices the money which Welbeck had taken from Watson's body and had entrusted to him to give them.[7] In his efforts to do good, he overcomes all opposition. He no sooner chances on one hazard and extricates himself from that situation than he is launched upon the next enterprise, which involves another peril and escape. He is absolutely disregardful of the usual social conventions: he enters homes, withstands threats and entreaties, when he knows that he is right, and imparts with perfect frankness every thought that comes to him. On the whole he does all that he set out to do, though penniless, and wins over as helpers some of the wealthiest people, of whom are Dr. and Mrs. Stevens, Mrs. Wentworth and Mrs. Fielding.

If Brown had in mind any other character than himself as the antetype of Arthur, this writer thinks it was Tom Jones. He was healthy, gallant, generous and humane, thrust out of his home with a sum of money, which he lost. He had many kinds of precarious adventures and did a number of helpful services, using

---

1. *Arthur Mervyn*, II, 7.
2. *Ibid.*, I, 135-6, 165-179.
3. *Ibid.*, II, 68, 193.
4. *Ibid.*, II, 174-5.
5. *Ibid.*, II, 106, 116, 117, 174.
6. *Ibid.*, II, 119.
7. *Ibid.*, II, 133-6, 157-163.

his sword and giving his money freely, seemingly at times without such resources. He is Fielding's natural man, good-hearted and uncautious, of whom he says:

"In fact, poor Jones was one of the best-natured fellows alive, and had all that weakness, which is called compassion. . . . If he doth not therefore find some natural means of fairly extricating himself from all his distresses, we will do no violence to the truth, and dignity of history for his sake; for we had rather relate that he was hanged at Tyburn . . . than forfeit our integrity, or shock the faith of our readers."[1]

In Brown's most well-contrived characterization, that of Arthur, the author identifies himself very fully with the character. He teaches that pure motives and unwonted heroism invariably frustrate all deceivers and that unswerving reason and good judgment triumph over all hindrances and dubitations. He surely displays his own native habit of kindness and generosity of heart in Arthur:

"I am incapable of any purpose that is not beneficent; . . . I reflected on the rectitude of my intentions, . . . my motives were unquestionably pure. . . . I pretend not to the wisdom of experience and age; to the praise of forethought or subtlety. I choose the obvious path, and pursue it with headlong expedition. Good intentions, unaided by knowledge, will, perhaps, produce more injury than benefit, and therefore knowledge must be gained. . . . I shall convince you of my good intentions."[2]

These last words seem an echo of Falkland's to Tyrrel in *Caleb Williams*: "I have great faith in the purity of my intentions."[3]

Replying to a question of his brother James in regard to the catastrophe, or denouement, in *Arthur Mervyn*, Brown wrote:

"Arthur is intended as a hero whose virtue, in order to be productive of benefit to others, and felicity to himself, stands in no need of riches. You may remember that he originally appears, in a pennyless condition. He is afterwards in possession of some thousand dollars. To maintain consistency and congruity, it was necessary that this sum should be lost. . . . Twenty thousand dollars are a large sum, but remember the belief of their being forged reduces the value to nothing, while their power to do mischief is proportionately increased. I have purposely left an opening for the

---

1. Fielding, *The History of Tom Jones*, II, 246, 367.
2. *Arthur Mervyn*, II, 114, 101, 107, 113.
3. Godwin, *Caleb Williams*, 36.

publication of a second part or sequel. The destiny of Wallace and of Mr. Hadwin is not mentioned. . . . Wallace, by his unseasonable journey, is thrown into a relapse, and dies upon the road. . . . Marriage with this youth is proved to be highly dangerous to the happiness of Susan. . . . Marriage with the youngest; the death of the elder by a consumption and grief, leaves him in possession of competence, and the rewards of virtue. This scheme, as you see, required the destruction of the bills."[1]

When pledged to silence, Arthur becomes the curious servant, like Caleb Williams under similar conditions; but he is superior to the latter in his frankly altruistic intentions and in the successful performance of his undertakings. A definite likeness between the two characters exists, in their plans and manner of expression.

"I (Caleb Williams) easily understood secrecy was one of the things expected from me. . . . These reflections of my friend Collins strongly tended to inflame my curiosity. . . . My thoughts fluctuated from conjecture to conjecture. . . . I determined to place myself as a watch upon my patron. . . . I was, as I had already been, watchful, inquisitive, suspicious. . . . I will watch him without remission. I will trace all the mazes of his thought. Surely at such a time his secret anguish must betray itself. . . . The vigilance even of a public and systematical despotism is poor, compared with a vigilance which is thus goaded by the most anxious passions of the soul."[2]   Arthur ponders his situation: "My companion (Welbeck) hinted that my own interest, as well as his, enjoined upon me silence to all but himself, on the subject of my birth and early adventures. . . . my curiosity was now awakened as to the motives which Welbeck could have for exacting from me this concealment. . . . I ought to mention that my departure from the directions which I had received was, in some degree, owing to an inquisitive temper. . . . I ruminated not superficially or briefly on this dialogue (with Welbeck). . . . Some inquietude now crept into my thoughts. . . . It seemed as if I were walking in the dark and might rush into snares or drop into pits before I was aware of my danger. Each moment accumulated my doubts, and I cherished a secret foreboding that the event would prove my new situation to be far less fortunate than I had, at first, fondly believed. . . . his wonted reserve gave place to a torrent-like and overflowing

---

1. Brown, Letter to his brother James, New York, Feb. 15th, 1799, in Dunlap, *op. cit.*, II, 97-8.
2. Godwin, *Caleb Williams*, 8, 10, 147, 167, 173, 190.

elocution. . . . I was placed in a scene that furnished fuel to my curiosity. . . . The business of writing was performed in the chamber on the third story. I had been hitherto denied access to this room. . . . The influence of prohibitions and an appearance of disguise in awakening curiosity is well known."[1]

Falkland and Welbeck are comparable. Their actions, good and bad, proceed from the same source—the love of money and reputation. Of the two, the latter is the more dastardly in the number of atrocious crimes deliberately planned and committed, like his infamous treatment of the heiress Madame Lodi and Watson's sister and in his more sordid motive in his relations with Arthur. He takes him into his house chiefly as an aid in working out his own villainous plots and incidentally to benefit him, as he states in his confession to Arthur:

"I have detained you in my service, partly for your own benefit, but chiefly for mine. I intended to inflict upon you injury and to do you good. . . . What it was that made me thus, I know not. . . . I can talk and can feel as virtue and justice prescribe; yet the tenor of my actions has been uniform. One tissue of iniquity and folly has been my life; while my thoughts have been familiar with enlightened and disinterested principles."[2]

"For a while," Arthur says, "the wondrousness of this tale kept me from contemplating the consequences that awaited us. . . . All was astounding by its novelty, or terrific by its horror. The very scene of these offences partook, to my rustic apprehension, of fairy splendour and magical abruptness. My understanding was bemazed, and my senses were taught to distrust their own testimony."[3]

Welbeck's worldliness and wickedness are clearly contrasted with Arthur's natural nobility and the homely morals of his country life, unsophisticated by society. Welbeck confides:

"I perceive in you a rectitude and firmness worthy to be trusted. . . . It may teach you to avoid the shoals on which my virtue and my peace have been wrecked. . . . Ease and the respect attendant upon opulence I was willing to purchase at the price of ever-wakeful suspicion and eternal remorse."[4]

---

1. *Arthur Mervyn*, I, 63, 64, 65, 71, 74, 82.
2. *Ibid.*, I, 86.
3. *Ibid.*, I, 108.
4. *Ibid.*, I, 86, 91.

The history of Welbeck reveals a man of selfishness, weakness, hypocrisy, lying and sensuality, producing the crimes of forgery, robbery, seduction and murder and leading to wretchedness, despair, imprisonment and a lingering, disgraceful death. Welbeck is called the *Nabob* a few times inquiringly;—it may be an appellation taken from the title of a novel by Mrs. A. M. Bennett:—*Anna; or, The Memoirs of a Welsh Heiress, interspersed with Anecdotes of a Nabob* (1785), written fourteen years before *Arthur Mervyn,* or from Edmund Burke's "Speech on the Nabob of Arcot's Debts" (1785). Welbeck had defrauded Wortley, whose name Brown may have chosen from that of the English writer, Mary Wortley Montagu, a cousin of Fielding.

The confession of Welbeck to Arthur has a precedent in the confession of Falkland to his servant Caleb. When Caleb discovers the murder of Tyrrel by Falkland, he decides to leave his employer, who thus speaks,

"You never shall quit it with life. If you attempt it, you shall never cease to rue your folly as long as you exist."[1]

Falkland and his henchmen pursue Caleb, arrest him on a trumped-up charge of robbery and cast him into prison. Caleb finally escapes and is pursued continually, until, driven to despair, he reveals his employer's crime and confronts him before a magistrate. The latter confesses, saying,

"I am the blackest of villains. I am the murderer of Tyrrel. I am the assassin of the Hawkinses. . . . I see too late the greatness and elevation of your mind. . . . I see that the artless and manly story you have told has carried conviction to every hearer. . . . My name will be consecrated to infamy, while your heroism, your patience, and your virtues will be forever admired." . . . "He survived the dreadful scene but three days."[2]

Godwin's theme is his theory of the unrelenting tyranny and ruthlessness of the rich over the poor.

Because of wealth obtained through no efforts of their own, Falkland and Welbeck gain supreme authority over certain individuals and oppress them. Imprisonment for debt of an unwanted person, like Miss Melville in *Caleb Williams,* is one part of the

---

1. Godwin, *Caleb Williams,* **211.**
2. *Ibid.,* 185, 450, 451.

tyranny of the rich. Brown partakes of the same prejudice, as in this discussion of riches and imprisonment by Miss Carlton, Mrs. Stevens and Arthur.

Miss Carlton: "My father was arrested by his creditor. . . . The creditor was obdurate, and would release him upon no condition, but that of receiving a bond from my brother."
Arthur: "You say he is rich and childless."   Miss Carlton: "He thinks himself wronged, and imprisons my brother, not to enforce payment, but to inflict misery. . . . In proportion to my brother's suffering is his gratification."   Arthur: "You draw an odious and almost incredible portrait."
Miss Carlton: "And yet such a one would serve for the likeness of almost every second man we meet. . . . I have found kindness and goodness in great numbers, but have likewise met prejudice and rancor in many."[1]

In this novel, Brown more than ever shifted to the background the Gothic influence. The yellow fever episodes and the benevolent acts of Arthur are the main features. His misfortunes in Welbeck's house, wherein lies the Gothic element, are foreign to the author's real purpose in writing and are nearly distinct from the setting of yellow fever. In Arthur's seeking refuge in Welbeck's house from fear of being carted off to the fever-hospital and in the burning of the Lodi bills the two strains cross. The midnight burial of Watson in the "darksome and murky" cellar and the concealed recess, entered by a ladder and a trap-door which "set me (Arthur) afloat on a sea of new wonders," are Gothic machinery.

Arthur Mervyn represents Brown's best and truest accomplishment in realism, for he had experienced the yellow fever disease himself and lived through two occurrences of the scourge, which equipped him for the work. One might well call this story a historical novel. In his descriptions of plague conditions, mostly in New York, he rivals Defoe's description of the plague in London and is not unlike him in the forcefulness of his narration; but he treats of real, dramatic happenings, not imaginary ones.

In the Preface, Brown says: "The evils of pestilence by which this city has lately been afflicted will probably form an era in its history. . . . the author of these remarks has ventured to methodize

---

1. *Arthur Mervyn*, II, 148-9.

his own reflections, and to weave into an humble narrative such incidents as appeared to him most instructive and remarkable among those which came within the sphere of his own observation. . . . It is but just to snatch some of these from oblivion, and to deliver to posterity a brief but faithful sketch of the condition of this metropolis during that calamitous period."

"In *Arthur Mervyn* he achieved a highly realistic description of the yellow fever epidemic in Philadelphia in 1798. It is Brown's one really good 'horror' job, and is not only the single thing he did worthy of remembrance today, but is probably also the high water mark of the entire Gothic school,"[1] asserted Charles Angoff.

The outspoken language in which Brown reproduced the shocking details of the yellow fever visitations is seemingly appropriate to its ghastly horrors and not a cause of censure by readers familiar with them. The author attained the presentation of the horrific, which so many other authors strove for, by the atmosphere of silence disturbed only by the rattling of the death-cart and by the fear of disease and death and starvation hanging over the panic-stricken city. His cumulative descriptions of distressing events give now a cumulative physical abhorrence and again a cumulative moral terror.

"In proportion as I drew near the city, the tokens of its calamitous condition became more apparent. Every farm-house was filled with supernumerary tenants, fugitives from home. . . . The passengers were numerous. . . . Some were on foot, bearing in their counte-nances the tokens of their recent terror, and filled with mournful reflections on the forlornness of their state. . . . some were without the means of paying for victuals or lodging for the coming night. . . . Families of weeping mothers and dismayed children . . . were carried in vehicles of every form. . . . (In the city many of the houses) were closed, above and below; dark, and without tokens of being inhabited. . . . Death seemed to hover over this scene, and I dreaded that the floating pestilence had already lighted on my frame. . . . I approached a house, . . . before which stood a vehicle, . . . a *hearse*. . . . Presently, a coffin, borne by two men, issued from the house. . . . One of them, as he assisted in thrusting the coffin into the cavity provided for it, said, 'I'll be damned if I think the poor dog was quite dead. It wasn't the *fever* that ailed

---

1. Angoff, *A Literary History of the American People,* 322-3.

him, but the sight of the girl and her mother on the floor'. . . .
(Such were) the *hearse-men*."[1]

"I wandered to the field where the dead had been, promiscuously
and by hundreds, interred. . . . Boards hastily nailed together formed
the best receptacle which the exigencies of the time could grant to
the dead. Many corpses were thrown into a single excavation, and
all distinctions founded on merit and rank were obliterated."[2]
"We ourselves enjoyed good health, and were hopeful
of escaping with our lives. Our measures . . . did not consist in
avoiding the receptacles of infection, for my office required me
to go daily into the midst of them; nor in filling the house with
the exhalations of gunpowder, vinegar, or tar. They consisted in
cleanliness, reasonable exercise, and wholesome diet. . . . This
house has no one to defend it. . . . the whole family, including
mistress, children, and servants, were cut off in a single week. . . .
Meanwhile, plunderers are numerous and active. A house thus
totally deserted, and replenished with valuable furniture, will, I
fear, become their prey. . . . The evils which had befallen this
city were obvious and enormous. Hunger and negligence had
exasperated the malignity and facilitated the progress of the pestilence."[3]   "The season advanced, and the havoc which
this fatal malady produced increased with portentous rapidity."[4]

When food was very scarce, pollenta was used, but that was not
an unknown dish in almost every home in the land in those early
days. Brown says of it:

"Pollenta, and hasty-pudding or samp, are preparations of the
same substance—a substance which she (Constantia) needed not
the experience of others to convince her was no less grateful than
nutritive. Indian meal was procurable at ninety cents per bushel.
By recollecting former experiments, she knew that this quantity,
with no accompaniment but salt, would supply wholesome and
plentiful food for four months to one person. The inference was
palpable. Three persons were now to be supplied with food, and
this supply could be furnished, during four months, at the trivial
expense of three dollars. . . . See this useful fact explained and
demonstrated in Count Rumford's Essays."[5]

---

1. *Arthur Mervyn*, I, 139, 140, 141, 156.
2. *Ormond*, 206.
3. *Arthur Mervyn*, I, 6, 152-3, 180.
4. *Ormond*, 47.
5. *Ibid.*, 46 and Footnote.

Most of the facts about yellow fever in Brown's novels are substantiated from authentic history, as has been proved by contemporary accounts of the same period. Besides, during the epidemic in New York, 1798, through which Brown remained, he kept up a strict correspondence with his brother James in England, describing the epidemic day by day. This selection from a letter, quoted in full by Dunlap, reads like a section from one of his novels, no more realistic and tragic:

"this pestilential air seems to be extending itself to all quarters. Things here wear a very gloomy aspect. Pearl and Water Streets are wholly desolate, and all business at a stand. The lowest computation supposes one half of the inhabitants to have fled. Notwithstanding, . . . I am sorry to add that the malignity increases and the number of deaths. . . . The number of physicians is rapidly declining, while that of the sick is as rapidly increasing."

Brown advised exercise and diet, "from which animal food and spirituous liquors are wholly excluded."[1] Pest-carrying mosquitoes had not yet been recognized.

In *A Pictorial History of the United States* (c. 1843), Samuel Griswold Goodrich gives a running account of yellow fever, cholera and consumption in America. The Indians suffered various outbreaks of the fever in the 1630's; in 1692, it raged among the colonists of New Hampshire, having been brought there in bags of cotton from the West Indies; it was prevalent in Charleston and in Boston, where in 1721 inoculation was first introduced. Dr. Boylston inoculated his family and was treated as a murderer; however, the inoculated disease was milder and few died of it. In 1746, it prevailed among the Mohegans and about one hundred died of it. In 1793, it was very fatal in Philadelphia and again in 1797 and 1798; in the latter year, it raged also in New York. Other outbreaks are listed.

"But the crowning discovery of all, as a preventive of this fearful disease, was that of vaccination, by Dr. Jenner, of England, late in the eighteenth century, and first made publicly known in 1796. Much praise should be accorded to Dr. Waterhouse for his

---

1. Brown, Letter to his brother James, Aug. 25th, 1798, in Dunlap, *op. cit.*, II, 5, 10.

successful efforts to introduce it in this country."[1]

This quotation from Miss Repplier, taken from a diary, it is understood, purports to be history of that same year:

". . . the story of Philadelphia is like the oft-repeated story of the Plague . . . it spread with horrible speed into every quarter of the town . . . there was a mad rush for the safety of the open fields. . . . Seventeen thousand people fled within a month. . . . People burned tar in the streets, and carried sprigs of wormwood. . . . The corpses were buried quietly at night . . . men and women . . . dug lonely graves. . . . In that vain frenzy of selfishness which stifles pity, those who were yet untainted thrust their sick and dying into the streets, or fled themselves from the squalid rooms where Death was busy with his work. . . . The tainted air was loaded with foul and nauseating odors. . . . When at last the cold weather checked the progress of the fever, it had counted nearly five thousand victims, a ghastly reckoning if we remember that the city, deserted by all who could escape, held less than thirty thousand inhabitants during the greater part of these terrible months. When the pestilence was at its height, two hundred victims were buried in a single day. . . ."[2]

Miss Repplier, also, testifies to the brilliancy of Philadelphia's social life in imitation of French society, at the time in which Brown wrote, and to the rapid return to social conditions after the fever had abated. In the same strain Brown says,

"Meanwhile, the dominion of cold began to be felt, and the contagious fever entirely disappeared. . . . Public entertainments were thronged with auditors. A new theatre had lately been constructed, and a company of English comedians had arrived during the prevalence of the malady. They now began their exhibitions, and their audiences were overflowing. . . . To my no small surprise, however, no vestiges of this calamity were to be discerned. All houses were open, all streets thronged, and all faces thoughtless or busy. The arts and the amusements of life seemed as sedulously cultivated as ever."[3]

"With a view to the possible recurrence of the same scene (yellow fever), as well as for its merits as a delineation of human nature as exhibited in our country, Arthur Mervyn is a work entitled to more than the common attention bestowed upon novels."[4]

---

1. Goodrich, *A Pictorial History of the United States*, 307.
2. Repplier, *Philadelphia, the place and the people*, 303, 304, 307.
3. *Ormond*, 59, 194.
4. Dunlap, *op. cit.*, II, 18.

Brown's fourth novel was *Edgar Huntly; or Memoirs of a Sleep-Walker,* so titled in the first edition (1799, Philadelphia). *Huntley* is given by the author in a letter to his brother James as reported by Dunlap, who repeats the same a score of times.[1] Otherwise, *Huntly* and *Sleep-Walker* are spelled variously in the different editions, according to bibliographers. Possibly Brown knew a Huntly family at Norwich, from whom came Lydia Huntly, born 1791, later the author, Mrs. Sigourney, when he tramped through Connecticut; just as he may have chosen the name Norwalk, in that state, a place not far from New York, for the scene of his novel laid in Pennsylvania, near the Forks of the Delaware. This romance is understood to embody some of the material from the earlier, unpublished *Sky-Walk,* the wild district of Norwalk of this story being the former Sky-Walk.

In this novel, Brown made a deliberate effort to provide events that may have happened in America and to display in majesty its scenery and to suit his descriptions of it to the conditions chosen. He perceived that he had added a new motif and a new background for American fiction. He was ambitious to depict in vivid and native colors the perils of the border settlements. He recites adventures that show the bitter hostility between the settlers in the states and the Indians and fails not to point out to the American public that the cause of that immitigable enmity was the unjust expulsions of the Indians from the lands by the pioneers. In his To the Public, he forthtells his purpose and resources:

"The sources of amusement to the fancy and instruction to the heart, that are peculiar to ourselves, are equally numerous and inexhaustible. It is the purpose of this work to profit by some of these sources; to exhibit a series of adventures, growing out of the condition of our country, and connected with one of the most common and most wonderful diseases or affections of the human frame. . . . The incidents of Indian hostility, and the perils of the Western wilderness, are far more suitable. . . . These, therefore, are, in part, the ingredients of this tale, and these he has been ambitious of depicting in vivid and faithful colours. The success of his efforts must be estimated by the liberal and candid reader."

---

1. Brown, Letter to his brother James, New York, July 26th, 1799, in Dunlap, *op. cit.,* II, 97.

In an editorial in Brown's magazine, *The Monthly Magazine and American Review,* where the Indian chapters of *Edgar Huntly* first appeared, Brown says:

"The following narrative is extracted from the memoirs of a young man who resided some years since on the upper branches of the Delaware. These memoirs will shortly be published. . . . Similar events have frequently happened on the Indian borders; but, perhaps, they were never before described with equal minuteness. As to the truth of these incidents, men acquainted with the perils of an Indian war must be allowed to judge. Those who have ranged along the foot of the Blue-Ridge from the Wind-Gap to the Water-Gap will see the exactness of the local descriptions. It may also be mentioned that 'Old Deb' is a portrait faithfully drawn from nature."[1]

A reprint of Brown's amusement-instruction idea appeared over fifty years later in the *Recollections* (I, 173) of Goodrich:

"I do not recollect to have discovered, before this time, that (children's) books contained inexhaustible sources of instruction and amusement."

So he wrote the "Peter Parley" books for little children.

The story unites accounts of contacts with the Indians and events founded on sleep-walking, or somnambulism, a malady whose strange effects were known to the people of America, but which were not yet sufficiently and convincingly explained by science. This cause or agent would produce occurrences at once astounding and mysterious. There were other ingredients, as the author suggests,—heredity, telepathy, insanity. The underlying purpose is the transformation of character.

In justice to Brown, a quotation from one of his letters gives his reflective opinion concerning the use of Nature's scientific rarities:

"Your remarks upon the gloominess and out-of-nature incidents of Huntley, if they be not just in their full extent, are, doubtless, such as most readers will make, which alone, is a sufficient reason for dropping the doleful tone and assuming a cheerful one, or, at least substituting moral causes and daily incidents in place of the prodigious or the singular. I shall not fall hereafter into that strain."[2]

---

1. Pattee, *The First Century of American Literature,* 1770-1870, 102-3.
2. Brown, Letter to his brother James, New York, April, 1800, in Dunlap, *op. cit.,* II, 100.

True to that promise, he gave his last two novels social and commonplace incidents, to their detriment.

The plot of *Edgar Huntly* breaks into two parts. The first centers around the assassination of Huntly's friend, Waldegrave, and the fortunes of Huntly as he tries to unravel that mystery and to connect with it the incomprehensible behavior of Clithero. Through the rest of the story, the center of interest in his adventures is related to the movements of the Indians. The story is full of a great variety of wild and picturesque incidents giving rise to wonder and suspense and succeeding each other with such breathless rapidity as to enchain the reader's attention and make him seem to partake of the amazing experiences, in which Brown's inventive power has been allowed to expend itself almost unrestrained.

The murderer of Waldegrave had disappeared and no trace of him had been found, though search had been made far and wide. Huntly tasks himself with finding the criminal. The story is the telling of his trials by letter to Mary Waldegrave, the sister of his friend.

"The fate of Waldegrave was as fertile of torment to thee as to me. His bloody and mysterious catastrophe equally awakened thy grief, thy revenge, and thy curiosity."[1]

Returning home one night, Huntly sees, by the light of the moon, a man digging under a well-known elm tree, the very tree under which the body of Waldegrave had been found, and stopping to give way to bursts of weeping and heart-rending moans. On approaching nearer he perceived "that this person was *asleep.*" The sleep-walker proves to be Clithero Edny, a taciturn foreigner employed in the neighborhood. Clithero keeps up this midnight practice, till the suspicion arises that he is the assassin of Waldegrave and that his conscience brings him in his dreams to the scene of his crime. Huntly determines to watch the queer actions of the man to seek a solution of his unusual conduct. Once when the digger had left, Huntly followed him a long distance through the woods till he disappeared into a cavern in the desert wilds of Norwalk. Huntly meets with several extraordinary adventures in the forest as he often tracked Clithero there. Finally, as a result of

---

1. *Edgar Huntly*, 2.

brooding over the matter, he, too, walks in his sleep. "On recovering from deliquium," he awakes one night to find himself at the bottom of a deep pit, from whence he emerges into a cavern, many miles from home. This pit as the clue to Poe's *The Pit and the Pendulum* is discussed in Chapter V. When he is about to leave the cavern, he sees a band of four Indians sleeping within. He kills, near the entrance, the guard and escapes, taking with him a young girl, a prisoner of the Indians. He has a number of affairs with the same pursuing Indians and kills the remaining four.

Surviving vast hardships and privations, Huntly reaches his home settlement:
"to perform the journey in that time (six hours) would demand the agile boundings of a leopard and the indefatigable sinews of an elk."[1]
He meets again the instructor of his youth and his dearest friend, Sarsefield. The story of Clithero, related by him to Huntly, shows him a young man of susceptible disposition, who was grief-stricken over the supposed death of Mrs. Lorimer, his benefactress, whose death he believed would occur simultaneously with the death of her twin brother, whom he had shot in self-defense. In a fit of remorse and fear, he had escaped from England to America. These English friends now appear, and Sarsefield is the husband of the former Mrs. Lorimer, Clithero's patron, to whose niece, Clarice Wiatte, Clithero had been engaged.

The mystery of the death of Waldegrave is cleared up by the explanation that he had been slain by one of the roving Indians who had been committing depredations in the neighborhood. The tale ends with all at peace; but the destiny of Huntly,—whether he married Mary Waldegrave, as was anticipated early in the story,—and of Clarice Wiatte is not settled. Edgar says:
"Marriage with thee was anticipated with joyous emotions, not merely on my own account or on thine, but likewise for the sake of those beloved girls (his two orphaned sisters) to whom that event would enable me to furnish an asylum."[2]

A link connecting Brown's novel with the writer of *The Castle of Otranto* may be noted, perhaps in the name Waldegrave. The

---

1. *Edgar Huntly,* 222.
2. *Ibid.,* 164.

Countess of Waldegrave, Maria Walpole, who married the Duke of Gloucester, was a niece of Horace Walpole. In London, 1829, there was published *Waldegrave: a novel* in three volumes, which will be discussed in Chapter V.

Edgar Huntly is affirmed to be the first American detective story. Godwin in England and Brown in America were the earliest to explore the mazes of the detection of crime. The basis of their detection consists in that of flight, in settings of terror, and pursuit, rather than detection in the modern sense. Eino Railo said of this subject:

"In this field of criminality, in which the question is no longer of traditional Gothecism as such, but of psychological analysis, with criticism of social justice as a background, Godwin was succeeded by the founder of American fiction, Charles Brockden Brown (1771-1810), who was a pupil of Godwin in his ideas of social philosophy."[1]

There is a detective element in *Wieland,* where Pleyel reads in a newspaper of a search for the convict Francis Carwin and then busies himself to verify the statements and to investigate later events connected with him and Clara Wieland. Brown identifies himself with the School of Terror by introducing into his stories mysterious crimes; yet he began the transition from the Radcliffe type of romance to the Indian tales of Cooper, by using American scenery for the landscapes instead of imaginary ones and American commonplace characters in place of her artificial villains and other conventional types. *Edgar Huntly* is superior to *Caleb Williams* in crime detection, but inferior to the detective stories of Edgar Allan Poe, a disciple of Brown. He might never have invented the short detective story, which forms the model of the modern detective story, if Brown's type of story had not preceded it.

The use of sleep-walking, or noctambulation, is incidental, rather than fundamental, to the plot; but as far as it enters into the problems of the story it is necessarily physical and not psychological. It serves to explain Huntly's first meeting with the Indians and his concealing the packet of letters and to convey Clithero on many nights to the foot of the tree; it is not absolutely needful to these

---

1. Railo, *The Haunted Castle,* 300.

occasions and therefore unimportant. However, it is interesting and carries out the author's plan, according to the alternate title of the book, to use happenings among his neighbors, that mystify them and cause questioning. The story would have been improved if Huntly had been the only sleep-walker, letting the unaccountable movements of Clithero be dependent upon his becoming the victim of an increasing dementia, over his worrisome obsessions. Clithero, like Wieland, represents an attempt of Brown to show the consistent advance toward insanity in a person of sensitive, self-disparaging temperament. Here the treatment of the progress toward insanity is almost as specific and nice as in the case of Wieland.

After the events heretofore related, Huntly, fearing some mischance to Clithero because of his long absence, seeks him in the forest and finds him in a starving condition. He ministers to him and finally accuses him of the murder of Waldegrave. Still laboring under the weight of supposed crime, Clithero unburdens his heart to Huntly, rising at times in his recital to the height of eloquence.

"But I came not hither to recriminate. I came not hither to accuse others, but myself. I know the retribution that is appointed for guilt like mine. It is just. I may shudder at the foresight of my punishment and shrink in the endurance of it; but I shall be indebted for part of my torment to the vigour of my understanding, which teaches me that my punishment is just. Why should I procrastinate my doom and strive to render my burthen more light? It is but just that it should crush me. Its procrastination is impossible. The stroke is already felt. Even now I drink of the cup of retribution. A change of being cannot aggravate my woe. Till consciousness itself be extinct, the worm that gnaws me will never perish."[1]

Clithero had been employed by Mrs. Lorimer, a wealthy widow, to whom he was deeply grateful. She is a character whom Brown carefully delineates (Chapter IV). From many privileges in her home and intimate conferences over business, he came to respect her as almost superhuman. He loved her niece Clarice and both the aunt and the girl approved. If he had been candid, all might

---

1. *Edgar Huntly*, 34.

have gone well, but he could not overcome the consciousness of his inferior rank and therefore decided to leave her service.

"I was habituated to consider the distinctions of rank as indelible. The obstructions that existed, to any wish that I might form, were like those of time and space . . . insuperable. . . . I knew what it was that duty exacted from me. To remain in my present situation was a chimerical project."[1]

The brother of Mrs. Lorimer, Arthur Wiatte, the father of Clarice, whose mother he had seduced, "whose heart was broken by the detection of his perfidy," and whose previous behavior to his sister had so exasperated her kindness to him that she had allowed him to be banished, for seven years, now, after nine years, returned for revenge. When he tried robbing Clithero of money he had charge of for Mrs. Lorimer, the latter in self-defense killed him.

"Such was the beginning of a series ordained to hurry me to swift destruction. Such were the primary tokens of the presence of that power by whose accursed machinations I was destined to fall. . . . Would to Heaven that my belief were groundless, and that I had no reason to believe my intellects to have been perverted by diabolical instigations!"[2]

Such was Clithero's unalterable belief in words spoken by Mrs. Lorimer that her death was inevitably connected with that of her brother. Arthur and Euphemia were identical twins:

"The resemblance between them was exact to a degree almost incredible." . . . "It was her obstinate persuasion that their fates were blended. . . . I read in it the condemnation of my deed, the agonies she was preparing to suffer, and the indignation that would overflow upon the author of so signal a calamity. . . . (She said) 'The stroke that deprives him of life will not only have the same effect upon me, but will set my portion in everlasting misery.' . . . The same blow that bereaved *him* of life has likewise ratified her doom. . . . A fatal sympathy will seize her. She will shrink, and swoon, and perish, at the news! . . . My fancy began to be infected with the errors of my understanding . . . All within me was tempestuous and dark. . . . Sable robes, sobs, and dreary solemnity encompassed me on all sides. I was haunted to despair by images of death, imaginary clamours, and the train of funeral pageantry. I could place the object in no light which did not corroborate the

---

1. *Edgar Huntly*, 49, 51.
2. *Ibid.*, 69.

persuasion that, in the act committed, I had insured the destruction of my lady. . . . Were they linked together by a sympathy whose influence was independent of sensible communication (telepathy)? . . . I had heard of such extraordinary co-partnerships in being and modes of instantaneous intercourse, among beings locally distant. . . . Had she already endured his agonies, and like him already ceased to breathe?"[1]

Clithero invades the rooms of Mrs. Lorimer to learn if she is well and while there conceives the idea that it would be an act of justice and compassion to kill her and, in a moment of temporary madness, attempts the deed, almost destroying Clarice instead, and prevented by Mrs. Lorimer just in time.

"The madness to whose black suggestions it bore so strong a contrast began now to make sensible approaches on my understanding. . . . Was it I that hurried to the deed? No. It was the daemon that possessed me. My limbs were guided to the bloody office by a power foreign and superior to mine. . . . Was it to this extremity of horror that my evil genius was determined to urge me? . . . What could I less than turn the dagger's point against my own bosom? . . . Murder was succeeded, in an instant, by the more detestable enormity of suicide." (Mrs. Lorimer thwarts him a second time and he tells her of her brother's death by his hand and she exclaims), "Then is the omen fulfilled! Then am I undone! Lost forever!"[2]

Thereupon Clithero abandons his friends and England for America.

"Yet I was anew distressed by the discovery that my thoughts found their way to my lips, without my being conscious of it, and that my steps wandered forth unknowingly and without the guidance of my will."[3]

So Clithero became a sleep-talker and a sleep-walker.

In this character especially, Brown exhibits his anatomical knowledge of human passions and of the mind. The complications of the plot of *Edgar Huntly* are based chiefly upon the supposed hereditary connection of twins, both as to their lives and deaths, and even as to their final eternal destinations. Mrs. Lorimer, the sister, is still alive and well and married.

"She . . . erroneously imagined that her fate was blended with his,

---

1. *Edgar Huntly*, 43, 75, 76, 77, 78, 79.
2. *Ibid.*, 83, 85, 87, 89.
3. *Ibid.*, 91.

. . . and that, therefore, whoever was the contriver of his death was likewise, by a fatal and invincible necessity, the author of her own. . . . she was indebted for her ruin to absurd opinions of the sacredness of consanguinity . . . The ignorance and prepossessions of this woman ("on this subject") were remarkable."[1]

Perhaps, Bayard Taylor, in his short story—*Twin-Love*—was influenced by Brown in his choice of subject.

Brown not only exhibits, exploits and explodes the idea of twin-destiny, but the fallacy of mental telepathy and the belief in an evil genius or daemon controlling the life. In the summer of 1801, Brown with a companion travelled through parts of New York, Massachusetts and Connecticut. In his account for Monday morning, July 20, from New Haven, he wrote:

"Yesterday in the morning we went to church, and heard Dr. Dwight preach an ingenious sermon to prove the reality of good and bad angels or genii. A very agreeable doctrine in which the fancy is more disposed to acquiesce than the understanding."[2]

Clithero, the villain of the story, has a greater claim to being called sleep-walker than Edgar Huntly, the hero, whose sleep-walking is less basic. The author provides another case of sleep-walking. The dream as an agent, named among those in *Wieland* and exemplified by Clara's dream, is found also in *Arthur Mervyn*. After Arthur grasped the fact that Achsa loved him, he could not sleep. He dreamed that Achsa's husband, now deceased, visited her; he rushed to her home, rang the bell, startled Eliza, now Achsa's protegeé, and was not admitted. He says in the morning, "I have little doubt that, in my feverish and troubled sleep, I actually went forth, posted to the house of Mrs. Fielding, rung for admission, and shortly after returned to my own apartment."[3] Dr. Stevens' wife had heard him leave and return.

Huntly learns from Clithero that he is guiltless of the murder of Waldegrave and that his former misdemeanors are largely imaginary and concludes that he is insane.

"Clithero is a maniac. This truth cannot be concealed. . . . I imagined that Clithero was merely a victim of erroneous gratitude, a slave of the errors of his education and the prejudices of his

---

1. *Edgar Huntly*, 302-3, 126, 289. (See also 279.)
2. Brown, Letter from New Haven, in Dunlap, *op. cit.*, II, 56.
3. *Arthur Mervyn*, II, 222.

rank; that his understanding was deluded by phantoms in the mask of virtue and duty, and not, as you have strenuously maintained, utterly subverted." "An agent from Hell had mastered his faculties,"[1] Sarsefield later admitted.

After his disclosure, Clithero conceals himself in the forest and tries to elude the solicitous care of Huntly; but, when Huntly, thinking to cure him of his remorse, tells him of the arrival of Mrs. Lorimer, he rushes to her home, bent on causing her death. He is apprehended as a lunatic and is being taken by boat from New York to the Pennsylvania Hospital at Philadelphia.

"Scarcely had we passed the *Narrows,* when the lunatic, being suffered to walk the deck, . . . threw himself overboard; . . . but, at the moment when his flight was overtaken, he forced himself beneath the surface, and was seen no more. . . . let our regrets and our forebodings terminate. He has saved himself . . . from lingering for years in the noisome dungeon of a hospital."[2]

Like Brown's other leading characters, Edgar Huntly has a passion for soliloquy: he goes over in his mind all the befallings that have led him to his present position and all the possibilities that will lead him out of each crisis. He is possessed, like Caleb Williams and Arthur Mervyn, of suspicions and restless curiosity. His maxim is, "Curiosity, like virtue, is its own reward."[3] Godwin wrote:

"Curiosity is a principle that carries its pleasures, as well as its pains, along with it. The mind is urged by a perpetual stimulus."[4]

In his self-appointed task of watching Clithero, Huntly says: "Henceforth this man was to become the subject of my scrutiny. I was to gain all the knowledge, respecting him, which those with whom he lived, and were the perpetual witnesses of his actions, could impart. For this end I was to make minute inquiries, and to put seasonable interrogatories. . . . I was to state the ground of my suspicions, and desire him to confute or confirm them. In doing this, I was principally stimulated by an ungovernable curiosity; yet, if I intended not the conferring of a benefit, I did not, at least purpose the infliction of evil."[5]

---

1. *Edgar Huntly,* 305, 291.
2. *Ibid.,* 308.
3. *Ibid.,* 13.
4. Godwin, *Caleb Williams,* 168.
5. *Edgar Huntly,* 12, 27.

The locked iron trunk, or magazine, that had excited Caleb's prying to his detriment has its counterpart in the chest which Edgar discovers that Clithero has been burying repeatedly under the elm, and in the box with the secret springs which Edgar finds in Clithero's chamber and opens through lawless desire, notwithstanding the consciousness of wrongdoing in the act.

The merits of this novel cause it to fulfil most nearly the author's purposes in writing fiction: to utilize American scenes, to amuse and to instruct. He placed its interest and dramatic scenes among savages in the wild forest and among the pioneers on the border of civilization. He has succeeded perfectly in constantly furnishing diversion by a rapid parade of excitant perils and narrow escapes, each relying for its interest on its own merits and yet forming parts of one whole. He has instructed by moralizing on sleep-walking, by proving that a prepossession regarding virtue or duty will unbalance the mind and by showing the process of making a killer.

"Hitherto the death of the savage, whom I had dispatched with my hatchet, had not been remembered without some remorse. Now my emotions were totally changed. . . . All my education and the habits of my life tended to unfit me for a contest and a scene like this (killing four Indians to save the life of the girl and his own). But I was not governed by the soul which usually regulates my conduct. I had imbibed, from the unparalleled events which had lately happened, a spirit vengeful, unrelenting, and ferocious. . . . Proofs of a just intention are all that are requisite to exempt us from blame."[1]
Edgar's own parents and an infant child had been killed by Indians.

The descriptions of scenery show Brown's love of nature and his intimacy with it as he had observed it in his walks, especially in his native Pennsylvania. The searchings of the hero for Clithero through cave, forest and river supply fine word pictures, though the varying scenes are often sketched rather than portrayed. He surpasses in wildness, but not in grandeur, perhaps, the scenic effects produced by Mrs. Radcliffe. She indulges in vague panoramic views; he, in close-ups, of which this of Norwalk is typical.

"The desert, lying on the north, has gained, by some means, the appellation of Norwalk. Canst thou imagine a space, somewhat

---

1. *Edgar Huntly*, 196, 201-2, 95.

circular, about six miles in diameter, and exhibiting a perpetual and intricate variety of craggy eminences and deep dells? The hollows are single, and walled around by cliffs, ever varying in shape and height, and have seldom any perceptible communication with each other. These hollows are of all dimensions, from the narrowness and depth of a well, to the amplitude of one hundred yards. Winter's snow is frequently found in these cavities at midsummer. The streams that burst forth from every crevice are thrown, by the irregularities of the surface, into numberless cascades, often disappear in mists or in chasms, and emerge from subterranean channels, and, finally, either subside into lakes, or quietly meander through the lower and more level grounds. Wherever nature left a flat, it is made rugged and scarcely passable by enormous and fallen trunks, accumulated by the storms of ages, and forming, by their slow decay, a moss-covered soil, the haunt of rabbits and lizards. . . . A sort of continued vale, winding and abrupt, leads into the midst of this region. . . . This vale serves the purpose of a road. It is a tedious maze and perpetual declivity, and requires, from the passenger, a cautious and sure foot. Openings and ascents occasionally present themselves on each side, which seem to promise you access to the interior region, but always terminate, sooner or later, in insuperable difficulties, at the verge of a precipice or the bottom of a steep. . . . I reached the mouth of a cave. . . . In a short time, my progress was stopped by an abrupt descent. I set down the advancing foot with caution, being aware that I might at the next step encounter a bottomless pit. . . . I stooped, and stretched my hand forward and downward, but all was vacuity."[1]

The recounting of Huntly's meeting with a panther, or the American cougar, is a good example of Brown's realism and shows how very nearly it approaches to the romantic. This account and a second one are particularly graphic and frightening. Huntly was just about to pass over a tree trunk, which he had previously felled as a bridge.

"Something was perceived moving among the bushes and rocks, which, for a time, I hoped was no more than a raccoon or oppossum, but which presently appeared to be a panther. His gray coat, extended claws, fiery eyes, and a cry which he at that moment uttered, and which, by its resemblance to the human voice, is peculiarly terrific, denoted him to be the most ferocious and untamable of

---

1. *Edgar Huntly*, 99, 100, 102, 103.

that detested race. . . . He sat on the brow of the steep, eyeing the bridge, and apparently deliberating whether he should cross it. . . . presently the animal scrambled down the rock and proceeded to cross it. . . . The evil of my present circumstances consisted chiefly in suspense. My death was unavoidable, but my imagination had leisure to torment itself by anticipations. One foot of the savage was slowly and cautiously moved after the other. He struck his claws so deeply into the bark that they were with difficulty withdrawn. . . . We were now separated by an interval of scarcely eight feet, . . . before me was this grim and terrific visage. . . . From this pause of horror I was aroused by the noise occasioned by a second spring of the animal. He leaped into the pit. . . . (Edgar then crossed by the trunk to the opposite side, and the trunk fell, recalling the animal to pursuit.) He saw me, and hastened to the verge of the chasm. He squatted on his hind-legs and assumed the attitude of one preparing to leap. . . . It seemed at first as if the rift was too wide for any power of muscles to carry him in safety over; but I knew the unparalleled agility of this animal, and that his experience had made him a better judge of the practicability of this exploit than I was. Still there was hope that he would relinquish this design as desperate. This hope was quickly at an end. He sprung, and his forelegs touched the verge of the rock on which I stood. In spite of vehement exertions, however, the surface was too smooth and too hard to allow him to make good his hold. He fell, and a piercing cry, uttered below, showed that nothing had obstructed his descent to the bottom."

"The grey cougar. This animal has all the essential characteristics of a tiger. Though somewhat inferior in size and strength, these are such as to make him equally formidable to man (Brown's note.)"[1]   "His escape from a panther is narrated in a manner pre-eminently entitled to praise" (Dunlap).

The second experience with a panther was in a cave.

"The darkness was no less intense than in the pit below, and yet two objects were distinctly seen. They resembled a fixed and obscure flame. They were motionless. Though lustrous themselves, they created no illumination around them. . . . These were the eyes of a panther. . . . There was no time for deliberation and delay. . . . Though tottering on the verge of dissolution, and apparently unable to crawl from this spot, a force was exerted in this throw (of a tomahawk) probably greater than I had ever before exerted.

---

1. *Edgar Huntly*, 128-32, 129 and Footnote.

It was resistless and unerring. I aimed at the middle space between those glowing orbs. It penetrated the skull, and the animal fell, struggling and shrieking, on the ground. . . . His cries and his convulsions lasted for a moment and then ceased. The effect of his voice, in these subterranean abodes, was unspeakably rueful."[1]

In the presentation of Indian behavior and encounters, Brown is equally vivid and full of powerful delineations. Yet they are delined by one dwelling in the settled sections, who has had little contact with frontier life and who knows the Indians only as they came to barter with the Whites or make trouble, except as from history or memoirs, as Brown stated.

"I knew that, at this time, some hostilities had been committed on the frontier; that a long course of injuries and encroachments had lately exasperated the Indian tribes; that an implacable and exterminating war was generally expected. . . . Here was every token of enmity and bloodshed. Each prostrate figure was furnished with a rifled musket and a leathern bag tied round his waist, which was, probably, stored with powder and ball. . . . The slumber of an Indian is broken by the slightest noise; but, if all noise be precluded, it is commonly profound. . . . Sleep usually comes at their bidding, and if perchance, they should be wakeful at an unseasonable moment, they always sit upon their haunches, and, leaning their elbows on their knees, consume the tedious hours in smoking. . . . I lighted on something which lay across the path. . . . It was the corpse of a girl, mangled by a hatchet. Her head, gory and deprived of its locks, easily explained the kind of enemies by whom she had been assailed. Here was proof that this quiet and remote habitation had been visited, in their destructive progress, by the Indians. The girl had been slain by them, and her scalp, according to their savage custom, had been torn away to be preserved as a trophy."[2]

Perhaps, Brown's most complete description of a person and of an aboriginal character is that of the Indian woman, Old Deb.

"This woman originally belonged to the tribe of Delawares, or Lenni-lennapee. . . . About thirty years ago, in consequence of perpetual encroachments of the English colonists, they abandoned their ancient seats. . . . This emigration was concerted in a general council of the tribe, and obtained the concurrence of all but one female. Her birth, talents, and age, gave her much consideration

---

1. *Edgar Huntly,* 174-5.
2. *Ibid.,* 182-3, 241-2.

and authority among her countrymen; and all her zeal and eloquence were exerted to induce them to lay aside their scheme. . . . Finding them refractory, she declared her resolution to remain behind and maintain possession of the land which her countrymen should impiously abandon. (She burned the wigwams of the departed tribe, retired into the fastnesses of Norwalk, and kept a dwelling free from interruption and intrusion.) Her only companions were three dogs, of the Indian or wolf species. . . . She governed them with absolute sway. They were her servants and protectors, and attended her person or guarded her threshold, agreeably to her directions. She fed them with corn, and they supplied her and themselves with meat, by hunting squirrels, raccoons, and rabbits. . . . The chief employment of this woman, when at home, . . . was to talk.

Though in solitude, her tongue was never at rest but when she was asleep; but her conversation was merely addressed to her dogs. Her voice was sharp and shrill, and her gesticulations were vehement and grotesque. . . . She seldom left the hut but to visit the neighbouring inhabitants and demand from them food and clothing, or whatever her necessities required; . . . to have her wants supplied was her prerogative, and to withhold what she claimed was rebellion. She conceived that by remaining behind her countrymen she succeeded to the government and retained the possession of all this region. . . . Being a woman aged and harmless, . . . her pretensions were a subject of mirth and good-humour, and her injunctions obeyed with a seeming deference and gravity. . . . She always disdained to speak English, and custom had rendered her intelligible to most in her native language, with regard to a few simple questions, . . . on the few ideas which she possessed. . . . The name by which she was formerly known was Deb; but her pretensions of royalty, the wildness of her aspect and garb, her shrivelled and diminutive form, a constitution that seemed to defy the ravages of time and the influence of the elements, her age. . . . her romantic solitude and mountainous haunts, suggested to my fancy the appellation of *Queen Mab.* . . . She dwelt in Norwalk upwards of twenty years. . . . Two years ago, some suspicion or disgust induced her to forsake her ancient habitation and seek a new one. . . . She was not molested in her new abode, and her life passed in the same quiet tenor as before. Her periodical rambles, her regal claims, her guardian wolves, and her uncouth volubility, were equally remarkable; but her circuits were new."[1]

---

1. *Edgar Huntly,* 216-220.

Her tribe and kinsmen came to visit her each autumn. New depredations were being made by the Indians and her disappearance about the same time, caused suspicion to fall upon her as the instigator.

Deb seems a unique character in fiction; such eccentric persons were not unknown. Goodrich in his *Recollections* of about 1807 tells of a strange woman who devoted herself to solitude, living in a cave within the limits of North Salem, many years, coming to the people occasionally to buy, and who died about 1810 or 1811. She went by the name of the Hermitess. Although Brown may have heard of her in his journeyings in Connecticut a few years before the writing of his romance, yet he states that Deb is "faithfully drawn from nature." One ought to call attention to Deb, or Queen Mab, as the antetype of Scott's Meg Merrilies.

In this story, Brown initiated that long line of tales of pioneer and border life west of the Atlantic seaboard, keeping pace with the movement of settlers westward, and gave American scenes and the American Indian their first entrance into popular literature. This is one romance surely that ought not die out of the reading of the American public. It deserves more consideration than is usually given it, because the author has demonstrated the substantial value of North American Indians as actors. This is said advisedly, taking into account what was said in Chapter II about stories in which the name Indian appears. They are used as examples rather than as participants in the actions narrated.

Edgar Huntly is historical and typically American, for its events could take place nowhere else. Brown's Indians and blood-thirsty animals belong here. History affords multitudes of instances of the burning of villages and the destruction of life by Indians, no more thrilling than the experiences of Huntly. Brown may justly be called the inventor of the Indian romance. Cooper and Irving followed him in the use of this material, making past events the basis of their tales amid American scenes.

In concluding a survey of this novel Dunlap said:

"I have by no means mentioned all the incidents, which the fertile invention of the author has introduced into this most interesting narrative. I would willingly induce the reader to seek a book full of moral instruction and fascinating amusement."[1]

"The four tales were unquestionably works of great genius, and were remarkable for the way in which natural causes were made to produce the semblance of supernatural effects. The superstitious terror of romance could scarcely be more strongly excited than by the perusal of *Wieland*. Brown wrote two other novels, *Jane Talbot* and *Philip Stanley,* in which he abandoned this system, and confined himself to the common business of life. They had little comparative success."[2]

Clara Howard (1801) and *Jane Talbot* (1801), Brown's last two novels, are very different from the four novels that preceded them.

Wieland, Ormond and *Edgar Huntly* are addressed as one long letter from one friend to another or to a group of friends, making them strictly autobiographical. The later stories consist of letters exchanged by the heroes and heroines and have an abundance of sentimentality, due to the conflicting loves of honorable, self-sacrificing young people. For the time covered, their correspondence gives the effect of having been written as the chief interest or business of life, to the exclusion of nearly everything else. Brown's purpose with reference to his early characters was to develop each of them mentally, for which end he found that the epistolary method was the best adapted. In *Clara Howard* and *Jane Talbot,* a greater emphasis is placed upon character traits than on psychological analysis. These novels have more regular plots than the former ones and a structure having better unity, proportion, climax and denouement, satisfactory to the reader and what he expects. The incidents are more probable than in the earlier novels and the language less full of peculiar words and forced, eloquent passages.

True to his promise to his brother James, Brown used "moral causes and daily incidents" instead of "the gloominess and out-of-nature incidents" of *Edgar Huntly,* which his brother had criticized. He wrote of social distinctions and commonplace life, to the lack of interest and individuality of the stories. The flash of his genius and the lively play of his imagination in the depiction of wild, free, bold scenery and startling and uncanny events are lacking.

---

1. Dunlap, *op. cit.,* II, 38.
2. *Peacock's Memoirs of Shelley,* 36.

Clara Howard; or, the Enthusiasm of Love,—formerly *Clara Howard in a Series of Letters* and *Philip Stanley* in England,— aims to reveal the mutual love of Clara and Philip. The problem that vexes the smooth progress of their love arises out of the sense of duty that each conceives is laid upon them of ascertaining what is due to Mary Wilmot, to whom Stanley had formerly been betrothed. The hero is an orphan boy, whose parents were poor, who with two sisters practically dependent upon him was left in the charge of an uncle. For a few years, a middle-aged English immigrant, named Howard, befriends and teaches Stanley. During the absence of this benefactor to his native country, Stanley completes an apprenticeship to a jeweler and becomes acquainted with the Wilmots, an orphaned sister and younger brother, who helps support his sister by teaching. At his death by drowning, he leaves his sister in very humble circumstances, except for a $5000 note, which he had never drawn and about which there was no explanation. Mary, now almost wholly dependent, though using a few dollars from the note, is engaged to Stanley, who is nine years younger than she. They agree that at the end of another six months, six months already having passed, they will marry if no claimant appears. A false claimant does appear and finally pretends to relinquish his claim in behalf of Mary.

Mr. Howard returns to America, bringing with him his recently-wedded wife and her daughter, Clara Howard, whose father was a cousin of Mr. Howard. He takes Stanley into his home with the expectation that he will wed Clara. The young people become attached to each other, as was hoped. When Stanley tells Clara of Mary, she rejects all thought of marrying him. He is interested in Mary's welfare, but he never really loved her, as he knew little about women at that time. Mary had been loved for six to eight years by an acquaintance, Sedley. She had never been able to love him because of her great love for Stanley. When she finds that Clara and Philip love each other, she disappears, leaving a note, saying, "Nothing but a sense of duty, nothing but a supreme regard to thy happiness, could suggest my design." They search for Mary and learn that she has promised to marry Sedley, her earlier lover, to whom belonged the $5000. He had deposited it with young Wilmot two years before, hoping that it would be used for

Mary, if there came any great need.

The correspondence for the most part is between Stanley and Clara, each writing alternately letters of upbraiding in which are stern demands and letters of repentance in which these demands are retracted. Stanley writes, grouping some of his remarks together,

"Your decision has made me unhappy. . . . It is the system of nature that deserves my hatred and my curses,—that system which makes our very virtues instrumental to our misery. . . . Conjugal claims and enjoyments are mutual. The happiness received is always proportioned to that conferred. . . . It was her duty . . . to contend with selfish regards, and to judge of the feelings of others by her own . . . to resign me, and she should derive more satisfaction from disinterested than from selfish conduct. She would not attempt to disguise her feelings and wishes, and extenuate the sacrifice she was called on to make; but she had no doubt as to what was right, and her resolutions to adhere to it would be immovable. . . . I do not pity you. You aspire to true happiness, the gift of self- approbation and of virtuous forbearance. . . . I believe you in the wrong. . . . Marry her I may, but I shall not love her, . . . because my affections are already devoted to one more attractive and more excellent than she. . . . Collected around the fire, and busied in music, or books, or discourse, the hours flew away with unheeded rapidity. The contrast which this scene bore to my past life perpetually recurred to my reflections, and added new and inexpressible charms to that security and elegance by which I was at present surrounded. Clara was the companion of my serious and sportive hours. I found in her character, simplicity and tenderness, united to powerful intellects. The name of children was often conferred upon us by my friend and his wife; all advances to familiarity and confidence between us were encouraged; our little plans of walking or studying together were sanctioned by smiles of approbation, and their happiness was evidently imperfect while ours was suspended or postponed. In this intercourse there was nothing to hinder the growth of that sentiment which is so congenial with virtuous and youthful bosoms. My chief delight was in sharing the society and performing offices for Clara; and this delight the frankness of her nature readily showed to be mutual. Love was not avowed or solicited, and did not frequently recur, in an undisguised shape, to my thoughts. My desires seemed to be limited to her presence and to participating her occupations and amusements. Satisfied in like manner with this, no marks of impatience or anxiety were ever betrayed by her but in my absence. . . . I was sprung from obscurity, destitute of property, of parents, of paternal friends; was full of that rustic diffidence, that inveterate humility, which are alone sufficient to divert from us the stream of fortune's favours. Such was I three years ago! Now am I rich, happy, crowned with every terrestrial felicity, in possession of that most exquisite of all blessings,—a wife, endowed with youth, grace, dignity, discretion."[1]

To which among Clara's replies are the following:

"In my eyes, marriage is no sensual or selfish bargain. I will never *vow to honour* the man who deserves only my contempt. . . . It shows you unable to comprehend that the welfare of another may demand self-denial from us. . . . I am in hopes that time and reflection will instil into you better principles. . . . Of that which I so hastily censured in you, I was guilty myself. . . . Human life, Philip, is a motley scene. . . . the truth of it, I think, has received new illustration in the little incidents on which thy last letters have commented. . . . I love you, Philip, as I ought to love you; I love your happiness, your virtue. I resign you to this good girl, as to one who deserves you more than I; whose happiness is more dependent on the affections of another than mine is. . . . for while Mary lives, and is not bound to another, I will never be to you anything but a friend. . . . (When marriage is possible, Clara writes Stanley to come.) This heart, with whose treasures thou art imperfectly acquainted, will pour all its sorrows and joys into thy honest bosom. My maturer age and more cautious judgment shall be counsellors and guides to thy inexperienced youth. While I love thee and cherish thee as a wife, I shall assume some of the prerogatives of an elder sister, and put my circumspection and forethought in the balance against thy headlong confidence. I revere thy genius and thy knowledge. With the improvements of time, very far wilt thou surpass the humble Clara; but in moral discernment much art thou still deficient; here I claim to be more than equal. But the difference shall not subsist long. Our modes of judging and our maxims shall be the same; and this resemblance shall be purchased at the cost of all my patience, my skill, and my love."[2]

After Mary had been discovered, she writes to Clara: "I am not grieved that Stanley and his Clara are subjected to trials of their magnanimity, since I foresee the propitious issue of the trial. I am not grieved that the happiness of Mary has been an

---

1. *Clara Howard*, 300, 304, 347, 378, 341, Introduction.
2. *Ibid.*, 301, 304, 306, 307, 362, 377, 409.

object of such value in your eyes as to merit the sacrifice of your own. I exult that my feelings are akin to yours, and that it is in my power to vie with you in generosity."[1]

Mary learns that Stanley is restored to Clara's favor and that their wedding date is set four weeks hence. She suggests that if they will wait one week more the two couples might be united at the same time.

The marriage of the humble Stanley and the gifted, unconventionally-educated, independent, noble-born Clara gives Brown a chance to comment on the difference between American and English social ideals, as quoted heretofore in connection with his love of country and of his appreciation of the influence of English writers. The comments are thoughtful and just and illustrate the triumph of those democratic ideals.

Clara is intended as an ideal representative of the newly-expressed rights of women. Her uncle says of her,

"She estimates the characters of others, not by the specious but delusive considerations of fortune or birth, but by the intrinsic qualities of heart and head. In her marriage-choice, . . . she will forget ancestry and patrimony, and think only of the morals and understanding of the object."[2]

In Stanley, Brown wishes to show that a worthy, industrious, sensible young man may rise from poverty and obscurity to riches and honor.

For some reason, Brown likes to arrange marriages of men of poverty and women of wealth, as exemplified in Clara and Philip. In *Edgar Huntly,* Sarsefield, having lost his money in misadventures, marries his friend Mrs. Lorimer, whom he eulogizes:

"Yes, Huntly, I am wedded to the most excellent of women. To her am I indebted for happiness, and wealth, and dignity, and honour. To her do I owe the power of being the benefactor and protector of you and your sisters."[3]

One cannot fail to recall Arthur Mervyn's peculiar love-affair and marriage to Achsa Fielding, who "lived in great affluence and independence," whom the "raw youth" adored:

"Was she not the substitute of my lost mamma? . . . Love her I *do* as I love my God; as I love virtue. To love her in another sense

---

1. *Clara Howard,* 397.
2. *Ibid.,* 327.
3. *Edgar Huntly,* 275.

would brand me for a lunatic."   So he marries her,
six years older than he, "a boy in age; bred in clownish ignorance;
scarcely ushered into the world; more than childishly unlearned and
raw; a barndoor simpleton; a plough-tail, kitchen-hearth, turnip-
hoeing, novice!" as he says.

Instead of Eliza, of the "age of delicate fervour, of inartificial love,"
but not of "marriage-seeking passion," Arthur prefers the widowed
Achsa and extols her:

"Her superior age (25), sedateness, and prudence gave my deportment a filial freedom and affection and I was fond of calling her
'mamma'."   "She thus splendidly endowed; thus allied
to nobles; thus gifted with arts, and endowed with graces." He,
as "wax in her hand," was to rely upon her tutelage, judgment,
guidance and property. "Direct me; prescribe to me."[1]

Clara Howard and Mary Wilmot are almost equally the heroines.
The experiences of these two girls, as well as those of Stanley, are
moral tests. Each, to secure her own self-approbation, unselfishly
relinquishes to the other, as she thinks, her highest hope of happiness. In creating such characters and that of Constantia Dudley
in *Ormond,* Brown portrays a new type of woman and should be
given credit for conceiving, so far in advance of its general acceptance, that which is now the common type. These women think
and act for themselves, as those who recognize their rights and
their place in the world.

Jane Talbot, A Novel has for its theme the continual contest in
Jane's mind between her duty and loyalty to Mrs. Fielder, her
benefactress, an exacting, possessive person, whom she calls mother,
and her excessive love for Henry Colden, whose known erratic
character, his quarrel with his wealthy father and his disbelief in
Christianity make him very distasteful to Mrs. Fielder. Jane writes
to Colden, "Ah! my friend! a weak—very weak—creature is thy
Jane. From excess of love arises that weakness."[2]

Five years old was Jane when her real mother died and she went
to live at the home of her mother's friend, Mrs. Fielder, who had
a considerable fortune, and no family. Jane says,
"My brother (Frank, three years older) and I passed our infancy

---

1. *Arthur Mervyn,* II, 213, 215, 219, 187-8, 179, 219, 212, 214.
2. *Jane Talbot,* 4.

in one unintermitted quarrel. We were never together but he played some cruel and mischievous prank, which I never failed to resent to the utmost of my little power."[1]

The unbusinesslike father provided Frank a good education but curbed him in no way.

"It was his maxim that all restraints were unworthy of a lad of spirit, and that it was far more wise to spend freely what his father had painfully acquired, than, by the same plodding and toilsome acts, to add to the heap."

So the worthless, scheming son, to whose control his father had intrusted his affairs, by imposture and fraud, spends all the fortune on gambling, women and gaming. By the same lying tactics, he inveigles from Jane $1500, half of her private legacy. When he can get no more money from his father and sister, he leaves Philadelphia, goes to France, procures a commission in the republican troops and enriches himself by speculations in the forfeited estates.

In childhood, Jane's father planned marriage for her with her cousin, Risberg, whom her father had reared. He is sent to study in Europe, is hated, defrauded and maligned by Frank. He wrote to Jane in boyhood, professing his love, and marries a woman of wealth in Europe, leaving Jane free of that noose. She writes,

"Experience had already taught me to set their just value on such professions. . . . most men of an ardent temper can be dying of love for half a dozen different women in the course of a year."[3]

Only once does Frank appear again in America. He calls on Jane late one night and tries to persuade her to go to France with him, to meet eligible young men. She refuses as her heart is knit with Colden's and she fears her brother's schemes. She retorts to his proposal:

"You would hardly, I imagine, allow your sister to prescribe to you in your marriage-choice, and I fear she will lay claim to the same independence for herself."[4]

Frank pays Jane the $1500 and leaves. The unity of the plot is broken by spending so much time on the brother.

"When my father and mother united their entreaties to those of

---

1. *Jane Talbot*, 7.
2. *Ibid.*, 9.
3. *Ibid.*, 20.
4. *Ibid.*, 126.

Talbot, my heart had never known a preference. The man of their choice was perfectly indifferent to me."[1]

Thus Jane is prevailed upon to betroth Talbot, a respectable, twice-her-aged man of religious principles. He leaves on a European business trip, after extorting from her a solemn promise. On his return he learns that Jane has become acquainted with a young man, Henry Colden. *Colden* is a name Brown had used in his unfinished *Romance* of Julia and Jessy for an eccentric character. Mrs. Talbot is faithful to her husband "after the marriage and during his absence on the voyage, which occasioned his death," although Miss Jessup, who had previously been in love with Talbot and pursues him shamelessly after his marriage to Jane, wrote a letter for his eyes, accusing Jane of unfaithfulness. This and other letters she wrote anonymously to Mrs. Fielder to complicate matters with suspicions of Colden and only on her death-bed did she acknowledge her interference and meanness. Concerning Miss Jessup, Colden queries:

"since she took so much pains to gain his favour, even after his marriage, is it not allowable to question the delicacy and punctiliousness, at least, of her virtue?"[2]

Mrs. Fielder disapproved of Jane's friendship with Colden during her husband's lifetime and now hears a rumor that Jane has married Colden. She writes hastily to Jane reminding her of her dependence as a daughter and promises to give her all the property at her own death and share equally while she lives, if Jane promises to think no more of Colden and converse no more with him personally or by letter. She did not reveal the sources of her information about Colden and refuses to see or write to Jane after receiving Jane's reply and threatens to disinherit her if she does not immediately forsake him, to whom she has become engaged. Colden is a man of unsettled habits and of no business, having been reared in luxury by his father and now driven from home because of his interest in Jane. Colden's father has been cognizant of the letters to Mrs. Fielder.

"I knew the motives," opines Mrs. Fielder, "that induced you to marry Lewis Talbot. They were good ones. Your compliance

---

1. *Jane Talbot,* 54-5.
2. *Ibid.,* 163.

with mine and your father's wishes in that respect showed that force of understanding which I always ascribed to you."[1]

There's the rub. Parental demands upon a daughter who has learned love and is emerging into womanly, modern independence. She never loved Talbot.

"It was not enough," continues Mrs. Fielder, "that this man had never been seduced into disbelief; that his faith was steadfast and rational without producing those fervours, and reveries, and rhapsodies, which unfit us for the mixed scenes of human life. . . . You wanted a zealot; a sectary; one that should enter into all the trifling distinctions and minute subtleties that make one Christian the mortal foe of another, while, in their social conduct, there is no difference to be found between them. . . . Colden, it is true, was not a faultless or steadfast character. No gross or enormous vices were ascribed to him. His habits, as far as appearances enabled one to judge, were temperate and chaste. He was contemplative and bookish, and was vaguely described as being somewhat visionary and romantic."[2]

Replying, Jane says, "Heaven is my witness that the happiness of my revered mamma is dearer to me than my own; no struggle was ever greater between my duty to you and the claims of another. . . . While you declare that Colden has been guilty of base actions, it is impossible to grant him my esteem as fully as a husband should claim. Till I know what the actions are which you impute to him, I never will bind myself to him by indissoluble bands. I have told him this. . . . He believes that you are misled by some misapprehension,—some slander."[3]

Jane intends to marry Colden and the contest is on, which becomes more strenuous and bitter. Excerpts are taken from letters written heretofore by Colden to his friend Thomson, who shows them to Mrs. Fielder.

"These letters showed Colden as the advocate of suicide; a scoffer at promises; a despiser of revelation, of Providence, and a future state; an opponent of marriage, and as one who denied (shocking!) that any thing but mere habit and positive law stood in the way of marriage. (Mrs. Fielder said to Jane that she would not be surprised if Colden's notions on moral and religious subjects as a youth were unsettled.) But widely and deplorably different was

1. *Jane Talbot*, 65. (See Edgar Huntly, 44.)
2. *Ibid.*, 67, 68.
3. *Ibid.*, 59, 63.

Colden's case. A most fascinating book (Godwin's Political Justice, Brown's note) fell at length into his hands, which changed in a moment, the whole course of his ideas. . . . The writer has the art of the grand deceiver; the fatal art of carrying the worst poison under the name and appearance of wholesome food; of disguising the impious, or blasphemous, or licentious, under the guise and sanctions of virtue. . . . His (Colden's) heart, his inclination, was perhaps on the side of religion and true virtue; but this book carried all his inclination, his zeal, and his enthusiasm, over to the adversary; and so strangely had he been perverted, that he held himself bound, he conceived it to be his duty, to vindicate in private and public, to preach with vehemence, his new faith. The rage for making converts seized him."[1]

Of Colden, in relation to his misdemeanors, Jane writes:
"Thou art the strangest of men, Henry. Thy whole conduct with regard to me has been a tissue of self-upbraidings. . . . In truth, there is no crime which remorse will not expiate, and no more shining virtue in the whole catalogue than sincerity. . . . Your deportment to me ought chiefly to govern my opinion of you; and have you not been uniformly generous, sincere, and upright?"[2]

After Colden had called on Miss Jessup, accused her of that base letter and received a letter for Mrs. Fielder, acknowledging her perfidy, he called on Mrs. Fielder and watched her as she read it:
"All was stern and inflexible. No wonder at the ascendency this spirit possesses over the tender and flexible Jane." (He then writes to Jane.) "Your mother's wishes, though allowed to be irrational and groundless, are to be gratified by the disappointment of mine, which appear to be just and reasonable. . . . I meant not to introduce myself into this letter,—self!—that vile debaser whom I detest as my worst enemy, and who assumes a thousand shapes and practises a thousand wiles to entice me from the right path. . . . You offer me your self. I love you. Shall I not then accept your offer? . . . I am not obdurate. I am not ungrateful. . . . All my doubts are connected with you. Can I compensate you for those losses which will follow your marriage?—the loss of your mother's affection,—the exchange of all that splendour and abundance you have hitherto enjoyed for obscurity and indigence? . . . In your

---

1. *Jane Talbot*, 70-1.
2. *Ibid.*, 54.

eyes, however, this mind and this person are venerable and attractive. My affection, my company, are chief goods with you. . . . You decide but reasonably. Fortune's goods ought not be so highly prized as the reason of many prizes them. . . . Not so I: I cannot labour for bread; I cannot work to live. In that respect I have no parallel. . . . My very nature unfits me for any profitable business. My dependence must ever be on others or on fortune. . . . I am not indolent, but my activity is vague, profitless, capricious. No lucrative or noble purpose impels me. I aim at nothing but selfish gratification. . . . How you have made yourself so absolute a mistress of the goose-quill, I can't imagine. . . . But you see what zeal will do for me. It has enabled me to keep drowsiness, fatigue, and langour at bay during a long night. Converse with thee, heavenly maid, is an antidote even to sleep, the most general and inveterate of all maladies. . . . For past faults and rectified errors, are not remorse and amendment adequate atonements?"[1]

To which Jane replies to Colden,

"I cannot help remembering the time when I reasoned like my mother; when the belief of a Christian seemed essential to every human excellence. All qualities, without that belief, were not to be despised as useless, but to be abhorred as pernicious. There would be no virtue, no merit, divorced from religion. 'Ah, Jane,' said my mother; 'rash and presumptuous girl, what a signal punishment hangs over thee! Thou wilt trust thyself within the toils of the grand deceiver. Thou wilt enter the list, with his subtleties. Vain and arrogant, thou fearest not thy own weakness.' . . . While reflecting on my debt to thee, my heart becomes too big for its mansion. . . . An upright demeanour, a self-acquitting conscience, are not sufficient for our safety. Calumny and misapprehension have no bounds to their rage and their activity. . . . Indeed, I have given up my mother. There is no other alternative but that of giving up you, and in this case I can hesitate, indeed, but I cannot decide against you. . . . Why did you conceal from me your father's treatment of you . . .? I will never be the cause of plunging you into poverty so hopeless. . . . But, thanks to Heaven, I am apprized in time of the truth. She (mother) carefully shunned the mention of atrocious charges. She dwelt only on the proofs which your past life and your own confessions had afforded of unsteady courage and unwarrantable principles."[2]

---

1. *Jane Talbot,* 194, 85, 86, 100, 101, 104, 109.
2. *Ibid.,* 131-2, 137, 142, 143, 144, 145.

Colden replies to Jane: "I supposed you willing to grant me the same independence of a parent's control which you claimed for yourself. . . . You exhort me to seek reconcilement with my father? . . . I have not been the injurer. Not an angry word, accusing look, or revengeful thought, has come from me. I have exercised the privilege of a rational and moral being. . . . Such is the lot of one that has forfeited his reputation. Having once been guilty, the returning path to rectitude is forever barred against him. His conduct will almost always be liable to a double construction; and who will suppose the influence of good motives, when experience has proved the influence, in former cases, of evil ones. . . . Jane Talbot is young, lovely, and the heiress, provided she retain the favour of her adopted mother, of a splendid fortune. I am poor, indolent, devoted, not to sensual, but to visionary and to costly, luxuries. How shall such a man escape the imputation of sordid and selfish motives? . . . But I can truly aver that my motives are disinterested. Will his averments of disinterested motives be believed? . . . Mrs. Fielder is averse to her daughter's wishes. While the aversion endures, marriage, instead of enriching me, will merely reduce my wife to my own destitute condition. . . . My own experience has taught me in what degree a luxurious education endears to us the means of an easy and elegant subsistence. . . . Yet why have I deliberately exhorted Jane to become mine? Because I trust to the tenderness of her mother. . . . The evil, she will think, cannot be repaired. . . . Intercession and submission shall not be wanting. Jane will never suffer her heart to be estranged from her mother. Reverence and gratitude will always maintain their place. . . . I begin to think it is vain to strive against maternal influence. What but momentary victory can I hope to attain? . . . I have now, indeed, no hope of even momentary victory. There are but two persons in the world who command her affections. Either, when present, (the other absent or silent) has absolute dominion over her."[1]

The type of heroine is seen in Colden's description of her above, and her own words to Colden:

"So easily swayed am I by one that is lord of my affections. No will, no reason, have I of my own. Such sudden and total transitions! In solitude I ruminate and form my schemes. They seem to me unalterable: yet a word from you scatters all my laboured edifices, and I look back upon my former state of mind as on something

---

1. *Jane Talbot*, 149, 176, 177, 151.

that passed when I was a lunatic or dreaming. . . . What a wretch am I! Feeble and selfish beyond all example among women! . . . Never was a creature so bereft of all dignity, all steadfastness. The slave of every impulse; blown about by the predominant gale; a scene of eternal fluctuation. . . . I was determined to raise you to affluence, by employing, in a way unseen and unsuspected by you, those superfluities which a blind and erring destiny had heaped upon me. . . . Oh, comfort me, my friend! plead against yourself, against me. Be my mother's advocate. Fly away from these arms that clasp you, and escape from me, even if your flight be my death. Think not of me, . . . by disclaiming, by hating, by forgetting, the unfortunate Jane. . . . I have nothing but evil to choose. There is but one calamity greater than my mother's anger. . . . I cannot put an impious and violent end to my own life. . . . My mother allows me, and even requires me, to write to you (urging Colden's reconcilement with his father). My reluctance to do so is only overcome by the fear of her displeasure; . . . Infer not from this reluctance that the resolution of being henceforward all that my mother wishes can be altered by any effort of yours. . . . My safety lies only in filling my ears with my mother's remonstrances and shutting them against your persuasive accents. I have therefore resigned myself wholly to my mother's government."[1]

After Jane's last letter to Colden, expressing her final resolve, he writes to his sister, Mary Montford, after he had decided to take a boat voyage:

"Whatever she feels for me, *I* am not her supreme passion. Her mother is preferred to me. *That* her present resolution puts out of all doubt. . . . The happiness of one or other must be forfeited. . . . I do not believe I shall ever return. If I did expect it, I know Jane too well to have any fears of her fidelity. While I am living, or as long as my death is uncertain, her heart will be mine, and she will reserve herself for me," and to Mrs. Fielder, "All that I fear is, that your efforts to console her will fail. I know the heart which, if you thought me worthy of the honour, I should account it my supreme felicity to call mine. Let it be a precious deposit in your hands."[2]

A year later, Mary writes to Jane of Colden's "voyage to the western coast of America and to China" with her husband's brother in his cargo ship.

---

1. *Jane Talbot*, 92, 178, 179, 180, 184, 209.
2. *Ibid.*, 215, 216, 154-5.

"They had been gone already upwards of a year. We have not heard of them since their touching at Tobago and Brazil." . . . (Jane and Mary become good friends and console each other, and Jane replies:) "I thank my God that I was capable of abandoning him on no selfish or personal account. The maledictions of my own mother; the scorn of the world; the loss of friends, reputation, and fortune, weighed nothing with me. Great as these evils were, I could have cheerfully sustained them for his sake. . . . I have regarded the promise that I made to the elder Colden and to my mother, as sacred. The decease of the latter has, in my own opinion, absolved me from any obligation except that of promoting my own happiness and that of him whom I love. I shall not *now* reduce him to indigence, and, that consequence being precluded, I cannot doubt of his father's acquiescence. . . . Her last words were these:— 'Thou hast done much for me, my child. I begin to fear that I have exacted too much. Your sweetness, your patience, have wrung my heart with compunction. I have wronged thee, Jane. I have wronged the absent; I greatly fear, I have. Forgive me. If you ever meet, entreat *him* to forgive me, and recompense yourself and him for all your mutual sufferings.' . . . (Jane revisits the country place near Wilmington, where she first met Colden and writes to Mary:) I have done expecting and repining, you know. Four years have passed since I was here,—since I met your brother under these shades. . . . The fields are sterile, the barn small, the stable crazy, the woods scanty. . . . It owes its power of bewitching us to the memory, the fancy, and the heart,"[1] as Jane contemplates buying the place.

In this interim, Jane meets again Mr. Cartwright, a schoolmate before boys and girls were separated to different schools. He used to wait for her at her school door and they kissed and wept when he was to leave to go to Europe, when Jane was scarcely fourteen. Jane writes to Mary:

"I will say to *you,* though my regard to his happiness will never suffer me to say it to him, that if three years more pass away, and I am fully assured that your brother's absence will be perpetual, and Cartwright's happiness is still in my hands,—that then—I possibly may—."[2]

Mary let Jane know that her husband's brother had returned

---

1. *Jane Talbot,* 211, 212, 213, 217, 218, 219.
2. *Ibid.,* 221.

alone from their unfortunate voyage. They shipped to the West Indies, remained some time at Nootka, prepared to cross the ocean to China, touched at the Sandwich Islands and landed near Japan. The crew mutinied and planned to kill Montford and Colden, but put Colden ashore on a coastal sandbar. When a Spanish ship bound for Manila approached, Montfort leaped overboard, swam to the Spanish ship and explained the mutiny. The Spanish ship seized the mutineers, taking them to Manila, and Montford sold his vessel and cargo there on very advantageous terms and returned to America.

Colden made his way to the chief city of Japan, Jedho, where he met a European, named Holtz, an agent of the Dutch East India Company in Japan, with whom he went to Batavia and for whom from there he reached Hamburg on business. There he met Cartwright, who gave him news of Jane. He returns to America, takes a swift stage from Boston, riding night and day, till within a mile of New Haven the carriage was overturned and his left arm shattered. He is detained by the surgeon and illness, but writes to Montfort, who notifies Jane of Colden's return.

All along Brown has been preparing his readers for a transformation in the character of Colden. He writes to his brother-in-law, James Montford:

"A state of doubt and indecision was, in every view, hurtful, criminal, and ignominious. Conviction, if it were in favour of religion, would insure me every kind of happiness. It would forward even those schemes of temporal advantage on which I might be intent. It would reconcile those whose aversion arose from difference of opinion; and in cases where it failed to benefit my worldly views, it would console me for my disappointment. . . . with all my confidence of a favourable reception from Jane,—her conduct now exempt from that irresistible control of her mother, and her tenderness for me as fervent as ever, (He wonders why she had not married Cartwright.)—that harmony of opinion on religious subjects, without which marriage can never be a source of happiness to hearts touched by a true and immortal passion, was perfect in *his* case. . . . If my reflections and experience had not changed my character,—if all *her* views as to the final destiny and present obligations of human beings had not become *mine*,—I should have deliberately ratified the act of my eternal banishment. Yes, my friend, this weather-beaten form and sunburnt face are not more unlike what you once knew, than my habits and opinions now and formerly. The incidents of a long voyage, the vicissitudes through which I have passed, have given strength to my frame, while the opportunities and occasions for wisdom which these have afforded me have made *my mind whole*. I have awakened from my dreams of doubt and misery, not to a cold and vague belief, but to the living and delightful consciousness, of every tie that can bind man to his Divine Parent and Judge. . . . You, who have had this experience, and who have always regarded me in this light, will not wonder that reflection has, at length, raised *me* to the tranquil and steadfast height of simple and true piety."[1]

A rich man's son who has kept in mind either Jane's inheritance or his father's wealth as a necessity and who had been sceptical about religion and the true values of life, in which Jane had been carefully instructed, after numerous attempts at explanation and reconciliation, the irresolute Colden weakly submits to the demands of Mrs. Fielder and of Jane and exiles himself to a distant part of the earth. Stranded on a bleak coast, tanned by a tropical sun and enured to four years of hardship, the hero, a sceptic no longer, returns, ill in body, to find that Mrs. Fielder had died and Jane waiting for him. He is married to Jane and they live on the fortune inherited from Mrs. Fielder. A modern young man in love would have married Jane first, with or without consent and without the inheritance, and been banished afterward if that had been decreed.

The story ends with Jane's letter to Colden:

"And are you then alive? Are you then returned? Still do you remember, still love, the ungrateful and capricious Jane? . . . I almost fear that joy will do what sorrow was unable to do. Can it be that Colden—that selfsame, dear, pensive face, those eyes, benignly and sweetly mild, and that heart-dissolving voice, have escaped so many storms, so many dangers? Was it love for me that led you from the extremity of the world? And have you, indeed, brought back with you a heart full of 'ineffable tenderness,' for *me?* Unspeakably unworthy am I of your love. . . . Tuesday evening —they say it can't possibly be sooner—I am with you. No supporters shall you have but my arms; no pillow but my breast. Every holy rite shall instantly be called in to make us one. And when once united, nothing but death shall ever part us again. . . . She died in my arms; and will it not give you pleasure to know

---

1. *Jane Talbot*, 205, 233, 234, 235.

that her dying lips blessed me, and expressed the hope that you would one day return to find . . . some recompense for all the evils to which her antipathies subjected you? She hoped, indeed, that observation and experience would detect the fallacy of your former tenets; that you would become wise, . . . deserving of the happiness and honour which would attend the gift of her daughter's hand and heart. My words cannot utter, but thy own heart perhaps can conceive, the rapture which thy confession of a change in thy opinions has afforded me. *All* my prayers, Henry, have not been *merely* for your return. Indeed, . . . union with you would have been *very* far from completing my felicity, unless our hopes and opinions, as well as our persons and hearts, were united. . . . Oh, what sweet peace, what serene transport, is there in the persuasion that the selected one will continue forever to commune with *my* soul, mingle with mine in its adoration of the same Divine Parent, and partake with me in every thought, in every emotion, both *here* and hereafter. Never, my friend, without *this* persuasion, *never* should I have known one moment of true happiness. Marriage, indeed, instead of losing its attractions in consequence of your errors, drew thence only new recommendations, since with a zeal, a tenderness, and a faith like mine, my efforts to restore such a heart and such a reason as yours could not fail of success; but *till* that restoration were accomplished, never I repeat, should I have tasted repose even in *your* arms. . . . I can write no more; but must not conclude till I have offered thee the tenderest, most fervent vows of a heart that ever was and always will be *thine own*. Witness, Jane Talbot."[1]

Moral causes make the conflicting motives in the heads and hearts of Jane Talbot and Henry Colden. Jane is a young woman trying to emancipate herself from tyrannical parental control and deciding to uphold her Christian principles against her love for a nonbeliever. She strives for independence but can only partially accomplish it. In *Jane Talbot*, more forcibly than in his former novels, Brown proclaims his complete breaking away from the influence of Godwin. A charge is brought by one of the characters that Colden is a disciple of Godwin, a discreditable fact. In presenting the hero in the end cured of his sceptical beliefs, Brown intended to renounce his dalliance with Godwin's philosophical heresy in respect to religion and his extravagant views in regard to marriage.

---

1. *Jane Talbot*, 235-7.

"The portrait of Jane is evidently a careful attempt to describe an affectionate, impulsive, unconventional creature, easily bent by an appeal to her affection, yet springing back toward a reliance on her own judgment. . . . Jane Talbot shares with Brown's other heroines the interest given by her apparent modernness in contrast to contemporary heroines,—blushing, sighing, and swooning. The author's intention is to make them women of a newer type, to let them speak and act and love for themselves, relying on their own judgment and not on the conventions of society."[1]

"A very stupid book," Lady (Mrs. P. B.) Shelley called *Jane Talbot*. She was displeased that any one would criticize the philosophic doctrines of her renowned father, Godwin, by denouncing *Political Justice*. Dunlap called *Jane Talbot* Brown's best novel.[2]

1. Loshe, *The Early American Novel*, 49.
2. Dunlap, in Dunlap, *op. cit.*, II, 67.

CHAPTER IV

METHODS OF COMPOSITION

The plots of Brown's novels are original, exceptional and forceful, though defective in unity of design. Each main narrative consists of a series of episodes slightly connected with each other, but all connected to the purpose and developing it. They are like clothes hanging on a line, grouped, however, as a good housewife would hang them. A contemporary of Brown, Royall Tyler, said of him:

"He never mastered the art of fiction well enough to produce a book that deserved anything more than the name of narrative."

Brown may have been negligent of his plots, but he certainly was never at a loss for a breath-taking adventure or for creating suspense,—not inferior to Cooper in this respect. The incidents of his novels are many of them dramatic, yet he made little attempt to dramatize his plots. He makes a conscious effort in *Edgar Huntly*. Dramatic terms are used in the story; for example,—

"To comprehend it (the "drama in which his mind was busy") demands penetration into the recesses of his soul. . . . Was the narrative of Clithero the web of imposture or the raving of insanity? . . . He had appeared. The strange being is again upon the stage." "I was left to mark the progress of the drama. . . . At length the drama is brought to an imperfect close, and the series of events that absorbed my faculties ("my mind had been the theatre") . . . has terminated in repose."

A few other times the words—drama, stage and scene—are found here and in his other novels, as in *Wieland*: "this the stage on which that enemy of man (Carwin) showed himself for a moment unmasked."

These words of the author are relevant in this connection, when the press was publishing each part as fast as he could supply it:

"I commenced something in the form of a Romance. I had at first no definitive conceptions of my design. As my pen proceeded forward, my invention was tasked, and the materials that it afforded were arranged and digested. Fortunately I continued to view this scheme in the same light in which it had at first presented itself. Time therefore did not diminish its attractions. The facility I experienced in composition, and the perception of daily progress, encouraged me, and my task was finished on the last day of December. . . . It was at first written in a hasty and inaccurate way. Before I can submit it to a printer, or even satisfactorily rehearse it to a friend, it must be wholly transcribed. I am at present engaged in this employment. I am afraid as much time will be required by it, as was necessary to the original composition."[1]

One might think he had in mind the words of Sterne when he began *Tristram Shandy*, "with no real idea of how it was to turn out." He also said in that novel (Chapter 19, p. 2): "Writers had need look before them, to keep up the spirit and connection of what they have in hand."

In strong contrast to this obvious irregularity of plot is Brown's ever-present, ever-evolving moral or psychological purpose, as illustrated in the treatment of Clithero mentioned above. The author always had a purpose, if not always a plan. Griswold wrote: "the metaphysical unity and consistency of his novels are apparent to all readers familiar with psychological phenomena."[2] This predetermined purpose or aim has the advantage of giving such an air of truth that his readers almost forget that they are not reading statements of some serious matter of fact and are unconscious of the abnormal phases of the subject. Brown "is inferior to all great story tellers in his sacrifice of universal truth to the situation, the moment,"[3] remarked Blake. It would seem that Brown had not sacrificed the truth, but rather had not sufficiently elaborated it or had too many truths.

"In sheer power of gripping plots and masterful climaxes Brown has few superiors. His weakness, on the other hand, lies in his inability to resolve his plots and scenes into their realizable effects," said David Lee Clark in his Introduction to *Edgar Huntly*.

One reason for Brown's lack of plot unity was his not having in

---

1. Brown, His Journal, in Dunlap, *op. cit.*, I, 107.
2. Griswold, *The Prose Writers of America*, 29.
3. Blake, "Brockden Brown and the Novel," in *The Sewanee Review*, XVIII, 436.

mind the completed story in the beginning, which led to necessary changes of plan in the prosecution of the work. Brown completed *Wieland* and three years after the romance itself wrote an additional chapter to clear up the unfinished incidents as promised at the close of the story and put the finishing touches on several characters— Clara and Pleyel, Carwin, Stuart and Maxwell. Another continuation of *Wieland* was made—*Memoirs of Carwin, the Biloquist, a fragment,* of which Brown says in the Advertisement of *Wieland*:

"The memoirs of Carwin, alluded to at the conclusion of the work, will be published or suppressed according to the reception which is given to the present attempt."

In similar fashion, Brown finished *Arthur Mervyn* with its theme of yellow fever and later wrote another volume to conclude the incidents of the first and to give Arthur time and opportunity to perform his benevolences. When Arthur has completed his projects and knows not that Achsa loves him and that he loves her, Dr. Stevens apprises him of the fact in dramatic terms: "This scene is quite new. . . . This is a necessary part of the drama," showing Brown's intention to unwind the story with the expected love-marriage ending. The episodical style in this book was due to the fact that Brown had published the early chapters as a series, as he had done with earlier writings, like *The Rhapsodist, The Rights of Women* and *Sky-Walk.* So this style became a habit. Besides, it was found effective in sustaining the interest of his readers. Parts of several of his novels were published in magazines serially, which accounts for the large number of striking incidents or crises at intervals,—also for the lack of well-developed plot construction and likewise for the author's lack of time for sufficient revision and transcription.

Dunlap, with whom Brown lived for a time and who knew him better than anyone else did, testified to his methods:

"He began to write a novel after having only determined upon one leading circumstance, character or idea, and trusted to the growth of one incident from another, and the appropriate sentiments from the incidents. One volume would be finished and printed before he had formed any plan for the beginning of the second, or any plan for the continuation, developement or denouement of the story. . . . It is very evident that this unsystematic mode of composition must give a motley appearance. . . . The parts must occasionally be disproportioned to each other, and incidents imagined which excite great expectations in the reader, and involve the story in mystery, which the author trusting to after thought for the explanation or the sequel, and not finding . . . any adequate solution of difficulty or termination of adventure, the event either does not answer the expectation raised, or the reader is put off with the intimation of a continuation at a future time."[1]

There are episodes which seem irrevelant, as it were, to the plot because they are based on the author's experiences and opinions. Brown was inexpert in portraying familiar characters against his real backgrounds. The portrayal of unusual characters with reality of settings produces an effect of confusion at times, seen not only in his construction of incidents, but in his designs.

Confusion is also occasioned by the use of the epistolary method, which requires a change of viewpoint with each different letter writer. Clara Wieland tells the Wieland story, but there are introduced confessions of Wieland and Carwin in their own persons. In *Arthur Mervyn*, Arthur relates the history of his own life and of the yellow fever; Dr. Stevens opens both parts of the story and enters at other times; Welbeck's two or three confessions are within Arthur's story; the early life of Arthur is told by a country neighbor woman and then he gives his version of it; in his attempts to alleviate the final distresses of all characters, there is conversation, presenting opposing viewpoints. Despite these "venial faults (dramatic bounds of time and action) the beauties of Arthur Mervyn are splendid,"[2] said Dunlap.

An additional cause of Brown's unskilfully wrought plots, involving cumulative incidents, unfinished incidents and narrative within narrative, was the celerity with which he wrote. Dunlap said that, in the year 1799, Brown had begun five novels, all of which were in a state of progression. Critics agreed that he had no time to perfect either plots or style, due to haste of composition.

The spur that set Brown on his extraordinary spree of writing five novels at once, after *Wieland* was begun, was the immediate popularity at home and abroad of its first chapters. Doubtless, these novels contain much material from his earlier writings or from his pre-contemplated plans and even outlines, as from social

---

1. Dunlap, *op. cit.*, I, 258, 259.
2. *Ibid.*, II, 29.

and political treatises, evident in *Wieland* and *Ormond,* from *Sky-Walk* in *Edgar Huntly,* from the *Romance* of Sophia and Jessy the Zisca incident in *Wieland* and so on. Brown's writing of all but one of his novels simultaneously speaks in a more forceful way than can any encomium upon the varied talents of the author. It was the exhilirating realization that he had now found a proper medium of expression for the teeming thoughts that circled in his brain and his exuberant youthfulness displaying itself with the thrill of accomplishment.

In a letter to his brother Armit, Brown wrote:
"Some time since I bargained with the publisher of Wieland for a new performance, part of which only was written, and the publication commencing immediately, I was obliged to apply with the utmost diligence to the pen, in order to keep pace with the press. . . . I call my book Ormond, or the Secret Witness. I hope to finish the writing and the publication together before new year's day, when I shall have a breathing spell."[1]

As a commentary justifying Brown's rapidity of writing are words from *Edgar Huntly*:
"In proportion as I gain power over words, shall I lose dominion over sentiments. In proportion as my tale is deliberate and slow, the incidents and motives which it is designed to exhibit will be imperfectly revived and obscurely portrayed."
Although Brown usually contrived thrilling incidents, his object was not the relation of the incidents but the recording of impressions. He uses the word "sentiments."

Scott's method a few years later reflects that of Brown. He said after completing the second volume of *Woodstock*:
"Now I haven't the slightest idea how the story is to be wound up to a catastrophe. . . . I never could lay down a plan. . . . I only tried to make that which I was actually writing diverting and interesting, leaving the rest to fate. . . . When I chain my mind to ideas which are purely imaginary, . . . I think away the whole vivacity and spirit of my original conception, and the results are cold, tame, and spiritless. . . . Wrote to the end of a chapter, and know . . . no more than a man in the moon what comes next. . . .

---

1. Brown, Letter to his brother Armit, New York, Dec. 20th, 1798, in Dunlap, *op. cit.,* II, 93.
2. *Edgar Huntly,* 1-2.

I love to have the press thumping, clattering, and banging in my rear; it creates the necessity which almost always makes me work best."[1]

Writing with the publishers always calling for copy forbade Brown's rounding out events, mysteries, incidents and characters, no doubt to his discomfiture. The words of Clara with regard to her relation by letter of the account of the Wieland family well applies to Brown himself:

"Yet I will persist to the end. My narrative may be invaded by inaccuracy and confusion; but, if I live no longer, I will, at least, live to complete it. What but ambiguities, abruptnesses, and dark transitions, can be expected from the historian who is, at the same time, the sufferer of these disasters?"[2]

One may readily speak of Brown as a sufferer, because of his lifelong uncertainty of health and his foreknowledge of consumption ever in the offing. However much the versatility and industry of the author may be admired, the loss of excellence and reputation that it occasions him and the loss of amusement and instruction to his readers must be forever deplored (Dunlap).

Many of Brown's characters are living, assertive beings. A few act as if they were the puppets of superior powers or the victims of a vague and dreadful fatality, almost subservient to the circumstances that surround them, which accords with the author's purpose to study character in unusual situations. He identifies himself with the working of their minds and develops each as a specific, psychological personality troubling himself little to individualize them in the details of their outward lives. He uses them as material in his hands to work out his purposes. In accordance with the characteristics of solitariness, mystery and gloom of his own temperament, he loves to present the heart as desolate, foreboding, self-dependent and at times plotting evil or good. When he would exhibit strength of mind or purpose to most advantage, he takes away all external succour and encircles the person with circumstances that rouse vague apprehensions of danger or uncertainty. The individual must then estimate the approaching evil, comprehend its worst consequences and act accordingly, thus revealing

---

1. Scott, *Journal*, 1825-1832, 117, 122, 151.
2. *Wieland*, 166.

the latent, potential virtue within him. Clara Wieland and Constantia Dudley, for example, have loving, gentle natures, but have also thinking minds, full of resourcefulness, constancy and courage. Arthur Mervyn with no money does many helpful services. Edgar Huntly reasons on the behavior of the panther and on his chances and on the necessity of killing the Indians, with no human aid at hand. Brown's women are equal to his men. Nearly all of them show minds of their own and somewhat of womanly devotion, helpfulness and self-sacrifice. Clara is almost as much the heroine of *Wieland* as her brother is the hero, in her education, independence, ability to meet situations, love-life and authorship. In comparison with Brown's female characters, a generation later Cooper's women are so limited by narrow conventions as to be insipid, helpless and ill-defined; to use his own phrase, they belong to the type "of religion and female decorum." They think, act and talk with fastidious propriety.

The principal characters of Brown's earlier novels are simple, impelled or motivated by some one ruling passion, which sets them apart, as it were, from their fellow men and drives them irresistibly to their doom, as Wieland, Carwin, Ormond, Welbeck and Clithero. Character grouping, whether in the social life of the city or country or in happy home relations, is a requisite for the true novel. Brown held himself aloof and probably did not perceive the value of it. He says, "my powers do not enable me to place the common place characters around me in an interesting or amusing point of view."[1] By nature and training, Brown was unacquainted with the complex relations of life, which are a necessary preparation to a novelist who would attain effective character grouping. His characters are more disposed to soliloquize than to talk. They deliberate. They bring before the mind all the pros and cons regarding a subject, which reveals their author's legal training, before they finally decide to act.

This process of reasoning, making mention of a thousand minute particulars, at times becomes tedious and seems affected; yet this being the way in which the larger part of the world reasons, Brown has convinced his readers of the truth of his facts and produces

---

1. Brown, Record of a Trip to Rockaway, in Dunlap, *op. cit.*, I, 66.

an atmosphere of circumstantiality. A modern novelist, like the dramatist, develops his characters more by action; but Brown more often has his characters make themselves known by their self-analyses and explanations, interspersed by his own comments. He uses dialogue sparingly, which correlates with the private musings of his characters. However, his chief characters speak in dialogue as befits them under proper conditions. Many of their conversations employ the thou-and-thee, old-style Quaker forms. One of the most natural conversations is that between Arthur Mervyn and the unlearned, indigent person from whom he tries to learn who owned the house where he was locked in. Arthur inquires of the name, profession, whether married. The man replies:

"It would be an odd thing if he was married. An old fellow, with one foot in the grave—comical enough for him to *git a vife!"* Concerning the death of the baby, he says: "She (the mother) is not quite out of *the dumps* yet. . . . I'll war'n' they'll have enough of them before they die."[1]

In his later works, Brown attempted a somewhat wider range of characters and personalities of mixed and complicated natures, rather than agents of a single, dominant control. Constantia Dudley, Queen Mab, Arthur Mervyn and Edgar Huntly are quite original in conception and evolution. Though at times the women are senti- mental and weakly portrayed, they are on the whole superior in strength and in reality to most of the women characters in the novels of the time; for example, Achsa Fielding in *Arthur Mervyn.* Mrs. Fielding is one of the author's choice characters, she who is the modern, refined, sensitive, well-educated woman, sharing as heroine with Eliza, the simple, unspoiled country girl. This is a case where an American, Arthur, marries an immigrant English lady, who is also a Jewess. The English seem to have become con- genial and reconciled to the Americans soon after the Revolution; or, perhaps, Brown is trying to help bring about better relations between them. Evidently, he chose the Hebrew name Achsa from the Biblical character, which indicates his familiarity with the Bible,— a fact that comes out in several instances.

Sometimes Brown introduces too many and too unimportant

---

1. *Arthur Mervyn,* I, 60-1.

characters for a single performance, as Harwick, Waring, the Walpoles, Keyser, Austin, Capper, in *Arthur Mervyn;* and important personages disappear altogether, as Mrs. Wentworth, Wallace and Eliza, abandoned both by the author and the hero, in the same novel. Again characters causing new complications are introduced unnecessarily, as Stuart, Maxwell and Dashwood, in *Wieland.* From a general study of Brown's novels, one can see that he is limited in the creation of characters and accepts some standardized models.

"Like some other dealers in fiction," Brown says, "I find it easier to give new names to my visionary friends, and vary their condition, than to introduce a genuine diversity into their characters."[1]

He brings in a large number of characters, but fashions fully only the opposing principals. Even in the case of those most fully treated, the treatment is chiefly mental to accord with his purposes and themes.

Supposing inheritances in names may be made a game, whether true or false. Fannie Burney's *Evelina* may have given Brown ideas besides the father-daughter incident,—as Arthur and the Villars family from the benevolent Arthur Villars, Louisa Conway from Lady Louisa, followed by the authoress of "Sabina" of her book *Louisa,* Lovel, mentioned but once by Brown, from her Lovel, and Clemenza from Clement. The same names are used in different novels: *Arthur Mervyn* and Arthur Wiatte in *Edgar Huntly,* in which Mary Waldegrave occurs; in *Ormond* are two Marys— Mary Mansfield and Mary Ridgefield; Talbot in *Ormond* and *Jane Talbot;* Watson, Wentworth, Lucy and Betsy in *Ormond* and *Arthur Mervyn;* Sarsefield in *Ormond* and in *Edgar Huntly;* Clara Wieland and Clara Howard. Following this author the name Wentworth is used by Dana in *Tom Thornton.* A few names have been noted heretofore.

In 1751, Mrs. Eliza Haywood published a novel, *Miss Betsy Thoughtless.* Betsy was of a scatter-brain nature, falling into trouble, flattered by lovers, meeting Mr. Trueworth, but losing him for a time by associating with a virtueless friend. She enters into a sham marriage with the worthless rascal and is finally rescued by

1. Brown, "Alcuin," in Dunlap, *op. cit.,* I, 74.

Mr. Trueworth. There may be a connection between her and Betty Lawrence in *Arthur Mervyn;* she was a loud, lover-possessed, ignorant person, whom Arthur's father was enticed into marrying, causing Arthur to leave home. The two Elizas in the same novel may take their name from Mrs. Haywood's given name, if Brown knew her novel.

Characters must be representative men and women to make them lasting fictional personalities. To invest them with the illusion of reality, whether factual or fictitious, they must be individualized by certain personal traits that distinguish them from all other representatives or members of their class. To make them interesting, they must act their parts,—be dynamic, not static. A few of Brown's best characters seem to measure up: Wieland, Ormond, Constantia, Dudley, Huntly, Queen Mab, Arthur Mervyn, Stanley, Carwin. These and, perhaps, others have been copied and handed down by later writers,—by Godwin, Shelley, Mrs. Shelley, Scott, Irving, Cooper, Poe, Maria Edgeworth, Wallace, Ainsworth, Meredith, of lasting fame.

Repetitions, confusions and inconclusions are not hard to find. Brown commits the fault of having two somnambulists in *Edgar Huntly.* Arthur Mervyn resembles both young Lodi and Clavering, with little reason for the fact in the story; and the purpose of the cockloft in Welbeck's home is unexplained. The author commenced a new novel before having completed a former one, thus repeating the same ideas without knowing it. Duplicate stories are found in the circumstances of Edgar Huntly and his two sisters and in those of Philip Stanley and his sisters. All are left orphans and provided for in each case by an uncle; but the young men are early compelled to shift for themselves. Each finds a friend and instructor in an English immigrant, who finally returns home to England, marries a former lady friend, a second marriage for her, and returns again to America.

The brother of Jane Talbot is like the brother of Mrs. Lorimer, in *Edgar Huntly.* Each recklessly squanders the patrimony of his father and tries to rob his sister. Jane says of her brother:
"My brother's temper grew more unmanageable as he increased in years. . . . I do not remember a single direct kindness that I ever received from him; but I remember innumerable ill offices and contempts. Still, there was some inexplicable charm in the mere

tie of kindred, which made me more deplore his errors, exult in his talents, rejoice in his success, and take a deeper interest in his concerns than in those of any other person."[1]   "Mrs. Lorimer had a twin-brother, . . . but the powers that in one case were exerted in the cause of virtue were, in the other, misapplied to sordid and flagitious purposes. Arthur Wiatte . . . had ever been the object of his sister's affection. . . . All her kindness was repaid by a stern and inexorable hatred. . . . He exceeded in depravity all that has been imputed to the arch-foe of mankind. . . . He seemed to relish no food but pure unadulterated evil. He rejoiced in proportion to the depth of that distress of which he was the author. . . . At their (parents') death the bulk of their patrimony devolved upon him. This he speedily consumed in gaming and riot."[2]

Parallel incidents are found in the brother of Mary Wilmot, in *Clara Howard,* and in Waldegrave, the friend of Huntly. Each receives and deposits money, dies, leaves an inheritance to his sister, and each deposit is sought by a claimant. Waldegrave left certain property in the care of Huntly. "It was money, and consisted of deposits at the Bank of North America. The amount was little short of eight thousand dollars. . . . His sister was his only kindred, and she is now in possession of it." Weymouth, a stranger to Huntly, on inquiring about the property, says:

"I invested the greatest part of my property in a cargo of wine from Madeira. The remainder I turned into a bill of exchange for seven thousand five hundred dollars. . . . To him (Waldegrave) therefore I determined to transmit this bill. . . . I remember when we parted, he was poor. He used to lament that his scrupulous integrity precluded him from all the common roads to wealth. . . . His religious duty compelled him to seek his livelihood by teaching a school of blacks. . . . It scarcely supplied the necessities of nature, and was reduced sometimes even below that standard by his frequent indisposition."   (Huntly replies:) "I was not only unapprised of any other employment of his time, but had not the slightest suspicion of his possessing any property besides his clothes and books."[3]

No conclusion is given of the return of the money to Weymouth;

---

1. *Jane Talbot,* 9.
2. *Edgar Huntly,* 43, 44, 46.
3. *Ibid.,* 147, 150, 148, 149.

and the difficulty of accounting for Morton's false claim in *Clara Howard* is unsolved. The brother of Mary Wilmot was drowned and he "was found to be credited in the Bank of P— for so large a sum as five thousand dollars." This credit had been given two years before his death. "This money was the gift of Mr. Sedley to my brother." His intimate associates had never heard the slightest intimation of his possessing anything beyond the scanty income of his school. His expenses were kept within his meager salary. Sometime afterward, Morton, a former acquaintance of Stanley, appeared and sought Wilmot, saying,

"His property he partly invested in a ship and her cargo, and partly in a bill of exchange for five thousand dollars. This bill he transmitted to his friend Wilmot."[1]

There is practically no true humor in Brown's novels to relieve the prevailing seriousness. The few attempts, particularly in *Arthur Mervyn*, are failures. One passage in the report of Brown's visit to Rockaway serves as an unconscious criticism in this respect, of his novels written later:

"As to our talk at dinner, there was perfect good humour, and a good deal of inclination to be witty, but I do not recollect a single *good thing* that deserves to be recorded."[2]   Dunlap said of Brown's humor: "He had no portion in himself, nor any adequate conception of it in others."

Clara Wieland contrasts herself, Catharine and Pleyel with her brother, in relation to humor:

"The images that visited us were blithesome and gay. . . . I scarcely ever knew him to laugh. He never accompanied the lawless mirth of his companions with more than a smile."

Quite a number of expressions refer to the mirth of Pleyel: "His gayety had flown. . . . His vivacity had indeed been damped; . . . His conversation abounded with novelty. His gayety was almost boisterous; . . . His conceptions were ardent but ludicrous, and his memory . . . was an inexhaustible fund of entertainment." . . . (He said) "They may doze away their days on the banks of the Schuykill; but, as for me, I go in the next vessel."[3]

Pleyel notices Carwin's effect upon Clara, who resents his

1. *Clara Howard*, 320, 389, 322.
2. Brown, Report of a Visit to Rockaway, in Dunlap, *op. cit.*, I, 66.
3. *Wieland*, 42, 43, 67, 68, 44-5, 64.

banter:

"It was a hint to rally me upon my prepossessions, and to amuse us with a thousand ludicrous anecdotes. . . . His conversation was occasionally visited by gleams of his ancient vivacity. . . . This would . . . call forth new railleries. His mirth, when exerted upon this topic, was the source of the bitterest vexation. . . . He was as whimsical and jestful as ever, but he was not happy. . . . The levity which had formerly characterized the behaviour of this man tended to obscure the greatness of his sentiments. . . . Pleyel was a devoted lover, but . . . a man of cold resolves and exquisite sagacity. To deceive him would be the sweetest triumph I had ever enjoyed (because of his distrust of her honor and his fierce upbraiding)."   (He said), "The spirit of mischievous gayety possessed me. I proceeded on tip-toe . . . till I was able to overlook your shoulder."[1]

Dr. Stevens investigated Arthur's boyhood and heard tales from a countrywoman:

"Here, in the chimney-corner, seated on a block, I found Arthur busily engaged in *knitting stockings!* I thought this a whimsical employment for a young active man. I told him so, . . . but he smiled in my face, and answered, without the least discomposure, 'Just as whimsical a business for a young active woman. Pray, did you never knit a stocking? . . . You see, though a man, I use your privilege, and prefer knitting yarn to threshing my brain with a book or the barn-floor with a flail.' . . . 'I wonder,' said I, contemptuously, 'you do not put on the petticoat as well as handle the needle.' . . . 'Do not wonder,' he replied, 'it is because I hate a petticoat encumbrance as much as I love warm feet'."[2]

The foolish colloquy of the ignorant continues in her report. Arthur, in speaking of his having left home and making up his bundle, says:

"My whole stock of linen consisted of three check shirts. Part of my winter evenings' employment, since the death of my mother, consisted in knitting my own stockings. Of these I had three pair."[3]

Brown uses a sort of humor when he has Dr. Stevens employ a bit of ridicule or sarcasm to open Arthur's eyes to his standing with Achsa:

---

1. *Wieland,* 81, 89, 96, 202, 229, 143.
2. *Arthur Mervyn,* II, 18.
3. *Ibid.,* I, 24.

"She can find nothing in you to esteem! . . . Incredible, indeed!
You, who are loathsome in your person, an idiot in your understanding, a villain in your morals! deformed! withered! vain,
stupid, and malignant. That such a one should choose *you* for an
idol!" to which Arthur replies, "Pray, my friend, jest not."[1]

This statement may smack of humor or irony: "He
was too old a bird to be decoyed into the net by *such* chaff,"[2]
speaking of Jamieson's financial dealings with Welbeck.

It has been said that the greatest novelist must be essentially a
humorist, just as the greatest romancer must be essentially a poet.
Certainly Brown was lacking in humor. He had tried his hand at
poetry and one can see poetical phraseology on many pages of his
novels, noticeably in his descriptions of nature.

The style of Brown's novels partakes of the style of those of his
contemporaries. He put great pains on his choice of words and on
the formation of his sentences, which emphasize the prevalent
pedantry of the times in letters exchanged between friends and
in the books that were written. His style contrasts singularly with
his natural simplicity of taste; and his care-free composition contrasts ofttimes with the preparation which he made in the study
of words and sentences. For Dunlap tells how Brown used to copy
in his Journal letters sent and received, besides other material,
to improve his composition. This policy of letter-copying is mentioned by Brown when he has Huntly write to Mary Waldegrave
of her brother's letters:

"The scheme of transcribing, for thy use, all the letters which,
during his short but busy life, I received from him . . . occurred
to my thoughts."[3]

On the whole Brown's words accord with the subject matter,—
solemn diction for morbid incidents, sentimental words for expression of feelings, heady words for psychological introspection.
Latin derivatives are used where Anglo-Saxon words would have
been just as forceful. Many unusual words and peculiar combi-
nations of words are to be found. The impression that the words
make remains with the reader rather than the words themselves,

---

1. *Arthur Mervyn,* II, 217.
2. *Ibid.,* II, 29.
3. *Edgar Huntly,* 135.

unless he rereads for the words' sake.

"His language was downright prose—the natural diction of the man himself—earnest—full of substantial good sense, clearness, and simplicity;—very sober and very plain, so as to leave only the *meaning* upon the mind. Nobody ever remembered the words of Charles Brockden Brown; nobody ever thought of the arrangement; yet nobody ever forgot what they conveyed."[1]

Some sentences are lengthy, run-on and awkward in grammatical construction. As if to offset the heaviness of such sentences, the author has fallen into the opposite extreme, using short, condensed statements, questions, exclamations and elliptical expressions, sometimes following one another in a series for a whole page, until they become monotonous.

The word *bombastic* was applied in a former chapter to Revolutionary-period writers' language. Like a goodly number of their predecessors, Brown does use inflated speech and magniloquent words when he wishes to make his characters seem impressive and learned. Their conversations often sound like set speeches. The language is then verbose, melodramatic or absurdly sentimental. At times one feels the incongruity between the strong, passionate, terrific enterprises of the characters and the pedantic language in which they are presented. He suddenly realizes that the author is doing the speaking.

"Simple, heart-felt expressions generally serve realism best," some one has said. Brown claimed to aim at realism; yet his fondness for long words and his avalanches of sentimental words are conspicuous on many a page. A few of his favorites are listed. *Ruminate* is used scores of times in place of think, which by inference has that meaning; but its frequent occurrence gives the impression that the speaker is putting on. Among words to watch, in alphabetical order, are adscititious, ambiguities, ambiguous, ambiguousness, animadvert, asperities, aspersions, assiduities, assiduous, attemper, austerities, bemazed, caprice, capricious, circuities, contumacious, conversible, deliquium, ductile (to her will), ebullitions, flagitious, immutable, incongruousness, indefatigable, inexhaustible, inexplicable, insuperability, interrogatories, lucubrations,

---

1. Neal, in *Blackwood's Magazine,* XVI, 421, October, 1824.

mellifluent, metamorphosed, mutable, mutate, mutations, nugatory, obsequiously, obsequiousness, opprobrious, panicful, pregnant (of meaning), presages, prognostics, prothonatory, punctilio, punctiliousness, pusillanimity, ratiocination, remediless, repugnant, sedulously, specious, spirituous, umbrage, undulation, unplausible.

Besides these there are hundreds of other words of four and five syllables and some of six and seven syllables. It is significant to recall how authors whom Brown influenced almost invariably used a score or more of his most unusual words. Nearly half of these listed words are found in *Caleb Williams,* showing either Godwin's influence or a common inheritance among writers.

Critics of Brown's language denounced it as melodramatic, involved, ornate, stiff and stilted. One would not want it otherwise, except that he did not take time to do as well as he knew—to substitute different words for those he uses so often. The so-called simple language of today would have made his writings out of place in his generation. A person need only read the fiction and the poetry of the years immediately succeeding Brown's short span of life to know that their language was far more ornate in expression, involved in construction grammatically and more impassioned in conversation than that of the present.

William H. Prescott, who wrote a memoir of Charles Brockden Brown for Jared Sparks' *American Biography* (1834), only twenty-four years after his death, in discussing his language, said:
"It must be remembered, too, that his novels were his first productions, thrown off with careless profusion, and exhibiting many of the defects of an immature mind, which longer experience and practice might have corrected."   He quoted a few of Brown's phrases—"fraught with the persuasion," "appended to it," "hoarser aspirations," "on recovering from deliquium," "fraught with the apprehension that my life was endangered," "his brain seemed to swell beyond its continent," "by a common apparatus, that lay beside my bed, I could instantly produce a light." "By this last circumlocution he meant to say that he had a tinderbox." Elsewhere Brown says, "a taper, a flint, tinder, and steel."

The spot-light might be turned on Prescott. By this circumlocutory remark, he said that Brown was born a Quaker:
"He was descended from a highly respectable family, whose ancestors were of that estimable sect, who came over with William Penn to seek an asylum, where they might worship their Creator unmo-

lested in the meek and humble spirit of their own faith."[1]

Here are additional typical Brownesque expressions. Arthur Mervyn struck his head and made a gash: "My ensanguined visage . . . my clothes were moistened with the unwelcome effusion." "My horse stood near, docile and obsequious." "This action was sufficiently conformable to my prognostics." "Washing was her trade"—the trade of kind Sarah Baxter—she "punctually visited the Dudleys once a week, and carried home with her whatever stood in need of ablution." "The voice was that of Constantia (after killing Ormond). It penetrated to my heart like an ice-bolt."

Corrode in literature is a pedigreed word. "The vexations and tumults of public affairs, which too frequently corrode the heart and vitiate the taste," are words of Mrs. Radcliffe. Godwin used "corrosive bitterness" in *Caleb Williams.* Clara Wieland says, when considering Carwin's words and Pleyel's suspicions, "But now my bosom was corroded by anxiety. I was visited by dread of unknown dangers." "Mr. Dudley's . . . features (were) corroded by his ceaseless melancholy." Brown said of himself, "Forget that any latent anguish or corroding sorrow" disquiet me, quoted more fully in Chapter I. After Brown, Godwin says, "corrode his vitals" and "corroding cancer" in *Mandeville,* and Maturin in *Fatal Revenge* says, "corroded mind" and "erosions of conscience."

Adders, vipers and scorpions slide through the pages of novels. "Viper in my bosom" of *Caleb Williams* becomes "adders lodged in my bosom" in *Wieland,* repeated by "viper in my bosom" in *Mandeville.* In *Tom Jones* (Fielding) many years earlier are the expressions: "a scorpion in her bosom" and "that wicked viper which I have so long nourished in my bosom." Lady Shelley in *The Last Man* carries on the tradition: "His praises were so many adder's stings infixed in my vulnerable breast," "and ideas, horrid as furies, cruel as vipers."

In relation to Brown's style, the words of Blake are appropriate: "His books, if they seem to us the crude expression of youth, are the expression of a literature's youth no less than the author's. . . . His language seems to us prolix and pretentious only if we go to

---

1. Prescott, "Memoir of Charles Brockden Brown," in Sparks, *Library of American Biography,* I, 119-80.

it direct, instead of from the reading of his British predecessors.
. . . Moreover, Brockden Brown was found remarkable—even in
his day and generation,—for writing in a style that is nervously
instinct with repressed energy. His sentences are short, like the
modern writer's, monotonously so; but experiment, even literary
experiment, is better than stagnation."[1]

---

    1. Blake, "Brockden Brown and the Novel," in *The Sewanee Review*
XVIII, 435.

CHAPTER V

INFLUENCE OF THE NOVELS

The recently-revived novels of Charles Brockden Brown were the first decidedly successful attempts at original fiction in America and are significant as illustrating the character and state of society on this side of the Atlantic. They were reprinted in England soon after their publication in America and immediately drew the admiration of Byron, Shelley and Scott. They were given earlier notice by the reviewers and critics of England than by those of America, though the criticism was often adverse. The early British magazines contain many flattering comments on the novels. For a quarter of a century after Brown's death, his novels were well known abroad and read with interest, profit and critical approval. The novels were reprinted in France and Germany, stated one commentator,—statement unverified except that the Library of Congress gives Edinburgh, Dublin and Paris imprints for *Edgar Huntley*, 1831. Although Brown received no pecuniary benefit from the reprints, yet four of his novels, *Wieland, Ormond, Arthur Mervyn* and *Edgar Huntley*, have a place in Bentley's *Library of Standard Romance* (1831). *Blackwood's Magazine* of 1824 gives Brown the first rank in American literature as an original writer and characteristically American and the first to obtain European celebrity.

Among the American critics who praised Brown highly were Prescott, Margaret Fuller, Duyckinck, Tuckerman, Griswold and others of that time. Their estimates of pioneer writers are still relied on, despite the remarks of Charles Angoff, with his backhanded cuff at the biographers:
"Brown's chief claim to our attention does not lie in what he did, but rather the preposterous importance which the older literary

historians have attached to him."[1]   "It seems hardly fair to sneer at the men and women who a century ago regarded Brown as a great and moving writer. His models were their standards, and they were right in perceiving that he measured well up to the Godwins and the Radcliffes. . . . They knew that their emotions had been deeply stirred, and that in some particulars at least the life around them had been faithfully set down."[2]

It was the struggles and undaunted hopes of this first of American novelists that encouraged that group of writers of the next generation to devote their lives to literature, art and science. They felt the influence of these previous efforts to create an American literature and were able to develop into mature artistic productions the materials of American life which Brown had treated fictionally amid the welter of political writings of the post-Revolutionary period. He foreshadowed the triumphs of Irving, Hawthorne, Cooper, Poe, of world-wide reputation, and of many authors of lesser renown, as Holland, Taylor, Tyler, Dana, Neal and Simms. His influence extended to writers across the water, among whom were Godwin, Shelley, Mrs. Shelley, Maria Edgeworth, Scott and Dickens.

In the preface to *The Early American Novel,* Lillie Deming Loshe said:
"The first forty years of American fiction (1789-1830) produced two novelists of real importance, Charles Brockden Brown and James Fenimore Cooper. . . . He (Brown) remains an interesting, but, as far as novel-writing is concerned, an isolated figure in the American literature of his time."
He had little affinity with his American predecessors and contemporaries and produced no real school of fiction for his followers, in the sense in which Cooper created a vogue among writers in the next thirty years. Richard Henry Dana said in the *Literary Gazette* (1827):
"For twenty years Brown's novels stood unrivalled—till 'Pioneers' and 'Pilot'—and traces of *Wieland* are to be found in Cooper."
Cooper was born in 1789 and did no literary work until ten years after Brown's death—until 1820,—leaving Brown the sole important novelist for thirty years, a generation nearly.

---

1. Angoff, *A Literary History of the American People,* 320.
2. Trent, *History of American Literature,* 211.

American novel writing was a series of experiments, unrelated to each other, rather than a steady growth from the first novel to Brown's novels. Like early writers he looked to England for his general forms, but, unlike them, because of his intense patriotism and plan to create an American literature, he employed native materials. The originality and power of his novels had little stimulation upon his successors. His greatest influence seems to have skipped over about twenty years until Cooper. A large number of now forgotten writers, to whom Brown gave an impulse to write, benefited in particulars from his novels. In listing the findings, in early novels, this writer has accepted the comments of Lillie Deming Loshe, *The Early American Novel,* by permission of Columbia University Press, because many of the books are unavailable, being rare copies in non-circulating collections.

As Brown was influenced by his predecessors, so he influenced his contemporaries and those following him. The influence of his novels upon American writers will be discussed first and then their influence upon European writers. Several works of fiction will be mentioned in time order and an endeavor made to show Brown's influence in each.

Constantia in *Ormond* has an heir in the title of a book by Helena Wells, published the year after Brown's: *Constantia Neville; or, the West Indian* (1800).
"Their aim (this book and *The Stepmother*), by pointing out the superior advantages of a religious education is to contrast the pernicious tendency of modern philosophy" (Loshe, p. 15).

In *The Gamesters; or, Ruins of Innocence* (1805) by Caroline Matilda Warren Thayer, Brown's influence can be detected, perhaps choosing the name of her heroine, Louisa, from *Wieland* and introducing Cato from *Arthur Mervyn*. The purpose of the book is to "blend instruction with amusement and at once to regale the imagination, and reform the heart" (Loshe, p. 14).
Brown says in To the Public of *Edgar Huntly*:
"The sources of amusement to the fancy and instruction to the heart that are peculiar to ourselves are equally numerous and inexhaustible."
The title "Gamsters" is given in some bibliographies.

Doesn't this title sound Brown-like: "the intricacies of the heart"? The author in *Jane Talbot* declares:

"I have always found an unaccountable pleasure in dissecting, as it were, my heart, uncovering, one by one, its many folds."
The above words are the alternate title of *Margaretta* (1807), published in Philadelphia six years after his novel, with no author designated (Loshe, p. 112).

One of Brown's contemporaries who followed in his "footsteps was George Watterston, whose first story, *The Lawyer, or man as he ought not to be* (1808), (is) a dreary tale of a very small and mean-spirited villain; *Glencarn, or the Disappointments of Youth* (1810) . . . shows more traces of Brown's influence, particularly in the use of ventriloquism" (Loshe, p. 51-2).
The hero's experiences in the den of robbers parallel Edgar Huntly's encounter with Indians in a cave.

The Asylum, or Alonzo and Melissa (1811), a romance by I. Mitchell, proclaims relationship to *Edgar Huntly*.
"He (the hero) crosses the moat (to the Gothic castle in which Melissa is immured) on a tree-trunk which the lightning had overthrown. . . . What is most striking about the tale . . . is the abundance and elaborateness of its description of scenery" (Loshe, p. 14), which is also characteristic of *Edgar Huntly*. Edgar Huntly provided his own tree-trunk bridge, which became a favorite makeshift to later authors, including Sedgewick, Scott and Bulwer-Lytton. Alonzo is a great friend of the brother of Melissa, whose name is Edgar. "They mourn together" over the lost Melissa.

It has been said that Brown was the first to begin the idealization of the Indian, in *Edgar Huntly*. A better word would be fictionization. Edgar says,
"I never looked upon or called up the image of a savage without shuddering," as upon those, "who long to feast on my heart's blood."
The only display of romantic sympathy that the author shows is in his word-portrait of the "shrivelled old woman," Queen Mab.

John Davis wrote in his Travels (p. 203):
"Arrived Philadelphia. I found Mr. B. (C. B.), who felt no remission of his literary diligence by a change of abode (from New York). He was ingratiating himself in the favor of the ladies by writing a new novel, and rivalling Lopez de Vega by the multitude of his works."[1]

---

1. Smyth, *Philadelphia Magazines and their Contributors*, II, c. 121.

In fact Brown completed two novels for the ladies in 1801: *Clara Howard* and *Jane Talbot.*

"Finding the author of Arthur Mervyn working in a dismal room, he (Davis) asked if Brown would not write with more facility were the prospect of the Lake of Geneva before him. . . . 'Sir,' said he, 'good pens, thick paper, and ink well diluted, would facilitate my composition more than the prospect of the broadest expanse of water, or mountains rising from the clouds' " (Loshe, p. 73-4).

Davis came from England to America in 1798 and became a prolific writer of tales, mostly American. In *Travels of Four Years and a Half in the United States of America,* published after his return to England (London, 1803), he recounts his American experiences. His chief enthusiasm was for the natural scenery, birds and animal life, like Edgar Huntly, and above all for the Indians, who

"want only an historian who would measure them by the standard of Roman ideas to equal in bravery and magnanimity those proud masters of the world."

His *The First Settlers of Virginia* pictures Indian manners and tells the story of Captain Smith and Princess Pocahontas, the work afterward condensed with this title. Brown, who seems to have inspired Davis, felicitated him in his Philadelphia *Monthly Magazine* and commends the subject

"which is pure American and which relates to two of the most interesting persons in Early American History."

In 1812, after his return to England, Davis wrote *The Post Captain* and *Walter Kennedy.*

"In the last of these he returns to the forest and the Indians . . . An Irish youth crossed in love . . . seeks peace of mind in the wilds of America, finally making his home among the Indians and marrying an Indian princess" (Loshe, p. 73, 75, 77).

Edgar Huntly is a story of the natural forest and of the Indians. Clithero is an Irish lad, who had lost the girl he loved and escaped into the wilds of America to flee the face of man and end his days in solitude.

"Several years after the publication of Davis' Indian tales appeared one of the most remarkable products of patriotic fervor and humanitarian zeal that ever celebrated the virtues of the guileless savage. *The History of the Female American, or the Extraordinary Adventures of Unca Eliza Winkfield, Compiled by Herself*" (Loshe,

p. 77-9).
Queen Mab is Brown's only female Indian. She could well furnish the inspiration for this romance or history.

The author of *The Old Oaken Bucket*, Samuel Woodworth, wrote *The Champion of Freedom, or the Mysterious Chief*, a romance of the War of 1812, in which a voice proceeding from the body of a fallen Miami Chief assured the father of the hero, "You have a son to redeem your vow"—that he would not relinquish his sword except with his life.   His sword hand was stricken off. Like the apparition of Carwin to Clara Wieland and his mysterious voices to warn and aid in distress, the similar feature of this tale is the voice of the majestic form of the dead Indian warrior who foretold the hero's birth and in times of stress and crisis always was heard to exhort and admonish or reprove (Loshe, p. 79-80).

"Neal said of the popular Irish novelist, Maturin, that he was 'haunted by the spirit of Byron and the Devil himself at the same time.'   By adding the spirit of Maturin to these two worthies, one might obtain the ghostly trio which followed the steps of Neal" (Loshe, p. 92).
Of Neal's first novel, *Keep Cool* (1817), she said:
"A portion of the action passes among Indians, into whose tribe the hero has been adopted.   Neal sympathized passionately with their wrongs in being driven from their lands, and a thirst for human gore was never any setback in his estimation."
In several of his novels, Neal introduced the American Indian. His next novel, *Logan* (1822) was more intentionally an Indian tale.
"It is as wild and incoherent as *Keep Cool* and far more bloody. . . . The complications of the tale are countless and totally unreasonable."
Brother Jonathan, or the New Englanders (1825), a novel of 1300 goodsized, solidly-printed pages,
"started out to be a study of New England customs, . . . but this intention was abandoned in favor of a man of mystery, an avenger of blood, an Indian Chief, a prophet, and a general incoherence of mystery" (Loshe, p. 92).

Neal counted Brown one of the three American novelists who were original; and he imitated Brown by adopting the Indian theme, as he said.   The first work that Neal seriously did was to index *Niles' Register*, concerning which he burst out:

"I labored upon the average sixteen hours a day . . . for full four months. . . . I, a poet, glowing with inward fire, and almost ready for a display of spontaneous combustion."
It looks as if Neal borrowed the term and another idea from Brown, even if he did not actually demonstrate it.

One other prose writer, who combined historical and Indian material, and two poets will be mentioned before Cooper with his full-fledged Indian romances.

N. M. Hentz, the author of *Tadeuskund, the last king of the Lenape* (1825), in subject matter seems to follow Brown; and his method is more complicated than Cooper's, whose *Pioneers* (1823) was his first Indian romance. Hentz's descriptions of the forest are of Pennsylvania, where Brown laid the scene of *Edgar Huntly* and his Indians are the Lenape, the same as Brown's Lenni-len-napee, or Delawares. The chief interest of the story is the warfare between the Indians and the troop of volunteer Indian fighters. The opponents of Brown's Indians are volunteers, also. Queen Mab is the last of the tribe as portrayed in *Edgar Huntly,* just as Tadeuskund is the last king. She exercised all the rights of a king. Tadeuskund is a friend of the Whites, but he is unable to restrain his people. Queen Mab was believed to have incited her kin against the Whites on their last annual visit to her. Possibly her power of restraint over them was gone.

Philip Freneau (1752-1832), like Cooper after him, treats in his poetry of the nobler and more romantic qualities of the Indians. He must have been a friend of Brown or, at least, an acquaintance. He lived in Philadelphia from the time of his graduation from Princeton, 1771, the date of Brown's birth, till 1810 probably, all of the latter's lifetime. He conducted *The Freeman's Journal* and was the only editor who remained at his post during the summer of 1793, the year of the yellow fever epidemic commemorated in *Arthur Mervyn,* whose alternate title is *Memoirs of the Year 1793.* Freneau is known as the "father of American poetry," as Brown is known as the "father of American fiction." He is unread today except for a few poems, among the best of which are two of his five about the Indians, *The Dying Indian* and *The Indian Burying Ground.* There is no concrete evidence that Freneau influenced Brown or even the reverse. A possible relation between them was suggested in Chapter I in Brown's contemplation of an epic on Columbus. Freneau was the first to touch upon the Indian poetically; and he pioneered in describing genuine native scenery. Brown introduced both subjects into his novels, but he did not glamorize them.

James K. Paulding (1779-1860), born eight years after Brown, lived in New York City and probably was known to Brown. He began to write about seven years after *Edgar Huntly* (1801) was published and wrote numerous novels and other prose and poetry. He mentions Indians frequently and his treatment is as Brown's, at least in this excerpt from *Passage Down the Ohio*:

> " 'Twas evening now . . .,
> Yet still they durst not seek the fearful shores,
> Lest watchful Indian crew should silent creep,
> And spring upon and murder them in sleep."

This recalls Edgar Huntly's swimming the river to elude Indians. Twenty shots were aimed at him from the precipice above when he raised his head above the surface. They were his friends who were searching for him; they mistook him for a fleeing Indian and showered him with bullets. Paulding was an ardent patriot, and the most noteworthy element in his writings was, perhaps, their distinctive national character, which was also the most notable element in Brown's political writings earlier. Following Brown, he made American scenery and American frontier character the background of his works. *The Backwoodsman* (1818), a narrative poem of six books, is devoted to American scenery, incident and sentiment.

The value of Indians as a literary asset was seen by Brown, who was seeking for some new thing that was typically American. He had a keener mind and a wider knowledge of literature than any of his predecessors and contemporaries in fiction. The picturesqueness of the scenery of Pennsylvania lent an appropriate setting to the Indians of the forest. They were thought of as shapes of terror rather than of grandeur, as they afterward became to writers who took their subject from him. To moderns so accustomed to out-of-door scenes, it is almost unimaginable how new were tales of Indians, savage attacks by them and by wild beasts and colonial Indian warfare.

"Although all these early attempts at historical romances and Indian tales are, with the exception of *Edgar Huntly,* always trivial and often absurd, they have a certain appeal to the interest of the modern reader. . . . The earliest American fiction had looked backward, finding its models in the school of Richardson and his contemporaries, already passing as a literary fashion. The stories of Gothic terrors and of political speculation merely kept abreast of the fashions of the day. But these tales of history and of Indian adventure look forward, however feebly and short-sightedly, to another great period of fiction" (Loshe, p. 80-1).

The influence of Brown upon Cooper will follow, although out of exact time order, to keep the progress of the Indian tales together. Brown aimed at realistic portraiture, realistic to him at least. For the Gothic elements of the Old World, he substituted the perils of settling the western wilderness, incidents of Indian hostility and cougars, in *Edgar Huntly.* The adventures are intriguing, animated and affrighting. They have local settings. In this respect the author anticipated and foreshadowed the more elaborate and skilful efforts of Cooper and Scott. However, they are objective, rather than subjective in their habits of thought. Instead of giving profound psychological studies, they give intimate detailed descriptions and racy narratives. It has been said that *Edgar Huntly* is objective and that, in contrast to the three novels preceding it, the plot-problems are physical rather than psychological. This writer grants the lavish use of more objective material. Nevertheless, the theme is not this outward display. A man thinks he has committed murder. Heredity is the theme, which would act with no scenery, no panther, no Indians.

X. Y. Z. accused two of plagiarism:

"Neal and Cooper also both stole his (Brown's) catamounts, and played the devil with his Indians. Neal is content with catching the idea and working it up. But Cooper steals the broom ready made. Neal is altogether too much of a poet; he overdoes everything. Cooper—the only catamount, that ever he ventured upon, was a tame one, escaped out of Brown's clutches, first, with his nails pared; and out of Neal's office with a bell on."[1]
This contrast was made by Neal himself, who signed his sketches

---

1. Neal, in *Blackwood's Magazine,* XVI, 421-6, Oct., 1824.

X. Y. Z.

The panther, or cougar, rapacious and daring as introduced by Brown in his romance, caused the subsequent use of it in Cooper's *Pioneers*, but Cooper's panther is partly tamed just as his Indians are partly civilized and idealized.

"They (Elizabeth and Louisa) saw the fierce front and glaring eyes of a female panther, fixed on them in horrid malignity, and threatening to leap. (Louisa fainted.)   A quarter-grown cub . . . now appeared, dropping from the branches of a sapling, . . . approached the dog, . . . exhibiting a strange mixture of the playfulness of a kitten and the ferocity of its race, . . . fell directly before the mastiff.   There was a moment of fearful cries and struggles, but they ended almost as soon as commenced, by the cub appearing in the air, hurled from the jaws of Brave. . . . (Then followed a struggle between the old panther and the mastiff, which was killed.)   Elizabeth now lay wholly at the mercy of the beast. . . . The eyes of the monster and the kneeling maiden met, for an instant, when the former stooped to examine her fallen foe; next to scent her luckless cub. From the latter examination, it turned, however, with its eyes apparently emitting flashes of fire, its tail lashing its sides furiously, and its claws projecting inches from her broad feet."[1]
At this critical moment, Natty Bumpo arrived and dispatched the panther. Not only did Cooper try to emulate Brown with his panther, but he borrowed his Louisa, as here and elsewhere. He casts a veil of ideality over the descriptions of his panther, his Indians and nature, which he had received from his predecessor with eye-witness forthrightness.

"The Indians of Cooper are not like those of Brockden Brown— mere streaks of red and of savagery upon the page; no glimmerings of kindlier humanities shine through them."[2]
This critic does scant justice to Brown in his estimate from the slighted reading he has done of the novels and the meager space he allows for his summary in comparison with most other critics.

The Blackwood's critic denounced Cooper's habit of giving accurate details of costumes and localities and said that a general account would have been far better.

---

1. Cooper, *Pioneers,* Chapter XXVIII.
2. Mitchell, *American Lands and Letters,* I, 236-7.

"It now turns out that this very habit has made Cooper's Indian a permanent and distinct figure in literature, while the so-called Indians of his predecessor, Charles Brockden Brown, were merely shadowy and unreal."[1]

Brown treats of Indians in their natural, uncivilized state, actuated to killing and pillage in revenge for the wrongs inflicted upon them, which is true to the ugly realism of American-Indian relations. He makes them neither too crafty nor too successful. They are savages who break into murderous revolt and are put down by superior civilization and order. They are untamed and are described in stern words with no sentimental tone. Nowhere does Brown give intimations of a generous nature, which Cooper discerned and which has since been recognized as a fact; yet he ascribes to them a certain amount of dignity and resourcefulness. A likeness between some of the principal characters of Cooper and those of Brown lies in their loneliness, their being set apart from their fellows—Leatherstocking, Chingachgook and Uncas. the "Last of the Mohicans"—and Deb, or Queen Mab, of the Lennilennapee in *Edgar Huntly,* the last of her tribe.

"Even after the rise of Cooper, it was long before some judges acknowledged him as Brown's superior. . . . In living among his own people and writing tales about them, the second of these writers (Brown) conceived his literary labors in what must today be recognized in a spirit wholly modern . . To its age, its execution was modern in no less degree. . . . Without losing sight of the highly colored—even morbid imaginativeness of Brown (indicated by the sub-title of *Edgar Huntly*), honor is due him as the painter of American scenes, the chronicler of American manners."[2]

"While so many men of genius disgrace themselves by envyings and detraction, this group ("The Chanting Cherubs") was executed by the first American Sculptor (Horatio Greenough), for one (J. F. Cooper) who, with C. B. Brown, stands at the head of American Novelists,"[3]
said Richard Henry Dana Sr. (1787-1879), a significant imitator of Brown.

---

1. Higginson & Boynton, *A Reader's History of American Literature,* 99.

2. Blake, "Brockden Brown and the Novel," in *The Sewanee Review.* XVIII, 432-3, Oct., 1910.

3. Dana Sr., *Poems and Prose Writings* (1833), 125.

Both in his verse and in his prose, Dana championed the romantic school. His early short novels, *Tom Thornton* and *Paul Felton*, were published first, with several others, in New York (1821-2), under the series title, *The Idle Man,* concerning which his editor informed him that he was "writing himself into debt." This series resembles Brown's series, *The Man at Home,* written some years previously.

In these novels, Dana makes free use of questions as abrupt sentences and causes his chief characters to analyze their feelings. An air of gloom and evil premeates the whole. Each story opens with sad and painful details, continues with sorrowful, bitter incidents and closes with the deaths of the principal actors. Like a few of Brown's characters, both those that exert some dreadful force over others and those that are wrought upon seem driven by some superior power and were said by one critic (Nichol) to have frightened rather than to have amused their readers.

Isaac Beckford in *Tom Thornton,* like Welbeck in *Arthur Mervyn,* from whom he may have received part of his name, gets control over a youth and outfits him with clothes. Welback says to Arthur,

"I have meditated to benefit as well as to injure you; but I do not desire that your demeanour should conform to any other standard than justice."[1]

His story is one of clamor for wealth, deceit, forgery, imprisonment and death. Beckford squanders wealth to sate his hate and lust and takes Tom, a former school fellow, as a dupe to his desires:

"What, my young *protege!*" . . . "soon I shall be a free man," he boasts, "and he must minister to my pleasure, as must every one whom I favour. I must see that he is brought up in the way that he should go. With a deliberate step and plotting mind," he welcomed Tom.   "Tom's brave, fiery, open temper, made young Beckford's sly, cautious and vicious disposition seem despicable and weak even to himself, and he was fixed upon revenge. He was one of that race who carry a hell within them. . . . though he had determined to make Tom a mere instrument for his own end, he hated him for that very preference which had been shown to him."

---

1. *Arthur Mervyn,* I, 108.

Thus he compassed the moral ruin of Tom, through riot, excess, drinking, gambling, loans, which ultimately led him to imprisonment for debt, violence and an agonizing death, and also of his fair cousin Fanny, Tom's wife, by threats, wiles, wasted fortune and betrayal. The evil life of Tom did not burn itself out alone; the grief of his father and mother over him caused their premature deaths, and his thirst for revenge made him a murderer of Isaac who defaulted a duel and whose body was never found.[1]

Paul Felton closely resembles *Wieland,* in plan and hero. Wieland was a man of gloomy, sensitive nature, who, in constant contemplation of the mysteries of this life and of the life after death, became melancholy, a religious maniac and the murderer of his wife and children. Good and evil spirits were a source of much speculation with him; and Carwin with his bilinguistic power, impersonating the Supreme Being, was the immediate cause of his madness and lent a tone of impending ruin to the story. Paul Felton, a youth of retired habits and moody, distrustful, self-accusing, passionate, intellectual disposition, questioned his own nature and became "a self-tormenter."

". . . the material world was a grand and beautiful mystery. . . . It was power, and intellect, and love calling out the sympathies of his being, and causing him to feel the living Presence throughout the whole. Material became intellectual beauty with him. . . . 'Must I only,' he cried, 'of all the works of God, be an outcast?' "

"As he advanced in life his passions waxed stronger, and he craved an object about which they might live and grow."
Paul meets Esther Waring, a beautiful girl of cheerful disposition, and soon they are married. Speaking to her,
"His voice was low, and thrilling, and admonitory," like Carwin's; "the affections (of Paul) were in motion; and, for a while, the sense that he was in fellowship with his kind thrilled through him with rapture."

Paul's oft-returning melancholy, his abstraction of mind and his distrust of his influence proved a source of mysterious foreboding to Esther and left an impression on her mind of some dread event awaiting her.

---

1. Dana Sr., "Tom Thornton," in *Poems and Prose Writings* (1833), 125, 179, 182, 188.

"But, so much as I doubt my powers to touch another's heart, so much the more, . . . must I have assurance of her love."
"No, Esther; but the very intenseness of love calls up misgivings."   "Yet there was something fearful and ominous to her in his gloom."   "My heart is fuller of joy than I well know how to bear—it aches to speak it to you," Paul confides.

A former friend of Esther, Frank Ridgely, calls and chats of his interests during two years away. Esther never loved him, but Paul is jealous of seeing her pleasure in meeting him.
"This was a poisonous thought to take root in a mind like his." (Esther enjoyed society; Paul did not.)   "Her gay laugh and cheerful voice were in some states of his feelings, like the hissing of an adder in his ear."   "He turned away, not only melancholy, but dissatisfied and doubting."

A wood near Paul's home was believed haunted by the Devil.
"And a foolhardy boy who had once been a birds'-nesting there, was ever afterwards looked on with suspicion, as . . . belonging to the Evil One," who instigated the boy, Abel, to steal crows' eggs.   A friend asked, "And the crow is the Devil's bird, Tom, isn't it?"   Another said, "O, Abel, you've been to that wood, and made yourself over to Him."
"He (Abel) believed himself the victim of some Demonic Power." Paul often frequented the grove and rocky heath and met the starving outcast boy. He furnished Abel food and from that time felt himself impelled in all his acts by the Master of the boy and that evil spirits were in strife for his allegiance.
"Twinned with me in misery, and bound to crime by chains that can't be broken, I'll feel a fellow's kindness for you while we're here."

Becoming more distraught in mind, Paul says to Esther:
" 'There's a fever here,' striking his forehead rapidly with his fingers, 'that must be cooled quickly, or 'twill sear the brain up', " like the elder Wieland's. Passing near his looking-glass, Paul started back.
" 'Have they not only changed my soul,' cried he, 'but transformed this body, too, that the world may know and shun me'," as Brown transformed Wieland.

Rushing madly out of doors one evening, Paul is sought for by Esther and others. Frank came to call and went to bring Esther back to the house. Paul sees him supporting her arm in arm.

Another evening he watches the house and sees Esther in the arms of a man, whom he thinks Frank. It was her father. Growing more distrustful of his wife's fidelity, he believes he is commissioned by the prevailing Evil One to kill her. He enters the house at night, finds Esther peacefully sleeping and stabs her in her heart with a knife. Paul falls forward on her bed and then to the floor dead. Abel is found dying on Paul's grave the evening of his burial.[1]

Wieland and *Paul Felton* are alike in that each gives a history of the soul. The heroes differ in that Wieland acts as if divinely impelled by God and Paul, as if supernaturally driven by the Devil. Wieland kills out of devotion to God; Paul, out of jealousy and revenge. Of the two stories, Brown's is the more masterly because he has succeeded in making readers sympathize with his hero in the growing disorder of his mind and perceive that the disorder is a natural result of inner soul devolution. Carwin's deceptions are extraneous and lack force as causes of Wieland's insanity, but rather corroborate what Wieland has already decided upon. Paul Felton's insanity seems the result of his own violent passions and uncontrolled thoughts, in league with actual supernatural beings. It is a hurried madness due partly to external circumstances.

The conversation of Wieland with God and with his wife runs on thus:

" 'Call her hither, and here let her fall.' . . . My wife! O God! substitute some other victim. Make me not the butcher of my wife. My own blood is cheap. . . . Undone! No; my duty is known, and I thank my God that my cowardice is now vanquished, and I have power to fulfil it. . . . I brought thee hither to fulfil a divine command. I am appointed thy destroyer, and destroy thee I must."   And his wife Catharine makes these replies: "My friend! my soul's friend. . . . Do I not merit to partake with thee in thy cares? Am I not thy wife? . . . Oh, Wieland! Wieland! . . . I see it; it is too plain; thou art undone,—lost to me and to thyself. . . . What mean you? Why talk you of death? Bethink yourself, Wieland, . . . and this fit will pass. Oh, why came I hither? Why do you drag me hither? . . . Surely Wieland,

---

1. Dana Sr., "Paul Felton," in *Poems and Prose Writings* (1833), 273-347.

thou dost not mean it. Am I not thy wife? and wouldst thou kill me? Thou wilt not; and yet—I see—thou art Wieland no longer! A fury resistless and horrible possesses thee:—spare me—spare—help—help—"
The colloquy occupies several pages,—Wieland with the spirit, with Catharine and with his sister Clara.[1]

Do not these passages sound verily like the words of Wieland and his wife?

"Thoughts, call you them? Visions, shadows, horrible, horrible shadows! Speak not of them; call them not round me again. . . . No 'tis not all dark; there's light beyond. . . . There they are, passing away, till swallowed up in the very brightness! Now they come again, hosts, myriads, and with the speed of fire!—The darkness, and the evil ones, too, are flying—they are gone! 'O, spare me, spare me!' he groaned out, throwing himself down and beating the ground madly with his arms. 'Let her die, if ye've ordained it so, but not by me! not by me!' (The fit of agony had passed.) ' 'Tis all in vain. I yield me to you, be it when you will' . . . The hour is coming, Esther—it breathes upon me now, when death will part us, and we shall never meet more, through all eternity. . . . Weep not for me; it can avail me nothing; the doom is on me.— Nay, ask me not what I mean. . . . I must be alone awhile. . . . Do not linger so. The time is coming when you would fain flee from me, and may not. . . . They hunt and drive me to the deed; and when 'tis done, will snatch the abhorred soul to fire and tortures. . . . Peace, peace, your promptings, ye that put me to this deed,— drive me not mad! Am I not about it?"   And Esther answers: "Paul, my husband, what is it? Why do you look so wild and lost? Rouse yourself; tell me what has happened. . . . Merciful Heaven! save him, save him! let him not go mad! Do with me what Thou wilt, but spare my husband! . . . O, my wretched, lost husband! . . . Is there no help for you? Will not Heaven have pity on you? . . . Why do you glare upon me so? Do you not know me, Paul?—Esther—your wife?"[2]

An author who took ideas from Brown's novels for her tales was Catharine Maria Sedgewick (1789-1867). In *A New England Tale* (1822), the hero, Mr. Lloyd, wishes to cultivate and employ a

1. *Wieland*, 187, 190-1.
2. Dana Sr., "Paul Felton," in *Poems and Prose Writings* (1833), 321-373.

"talent for doing good." "All that was left of Jane's hopes and plans was the consciousness of having acted right—from right motives." These quotations call to mind the good deeds and right intentions of Arthur Mervyn.

Comparable to the peculiar Indian character, Old Deb, in *Edgar Huntly,* is the wandering, half-insane vagrant, Crazy Bet. "She was often seen by moonlight, wandering in the churchyard, plucking the nettles from the graves, and wreathing the monuments with ground pine. She would watch for whole nights by the side of a grave in her native village, where twenty years before were deposited the remains of her lover, who was drowned the day before they were to have been married. She would range the woods, and climb to the very mountain's-top, to get sweet flowers." She aids others, does errands on occasion and goes from one family of friends to another for shelter and food. One night she conducts Jane, the young heroine, at midnight, through narrow passes in the mountains, by rocks, streams, caves and caverns, similar to scenes described in *Edgar Huntly.* Previously, Jane had crossed over a stream on a slippery tree-trunk fallen across as a foot-bridge, —similar to the panther's and Edgar's walk across a chasm. Crazy Bet and Jane visit a dying woman, Lucy, and her babe, taken into their hut by an aged couple. "Old John, who believes in the Author of nature" ("the Author of my being," Wieland says), discovered the woman, seduced by David Wilson, a young scoundrel, who had abandoned her and their child, as Welbeck in *Arthur Mervyn* had abandoned Clemenza and their child, whom Arthur discovers.

Miss Sedgewick transforms her chief characters largely by her comments,—not by self-revelation and psychologically, as Brown does. Deceit and duplicity are terms applied to David. He robs his mother of $500, after being involved with two fellows in forgery, altering bills, and threatens suicide, using almost the exact words of Clithero in *Edgar Huntly*: I will be "beyond the reach of human tribunals." He is caught when engaged in a mail-coach hold-up, is imprisoned, escapes, goes to Europe and writes his mother, cursing her for all his troubles: "You taught me . . . that there was no difference between doing right and doing wrong, in the sight of the God you worship; you taught me that I could do nothing acceptable to him. . . . I have only acted out the nature totally depraved (your own words) that he gave me."

David seems patterned after Arthur Wiatte in the same novel, save for the Calvinistic doctrine, which undermined his and Wieland's characters.

David's mother, Jane's aunt, like Wieland, is very religious, pious and self-deluded, but she is a hypocrite, a pharisaical, canting bigot of the old orthodoxy. All her children

"produced such fruits as might be expected from her culture. The timid among them had recourse to constant evasion and to the meanest artifices to hide the violation of laws which they hated; and the bolder were engaged in a continual conflict with the mother, in which rebellion often trampled on authority."

She murdered their minds worse than Wieland murdered his wife and children. Martha married secretly and soon dies; Elvira, against her mother's command, ran off and married a no-count French actor; David is depictured a deceiver, seducer, forger, hold-up and an escaped convict.

These words of Jane to Mrs. Wilson sound like Brown's through the voice that tried to undeceive Wieland after his murders:

"Oh, Aunt, do not—do not, for your soul's sake, indulge any longer in this horrible delusion. ("Oh, brother! spare me! spare thyself," says Clara; "Man of errors! cease to cherish thy delusion," commands the voice.) You have more children . . . be pitiful to them; be merciful to your own soul. You deceive yourself ("Not heaven or hell, but thy senses, have misled thee to commit these acts," says the voice.). You may deceive others, but God is not mocked . . . her faith, her prayers, her pretences, her meeting going, were nothing . . . in the sight of Him, who cannot be deceived by the daring hypocrisies, the self-delusions, the refuges of lies, of his creatures."   Mrs. Wilson is transformed from worse to worse all her life until "betrayed by the secret gnawings of her conscience"; but "she quelled her convictions."

"There is nothing more subtle, more inveterate, than a habit of self-deception. . . . I don't like lip-prayers—it is nothing but a mockery," declares Sukey, Mrs. Wilson's negro housemaid.

Jane Elton is a character in direct contrast to Mrs. Wilson. Like Jane Talbot, after whom she may have been named, she was left a penniless orphan, who becomes an unwelcome inmate of her rich aunt's home, is reminded often of her state, given much work to do, is led along step by step to perfection, by the exacting discipline, severity and oppression of her aunt and by patience, suffering unjust suspicion and temptation on her part, until Old John says of her, she is "the wisest, and discreetest, and gentlest." Jane Talbot was trained in a strictly orthodox way by her wealthy foster-mother, Mrs. Fielder. Miss Sedgewick's Jane was truly religious and finally becomes a Quaker to marry Mr. Lloyd, because of the Quaker "custom of restricting their family alliances within the limits of their own sect," a statement made also by Brown in *Arthur Mervyn* (I, 125). Brown was brought up in the Quaker faith and suffered from a disregard of this custom. Mr. Lloyd, like Brown, pondered what course to pursue,—law-writing it is later called.[1]

With "indefatigable" "assiduity," Miss Sedgewick may be said to follow Brown's lead. *A Berkshire Tradition* is another story of seduction and wrong. William Freeman goes off to war, leaving in his home a very young wife, his sister and a tutor for his six-year-old son, Stanton Oakley, a friend, a scholarly man, beautiful—"an idle man—with all the qualities pleasing in the eyes of a young woman." Like William Colvill, a teacher in Arthur Mervyn's home, who betrays his sister, Lucy Freeman is betrayed. William, Lucy and perhaps Stanton for Stanley are Brown names. Oakley goes to Europe and sends to William one thousand pounds sterling to ease his conscience of the wrong, which William rejects. The child born dies at one year of age and Lucy lives four years of unreality, thinking all people are shadows.[2]

The White Scarf, in which good and evil spirits occur, is the story of a young girl, who finally marries an Italian after escaping from an abduction plot by French "persons of rank."[3] Lettie, from her name Violette, is similar to Brown's Letty; and also her Fanny McDermott in *Fanny McDermott* to his Fanny. Fanny is orphaned, young, enticed, forsaken by her seducer Stafford and with their child dies,—the mother with a terrible burning in her head, somewhat like the elder Wieland's brain "scorched to cinders."[4]

1. Sedgewick, *A New England Tale,* 17-242.
2. Sedgewick, "A Berkshire Tradition," in *A New England Tale,* 245-294.
3. Sedgewick, "The White Scarf," in *A New England Tale,* 295-334.
4. Sedgewick, "Fanny McDermott," in *A New England Tale,* 335-388.

The title of Miss Sedgewick's novel, *The Poor Rich Man and the Rich Poor Man,* published sixteen years after Brown's death, definitely links her work to his. Doesn't this title easily connect her novel with his first plan for fiction writing? *Sophia and Jessy* was an early uncompleted romance, composed of letters written and received by Sophia, the rich girl, full of leisure, restless and sometimes of arrogant manner, and by Jessy, the poor girl, meek, quiet, humble, hard-worked, caring for an invalid mother, refusing to marry Courtland because of family duties and anguish over the death of a sister.

"There is that maketh himself rich, yet hath nothing; there is that maketh himself poor, yet hath great riches,"
is the theme of her story. The poor man's charities, which consist of doing kindnesses, are contrasted with the skimpy gifts of money forced grudgingly from the rich man. Several names are significant. Susan May and her father Philip may have been named from Susan in *Arthur Mervyn* and Philip in *Clara Howard,* Louisa from Louisa in *Wieland,* Beckwith, a partial use of Welbeck in *Arthur Mervyn* and Courtland from Courtland in *Ormond.* Welbeck was a forger and finally imprisoned, abandoning Clemenza and their child; Mr. Smith in Miss Sedgewick's story was a forger, imprisoned and leaving Paulina, dying of consumption, and their child and a mysterious black trunk, like the trunk of Craig in *Ormond* and the chest of Clithero in *Edgar Huntly.*

Neal, in speaking of the *Adventure of Sam, the Black Fisherman* in Irving's *Tales of a Traveller* (1824), asserted that
"Irving has purloined a head and a scene, from Brown, probably without knowing it; as Brown purloined from Godwin. . . . In *Wieland,* there is a description of a murderer's face; Irving makes direct use of this head, in a negro, looking over the rock; and, indirectly, in his account of the picture, which, in its frightful distinctness, is not only very like Brown, but wholly unlike Irving."[1]

The "Tales" by Geoffrey Crayon, Gent., consist of shortened, imported German tales and some American. Of them, Cross said: "Irving was too much of a common-sense realist to deal with superstition. His moving portraits, phantom faces, and dancing

---

1. Neal, in *Blackwood's Magazine,* XVI, 421-6, 1824. (Signed X. Y. Z.)

furniture were in intention comic, and always carried an obvious explanation,"[1] which, of course, is true of Brown's mysteries.

"Irving met Brown and was impressed by his patience and aspiration. He acknowledged his indebtedness to this early fictionist for an example of courage and literary purpose."[2]
He drew inspiration to persist in literary endeavors and to expand the mental horizon of Americans by acquainting them with foreign culture.

Dana said, "what . . . would Mr. Crayon have brought to pass, had he . . . attempted to write like that extraordinary man, Charles Brockden Brown?"[3]

A number of passages in Irving's tales might be chosen to show that he had read the novels of his compatriot. This tends to prove Brown's spectacular influence,—perhaps, to arouse curiosity as he wished. In *Notoriety,* Irving averred:
"There is a constant demand in the fashionable world for novelty; every nine days must have its wonder, no matter of what kind. At one time an author; at another, a fire-eater; at another, a composer, an Indian juggler, or an Indian chief."
Maybe he had Brown in mind for the author and his Indians in *Edgar Huntly* as a chief.

The face in question was of Carwin whom Clara Wieland glimpsed when she revisited her deserted house at dusk.
"The face was turned towards me. Every muscle was tense; the forehead and brows were drawn into vehement expression; the lips were stretched as in the act of shrieking, and the eyes emitted sparks, which, no doubt, if I had been unattended by a light, would have illuminated like the coruscations of a meteor."[4]
In *The Mysterious Picture,* a face is made use of by Irving:
"It consisted merely of a head, or rather a face, staring full upon me with an expression that was startling—an accursed visage, with its horrible and mysterious expression still gazing and gazing upon me."
The owner had put one of his guests, chosen by lot, into the room where the picture was. In *The Black Fisherman,* a group of sup-

---

1. Cross, *Development of the English Novel,* 160.
2. Marble, *Heralds of American Literature,* 318.
3. Dana Sr., "The Writer of 'The Idle Man' to his old friends," in *Poems and Prose Writings* (1833), 147.
4. *Wieland,* 166-7; also, 199, 213.

posed murderers looked up from digging a grave to behold
"the round, black head of Sam (a negro) just above them. His
white eyes strained half out of their orbits. . . . He scrambled
over rock and stone, through brush and brier; rolled down banks
like a hedge-hog; scrambled up others like a catamount," probably
a reference to Brown's panther.

In *Wolfert Webber,* the story of a Dutchman, at a rural inn, the
favorite resort of the Dutch, after a certain explosion,
"an old negro's bald head thrust in at the door, his white goggle
eyes contrasting with his jetty poll, which was wet with rain, and
shone like a bottle," suggesting the gleam from Clara's candle.

Two of the *Tales of a Traveller* seem to be patterned after
Wieland in character hero and in means of transformation: *Adventure
of the German Student* and *Wolfert Webber.* The student
wandered in speculative doctrines until he thought "there was an
evil influence hanging over him," as Wieland wrought himself
into believing. He became haggard and desponding. His friends
discovered the mental malady preying upon him and determined
that the best cure was a change of scene. He went to Paris. While
returning home late one night near the scaffold of the guillotine,
he discovered the form of a woman and took her home. She apparently
died. He lifted her from the bed. The police were summoned
and exclaimed, "She was guillotined yesterday." The
student became possessed with the frightful belief that an evil spirit
had re-animated the dead body to ensnare him. He went distracted
and died in a madhouse. Wieland lifted the corpse of his wife and
laid it on the bed and gazed upon it. He was judged insane and imprisoned.
He escaped and killed himself.

The hero in *Wolfert Webber* is changed from a substantial
cabbage-grower, like his family for generations, into an almost
insane person over his cupidity for gold, thought to have been
concealed by pirates. He first upturned all his cabbages, in vain.
Listening at the inn to tales of a chest and a supposed drowned
buccaneer, his cupidity was once more awakened by the possibility
of at length getting trace of some of this lurking wealth. Indeed,
his infected fancy tinged everything with gold. He was now in a
worry of trepidation and impatience, fearful lest some rival adventurer
should get a scent of the buried gold. He decided privately to
seek out the black fisherman. They went to a cove and located the

place, known by a ring to which boats were tied up and three crosses, but decided to wait until some dark night.

"The leading anxiety which had hitherto absorbed every feeling, being now in some measure appeased, fancy began to wander and conjure up a thousand shapes and chimeras as he returned through the haunted region." *Chimera* is a Brown word.

Webber became really ill and saw the apparition of the buccaneer:

"The figure moved slowly on, ascended the bank, and stopped at the very door of the sepulchral vault. Just before entering it he looked around. What was the affright of Wolfert when he recognized the grisly visage of the drowned buccaneer. . . . What a conflict of mind did he suffer! His rest was broken and when he fell asleep, a nightmare in the shape of a huge money-bag sat squatted upon his breast. He babbled about incalculable sums; fancied himself engaged in money-digging; threw the bedclothes right and left, in the idea that he was shoveling away the dirt; groped under the bed in quest of the treasure, and lugged forth as he supposed an inestimable pot of gold."

These nightmarish ravings remind one of Clara Wieland's abberations which she suffered when ill of fever; and the digging is suggestive of the nightly burying the chest and digging it up again, by Clithero, a sleep-walker in *Edgar Huntly.*

"It was a moving sight to behold him wasting away day by day; growing thinner and thinner, ghastlier and ghastlier. . . . Dirk Waldron (his daughter's lover) was the only being that seemed to shed a ray of sunshine into the house of mourning. He came with a cheery look and manly spirit, and tried to re-animate the expiring heart of the poor money-digger, but it was all in vain."

Webber became so distraught that his wife and daughter consulted a Doctor. When he learned the symptoms, he listened intently. When they came to mention his raving about money, he pricked up his ears. His mind was stored with all kinds of mystic lore— astrology, alchemy, divination,—so he offered to go with Webber, made and took a divining-rod, his book, herbs to make a fire and so forth. Irving, like Brown, in his footnote explanation of ventriloquism, has a footnote to testify to the scientific value of the divining-rod, if used properly. The above quasi-scientific beliefs parallel the delirium, insanity, good and evil spirits and biloquium, in *Wieland* .

Webber and the Doctor went to the cove under the over-hanging rocks, having brought with them the negro to do the digging. When Webber told his wife and daughter to go to bed as he might be out late, his wife tried to persuade him not to go, as the wife of the elder Wieland urged her husband not to go at midnight to his temple. She sent Dirk to follow them. He fought a man who was scouting above the diggers, threw him into the river and rescued Webber, who had had a fall. This recalls the rescue of the elder Wieland after the fire and the stroke on his arm.

Wolfert called for a lawyer to make his will and commended his daughter to Dirk. When the lawyer told of the street to be opened through the Webber property and the land on both sides of it to be cut up into town lots, Webber quit his will-making and dying, rose from his bed and was well again, living many years on the wealth from the sale of lots.

Of necessity, Irving's transformations of character occupy a smaller space of writing time than Brown's. He registers changes in his heroes by statements made by the author; the characters in Brown's novels reveal their transformations by action to a certain extent, but more by their soliloquizing.

There is more than a possibility that William Gilmore Simms (1806-1870), who gave up law for literature, was influenced by Brown in his early novels. He resided at Hingham, Mass., during 1832-33, and wrote his first novel, *Martin Faber, the Story of a Criminal* (1833) there. The novel, as stated in the Advertisement, delineates two characters, "put in direct opposition, not less with the view to contrast and comparison, than incident and interest." Their development shows the nature of the education given them, in their homes, where "the affections and moral faculties are to be tutored," and goes "to impress upon us the necessity of prayer and early education."

Martin Faber, like Carwin in *Wieland,* commits one crime after another, beginning with those suited to childhood years, the meanwhile struggling against the necessity which he feels drives him on, due to erroneous early education.
"The demon was not of me; though presiding over, and prevailing within me. . . The only child, I was necessarily a favorite. . . . The pet of mama, the prodigy of papa, I was schooled to dogmatize

and do as I pleased from my earliest infancy. . . . I had no respect for authority—no regard for morals. I was a brute from education." Like Welbeck in *Arthur Mervyn,* "One tissue of iniquity and folly has been my life."[1]

William Harding, his associate, is a "susceptible, gentle youth," who is free even from the thoughts of sin, till the time when Martin reveals to him a murder. The revelation so preys upon his mind as to destroy his peace and mental equilibrium, and he begs Martin either to own up that he did not commit the deed or to give himself up to justice. From that time the purpose, the all-absorbing, over-powering passion, of Harding's life, which altered his habits, his temper and his hopes, is to solve the murder. He does this with more masterful ingenuities than Edgar Huntly in searching for the slayer of his friend Waldegrave or Godwin's Caleb Williams in discovering Falkland to be a murderer,—thus making a sequence of three among the first three detective stories.

Certain particulars throughout the book call to mind similar particulars in Brown's novels. Martin says of William's attempt to prove his guilt: "Search was made under the tree where my victim was alleged to have been buried."[2] In *Edgar Huntly,* the weeping sleep-walker Clithero digs nightly under an elm tree, where the mutilated body of Waldegrave had been found, supposedly in connection with the murder. Edgar says, "Henceforth this man was to become the subject of my scrutiny."[3]

Harding "had lived upon the breath of fame—he was jealous of high reputation. . . . (He says) You know that for years . . . I have been contending for glory—for a name."[4]
Arthur Mervyn's statement gives a precedent to Martin: "I must build a name and a fortune for myself" and Welbeck expresses his ambition thus: "The esteem of mankind was the spring of all my activity, the parent of all my virtue and all my vice. . . . My ambition has panted, with equal avidity, after the reputation of literature and opulence."[5]

"It is strange, that, with my extended and perfect knowledge of

---

1. *Arthur Mervyn,* I, 86.
2. Simms, *Martin Faber,* 105.
3. *Edgar Huntly,* 12.
4. Simms, *Martin Faber,* 106,113.
5. *Arthur Mervyn,* I, 25, 90, 101.

human character, and my great love of mental and moral analysis, I should have suffered myself to be taken in by these external shows on the part of my victim,"[1] muses Martin.

The name Constance for the name of Martin's wife shows imitation of Constantia in *Ormond*.

The book is divided into two parts, like *Ormond* and *Arthur Mervyn*, for example. The first relates the life of Martin and his career of crime; the second part serves "to record the progress of Harding in the newly assumed duties of his life."[2]

Simms' novel, *The Yemassee,* is an Indian story, in which the character of the red men is less idealized than Cooper's, more nearly like that of Brown.

One of the most conspicuous evidences of Brown's influence is in the title of this anonymous novel, *Stanley, or the Recollections of a Man of the World* (1838),—named after Philip Stanley in *Clara Howard,* which was published in England as *Philip Stanley*. Being unable to secure a copy of the book, a quotation by the joint authors, Higginson and Boynton, concerning it will be given.

"Undoubtedly Brown's tales furnished a point of transition from Mrs. Radcliffe, of whom he disapproved, to the modern novel of realism, although his immediate influence and, so to speak, his stage properties, can hardly be traced later than the remarkable tale, also by a Philadelphian, called *Stanley; or the Man of the World,* the scene of which is laid in America, though it was first published in 1839 in London. This book . . . was soon understood to be the work of a young man of twenty-one, Horace Binney Wallace. It is now forgotten, except one sentence: 'A foreign nation is a kind of contemporaneous posterity' (II, 89). In this book the later influence of Bulwer and Disraeli is palpable, but Brown's concealed chambers and aimless conspiracies and sudden mysterious deaths also re-appear in full force, not without some lingering power; and then vanish from American literature for-ever."[3] It may be that Brown's "stage properties" have disappeared, but his influence continues to this day.

---

1. Simms, *Martin Faber,* 119.
2. *Ibid.,* 129.
3. Higginson & Boynton, *A Reader's History of American Literature,* 72-3.

Information varies regarding this work. "Wallace, Horace Binney, *Stanley,* 2 vols. First published in London in 1839" is given by Higginson, Thomas Wentworth, and Boynton, Henry Walcott, in *A Reader's History of American Literature.* Houghton, Mifflin & Co., c. 1903. p. 72. In *American Fiction, 1774-1850, a contribution towards a bibliography* by Lyle H. Wright, San Marino, California, 1939, is given "Philadelphia, Lea & Blanchard, 1838. 2 vols." The latter statement is probably correct, as that library is a depository of many original books and manuscripts.

Attention has been directed to Poe's indebtedness to Brown, whose use of unusual scientific phenomena appealed to Poe's fancy and led him, no doubt, to choose the agents of his stories from similar sources. He employed mesmerism, suspended animation, phrenology, telepathy, metempsychosis, aerial navigation, ventriloquism, with nightmarish details. Brown's influence was not limited to suggestion merely; he loaned specific ideas.

In Poe's *Facts in the Case of M. Valdemar,* he says: "My attention, for the last three years, has been repeatedly drawn to the subject of mesmerism." The speaker then performs upon his friend, M. Ernest Valdemar (whose name sounds like Huntly's friend Waldegrave), putting him to sleep on a few occasions. In this story, "cases of sleep-waking," "change of countenance of the sleep-waker," "the sleep-waker remained exactly as I have described him" are comparable to Brown's sleep-walkers and confused somnambulistic wakenings.

The denouement in Poe's tale, *Thou Art the Man,* is dependent upon ventriloquism, which Brown used in *Wieland.*

"I confidently depended upon my ventriloquial abilities, for the effect . . . upon the conscience of the murderous wretch."

When Goodfellow looks upon the corpse of his victim, Shuttleworthy, and it seems to say, "Thou art the man," he is convicted forthwith. Carwin's last "Hold!" to Wieland and his saying, "Man of errors! . . . Be lunatic no longer," cause Wieland to kill himself.

Poe's use of telepathy in *The Murders in the Rue Morgue* may have been anticipated by Brown in these words uttered by Clithero: "Were they (the twins) linked together by a sympathy whose influence was independent of sensible communication?"[1]

In *A Tale of the Ragged Mountains,* Poe describes "Bedloe's eyes like those of a cat . . . emitting luminous rays, of an intrinsic luster, not as a candle,"—which imitates Brown's panther whose eyes were "glowing orbs . . . though lustrous themselves . . . created no illumination around them." Instead of a panther, Poe introduced a beast "with open mouth and glaring eyes. . . . I could not be mistaken in its character. It was a hyena." A wild hyena in America!

Stronger, perhaps, than the influence of Brown's scientific element over Poe his analyses of the motives and feelings of his characters under some mental strain. In his autobiographical story, *William Wilson,* Poe made use of the effects of whispers, recalling Carwin's whispers at Clara Wieland's ear:

"And his singular whisper, it grew the very echo of my own. . . . It was the pregnancy of solemn admonition in the singular, low, hissing utterance . . . which struck upon my soul, with the shock of a galvanic battery."

As Clara drew aside the bed-curtains and discovered the murdered wife of Wieland, so William drew the bed-curtains where his namesake was sleeping and "shuddered to behold, his breath heaved, his knees tottered with horror." As the Wielands were pursued by the voice of Carwin, William was pursued by his double and the

"damnable whisper" . . . "From his inscrutable tyranny . . . panic-stricken, as from a pestilence (suggestive of Brown's yellow fever); and to the very ends of the earth *I fled in vain.*"

Exasperated beyond endurance, William murders his friend, who dooms him to a living death:

"Thou hast murdered thyself, henceforward thou art also dead,—dead to the world, to Heaven, and to hope."

Poe calls it self-murder, as Wieland killed himself. The victim is, of course, the conscience of William. Poe seems to portray his own wasted life, with its blasted opportunities, remorse and ruin.

Unquestionably, Poe's *The Pit and the Pendulum* grew out of his reading of Edgar Huntly's sleep-waking experiences in the

---

1. *Edgar Huntly,* 79.

pit—a real pit—with no light, in chilly atmosphere, half-clad, bruised, anhungered, stunned unconscious. Edgar imagines himself in a tomb, with rocks in the bottom and steep, *untenable* sides; he gropes round and round; a hundred times he ascends a few feet only to have to relinquish his hold; a hundred times he throws himself, exhausted by fatigue and his pains, on the ground. "Had two days and a half been consumed in my subterranean prison? Surely my senses were fettered or depraved by some spell. I was still asleep, and this was merely a tormenting vision; or madness had seized me, and the darkness that environed and the hunger that afflicted me existed only in my own distempered imagination."[1]   "I shuddered as if I had beheld suspended over me the exterminating sword,"[2] words of Clara after Carwin's threatening warning and Poe's *cue*.

Poe's story is well known: its black vault, bottomless pit and swinging pendulum with the sharp blade just over the rack on which the victim was fettered with chains and gradually being lowered closer and closer to wreak retribution. Like Brown he speaks as one who has experienced the sensations himself and concentrates on trifles, as the shape and size of the dungeon, when the mind is wracked unendurably. All of Chapter XVI of *Edgar Huntly* displays Brown's animated descriptive ability.

Some of Brown's pet words were appropriated by Poe,—ratiocination, ruminate, ebullition, assiduously, animadversion, chimeras, pregnancy (as above) and conversible.

It was left to Poe and Hawthorne to create the perfect short story, but Brown had used such forms in his contributions to magazines,—in fact, a portion of *Edgar Huntly* was so published, which may have given Poe a hint, leading to the standardized type of short story.

Poe's stories are ingenious and artistically, artificially perfect in plot construction, for one is forced to recognize his deliberate effort to create them so. In minuteness of details and power of graphic description he rivals, or outrivals Brown. He out-Browned Brown also in portraying the weird, morbid, dismal, horrible,— the death throes of his victims. Brown used imagination rather than

---

1. *Edgar Huntly,* 221, 166-73.
2. *Wieland,* 84.

fancy, terror rather than horror *per se*. He shows sympathy and moral consciousness and gives lessons in practical wisdom; whereas Poe reveals none of these purposes.

Richard Henry Stoddard in *Recollections, personal and literary*— "Meetings with Poe," said concerning him: "His first master in verse was Byron, in prose Charles Brockden Brown, and later Hawthorne."

As Brown anticipated Cooper in local color and Poe in the explication of eerie and morbid conditions, so he anticipated Hawthorne in psychological analysis. Men of such superior merit are not the first in their particular fields. Pioneers are needed to break the way and develop a standard by which followers may compare, avoiding that which is mediocre and imitating that which is excellent. Brown was such a pioneer or forerunner to these men as he was to other writers in the various phases of American literature. Many things were lacking to Brown, which helped his successors a generation later.

While Brown's contemporaries were using haunted castles, he used accessible American settings. Hawthorne was a genuine romancer, but rather than confine himself to American conditions, he laid the scene of *The Marble Faun* in a distant foreign land and in the remote romantic past. He said in the Preface of *The Marble Faun*: "No author, without a trial, can conceive of the difficulty of writing a romance about a country where there is no shadow, no antiquity, no mystery, no picturesque and gloomy wrong, nor anything but a commonplace prosperity, in broad and simple daylight, as is happily the case with my dear native land."

There need be no hesitation in believing that Hawthorne was pleased with Brown's novels and was affected by them. Brown preceded Hawthorne in the study of those mental transitions which the latter afterward traced so fundamentally. He watched the actions and psychological states of his characters and produced what seems to be a true history of the mind, but he made no great attempt to separate moral and mental interests. He failed at times to connect act and character, as when Edgar Huntly kills the Indians without a question of right or wrong, but of who should die, they or he. He shrinks from the deed, because he had never done the like before; by others, it is accounted to him as a feat of skill and courage.

Hawthorne had a finer insight into the essence of human nature than Brown. He would have made such changes of mind as Brown used wholly the result of individual choices, as in *The Scarlet Letter* (1850). The climactic chapter of this book, entitled "The Interior of a Heart," proclaims relationship to Brown, who says, "I have always found an unaccountable pleasure in dissecting . . . my heart." Hawthorne dissects the heart of Hester Prynne, the outcome of which is represented by the wearing of the letter **A** over her heart; and he has Chillingworth probe the guilty mind and heart of Arthur Dimmesdale, until it results in his death. It is a tragedy of sin and remorse.

Hawthorne dwelt upon the subject of heredity rather than upon the older belief of fate and necessity, as in *The House of the Seven Gables* (1851). The wrong-doing of one generation lives into succeeding ones. He was interested chiefly in the moral responsibility and spiritual development of his characters and recorded the struggles of their souls. He was profoundly reverent. He spiritualized everything he touched and surrounded his characters with uncombatable influences to watch the re-actions in their souls and minds.

The Marble Faun was sketched in Italy, rewritten in England and published there under the name *Transformation,* which the author disliked, in February, 1860. In an advertised list of books of the York library, a new series of reprints, is Hawthorne's *Transformation* (The Marble Faun), found in a volume of Schiller's Works, Bohn's Standard Library, London (1912). *The Transformation* is the alternate title of *Wieland.* The climactic chapter of Hawthorne's story is "The Faun's Transformation," proving that his theme is the same as in *Wieland.* He planned to do for Donatello what Brown had done for Wieland. Donatello killed the persecutor of Miriam, following the example of Wieland, and from that time his sense of guilt pursues him like a curse until he is changed from an innocent, light-hearted youth to a haunted misanthrope, who finally gives himself up as a murderer and is confined in a dungeon for life.

"Out of his bitter agony, a soul and intellect, I could almost say, have been inspired into him."   (Miriam was a witness and consented to the death with her eyes.) "Our fates cross and are entangled. . . . We are bound together, and can never part again. . . . The deed knots us together for time and eternity."

These words bear out Brown's twin-destiny idea in *Edgar Huntly*. Hawthorne's moral seems to be that perfect culture is unattainable in a state of innocence and that the noblest character can be developed only through spiritual conflict involving crime. The theme of *The Marble Faun* must have struck the publishers as reminiscent of *Wieland; or, the Transformation* or they would not have titled the book, *The Transformation*. Hawthorne's chosen title was *A Romance of Monte Beni* after the Count (Faun) of Monte Beni.

These are strange words unless the author had in mind the spontaneous combustion of Wieland. The artist Hilda, after she had seen the assenting look of her friend's (Miriam's) eyes, is overwhelmed and pining with grief. In an art gallery one day, an old German artist, who had seen Hilda often, says,
"Some fine morning, I shall come . . . and shall look for my little American artist. And what shall I behold? A heap of white ashes on the marble floor. . . . Nothing more, upon my word! The fire, which the poor child feels so fervently, will have gone into her innermost and burnt her up!"[1] Brown says, "a heap of ashes."

Words and phrases might be chosen recalling Brown's expressions, like "Obey my bidding" for Carwin's "Mark my bidding," "attempered" for "attemper," and "My heart, it has none but pure motives" for "my motives . . . were pure."

Hawthorne's three great romances were written between his forty-sixth and fifty-eighth years, years of ethical, spiritual and artistic maturity, and after more than fifty years of American literature had passed. Brown wrote his six romances or novels between his twenty-seventh and thirty-first years, at the dawn of his powers and as creator of American Literature. Brown was the father of American romance; Hawthorne became the master of American romance.

In speaking of Brown in relation to Poe and Hawthorne, Dr. Walter Just said:
"Jedenfalls aber hat Brown . . . als einer der ersten in der Weltliteratur es gewagt, die Nachtseiten der Natur zum Gegenstand künstlerisch Darstellung zu machen. Dass er damit einen guten Griff getan hatte, bewies sein grosser Erfolg—er galt ungefähr

---

1. Hawthorne, *The Marble Faun,* Chapter XXXVII.

zwanzig Jahre lang für den ersten Amerikanerischen Romanschriff-steller—und er hat auf diesen Gebiete Poe und Hawthorne vor-gearbeitet."[1]

Brown is one of the first to use seriously and fictionally historical material, in his novels,—perhaps, the first in America,—in his employment of yellow fever. An evident result of his use of the theme was *Laura* (1809). By a Lady of Philadelphia. She exploits the subject in Brown's home city ten years after his accounts of it in *Ormond* and in *Arthur Mervyn.*

A late influence of Brown's treatment of yellow fever may be seen in its introduction by S. Weir Mitchell in *The Red City* (1909), a century after *Laura.* The story includes the year 1793 and a visit of the plague to Philadelphia. It began in August and subsided in November. Of the city's population of 45,000, 24,000 left the city for the country. The plague was limited largely to two miles along the water front and exposure at night was almost fatal in its consequences. The author tells of the great fear and the burning of pitch and of fence-paling fires in the streets until a pall of smoke hung over the city. Vehicles came endlessly over the middle-ferry floating bridge and tents were erected across the river. Grass grew in the streets. Hearses and push-carts passed all night long bearing the dead away. Negroes were practically immune to the disease and were employed as nurses in the hospitals, buriers of the dead, purveyors of food. The disease was called *El Vomito.*

During the centenary year of Brown's death, that event was the inspiration of a number of articles by Warren Barton Blake: "Brock-den Brown and the Novel" in *The Sewanee Review,* October, 1910; "Fiction and Yellow Fever" in the *Boston Evening Transcript,* Feb. 26, 1910; and "A Novelist of Plague Days" in the *New York Evening Post,* March 19, 1910.

Herman Melville can be said to have been influenced by the novels of Brown. His autobiographical novel, *Redburn,* and *Pierre* will be related to Brown's novels.

Redburn: His First Voyage (1849) definitely shows the influence of *Wieland* in that spontaneous combustion combusts into a story

---

1.   Just, *Die Romantische Bewegung in der Amerikanischen Literatur—Brown, Poe, Hawthorne,* 51.

again. Melville purports to give his actual experiences on a round trip from New York to Liverpool as a sailor-boy in the Merchant Service. The author incenses the thought of combustion in reddening the sailor Max, who has red hair, red whiskers, red cheeks and wears a red shirt; he says of him: "he was altogether the most combustible looking man I ever saw."[1]

It was customary to recruit sailors in Liverpool to replace any who for some reason did not make the return trip. If volunteers did not offer themselves, certain men and women about the wharves known as *crimps* procured drunken sailors at the last and brought them aboard. One such helpless was stowed in a bunk. When he did not report for duty, an investigation was made.

"The eyes were open and fixed; the mouth was curled like a scroll, and every lean feature firm as in life; while the whole face, now wound in curls of soft blue flame, wore an aspect of grim defiance, and eternal death. . . . No, he's not dead; . . . hardly had the words escaped, when, to the silent horror of all, two threads of greenish fire, like a forked tongue, darted out between the lips; and in a moment, the cadaverous face was crawled over by a swarm of worm-like flames. . . . The mate sprang down in a rage; but recoiled at the burning body as if he had been shot by a bullet. . . . 'Take hold of it,' (barked Jackson) . . . 'it must go overboard,' . . . and smothering it all in the blankets, he pulled it partly out of the bunk. A few minutes more, and it fell with a bubble among the phosphorescent sparkles of the damp night sea, leaving a coruscating wake as it sank."[2]
Brown uses some form of the word *coruscate* two or three times.

One sailor said he believed the crimp had brought on board a corpse, for the sake of the month's advance (pay). Jackson was heard to claim

"that he had known of such things having been done before. But that a really dead body ever burned in that manner, I (Redburn) can not even yet believe. But the sailors seemed familiar with such things; or at least with the stories of such things having happened to others. For me, who at that age had never so much as happened to hear of a case like this, of animal combustion, in the horrid mood that came over me, I almost thought the burning body was a

---

1. Melville, *Redburn,* 80.
2. *Ibid.,* 246, 247.

premonition of the hell of the Calvinists, and that Miguel's earthly end was a foretaste of his eternal condemnation. . . . Jackson . . . would look toward the fatal spot, and cough, and laugh, and invoke the dead man with incredible scoffs and jeers. He froze my blood, and made my soul stand still."[1]

These last words remind one of Brown's words when he saw the ocean for the first time: "My soul was suspended for half an hour."

That other suggestions came to Melville from Brown's novels is likely. He brings in dreams and sleep-walking. A young man named Blunt, with graying hair, used two kinds of restoratives. "He was so smitten with his hair oil . . . that he had gotten out of bed, even in his sleep, . . . seized the precious bottle, applied its contents, and then to bed again, getting up in the morning without knowing anything about it."[2]

Blunt would dream and get up at other times. Redburn became acquainted in Liverpool with a Londoner, Harry Bolton. With him he went to London, where Harry gambled, leaving Redburn to wait and rest:

"I did not sleep; but, like a somnambulist, only dozed now and then; starting from my dreams."[3]

Music occupies quite a prominent role in the story, as music does in Brown's novels. The author says:

"Now, music is a holy thing, and its instruments, however humble, are to be loved and revered. Whatever has made, or does make, or may make music, should be held sacred. . . . Musical instruments should be like the silver tongs, with which the high-priests tended the Jewish altars. . . . And there is no humble thing with music in it, not a fife, not a negro-fiddle, that is not to be reverenced as much as the grandest architectural organ. . . . For even a Jew's harp may be so played, as to awaken all the fairies that are in us, and make them dance in our souls."[4]

The Italian boy Carlo played an elaborately carved organ, which had parades of martial men, tumblers—Nubian slaves,—knights and ladies. He played almost any piece called for by the sailors and passengers and played for dances by the cabin-passengers. Redburn's friend, Harry Bolton, was a charming singer with his "gentle

---

1. Melville, *Redburn,* 247-8.
2. *Ibid.,* 89.
3. *Ibid.,* 238.
4. *Ibid.,* 250-1.

and liquid" voice.

There was a plague or pestilence among the steerage passengers, that carried off about thirty of them. Brown used yellow fever. Two sets of twins are described (really two sets of triplets), a phenomenon which Brown employs. Melville must use the word *corrode*— "corrode their secret hearts."

In *Pierre* (1852) are names and thoughts which may refer to similar details in the Brown novels. Pierre's cousin's name is Glendinning Stanly, Stanley appearing in *Clara Howard,* and his early sweetheart's name is Lucy, perhaps, named from Brown's Lucys. *Transformation* is a theme used. Both the cousins are changed by fate; for Fate is the underlying agency. Glen was changed from exhibiting a friendly, companionable fellowship with Pierre into exercising hatred through indulgence and a love of wealth. He became an infernal impostor, which is Brown's designation of Carwin in *Wieland.* Pierre himself is transformed from a light-hearted, pietistic son by a secretive obedience to Fate and an obsession of generosity to his disclaimed half-sister Isabel, a sort of twin-relationship, as in *Edgar Huntly,* into a broken man, who became insanely mad, killed his cousin, was jailed and committed suicide, a series of disasters in the manner of *Wieland.*

These expressions are reminiscent of Brown's novels. Pierre says, "I believe I was dreaming—sleep-walking" and "He crumpled Glen's and Frederic's letter in his hand—as it were somnambulously," recalling the same malady in *Edgar Huntly.* Pierre says: "In my bosom a secret adder of self-reproach and self-infamy would never leave off its sting," and his mother says of him: "Oh viper! had I thee now in me, I would be a suicide and a murderer with one blow." The two had had an unnatural mother-sister, son complex; "in the very summer-house where of July mornings, he had sat chatting and drinking negus with his gay mother," he heard of Glen's pretended love-making to Lucy, now his betrothed. There was trouble,
"remembering that in love matters jealousy is as an adder . . . jealousy of Glen was double-addered by the extraordinary malice."[1] Vipers, adders, the summer-house and the overhead love-tangle are

---

1. Melville, *Pierre,* 377, 214, 328, 374.

in *Wieland.*

An early picture of Pierre's father, which looked frankly, cheerfully, ambiguously, mockingly at him, may have been suggested by Clara Wieland's drawing of Carwin's face, which she contemplated endlessly. "In the privacy of his closet, he would stand, or lean, or sit before it all day long . . . and keep thinking." The alternate title of the book, *the Ambiguities,* which theme is generally maintained, is typically illustrated by the picture: "Consider; for a smile is the chosen vehicle for all ambiguities, Pierre," proverbed his aunt Dorothea, who had given him the picture.

A study of the emotions of the heart is one of Brown's hobbies. Maybe, imitating that idea, Melville says: "The heart! the heart! 'tis God's anointed; let me pursue the heart!"[1] That is what Pierre did, which led him into all his troubles because he did not use his head at the same time.

English novelists who were influenced by Brown's novels will now be considered, a few slightly out of time order to permit the treatment of certain ones together,—Scott and Edgeworth, Shelley and Mrs. Shelley. It is not only best to speak first of William Godwin (1756-1836), whom Brown so much admired, but he was among the first to be influenced by Brown.

"It has been the custom to liken Brown to Godwin," said Margaret Fuller Ossoli. "But there was no imitation, no second-hand in the matter. They were congenial natures, and whichever had come first might have lent an impulse to the other."[2]

The influence of Godwin, as set forth in Brown's novels, has been made quite forcible. Turn about is fair play. *St. Leon: A Tale of the Sixteenth Century* (1799), coming out the year after *Wieland,* shows borrowings from it. The hero, a French nobleman, an amiable person, but lacking stability, secretes a beggarly stranger in his summer-house,—reminding one of the uncouth Carwin and his frequenting the Wieland summer-house nights. His little daughter complains:

"Papa, I wish you would not let a man get into the summer-house (the children's play-house), who shuts all the shutters and locks the door."[3]

---

1. Melville, *Pierre,* 90.
2. Ossoli, *Papers on Literature and Art,* Parts II, 147.
3. Godwin, *St. Leon,* 131-2.

The stranger remained about two months, cared for only by St. Leon, and died leaving a secret legacy to him, the philosopher's stone for transmuting metals into gold and the *elixir vitae,* which would restore his youth. The gift creates the mystery of the plot. It follows the hero like a curse and transforms him, as Wieland was transformed. Godwin uses the words *metamorphosis* and *transition.* These supernatural elements make *St. Leon* a quasi-scientific, quasi-historical mediaeval tale. "St. Leon is Godwin faintly disguised," wrote C. H. Herford in the *Age of Wordsworth,* Chapter V. Just before the old man died he named two persons, Clara and Henry, not mentioned otherwise. They are the names of Clara Wieland and her lover, Henry Pleyel.

The most evident influence of *Wieland* and *The Rights of Women* is seen in Godwin's right-about face regarding marriage and benevolence, from his ideas in *Political Justice* and *Caleb Williams* to his ideas in *St. Leon* and *Fleetwood.* "Godwin the philosopher stands rebuked by this discovery of Godwin the novelist,"[1] quipped Raleigh. Godwin says:

"I apprehend domestic and private affections inseparable from the nature of man, and from what may be styled the culture of the heart. . . . True wisdom will recommend to us individual attachments . . . and it is better that man should be a living being, than a stock or a stone. . . . Nay, by kindling his sensibility, and harmonizing his soul, they may be expected, if he is endowed with a liberal and manly spirit, to render him more prompt in the service of strangers and the public."[2]

As Carwin's secret power of ventriloquism brings disaster in its wake, so the magic endowments, partly because of the stipulation that St. Leon is to tell no one, bring ruination to every person with whom he becomes intimate and to every benevolent project. His wife, Marguerite, gentle, aristocratic, perfect, dies of grief; their son leaves home at age seventeen, lives under an assumed name because of his father's reputation and makes good in the world, like Arthur Mervyn; his three daughters are under a cloud: one dies, the other two remain unmarried. St. Leon is pursued as if by furies, —is imprisoned because thought to have murdered the stranger for

---

1. Raleigh, *The English Novel,* 246.
2. Godwin, *St. Leon,* Preface, Nov. 26, 1799, IX-X.

his wealth, escapes with the negro turnkey to Italy, has his mansion burned and the negro killed, is imprisoned in an Inquisition dungeon for twelve years, is sentenced to be burned, escapes. He tries to use his wealth in a project for the revivescence of Hungary and coming under suspicion is again endungeoned for his efforts, but soon escapes.

St. Leon gives himself the gift of young manhood and becomes a voluntary vagabond, separated from all people, suspected and solitary. He would, like Wieland, take his own life; however, being immortal, he is unable, unless he can find some one else to whom he may impart the gift. The author's purpose is to show how miserable a man would become, living from century to century, when his exemption from mortality would cut him off from the dearest ties on earth and make him incapable of sympathizing with his fellowmen. Wieland was transformed, as already explained; St. Leon was changed from a rather weak, moody, indulgently-trained man to one of ageless wretchedness. Many morphoses of Godwin's characters are well and subtlely drawn; yet the supernatural agencies interfere with their natural development, which is not the case with any of Brown's characters.

Other details might be mentioned. Godwin used many of the word favorites of Brown in various forms; and in numerous expressions he substituted words which are synonymous to Brown's. There are similar phrases, like "corroded my heart," "unaccustomed as I was to regard my person or mind as a machine fitted for productive labour," "check your rash and rude curiosity," "being communicated by a sort of electric stroke," like the elder Wieland's. How does this sound compared to Brown's apostrophe to his pen? Godwin even copies the Quaker *thou* and *thee*.

"Senseless paper! be thou at least my confidant! To thee I may impart what my soul spurns the task to suppress. The human mind insatiably thirsts for a confidant and a friend. . . . They afford at least the semblance of communication and the unburthening of the mind; and I will press the illusion fondly and forever to my heart."[1]

Fleetwood; or, The New Man of Feeling (1805), published four years after Brown's novels were completed, shows the latter's

---

1. Godwin, *St. Leon*, 161-2.

influence strongly. After publishing *Edgar Huntly*, Brown wrote his brother that he would hereafter use more commonplace incidents, which he did in *Clara Howard* and *Jane Talbot*. In the Preface of *Fleetwood*, Godwin asserts:

"In the present volume I have served you with a dish agreeable to your receipt. . . . The following story consists of such adventures, as for the most part have occurred to at least one half of the Englishmen now existing, who are of the same rank of life as my hero . . . college excesses . . . gauntlet (sic) of dissipation; most have married . . . misunderstandings with their wives. . . . In this little work, the reader will scarcely find anything to 'elevate and surprise'; and, if it has any merit, it must consist in the liveliness with which it brings things home to the imagination and the reality it gives to the scenes it pourtrays."

Yet Godwin aimed at novelty. His hero tells of participating in drinking parties and humiliating the underclassmen. In one of these the performer uses the voice of a ventriloquist to imitate the professor to threaten an innocent lad, who afterward kills himself, as Wieland did after he had heard the biloquistic voices of Carwin.

A long digression tells of an orphan boy of eight years, bereft of his father's provision for him by a scheming uncle, working in a Lyons linen mill, escaping and being brought up in Wales by a wealthy man, as and with his own son. A similar digression is Arthur Mervyn's story of his uncongenial home with his father and stepmother and his leaving, later to get into the toils of Welbeck.

"Certain persons . . . will perhaps remark with exultation on the respect expressed in this work for marriage."[1] It is quite a transformation in the author who once said of marriage, "never to practice, but with the greatest caution," to his advocating marriage, as the theme of this book, after having discarded the idea of relations out of marriage. Godwin transforms (metamorphizes) his hero from a confirmed misanthropic bachelor, who thinks all women artificial and sensual, whom he helped to make so, into a decent husband, after many months of suspicions, vacillations and cruelties, egged on by the scheming imposture of a nephew.

Many words and phrases are Brown-istic. "All was dark and

---

1. Godwin, *Fleetwood*, Preface, XVI.

dreary and sable around me. I wandered in the pathless wilds";
"That arch deceiver"; "saturnine disposition" for contemplative
melancholy. Fleetwood was destined for the profession of law, but
he "ultimately declined this pursuit, from an aversion, as he said,
to disputes and sophistry and the deriving a subsistence from the
misfortunes of others," as Brown did. "The generous sympathy
which animated my charitable deed was pure," like Arthur Mervyn's
motives.

Mary, left orphaned and penniless through the loss at sea
of her parents and two sisters and their fortune, wrote a letter
to Fleetwood very similar to orphaned Eliza Hadwin's to Arthur
Mervyn: "What shall I do alone in the world?" "Ye have made
me tenfold a vagabond and a beggar upon the earth!" speaking
to the sea. Does not one recall the two sisters, Susan and Eliza
Hadwin, who harmonized like music in different keys? Godwin
writes: "At the same time we are like instruments tuned to a cor-
respondent pitch." "His researches, especially in the human heart,
were profound," said of Gifford, the designing, hypocritical nephew.
Like Catharine and Wieland, Mary and Fleetwood carry on a
several-page colloquy, when he accuses her wrongfully:
"If you loved me, you would not make me a stranger to your
thoughts". . . . "You will know them too soon". . . . "Fleetwood,
I am your wife. . . . I have a right to know your thoughts, and share
your sorrows." "I turned upon her enraged at her duplicity. 'Be
gone! How dare you torment me thus!' . . ." (Mary heard me with
astonishment and burst into tears.) "Fleetwood, is it come to this?
This is too much—too much! . . . If ever you had compassion on the
wife of your bosom." (I shook her from me.) "Will you not leave
me?"[1] Then Fleetwood raves on about his being a "brute" . . .
"demons of hell!" in contrast to Wieland who feels himself under
the power of the Almighty.

Fleetwood is dominated intellectually by his opinions and by
the rascality of Gifford. His thoughts he never tells to Mary, though
playing fast and loose with her emotionally. Wieland also lives
apart from Catharine in his mind and religion, but is a kind husband. In *St. Leon,* Godwin expresses a similar view. St. Leon
kept the fatal secret to himself, though protesting all the time his
whole-hearted love for his wife. This sentence by him seems to

---

1. Godwin, *Fleetwood,* 322, 340.

express the idea in the alternate title of *Fleetwood, The New Man of Feeling*: "I poured forth to Marguerite, not the secrets of my understanding, but the overpowering emotions of my soul."[1]

In the Preface of *Mandeville: A Tale of the Seventeenth Century* (1817), Godwin makes a frank statement of his indebtedness to Brown.

"Every author, at least for the last two thousand years, takes a hint from some suggestion afforded by an author that has gone before him, as Sterne has very humorously observed (Tristram Shandy, Vol. I, Chap. XXI. Edition 1775); and I do not pretend to be an exception to this rule. The impression, that first led me to look with an eye of favour upon the subject here treated was derived from a story-book, called Wieland, written by a person, certainly of distinguished genius, who I believe was born and died in the province of Pennsylvania in the United States of America, and who calls himself C. B. Brown.

"It is the express purpose of the narrative in which I am engaged, to show how the concurrence of a variety of causes operate to form a character: and if I were to omit any circumstance, . . . the person, into whose hands this story may happen to fall, would have an imperfect picture of the man who is set before him."[2]

Few circumstances were omitted in the nearly thousand pages of the narrative. Repetitional ideas stated in a hundred ways and recapitulations of the past "to enforce the present gloom" are frequent.

Charles Mandeville, the hero, was born in North Ireland (1638) of English parents who were massacred in the patriotic rebellion of the Irish Catholics against their English Protestant overlords (1641). The rebels were severely punished by Cromwell in 1649. Mandeville is comparable to Wieland. His formation from the age of three to short of the legal age of twenty-one into a religious madman is based upon his seeing the bloody slaying of his parents and many other Protestants and his being snatched from the arms of his Irish nurse Judith and the nine-year tutorage of the English parson, Hilkiah Bradford, who instilled into him a terrible, undying hatred of everything papist as satanic.

1. Godwin, *St. Leon*, 176.
2. Godwin, *Mandeville*, I, 220.

The author does not let the reader forget apparitions and visions, such as are in *Wieland*, or sleep-walking as in *Edgar Huntly*. The tutor acquaints Charles with the apparitions of the slaughtered Protestants driven into the river, seen nightly on the surface, upright in the stream; and that the spirits uttered hideous and terrifying cries and imprecated revenge on their murderers. The boy was immured in a gloomy, desolate, fog-girt castle of a wealthy uncle, a recluse whom he seldom saw, shut up to his tutor alone. He says: "I never was a boy." All I remembered of Ireland was "tumultuous and tragic, and distracting and wild." The tutor's "representation of all imaginable cruelties, racks, pincers . . . kept me awake whole nights . . . and made me wander like a meagre, unlaid ghost (sleep-walker), to the wonder and alarm of the peaceable and well-disposed inhabitants of my uncle's house. . . . (When appointed menial tasks by my tutor) I submitted outwardly, . . . but I retained the principle of rebellion entire. . . . My displeasure brooded, and heated, and inflamed themselves, at the bottom of my soul."[1]

Once, his sister Henrietta, a year younger than Charles, "as good as she was beautiful," whom Charles seems not to have remembered, was invited to visit him. Did Godwin choose the name Charles from Brown, Henrietta from Brown's first betrothed, Judith from Clara Wieland's maid and Clifford's friend Calvert from Brown's story, *Stephen Calvert?* Charles blazed with awareness.

"I felt as if this were the first day in which I had known what it was to be truly alive. . . . Henrietta talked best, but I loved most. . . . I had a heart for love, oh, for what transports and turbulence of love."[2]

His possessive love for Henrietta and his hatred of Lionel Clifford, whom he singled out in Winchester College, a youth, fascinating, irresistible, vivacious, healthy, are the complicating elements in Mandeville's character, with conflict of Royalists and Commons, Catholics and Protestants, as background.

"Clifford is my fate," Charles iterates, as the main theme of the story. The fates of the two as boys and men are linked together. Clifford represents all joy, beauty and kindness—the ideal man. Charles represents the misanthrope, all gloom, bitterness and

---

1. Godwin, *Mandeville*, I, 136, 156, 158.
2. *Ibid.*, I, 203, 178; II, 21.

malignity. This theme follows one in *Edgar Huntly,* by which the fate of twins is thought inextricably connected. Henrietta is the ideal woman, the good angel, who tries to inspire Charles with the principles of benevolence and subdue his growing lunacy,— insanity Brown named the same derangement. "I must kill him; or he must kill me."

In college Charles was accused of having and concealing a book of caricatures of King Charles, for which he was punished. The real culprit makes a confession to Charles later, after the method of Wieland and Carwin. Young Mandeville, like Arthur Mervyn, cares for a fellow student who dies of consumption. Doesn't this sound like Brown at ten years of age: "Why does he call me boy?" Charles was ambitious. At seventeen years, he says, "Already I counted myself for man." He applies for the secretaryship to a plot-leader to put Cromwell down and Clifford is given the place. Charles ruminates:

"Was not this infernal malice?" . . . (and he entreats a friend) "Come now let us curse a little. . . . I had arrived at seventeen years. . . . I had no place in the world of mankind. . . . I felt ease in proportion as I withdrew from the haunts of men (almost Brown's words)."[1]

For page after page Mandeville rages on until he gets into a fever and wanders distractedly.

"The next morning I was found by one of these woodsmen, stretched my length at the bottom of a pit, extenuated, vacant, scarcely able to help myself. . . . All comes to my recollection, with the violence, the cords, the harsh language, the blows, it had been judged necessary to employ for my restraint, and my cure."[2]

How like Huntly's sleep-walking into a pit! Charles' sick spell, frenzy, an attack of lunacy and being taken to an infirmary have a parallel in Clara Wieland's illness and fever illusions and the prison treatment of Wieland as a maniac. Charles reveals the cause of his distress to his watchers, his sister among them, to be his hatred of Clifford.

Clifford had become interested in Henrietta and finally marries her. Henrietta pleads with Charles to lay aside his unnatural and

---

1. Godwin, *Mandeville,* II, 68, 107, 108.
2. *Ibid.,* II, 110-1, 114-5.

uncalled-for hatred:

"No, Clifford is my fate. Present or absent, waking or sleeping, I can never get rid of him. . . . Hatred, bitter and implacable hatred became now more than ever the inmate of my bosom. I lived but for one purpose, the extinction of Clifford. This was the first object of my existence. . . . (Clifford became a Catholic, to add the last straw to Charles' consuming hatred.) Thank God. . . . I may now hate him as much as I please with a safe conscience. . . . Yes, I feel an instinctive antipathy to the wretch: but it is the voice of God, warning me of my danger."[1]
All along Wieland considered himself doing God's will, even to the destroying of his own family; Mandeville's misanthropy was instilled into him and his idea of the voice of God was anti-papal teaching.

The uncle, Dudley Mandeville (Dudley probably taken from the Dudleys in *Ormond*), before his death, had placed the estates of Charles and Henrietta into the hands of a scoundrelly lawyer, Holloway, whose ruling passion, like Welbeck's in *Arthur Mervyn,* is to get wealth. With his nephew, Mallison, as accomplice and tool, a fellow student of Charles at college, a bully and evil-natured, he subjects Mandeville, during his four years' minority, to all kinds of machinations and impostures, sometimes urging him on to rages and supposed lunacy and sometimes trying to get him to take over certain powers over the estate in collaboration.

Such deceit and impostures resemble the behavior of Carwin to the Wieland family with his ventriloquistic power. Godwin doesn't mention that faculty, but replaces it with mimicry. Mandeville suffered a broken leg, by being thrown from a horse.
"I wore a wound in my heart to which the fracture I had sustained in a limb was nothing. . . . (Mallison was assigned to care for him and added to his other accomplishments that of mimicry.) I had scorned so inglorious and plebeian a talent; but what will not a sick-bed reduce us to? Add to which, there is something in mimicry that is irresistible. . . . Mallison was an admirable mimic, an excellent actor."[2]
The "talent of mimicry" had entered the story before this. Charles' friend who had sponsored him for the secretaryship, had to save the

---

1. Godwin, *Mandeville,* II, 217, 240, 241; III, 51; II, 207.
2. *Ibid.,* III, 85-6, 97, 123.

life of a Royalist on one occasion: "Among the many convivial qualities of my patron, one was that he was an admirable mimic. . . . The place of his confinement was a summer-house in the garden." Brown's summer-house inevitably appears. Of course. Carwin's voices usually took the form of mimicry of members of the Wieland family. Brown gives an instance of mimicry as well as of ventriloquism in *Arthur Mervyn.* Arthur heard distinctly in Welbeck's house the tones of the teacher Colvill. Welbeck was imitating him, hoping to decoy Arthur if he was within hearing. The hut of the laborer recalls Wieland's hut of the caretaker; the chimney-sweep follows Ormond's disguise as a chimney-sweep.

Charles was outshone in college by Clifford, outwitted of the secretaryship by him and outmaneuvered by him, a Catholic, in his wooing of Henrietta. He moralizes,
"Pride, the infirmity through which the angels fell, was my ruin. . . . My error was misanthropy. She (Henrietta) endeavored to inspire me with a contrary principle."[1]
Often the conversation between Charles, when he threatens her for yielding to a Catholic, and Henrietta in her beseeching seems like Catharine's or Clara's pleadings with Wieland. "A cursed disposition is its own punisher," imitates Brown's virtue or curiosity is its own reward. The errors of a false education are strongly emphasized by the author, one of Brown's themes.

In the ending of the story, Charles' attempt, with the help of some troopers, to kidnap Henrietta on her wedding eve to prevent her marriage, is foiled by Clifford and his friends. He curses Clifford with bitterness and malignity, tries to kill him and says—"I remember no more." In the development of character Godwin used metamorphosis instead of Brown's transformation. One might go on finding suggestions from Brown, but, in most instances of similarity, Godwin has outdone Brown by being more outspoken in portrayals and more drastic in each item of behavior. He is more Gothic in spirit than Brown.

In *The Fatal Revenge; or, The Family of Montorio* (1807) by Charles Robert Maturin (1782-1824) are many details that remind one of the disasters in the Wieland family. There can be

---

1. Godwin, *Mandeville*, II, 5, 136-7.

little doubt that the author had read Brown's novels with appreciation and benefited positively thereby. His purpose is to show "the hollowness, the worthlessness, the nothingness of that for which he (Montorio) had sold himself under sin, . . . he was a miserable man—substantially wretched—wretched from suspicion—wretched from fear—wretched from the conviction that he had destroyed himself for nothing."[1]

He had committed murder and disinherited his older brother and his two nephews through unlawful ambition. His brother, Orazio, whom he thought he had killed, represents revenge and becomes the avenger. He confesses:

"To one demon passion I have sacrificed the whole of existence; in revenge I butchered Verdoni, in revenge I murdered my wife, in revenge . . . I have destroyed my innocent sons. I have been sated with revenge, and let revenge be now sated on me."[2]

In connection with this, his first romance, Maturin said:
"I have presumed to found the interest of a romance on the passion of supernatural fear, and on that almost alone—fear . . . especially the fear arising from objects of invisible terror, is universal and irresistible in its appeal."

The disguised avenger, with his distorted determination, surely shows great subtlety in his manipulations, by power of suggestion and by imitating supernatural manifestations, to annihilate the peace and compass the downfall of Montorio and his scheming wife and to ruin the two young nephews—his own sons—mentally. He operates almost entirely upon the minds of his victims to create blighting terror, meanwhile using, of course, the customary Gothic machinery. The brothers' characters are transformed through their unrestrained passions and are fatally destroyed body and soul. The betrayal of the boys' characters by the avenger is exceedingly acute.

Ippolito, the older nephew, says:
"My blow cannot be averted, my victim cannot resist . . . yet I linger—yet I would shrink—yet I would retreat: but my fate cannot be resisted. No, no, no—my fate cannot be resisted. . . . Author of my being (Brown's exact words) and of my fate! hear my groans! hear my despair! Father, these are not the groans of a

---

1. Maturin, *The Fatal Revenge,* 240.
2. *Ibid.,* 251.

rebel heart! . . . but spare me, spare me!" . . . "Hold, hold! What, oh, what are you?" . . . "Be bold and reckless." . . . " 'Tis almost twelve. . . . Then my hour is very near; I feel its summons coming on. A fire is kindled in my heart."[1]

These words recall the contemplations of Wieland, before he murdered his wife and children, Clara's reply at his attempt upon her life: "Oh, brother! spare me! spare thyself!", Carwin's wonted cry, "Hold!", and the elder Wieland's fate at twelve with a fire in his brain.

"I can hardly breathe. I can scarce hold my pen; these are the last lines it shall ever trace." Such words are similar to Clara Wieland's when she expressed here and elsewhere reluctance to write the family story: "I imagined that I had forever laid aside the pen. A few words more and I lay aside the pen forever."

The Fatal Revenge was written only nine years after *Wieland*. Maturin explains, as Brown does, the apparently miraculous incidents, but some of his solutions are pitifully incredible and trifling. Other Maturin novels have been linked with Brown's influence; but this author has been unable to secure them.

In Clara Wieland's defense of herself because of Carwin, Pleyel, her lover, admits,
"Your principles were eminently just. Had not their rectitude and their firmness been attested, by your treatment of that specious seducer Dashwood,"[2] the only use of the name Dashwood by Brown. In one word he describes the betrayer as presenting a pleasing appearance; for *specious* means superficially fair, just, and correct, but not so in reality. Where Brown got the name is a conjecture. A Sir F. D (ashwood) is mentioned by Sterne in reporting the first debate in the House of Commons (1761?) on the German war after the Great Commoner retired from office: "Sir F. D (ashwood) maintained the German war was most pernicious."[3]

The year following Brown's death (1810), a novel was published anonymously in England, whose heroines were sisters, the Misses

---

1. Maturin, *The Fatal Revenge*, 43, 44, 64.
2. *Wieland*, 143.
3. Sterne, Letter in *Life of Laurence Sterne* by H. D. Traill, bound with *A Sentimental Journey*, 80.

Elinor and Marianne Dashwood, representing Sense and Sensibility, which make up the title of the book. The author, Jane Austen, begins with the history of the Dashwood family, against a background of property, for wealth or the lack of it influences the behavior of the chief characters. It is demonstrable that the writer had Brown's novels in mind, because many details of likenesses may be found besides the family name whose mere mention of it may have piqued her desire to elaborate.

In the Introduction to the novel (*Macmillan* 1796 . . . 1809), Austin Dobson says the story was begun as *First Impressions* (1792), revised as *Elinor and Marianne* (1797-8), and remodeled again before its publication in 1811. That would bring the first revision in the year that *Wieland* was published (1798).

The pretended lover of sweet-sixteen Marianne is Willoughby, who, while hunting, discovers her with a sprained ankle. Like Welbeck in *Arthur Mervyn,* he makes a great show of wealth, waiting for his aged cousin, Mrs. Smith, to appoint him her heir and then die. He had betrayed a young girl, Eliza Williams, and deserted her and their baby daughter Eliza. She died of consumption. Willoughby makes a speedy love-affair with Marianne, who does nothing by halves and thinks him perfect. After weeks of intimate companionship, he bids goodbye hastily with no excuse, finally jilts her and marries a wealthy girl for money, not love. Like Welbeck, too, he makes a complete confession to Elinor, the girl of sense, who ever advises her mother and two sisters, Marianne and Margaret, thirteen. He is more than half forgiven by the sisters and receives the inheritance, though formerly under the ban of Mrs. Smith's puritanism, which he sees now he might probably have had if he had "behaved with honour toward Marianne." He retained his regard for her and "made her his secret standard of perfection in woman." The author sums up in the words of Willoughby the theme of riches throughout the book:

"My affection . . . was all insufficient to outweigh that dread of poverty, or get the better of those false ideas of the necessity of riches."[1]

Are not these two cases similar, Miss Austen's following

---

1. Austen, *Sense and Sensibility,* Chapter XLIV.

Brown's? Arthur, in speaking of Clemenza to Welbeck, says,

"her . . . I formerly met under your roof blooming and gay, but whom calamity has tarnished and withered. I saw her in the raiment of poverty, under an accursed roof; desolate; alone; unsolaced by countenance of sympathy of human beings; approached only by those who mock at her distress, set snares for her innocence, and push her to infamy. I saw her leaning over the face of her dying babe."[1]   "He (Willoughby) had left the girl whose youth and innocence he had seduced in a situation of utmost distress with no creditable home, no help, no friends, ignorant of his address! He had left her, promising to return; he neither returned, nor wrote, nor relieved her. . . . His character is now before you—expensive, dissipated, and worse than both."[2]

Like Welbeck and also Ormond, Willoughby appeared at first to be upright, frank and amiable.

Education, as a subject, is not neglected by Miss Austen. She compares the education of two brothers, Edward and Robert Ferrars: Edward was believed kept from mixing in proper society

"much less from any natural deficiency than to the misfortune of a private education"; while Robert without "any material superiority by nature, merely from the advantage of a public school, was as well fitted to mix in the world as any other man."[3]

In speaking of professions, Edward says: "But I had no inclination for the law, even in this less abstruse study of it which my family approved."

This echoes Brown's distaste for law and his family approval. Contrasts in the education of women are given by the author:

"her (Lucy's) powers had received no aid from education (like Arthur Mervyn's stepmother Betty): she was ignorant and illiterate; and her deficiency of all mental improvement, her want of information in the most common particulars, could not be concealed from Miss Dashwood."[4]

The distinction between the two sisters comes out clearly in their love affairs. Recalling Clara Wieland's soliloquy on her love for Pleyel, Miss Austen has Elinor (Sense) repeat almost the same words:

---

1. *Arthur Mervyn*, II, 121.
2. Austen, *Sense and Sensibility*, Chapter XXXI.
3. *Ibid.*, Chapter XXXVI.
4. *Ibid.*, Chapter XXII.

"till his sentiments are fully known, you cannot wonder at my wishing to avoid any encouragement of my own partiality, by believing or calling it more than it is. In my heart I feel little, scarcely any, doubt of his preference."[1]

Drawing occupies this eldest sister, as it does Clara, and music and books occupy Marianne (Sensibility), leading Willoughby to confessing a liking for them. She ironizes herself:

"I have been too much at my ease, too happy, too frank. I have erred against every commonplace notion of decorum, I have been open and sincere, where I ought to have been reserved, spiritless, dull, and deceitful." . . . "She played over every favorite song that she had been used to play to Willoughby . . . till her heart was so heavy that no further sadness could be gained; . . . but these employments . . . still produced occasional effusions of sorrow as lively as ever. . . . In such moments of precious, of invaluable misery, she rejoiced in tears of agony . . . wandering from place to place, in free and luxurious solitude . . . in the indulgence of such solitary rambles."[2]

This reminds one of Achsa's playing to Arthur Mervyn his favorite ditty, but whose "cheerfulness would not return at her bidding."

Marianne "had depended on a twilight walk to the Grecian temple," imitative of Wieland's temple of prayer. She took two delightful walks,

"not merely on the dry gravel of the shrubbery, but all over the grounds . . . where there was something more of wildness than in the rest, where the trees were the oldest, and the grass was the longest and wettest. . . . Though heavy and feverish, with a pain in her limbs, and a sore throat." . . . "He (the apothecary) came, examined his patient, and though encouraging Miss Dashwood, . . . yet, by pronouncing her disorder to have a putrid tendency, and allowing the word 'infection' to pass his lips, gave instant alarm."[3]

Brown uses the word *putrefaction* in connection with the elder Wieland's death. Fever is mentioned, but not yellow fever. Elinor says to Marianne: "Is there not something twice interesting to gain in the flushed cheek, hollow eye, and quick pulse of fever." Later Marianne nearly died of a fever after Willoughby had so broken

---

1. Austen, *Sense and Sensibility,* Chapter IV.
2. *Ibid.,* Chapters X, XVI, XLII.
3. *Ibid.,* Chapters XLII, XLIII.

her heart, just as Clara Wieland had nearly died of fever after Pleyel had accused her wrongfully.

One might note here the use of names and expressions similar to Brown's: Dashwood, Lucy compared to Lucy Villars and two Eliza Williamses to two Elizas in *Arthur Mervyn,* the elder Eliza dying of consumption so feared in the American novels, a Sophia, a Betty and even Queen Mab, which, by Miss Austen, is the name of a horse promised by Willoughby to Marianne, for name of the old Indian woman in *Edgar Huntly.* Mrs. Jennings says to her husband after the Misses Dashwood had returned home: "Lord! we shall sit and gape at one another as dull as two cats."[1] Eliza writes to Arthur Mervyn: "I am altered of late! . . . I am now demure as our old *tabby*—and not half as wise. Tabby had wit enough to keep her paws out of the coals."[2] *Puss the cat* occurs in Brown's unfinished Romance of Sophia and Jessy.

Miss Austen describes charmingly her characters in their every-day family life, in the country and in their spending winters in London; Brown's characters act more independently with very little influence upon each other. Her characters analyze their feelings and usually tell them to others, except Elinor; while Brown's muse within themselves. In *Sense and Sensibility,* the author presents all the characters from a sentimental standpoint and satirizes their ambitions and foibles with most delicate humor, as when loquacious, vulgar, match-making Mrs. Jennings and Elinor consume several pages in talking on different subjects, Mrs. Jennings not realizing they are not discussing the same subject. Brown lacked humor, but he and his characters repudiate in plain words the romantic and sentimental excesses of his contemporaries and the extreme teachings of Godwin, finally. The whole class of sensibility novels came under Miss Austen's satire. Her last works, fragments, among which were *Lady Susan* and *The Watsons,* may have borrowed their titles from characters in *Arthur Mervyn,* seemingly her favorite among Brown's novels.

Among the writers whom Brown influenced in England, Scott is the most noteworthy. Several critics made the statement that he read Brown's novels with delight and appreciation. One who reads

---

1. Austen, *Sense and Sensibility,* Chapter **XXXIX**.
2. *Arthur Mervyn,* II, 183.

Guy Mannering; or, The Astrologer (1815), with the idea of comparison with Brown's novels in mind, may find many suggestive elements. In imitation of Brown's use of scientific phenomena, Scott planned to employ astrology in the same capacity. He diverges from his purpose, perhaps, owing to the declining belief in astrology.[1] Astrology, as introduced, plays only an inferior part. Colonel Mannering observed at the birth of Henry Bertram "that three periods would be particularly hazardous,—his fifth, his tenth, and his twenty-first years." Little Henry was kidnaped in his fifth year and he returned to his native land in his twenty-first year; the mystery of his name and ancestry was cleared up by the discovery, in a velvet bag he had worn all these years, of the very paper on which Colonel Mannering has composed this prophecy. The gypsies and their robberies form a close parallel to the Indians and their depredations in *Edgar Huntly,* and the gypsy Meg Merrilies makes as interesting a character study as does Queen Mab among Brown's Indians.

More significant than the facts above are the names of Scott's characters. The hero of the tale is a man named Brown. The elder Brown was the smuggler who took little Henry Bertram to bring up and gave him his own name Vanbeest Brown. Vanbeest Brown turns out to be the true Henry Bertram in the denouement of the story, under the assumed name Brown, a captain in his Majesty's service, the serenader of Julia Mannering, the friend of the gypsies, a solitary wanderer. Like Charles Brockden Brown, he is a lover of magnificent, inspiring scenery.

The words of Vanbeest Brown in regard to Julia are quite comparable to Arthur Mervyn's about Eliza Hadwin. Arthur says: "Eliza's mind was quick, active, and sagacious; but her total inexperience gave her sometimes the appearance of folly. She was eager . . . to resign herself and her property, without limitation or condition, to my control. . . . 'Ah!' thought I, 'sweet, artless, and simple girl!' " Thinking of marriage, he says, "Could I rely upon the permanence of her equanimity and her docility to my instructions? What qualities might not time unfold, and how little was I qualified to estimate the character of one whom no vicissi-

---

1. Scott, *Guy Mannering,* Introduction by the author, Abbotsford, August 1, 1829.

tude or hardship had approached before the death of her father,—
whose ignorance was, indeed, great, when it could justly be said
even to exceed my own!"[1]   Vanbeest Brown says:
"There is only one circumstance that chills me a little—Julia is
young and romantic. I would not willingly hurry her into a step
which her riper years might disapprove.—No;—nor would I like to
have her upbraid me, were it but with a glance of her eye, with
having ruined her fortunes—far less give her reason to say . . .
that, had I left her time for consideration, she would have been
wiser and done better. . . . The picture presses close upon me,
because I am aware a girl in Julia's situation has no distinct and
precise idea of the value of the sacrifice she makes."[2]

The title of Brown's novel, *Arthur Mervyn,* is applied by Scott
to a kindly elderly country gentleman, friend of Colonel Mannering, in whose charge his daughter Julia had been placed. A letter
addressed to "Arthur Mervyn, Esq. of Mervyn-Hall, Llanbraithwaite,
Westmoreland," gives his status.[3]

Dudley in *Ormond,* is an artist of broken fortune, the father of
Constantia. The name is given by Scott to the travelling companion
of young Brown, of whom he says:
"(He is) a young English artist. . . . A fine fellow this . . . —
he paints tolerably, draws beautifully, converses well, and plays
charmingly on the flute; and, though thus well entitled to be a
coxcomb of talent, is, in fact, a modest, unpretending young man."
                "During the summer of my year," says Dudley, "I
am as free as a wild Indian, enjoying myself at liberty amid the
grandest scenes of nature; while, during my winters and springs,
I am not only cabined, cribbed, and confined in a miserable garret,
but condemned to as intolerable subservience to the humor of others,
and to as indifferent company, as if I were a literal galley-slave."[4]
Brown's Dudley was a player on a lute.

Who cribbed from whom? Shakespeare said in 1606:

"But now I am cabin'd, cribb'd, confined, bound in
To saucy doubts and fears."[5]

Brown wrote this in 1798: "It is true that I hated school. . . . I

---

1. *Arthur Mervyn,* II, 68, 76.
2. Scott, *Guy Mannering,* Chapter XXI.
3. *Ibid.,* Chapter XII.
4. *Ibid.,* XXI.
5. Shakespeare, *Macbeth,* Act III, Sc. 4.

hated to be classed, cribbed, rebuked, and feruled."[1] It looks as if Brown knew his Shakespeare and Scott knew both Brown and Shakespeare, for his character Dudley is the speaker. Bulwer-Lytton carried on the tradition. In *Zanoni,* of Clarence Glyndon it is said,

"The dull walls within . . . seemed now cabined and confined as a felon's prison . . . in the cabined darkness of the hour"; in *Pelham* are the words: "cooped, chained, and confined in cities and slavery."

On leaving Oxford, Fleetwood says, "I had elbow room, and could expatiate as I pleased. I was no longer cooped and cabined in a sort of menagerie."

Like Brown's, Godwin's words pertain to school.

The following delineation might have been applied to Brown himself, the designer and dabbler in poetry.

"Did you know that Colonel Mannering was a draughtsman? . . . He draws beautifully, however. . . . Dudley says he has seldom seen anything so masterly, though slight; and each had attached to it a short poetical description." . . . "Colonel Mannering write poetry!— Why, surely this man must have taken all the pains to conceal his accomplishments, that others do to display theirs. How reserved and unsociable he appeared among us!—how little disposed to enter into any conversation which could become generally interesting!"[2]

Scott mentions American Indians several times.

"These tribes were, in short, the *Parias* of Scotland, living like wild Indians among European settlers, and, like them, judged of rather by their own customs, habits, and opinions, than as if they had been members of the civilized part of the community. . . . A tribe of these itinerants, to whom Meg Merrilies appertained, had long been as stationary as their habits permitted."[3]

Meg Merrilies, it will be recalled, is thought patterned after Brown's Queen Mab. Glossin, one of the kidnapers of young Bertram,

"suffered . . . yet his pride and interest, like the fortitude of a North American Indian, manned him to sustain the tortures . . . of a guilty conscience, of hatred, of fear, and of suspicion."[4]

"He (Donald Bean Lean's Lieutenant) then placed

---

1. *Arthur Mervyn,* II, 125.
2. Scott, *Guy Mannering,* Chapter XXI.
3. *Ibid.,* Chapter VII.
4. *Ibid.,* Chapter XLI.

himself at the head of the party, who moved up the pathway in single or Indian style, Waverley being placed nearest to their leader."[1]

In 1816, *The Antiquary,* dealing with Scotch and English society around 1800, was published. Like the former work, it shows unmistakably the influence of Brown. The description of the evening walk taken by Miss Wardour and her father along the beach reads like the account of some of the experiences of Edgar Huntly, when he tried to escape from the pit of the cavern into which he had fallen or when he had crossed by a tree-trunk bridge to an opposite cliff to avoid the onslaught of the panther which leaped and tried to scramble up the slippery surface or when he threw himself down from a steep precipice into a raging stream to prevent his capture or death by a supposed band of Indians. Scott writes, "A storm came up and the sea almost reached the cliffs." They were between "a raging tide and an insurmountable precipice." Finally they are met by the beggar, Edie Ochiltree, who helps them to a ledge of rock above the roaring billows. At length a halloo is heard from above. It is the adventurer Lovel who is traversing the verge of the precipice in search of them. An anxious group is now gathered above. Certain fishers make, of the mast of a ship and a yard across it, an extempore crane, "which afforded the means of lowering an armchair," fashioned of rope. Then follows a description of the hazardous, perpendicular ascent of each member of the party, through the vacant atmosphere, in the darkness and storm, in constant fear of being dashed against the rugged, projecting cliffs of the face of the precipice. All are finally safe.[2]

The description of the cave into which the beggar and Lovel take refuge from the sheriffs makes a scene somewhat similar to that of Edgar Huntly's adventures in the cavern, his encounters with the panther, the bound girl and the Indians. The beggar and Lovel spend the night on the Gothic staircase, but at midnight are disturbed by the sound of voices below. They witness the leger-demain tricks of the thief Dousterswivel and the anxiety and terror of Sir Arthur Wardour. Edie Ochiltree emits an irre-

---

1. Scott, *Waverley,* Chapter XXXVIII.
2. Scott, *The Antiquary,* Chapters VII, VIII.

pressible sneeze and several unearthly groans and deplorable whines which cause most violent trepidation and superstitious fear in the two visitors. Tremblingly they withdraw from the cave, terrified by the supernatural beings by whom they suppose themselves surrounded.[1] The cave was beneath St. Ruth's Abbey.

Into the body of the novel, Scott has introduced a tale, "The Fortunes of Martin Waldeck." The name "Waldeck" is used for "Welbeck" in some of the editions of *Arthur Mervyn* and is so used by Griswold and Vilas in their criticisms. Waldeck, or Welbeck, in *Arthur Mervyn* is an apparently wealthy person who has committed many kinds of crimes and who, to keep up appearances in the eyes of the world, has stolen the fortune of the young girl whom he makes his mistress. Scott's tale is taken from the German. There was a belief current that the Hartz forest was haunted by a sort of tutelar demon, in the shape of a huge wild man. Traveling priests often warned the people against any intercourse with fiends, witches, fairies and especially with the woodland goblin of the Hartz. Martin Waldeck, a rash, impetuous youth, determines to defy the doctrines of the priests and the timidity of his brothers, Max and George, and seize upon any gold or silver that the demon should point out to him. The three boys prepare charcoal for smelting furnaces and take turns watching the fire by night. One night Martin allows the fire to go out, but sees at a distance the fire of the demons. He goes three times and carries away huge pieces of burning wood, but cannot rekindle the fire. In the morning his brothers find the fire out and three masses of gold among the embers. Waldeck, always bold and daring, is now rendered harsh and presuming by prosperity. He buys lands and forests, builds a castle and obtains a patent of nobility. At a tournament of nobles he has the presumption to appear, with a gallantly-equipped retinue. Being odious to the nobles and hewing down a herald with his sword, he is seized, tried, condemned to have his right arm struck from his body and driven from the lists by the rabble. His brothers carry him off in a cart to a nearby convent. On the way the demon appears and asks, "How like you the fire MY coals have kindled?"

---

1. Scott, *The Antiquary*, Chapter XXI.

Being charitably received at the convent, Waldeck makes his first confession to the very priest whom he had helped to stone out of the Hartz forest, three years before. He dies, and Scott concludes:

"Thus were the miseries attendant upon wealth, hastily attained and ill employed, exemplified in the fortunes of Martin Waldeck."[1] Brown's Waldeck ends his miserly and criminal career in a prison.

Do not these portrayals sound somewhat alike?

"I found Welbeck . . . at the breakfast-table. . . . He then said, turning to me, 'A lady will enter presently, whom you are to treat with the respect due to my daughter.' . . . I so far conquered my timidity, however, as to snatch a look at her. . . . Perhaps the turban that wreathed her head, the brilliant texture and inimitable folds of her drapery, and nymphlike port, more than the essential attributes of her person, gave splendor to the celestial vision. . . . I could only remark that her accents were thrillingly musical. . . . Breakfast being finished, the lady, apparently at the request of Welbeck, sat down to a piano-forte. . . . She played without a book, and, though her bass might be preconcerted, it was plain that her right-hand notes were momentary and spontaneous inspirations."[2]

"The old man led the way into a summer-parlor, where a frugal meal was placed on the table. As they sat down to the board, they were joined by a young lady about eighteen years of age, and so lovely, that the sight of her carried off the feelings of the young stranger from the peculiarity and mystery of his own lot, and rivetted his attention to every thing she did or said. She spoke little, and it was on the most serious subjects. She played on the harpsichord at her father's command, but it was hymns with which she accompanied the instrument."[3]

Similar accounts are these of hidden monies.

"My tumultuous curiosity was suddenly checked by the following leaves (of the manuscript) being glued together at the edges. . . . The edges were torn away, and the leaves parted. . . . The object that my eyes encountered . . . was beyond the power of the most capricious or lawless fancy to have prefigured. . . . *a banknote!* . . . *Twenty thousand dollars!*"[4]   "It must be in the book still, whatever it is," thought Pleydell; "and again applied himself

---

1. Scott, *The Antiquary,* Chapter XVIII.
2. *Arthur Mervyn,* I, 52-3, 54.
3. Scott, *Guy Mannering,* Introduction, 1829.
4. *Arthur Mervyn,* I, 127-8.

to the pocket-book, until he discovered, on a narrow scrutiny, a slit, between the pasteboard and leather, out of which he drew three small slips of paper."[1]

There are many points in common between Brown's Carwin and Scott's Dousterswivel, the Adept, of *The Antiquary*. Carwin, the biloquist, enters the story with no very clear excuse; by his gift of ventriloquism he induces the deaths of Wieland's family, as it were by proxy; and he escapes punishment and makes his exit to no destination in particular. Dousterswivel, whom Scott satirizes as Dousterdevil and Dustanshovel, is a German knave, who makes a mysterious, unknown entrance into England and carries on his machinations by leading a double existence and working upon the superstitions of his neighbors. He defrauds Sir Arthur Wardour and others by getting them into his debt by promising to change lead into gold. He operates nights from the ruins of the Abbey of St. Ruth. He is captured as an impudent, fraudulent, mendacious quack, and questioned for his roguery and let depart. Both characters go among their acquaintances by day and practice their quasi-scientific powers by night.

Lord Glenallan in the same novel is a character whom Scott transformed after the manner of Brown's Wieland. From a kind, noble young man, he becomes a recluse, a wreck in body and almost in mind—brooding over his secret marriage, a horrible invention of his mother in regard to it, death by suicide of his wife, kidnaping of his child, travel wildly about Europe, sickness and slow recovery, inquiry of the authorities into the death of his wife and bafflement by the family. For twenty years, till his mother's death, the poison of her fabricated lie and fraud rankled in him;—unrefreshed by sleep, unnourished by food, uncomforted by devotions, he deplores:
"I vegetated on as I could in the same spot, fancy, feeling, judgment, and health, gradually decaying, like a tree whose bark has been destroyed."[2]

Scott's fourth novel, *Rob Roy* (1817), may also be thought to reflect some of Brown's ideas, without being directly quoted. In his Introduction to the 1829 edition, Scott says of Rob Roy:

---

1. Scott, *Guy Mannering,* Chapter LVI.
2. Scott, *The Antiquary,* Chapter XXXIV.

"Thus a character like his, blending the wild virtues, the subtile policy, and unrestrained license of an American Indian, was flourishing in Scotland during the Augustan Age of Queen Anne and George I. . . . The devoted sept (Mac Gregors, Rob Roy's clan), ever finding themselves iniquitously driven from their possessions, defended themselves by force, and occasionally gained advantages, which they used cruelly enough. This conduct . . . was studiously represented . . . as arising from an untameable and innate ferocity, which nothing, it is said, could remedy. . . . Hence they became versed in predatory forays, and accustomed to bloodshed."

This describes quite accurately the Americans dispossessing the Indians and their retaliations.

"Do not, therefore, throw away your pretty sayings—they serve fine gentlemen who travel in the country, instead of the toys, beads, and bracelets, which navigators carry to propitiate the savage inhabitants of newly-discovered lands."[1]

This was a practice of the explorers of America. The Baille, in a fight with the Highlander, picked up a red-hot coulter, using it as a weapon. After the fuss was over, the Highlander says,

"But, honest gentleman, neist time ye fight . . . let it be wi' your sword . . . and no wi' thae het culters and fire-prands, like a wild Indian."[2]

Rashleigh Osbaldistone, the villain of Scott's story, seems to be a combination of Brown's Carwin in *Wieland* and Welbeck in *Arthur Mervyn*.

"The features of Rashleigh were such as, having looked upon, we in vain wish to banish from our memory, to which they recur as objects of painful curiosity, . . . and even of disgust. His features were . . . irregular; . . . his keen dark eyes, and shaggy eyebrows, redeemed his face from the charge of ugliness. But there was in these eyes an expression of art and design, and a . . . ferocity tempered by caution. . . . Rashleigh Osbaldistone was possessed of a voice the most soft, mellow, and rich in its tones I ever heard,"[3] says his cousin Francis.

Clara Wieland was thrilled at the "mellifluent" tones of Carwin's voice and was fascinated by his Spanish appearance:

"shaggy locks . . . eyes lustrously black, and possessing, in the

---

1. Scott, *Rob Roy,* Chapter VI.
2. *Ibid.,* Chapter XXVIII.
3. *Ibid.,* Chapter VI.

midst of haggardness, a radiance inexpressibly serene and potent,
. . . which served to betoken a mind of the highest order";[1] and
she sketched his likeness for future contemplation.

The father of Rashleigh admonishes him:
"Rashleigh, thou art a sly loon—thou hast ever been too cunning
for me, and for most folks. Have a care thou proven too a cunning
for thysell—two faces under one hood is no true heraldry."[2]
Carwin had two voices in one mouth, to his own shame and to the
consternation of the Wielands,—using his accomplishment of ventriloquism to terrify them, driving Wieland farther on his way
to insanity and Clara to oppose him by prudence, as Scott's Diana
does.

In his way, Scott attempts transformation of character. Diana,
Rashleigh's cousin, is the product of her education. From him
she learned Greek and Latin and most of the modern languages
of Europe, whose moral instincts he tried to undermine. She
deprecates his guidance:
"he pursued that purpose from year to year, without one single
momentary pause of remorse or compassion—the purpose for which
he would have converted into poison the food he administered to
my mind . . . under the arts of this accomplished villain! . . .
there is a mystery connected with Rashleigh, of a dangerous and
fatal nature. . . . You . . . must . . . foil his artifices by opposing
to them prudence, not violence."[3]

Later, in the employ of his uncle, Francis's father, Rashleigh
steals ready money and papers of credit, plays fast and loose with
Rob Roy, tries to break the will of his father and plans treason
against his country while assuming both merit and influence. When
he tries to seize Osbaldistone Hall, willed to Francis, by force and
captures Diana and her father, he (Sir Frederick Vernon) says:
"Rashleigh, thou art a detestable villain!" and Diana says, "Rashleigh, I pity you—for, deep as the evil which you have labored
to do me, and the evil you have actually done, I cannot hate you so
much as I scorn and pity you."[4]

Rob Roy arrives on the scene, rescues the captives and wounds

---

1. *Wieland*, 73.
2. Scott, *Rob Roy*, Chapter XI.
3. *Ibid.*, Chapter XIII.
4. *Ibid.*, Chapter XXXIX.

Rashleigh fatally. Francis attempts to save him. Rashleigh, among some of his last words, execrates:
"I hate you with a hatred as intense, now while I lie bleeding and dying before you, as if my foot trode on your neck. . . . My very patrimony has become yours—Take it . . . and may the curse of a dying man cleave to it."[1]

Welbeck in *Arthur Mervyn* kept the Italian Clemenza from learning English that he might dominate her, seduced her and left her in poverty, hired Arthur to aid him in his money schemes, stole the papers representing Clemenza's estate, railed at Arthur frequently for his curiosity and suspicions, cursed him when he visited Welbeck in prison and died relinquishing other money stolen from the interred body of Watson, whom he had murdered and buried.

In one of Scott's *Tales of My Landlord—Old Mortality* (1816), the year of *The Antiquary,* one may almost assert the relationship between Brown's account of Huntly's meeting with a panther, a quotation from which is given in connection with the discussion of that novel, and Scott's recounting the visit of Morton to the Old Covenanter Burley, living in a cave.

Brown speaks of craggy eminences, deep dells, hollows, cavities, caverns and caves in a wild region far from home and a tree-trunk bridge Edgar felled across the crevass. The panther crossed the trunk and entered a cave eight feet from Edgar. Then he crossed the trunk and it fell. The panther in pursuit made a mighty leap and fell short. Scott describes the cavern hidden
"among dells and thickets, caves and cataracts . . . lying in a remote and wild district. . . . But crossing in the very front of the fall, and at scarce three yards distance from the cataract, an old oak-tree, flung across the chasm in a manner that seemed accidental, formed a bridge of fearfully narrow dimensions and uncertain footing. The upper end of the tree rested on the platform on which they (a young girl and Burley) stood—the lower or uprooted extremity extended behind a projection on the opposite side, and was secured, Morton's eye could not discover where. . . . As . . . he began to consider how he should traverse the doubtful and terrific bridge, which, skirted by the cascade, and rendered wet and slip-

---

1. Scott, *Rob Roy,* Chapter XXXIX.

pery by its constant drizzle, traversed the chasm above sixty feet from the bottom of the fall, . . . (the young girl, barefoot, led the way, and), fixing his eye firm on a stationary object on the other side, without allowing his head to become giddy, or his attention to be distracted by the flash, the foam, and the roar of the waters around him, he strode steadily and safely along the uncertain bridge and reached the mouth of a small cavern on the farther side of the torrent."[1]

Burley was standing, sword in one hand and Bible in the other, and talking aloud as if to friends or spirits. Morton speaks to him as an acquaintance at the fight of Bothwell Bridge and entreats him to surrender a paper for property belonging to the rightful owner. Burley casts the document into a small fire burning to keep the cave warm and dry. This recalls Eliza's burning of her father's will. The men scuffle and Burley tries to kill Morton, as his secret hiding-place is now known. Morton leaves and Burley by "one spurn" of his foot overwhelmed the tree-trunk drawbridge, with a thundering and crashing, into the abyss below. Morton by a mighty leap, like that attempted by the catamount, sprang clear across the fearful chasm which divided the mouth of the cave from the projecting rock on the opposite side and safe from his enemy.

These descriptions are striking illustrations of the harmony between scene and incident, between mental and spiritual states. The spiritual terror of the Old Covenanter inspired by his frenzied struggle with imaginary fiends and his continual fear of enemies accord well with the gloominess, wildness and inaccessibility of his surroundings. Morton's mental disquietude as to how he shall find his friend Burley and how he shall get across to the cave are paralleled by the physical terror of the deep gulf and a roaring flood spanned by a slippery tree trunk. Huntly had had to make mental calculations as to the panther's plan and had suffered the trepidation and solitariness of his condition and the physical considerations of the cave, the slight tree-trunk bridge and the gulf. Burley's growing religious fanaticism parallels Brown's transformation of Wieland into a religious madman.

A discussion of names is enlightening. The first three of Scott's novels—*Waverley*, 1814; *Guy Mannering*, 1815; *The Antiquary*,

---

1. Scott, *Old Mortality*, Chapter XLIII.

1816, written while Brown's novels were still best sellers in England, have some names the same as he used and other modified. Names used unchanged are Brown, Arthur Mervyn, Dudley, Morton, Lovel, Wardour, Waldeck, Stanley, Wilmot, Lucy, Talbot, Gabriel, Eliza, Sophia, Louisa and Wieland. Wardour, Lovel, Stanley and Wilmot are characters in *Clara Howard.* "I met Mr. Lovel," said Julia (Wardour), slightly coloring, "when I resided this last spring with my aunt Mrs. Wilmot." It will be remembered that to Mary Wilmot, Philip Stanley was affianced before his meeting with Clara Howard. Scott's Stanley may have been suggested from the fact that *Clara Howard* had been published in London in 1806 under the title *Philip Stanley.* Scott's Philip Talbot may come from both *Philip Stanley* and *Jane Talbot,* his Lucy Talbot from *Jane Talbot* and Lucy Villars in *Arthur Mervyn,* Sir Arthur from Arthur Mervyn, Sophia Wellwood from Sophia Westwyn. Modified similar names include Pleydell for Pleyel, Teresa for Theresa, Misticot (whom Sir Arthur said should be Misbegot or Mishdigoat) for Medlicote, Corsard for Carsol. Once in *Rob Roy,* Scott brings in the name Ormond, in speaking of the Duke of Argyle: "He was an honest Tory in those days, and hand in glove with Ormond." This writer has been unable to find any reference to Brown's or Miss Edgeworth's choice of the title *Ormond.* Scott speaks of genii, spirits, witches, the panther (in his poetic headings), scarlet fever and the plague,—perhaps in place of Brown's yellow fever.

Waverley has been somewhat indiscreetly called "The Castle Rackrent of Scotland." Scott acknowledged his indebtedness to Maria Edgeworth and desired to do for Scotland what she was doing for Ireland. Her three novels—*Castle Rackrent,* 1801; *The Absentee,* 1812; and *Ormond,* 1817,—are national in subject, giving precise pictures of Irish life, which Scott said gave him the idea of preserving Scottish legends. They opened up a new field of sane, excellent material and characters; and as Saintsbury commented: "Corny the 'King of the Black Isles' in *Ormond* actually adds a new province and a new pleasure in fiction." Miss Edgeworth, for more than sixty years, both preceding and following Scott's production of novels, wrote short stories, novels and Irish studies.

Her romance, *Ormond,* claims attention in this work. Did she take

its title from Brown's *Ormond* or did she, Brown and Scott, all three take the name from the Duke of Ormond? *Ormond, a Tale* written eighteen years after Brown's novel, seems to follow it more closely than merely in name. However, the Ormond of the later novel is a youth wholly unlike Brown's Ormond. Harry Ormond is like Arthur Mervyn, uneducated by schooling, naive, kind-hearted, virtuous, genuine. The author transforms him, following Brown's general theme, by his experiences, one after another,—inculcating studiousness; politeness; dislike of casuistry, scandal and sham; self-control; sense in place of sensibility, sensation and sensualism,— "confirming his principles, settling his character and deciding for ever his taste and judgment until he should maintain that high character, which, in spite of his neglected education, and of all the adverse circumstances to which he was early exposed, he had *formed* for himself by resolute energy."[1]
He marries the titled, well-educated lady of his choice, after her choice of him before and after his being perfected.

Arthur Mervyn, a country youth with desultory learning, is led through a similar sequence of experiences until he is fitted to wed the titled, polished, educated Achsa Fielding, by her choice of him. Both youths were dominated at times by rascally, cynical, unscrupulous men. Both became benevolent agents,—Arthur in numerous adventures to aid those in distress, Ormond in the treatment of the Irish peasants on his estates.

At one time Ormond was full of *Tom Jones*. He compared his cousin Dora to Sophy (Sophia) Western, a name handed down from Fielding to Brown, using Sophia Westwyn. Naively Arthur says: "I felt no scruple on any occasion to disclose every feeling and every event";[2] so with Harry: "the ingenuous young man directly opened his whole heart to him (his uncle)."[3]

Miss Edgeworth's influence was very great, destined to tempt many imitators,—among them Scott, Charles Reade, Samuel Lover, Frances Burney, Jane Austen and Maturin, a compatriot of hers. Both Miss Edgeworth and Maturin, were romanticists, but she slightly satirized the pseudo- or Gothic romance and he made

---

1. Edgeworth, *Ormond*, 244.
2. *Arthur Mervyn*, II, 179.
3. Edgeworth, *Ormond*, 220.

Gothecism run riot in his romances and earned title to the headship of the School of Terror. Saintsbury denounced the habit of some critics to compare authors—"these attempts to rank the 'light white sea-mew' as superior or inferior to the 'sleek black pantheress'," meaning the attempt to rank Maria Edgeworth with Charles Maturin. One wonders if Saintsbury took a hint from Brown's American romance, *Edgar Huntly,* in choosing the epithet *pantheress.*

In most of Brown's novels some man is conceived of as a being of inordinate desires, which at a later time has been given the name Byronic. Ormond and Welbeck are of this type,—exceedingly passionate and of unrestrained wickedness. They may be called pre-Byronic, just as Walpole's hero and several of Mrs. Radcliffe's may be so designated. However, it is not with Byron, but with Shelley (1792-1822), that Brown's name is forever to be associated. His heaping up of original and impulsive incidents is matched only by Shelley in his romances, distinguished by grand picturesqueness and a bold, grotesque, untempered imagination. Peacock in his *Memoirs of Shelley* (1860) said:

"He was especially fond of the novels of Brown—Charles Brockden Brown, the American, who died at the age of thirty-nine. . . . Brown's four novels, Schiller's *Robbers,* and Goethe's *Faust* were, of all the works with which he was familiar, those which took the deepest root in his mind and had the strongest influence in the formation of his character. . . . The first of these novels was *Wieland.* Wieland's father passed much of his time in a summer-house, where he died of spontaneous combustion. This summer-house made a great impression on Shelley, and in looking for a country house he always examined if he could find such a summer-house, or a place to erect one. . . . The second was *Ormond.* The heroine of this novel, Constantia Dudley, held one of the highest places, if not the very highest place, in Shelley's idealities of female character. . . . The third was *Edgar Huntley; or, the Sleep-walker.* In this his imagination was struck by, captivated by the picture of Clitheroe in his sleep digging a grave under a tree. . . . The fourth was *Arthur Mervyn*: chiefly remarkable for the powerful description of the yellow fever in Philadelphia. . . . No descriptions surpass those of Brown. The transfer of the hero's affections from a simple peasant girl to a rich Jewess displeased Shelley, and he could only account for it on the ground that it was the only way Brown could bring his story to an uncomfortable conclusion. The three preceding tales had ended tragically. . . . He devotedly admired Wordsworth and Coleridge, and in a minor degree Southey, . . . but admiration is one thing and assimilation is another; and nothing so blended itself with the structure of his interior mind as the creations of Brown. Nothing stood so clearly before his thoughts as a perfect combination of the purely ideal and possibly real in Constantia Dudley."[1]

Shelley found his summer-house. He lived in Byron's house at Estes near Venice:
"The house was cheerful and pleasant: a vine-trellised walk . . . led from the hall door to a summer-house at the end of the garden, which Shelley made his study."[2]
Either Mrs. Shelley shared her husband's desire for a summer-house or she continued to frequent his after his death. In *The Last Man,* she has Adrian take his family to France and then to Italy after the plague had subsided in London. Clara goes along to care for the children, Lionel and Evelyn. A little summer-house is frequented by the children and death stalks even there.[3]

Though the summer-house that Shelley finally found may not have come up to his ideal, he had no trouble in describing imaginary ones. Brown sponsored a long line of such houses or pavilions. The elder Wieland had what
"seemed a summer-house—three hundred yards from his house, on the top of a rock . . . sixty feet above the river. . . . The edifice was slight and airy . . . a circular area, twelve feet in diameter . . . edged by twelve Tuscan columns. . . . This was the temple of his Deity."[4]

In *Rosaland and Helen* (1817)—Helen perhaps named from Brown's Helena—
"they came to a stone seat beside a spring; o'er which the columned wood did frame a roofless temple." . . . "Amid a bloomless myrtle-wood on a green and seagirt promontory . . . there stood . . . an altar and a temple bright circled by steps." (This was built by Lionel's mother.) "Each new moon, that lady did, in this lone fane, the rites of a religion sweet whose god was in her heart and brain." The likeness can be noted at once. At first it was a place of solitary, individual worship, like the elder Wieland's; later it became

---

1. *Peacock's Memoirs of Shelley,* 35-7.
2. Shelley, Mrs. P. B., *Shelley Memorials,* 93.
3. Shelley, Mrs. P. B., *The Last Man,* III, 272.
4. *Wieland,* 31.

a meeting-place for friends, like that of the Wielands, Pleyel and Carwin.

Previous to Shelley's literary summer-house, but after Brown's, others had appeared. In Lewis' "Anaconda" (Romantic Tales, 1806), eight years after *Wieland,* there is described a "small, circular pavilion," a few hundred yards from Seafield's dwelling, "situated on a small eminence" and surrounded by "a circle of palm-trees, resembling a colonnade." In Leigh Hunt's *Story of Rimini* (1816), Canto III, is described Francesca's favorite retreat:

"And in the middle of those golden trees, half seen amid the globy oranges, lurked a rare summer-house, a lovely sight,—small, marble, well-proportioned, creamy white. . . . The rest was domed on top, and circular . . . 'twas a temple . . . built to the nymphs that haunted there of old."

As a social philosopher, romancer and employer of curious scientific phenomena, Brown had a three-fold interest for Shelley. Being extravagantly romantic in his youth, Shelley was keenly delighted by Brown's romances. He may be said to have launched the true romanticism in England. Shelley had an inborn passion for reform, and Brown's re-iteration of Mary Wollstonecraft's doctrine of equal education and of the same rights for men and women was enough to win Shelley's attention, not to speak of the fact that she was the mother of Shelley's wife. Science was one kind of the marvellous that enravished Shelley.

"His greatest passion at Eton was for chemistry. . . . The chemical experiments which the young student eagerly pursued at Eton were not discontinued when he was at home. . . . We (his sister speaking) were placed hand in hand round the nursery table to be electrified. . . . His own hands and clothes were constantly stained and corroded with acid."[1]   The writer of an article in the *Atlantic Monthly* surmised that "he (Shelley) perhaps pursued chemistry as much with the hope of raising a ghost as from any other motive."[2]

So far as is known Shelley had an interest in natural philosophy and chemistry only for the amusement they afforded him. Brown's

1. Shelley, Mrs. P. B., *Shelley Memorials,* 5, 10.
2. *Atlantic Monthly* 61: 714.

spontaneous combustion, ventriloquism, good and evil spirits, insanity, somnambulism and yellow fever were the kind of science that intrigued Shelley and lured him on to use it in his writings.

The novels of Godwin, Mrs. Radcliffe and Lewis also pleased Shelley. He said:

"From a reader, I became a writer of romances; before the age of seventeen, I had published two, *St. Irvyne* and *Zastrozzi,* each of which, though quite uncharacteristic of me as now I am, yet serve to mark the state of my mind at the period of their composition. . . . My age is now nineteen. . . . You (William Godwin) will perceive that *Zastrozzi* and *St. Irvyne* were written prior to my acquaintance with your writings. . . . I had, indeed, read *St. Leon* before I wrote *St. Irvyne,* but the reasoning had then made little impression."[1]

The two stories, published 1810 and 1811 respectively, while Shelley was a freshman at Eton, are of the extreme Gothic type and reflect his crude, excitable, enthusiastic, violent imagination. They are morbid, unreal, full of absurd situations, wordiness and immaturity. They provide such undigested materials as he would afterward use. The horrors in his tales are probably partly a reaction from the natural shrinking he experienced against the floggings of his teachers and the fagging and torments he rebelliously endured from most of the fellows in college. He borrowed characters, incidents, Gothic machinery, even names from writings of this type.

The opening scene of Zastrozzi where Zastrozzi has Verezzi borne into a "deep chasm, which yawned in a dell close by," in "an immense forest," reminds one of the cavern into which Edgar Huntly fell as a sleep-walker. His painful sensations on awaking: "my thoughts were wildering and mazy"; and his subsequent encounters with a maiden bound in the cave, four sleeping Indians and an Indian at the mouth of the cave have a parallel in the following passage:

"Verezzi followed as fast as his frame, weakened by unnatural sleep, and enfeebled by recent illness, would permit; yet, scarcely

---

1. Shelley, Letters to William Godwin, London, from Keswick, Jan. 10 and 16, 1812, in T. J. Hogg, *Life of Percy Bysshe Shelley,* 1858, II, 55, 62.

believing that he was awake, and not thoroughly convinced of the reality of the scene before him, he viewed everything with a kind of inexplicable horror which a terrible dream is wont to excite. . . . Verezzi for the first time, saw the masked faces of his persecutors. . . . His triumphant persecutor bore him into the damp cell, and chained him to the wall."[1]

Both he and Huntly awake from a strange sleep, with the resulting mystery and confusion. Verezzi was later taken by his captors from the river cavern to a lonely cottage and put under the charge of an old woman. Finally escaping, he was

"overcome by languor, sank on some stone steps, which led to a magnificent mansion, and resting his head on his arm, soon fell asleep."

Edgar, after rescuing himself from the pit and the captive white girl from the Indians, goes to a small hut or cabin, inhabited by the old Indian woman Deb. Verezzi's experience is also like that of Arthur Mervyn, who came to the city, was taken ill of yellow fever, found by Dr. Stevens, "reclining against the wall"; "rousing him from his stupor. . . . The lethargy into which he was sunk . . . he fixed his languid eyes upon me,"[2] said the doctor.

Uncontrollable revenge swayed Zastrozzi, and love for Verezzi and jealous hate of Julia swayed Matilda. Zastrozzi drifts into a castle, and, idly picking up a paper that lay on the floor near an escritoire finds through its means an old associate, Matilda,— which imitates Huntly, who, returning home from his Indian encounters, enters a farm house, finds an escritoire and his own packet of papers near by and encounters his old friend and teacher Sarsefield. Matilda's attempt to commit suicide in the Danube and her rescue by Verezzi took its rise from Welbeck's attempted suicide in the Delaware and his swimming to save his cowardly self. Curiosity is a common attribute with both authors. Verezzi spies upon Zastrozzi and Matilda; and Edgar spies upon Clithero.

In *St. Irvyne; or, The Rosicrucian,* Wolfstein's thoughts of suicide and the manner of expression may have been suggested by Brown's novels:

"What, what is death? Ah, absolution! thy pang is blunted by the

---

1. Shelley, *Prose Works,* I, 56, 61, 66, 82. (Cf. Edgar Huntly, 165-79).
2. *Arthur Mervyn,* I, 5-7.

hard hand of long protracted suffering—suffering unspeakable, indescribable. . . . For what then should I longer drag on the galling chain of existence?"
Seduction, crime, misery, disbelief in immortality govern the book.

This presentment of impressions is somewhat similar to that of the effects of Carwin's appearance upon Clara Wieland:
"For the ideas which the countenance of this man (Nempêre) inspired Eloise, she in vain endeavored to account. It appeared to her that she had seen him before; that the deep tone of his voice was known to her; and that eye—found some counterpart in herself. . . . Her thoughts were not within her control and she trembled as she reflected on the appalling and mysterious influence which the image of a man, whom she had seen but once, and whom she neither loved nor cared for, had gained over her mind. . . . She felt no prepossession in his favor; she rather detested him, and gladly would never have again beheld him."[1]
The subsequent history of these two characters resembles in many respects the intercourse between Carwin and Clara Wieland, each girl meeting the man in a lonely place at a late hour. Eloise, like Sophia Westwyn in *Ormond*, accompanying her ailing mother for four years on journeys through Europe and Italy where she dies, accompanies her dying mother and meets a mysterious stranger, Nempêre, in a lonely house where they take refuge.

Carwin's knowing of the movements of Clara and Ormond's uncanny watching of Constantia with malicious self-conceit and his apparently supernatural powers have their counterpart in Ginotti's specific knowledge of Wolfstein's life and thoughts. The fiery decease of Ginotti and Wolfstein shows a resemblance to Wieland's father's death by spontaneous combustion. Both Ginotti and his victim are blasted by lightning:
"on a sudden Ginotti's frame mouldered to a gigantic skeleton, yet two pale and ghastly flames glared in his eyeless sockets. Blackened in terrible convulsions, Wolfstein expired; over him the power of hell had no influence. Yes, endless existence is thine, Ginotti— a dateless and hopeless eternity of horror."

When asked by Stockdale, publisher of *St. Irvyne*, the cause of

---

1. Shelley, *Prose Works*, I, 116, 172, 178, 179. (Cf. Wieland, 70-75, 156-170, etc.)

Ginotti's death Shelley first replied (Nov. 14, 1810):
"Ginotti, as you will see, did not *die* by Wolfstein's hand, but by
the influence of that natural magic which, when the secret was
imparted to the latter, destroyed him."   Later Shelley
said: "On a re-examination you will perceive that Monfort physically
did kill Ginotti, which must appear from the latter's paleness."
Shelley stated that Nempêre is Ginotti.

Shelley's two stories show his trial at abandonment of orthodox
morality, rebellion against God and the beginnings of free love.
He far surpasses the comparative conservatism of Brown. His
use of terrifying characters and horrible incidents outstrips contemporary fiction in ultra-Gothecism.

"It is interesting," commented Smyth in *Philadelphia Magazines
and Their Contributors* (p. 152—),
"to find young Shelley confessing his obligations to the Philadelphia
novelist, and saying that Brown's novels influenced him beyond any
other books. Traces of *Wieland* are to be found deeply stamped
upon *Zastrozzi* and *St. Irvyne*. It is a singular chapter in literary
history that records the progress of Godwin's social theories and
tales of horror across the Atlantic to an abscure house in Philadelphia and their return in a new literary form into the hands of
Godwin's son-in-law, Percy Bysshe Shelley, himself a poet of
American descent"—on his mother's side.

Among Shelley's poems, written in 1817, is one entitled "To
Constantia, Singing," and among a group of poems called "Fragments," clearly unfinished, collected and revised by William M.
Rosetti, is the poem "To Constantia." Evidently in the opening
stanza of the former poem, Shelley refers to Constantia's last contest with the villain Ormond:

> "Thus to be lost and thus to sink and die
> Perchance were death indeed!—Constantia, turn!"

The rest of the poem describes the bewitching power of her singing:

> "Her voice is hovering o'er my soul—
>
> . . .
>
> The blood is listening in my frame,
>
> . . .
>
> I am dissolved in these consuming ecstasies!"[1]

---

1. Shelley, *Complete Poetical Works*, 405-6, 502.

Through Sophia, Brown likewise testifies to Constantia's musical ability:

"If ever human tones were qualified to convey the whole soul, they were those of Constantia when she sung:

'The breeze awakes, the bark prepares
To waft me to a distant shore;
But far beyond this world of cares,
We meet again to part no more'."[1]

The two Constantia lyrics were addressed by Shelley to Claire Clairemont, who must have cherished the nickname Constantia, for she added it to her other names and signed herself Clara Mary Constantia Jane Clairemont. Like Claire, Constantia had a lovely, natural singing voice. She sang to her father's playing the lute to comfort him in his blindness. She and Sophia used to sing together the above song, the singing of which by Sophia later led to their finding each other.

No doubt the character of Constantia, the result largely of her education, as detailed by Brown in *Ormond* and relayed to the readers by this writer in the discussion of that novel, appealed to Shelley, knowing so well *A Vindication of the Rights of Woman* (Wollstonecraft) and Brown's *The Rights of Women*. Her staunch independence, her ability to earn a subsistence, her capacity to think and decide, her unconventional conclusions and acts and her tastes in reading corresponded to his own traits and the qualities he hoped to attain.

"This daughter had already exhibited proofs of a mind susceptible of high improvement, and the loveliness of her person promised to keep pace with her mental acquisitions. He (her father) charged himself with the care of her education. . . . Miss Dudley's notions had little in common with those around her. . . . Not that she was perfectly exempt from intervals of weakness or from the necessity of painful struggles . . .; but its tumults were brief, and speedily gave place to quiet thoughts and steadfast purposes. . . . She had been taught a very different lesson. Marriage included vows of irrevocable affection and obedience. It was a contract to endure for life. . . . She knew the fascination of wealth, and the delusiveness of self-confidence. . . . This change in her condition she treated lightly, and retained her cheerfulness unimpaired. . . . to the

---

1. *Ormond*, 155.

alleviation of her parents' sorrows. . . . she began to deliberate what conduct was incumbent on herself, . . . and blunt the edge of this calamity by the resources of a powerful and cultivated mind. . . . Her mother's disposition was soft and pliant, . . . She died a victim of discontent. She (Constantia) did not despair. Her sweetness and patience was invincible, . . . but her fortitude did not exceed the standard of human nature. . . . She was embued with an ardent thirst of knowledge, and, by the acuteness of her remarks and the judiciousness of her inquiries, reflected back upon his (her father's) understanding as much improvement as she received. . . . The mind of Constantia was a stranger to pusillanimity. Death, as the common lot of all, was regarded by her without perturbation."[1]

The word-painting that Constantia gives of Ursula Montrose was applied to Constantia—figure small, of exquisite proportions, glowing tints of her cheeks veiled with darkness from the influence of the torrid sun, features irregular:

"if we substitute a nobler stature, and a complexion less uniform and delicate, it is suited, with the utmost accuracy, to herself. . . . Her sweetness and gentleness were uniform. . . . Constantia did not form her resolutions in haste, but when once formed they were exempt from fluctuation. She reflected before she acted, and therefore acted with consistency and vigor. . . . When her heart is once set upon a thing, all the devils will not turn her out of her way. . . . I know she'll do what she promises. . . . Her reasonings might be fallacious or valid, but they were so composed, arranged, and delivered, were drawn from such sources, and accompanied with such illustrations, as plainly testified a manlike energy in the reasoner. In this indirect and circuitous way, her point was unanswerably established. . . . Constantia could not but accept this bequest . . .; she justly regarded the leisure and independence thus conferred upon her as inestimable benefits."[2]

It was her cheerfulness in poverty, a powerful and cultivated mind, thirst for knowledge and patience invincible that enraptured Shelley. The ideal Shelley sought in women, in those whom he married and divorced in life and in his imagination, was an accordant union of perfect physical beauty and perfect spiritual beauty. The delineation of Constantia's character reveals Brown's

---

1. *Ormond*, 9, 17, 18, 19, 21, 24, 35.
2. *Ibid.*, 63, 67, 121, 79, 80, 131, 144.

self, specifically in her reasonings with "manlike energy."

A third direction, at least, which Shelley's debts to Brown took, was in the way of science, or pseudo-science, if one may so relate the subject of yellow fever, as an example. In *The Revolt of Islam* (written as Laon and Cythna, 1817), Shelley shows that he had read not only Brown's accounts in *Ormond* and *Arthur Mervyn,* but Defoe's tale and Wilson's drama. In both novels Brown dwells on the panic of anticipation of the scourge; some sickened and died even before the plague reached their district. Shelley suggests some going to the length of suicide through fear:

> "It was not thirst, but madness. Many saw
>   Their own lean image everywhere; it went
> A ghastlier self beside them, till the awe
>   Of that dread sight of self-destruction sent
> Those shrieking victims.
>
> . . .
>
> Strange panic first, a deep and sickening dread,
>   Within each heart, like ice, did sink and dwell.
>
> . . .
>
> There was no food.
>
> . . .
>
> There was no corn."[1]

Both authors speak of famine, victims running through the streets, rich and poor leveled by death. Constantia bought Indian corn and made cornmeal mush or samp.

Brown spoke of shrieks and the burial of some not quite dead. Arthur Mervyn was in danger twice of being picked up by the death-cart. At Welbeck's house he hid in a loft to prevent premature seizure and in a house where robbers were at work he was struck unconscious; but for the timely intervention of Estwick, a Quaker nurse, he would have been carted away to the horrid hospital or worse. Undoubtedly Shelley and Mrs. Shelley read together Brown's novels and were influenced, she as shall be seen in the discussion of *The Last Man.*

Because of Shelley's intense liking for Brown's novels, one would be inclined to find in his youth the outcropping of ideas from

---

1. Shelley, *The Revolt of Islam,* X, 22, 16, 18, 19. (Cf. Arthur Mervyn, I, Chapter XIV.)

the novels. **Might** it be that Shelley's love-affairs were modeled after those in *Ormond?* Ormond loved Helena, though
"Nature seemed to have set impassable limits to her attainments . . . mediocrity of understanding."[1]   When he met Constantia, "Her discourse tended to rouse him from his lethargy, to furnish him with powerful excitements, and the time spent in her company seemed like a doubling of existence."[2]
He cast Helena off, saying, "I am molded by circumstances. . . . I will guard thy ease and thy honor with a father's scrupulousness. Would to heaven a sister could be created by adoption! . . . I will own thee to the world for my sister. . . . All other claims are swallowed up in a superior affection. . . . there exists one whom I love with unconquerable ardor."[3]
Helena committed suicide by taking laudanum.

Shelley married Harriet Westbrook and abandoned her and their two children,—however providing for them,—because of a mental infatuation for Mary Godwin, with whom he lived and whom he married after the suicide of Harriet by drowning. Both Ormond and Shelley had had an earlier love-affair than these mentioned. Does not Shelley reflect Brown's sister idea in his *Epipsychidion* in these words:

> "Would we two had been twins of the same mother!
> Or that the name my heart lent to another
> Could be a sister's bond for her and thee,
> Blending two beams of one eternity!"

Unhesitatingly one may say that Brown's "men of soaring passions and intellectual energy" did for Shelley what the author hoped it would do for all—"enchain the attention and ravish the souls of those who study and reflect."

Besides memorializing Shelley and connecting the influence of Brown's novels upon him, Peacock himself seems to have read the novels and been influenced also. Leastwise, he uses certain ideas or expressions. In *Crotchet Castle,* a robber being caned by Rev. Dr. Folliott yells: "Hold! Hold! reverend sir, I am disabled already in every finger, and in every joint."[4] In *The Fortunes of Elphin,*

---

1. *Ormond,* 106, 121.
2. *Ibid.,* 131.
3. *Ibid.,* 134, 135, 137. (See also Arthur Mervyn, II, 186.)
4. Peacock, *Crotchet Castle,* Chapter VIII.

a voice of warning is heard at various times by Elphin: "Beware of the oppression of Gwenhidwy (signifying the mermaid lure or power of the sea)." Elphin goes to warn the Lord High Commissioner of the Royal Embankment, of the rottenness of the dike and need of repairs. That night a terrible storm breaks down the sea-wall. Elphin and Angharad, the Commissioner's daughter, together hear the voice of warning and escape, with a few others. Many are drowned. The Commissioner saves himself by throwing his arms over two empty barrels. No explanation of the voices is given at this time in relation to these warnings; but it was said that king Gwythno was not fond of the sea: that a moonstruck bard had warned him long ago to beware of the oppression of Gwenhidwy.

"By the name of the Yellow Spectre, Taliesin (foster son of Elphin and Angharad) designated a pestilence, which afterwards carried off great multitudes of the people."[1]

Brown names *yellow* fever. There seems no reason other than Brown's use of *yellow* for Peacock's using "Yellow."

The influence of Brown is evident not only in Shelley's works, but confessedly in the romances of Mrs. Shelley. *Frankenstein, or the Modern Prometheus* (1818) gives an exaggerated treatment of scientific material. She followed Brown in the use of science as an agent in her romance, but she adapted its methods to the peculiar purpose of the novel of terror. She wanted to frighten her readers as she had been frightened by reading current Gothic romances, Lewis' *The Monk,* in particular.

Frederic C. Prescott, in his "Wieland and Frankenstein," American Literature, II, 172-3, May, 1930, says that he thinks that the germinal idea of *Frankenstein* may have come from Carwin's words to Clara Wieland in his confession:

"Catharine was dead by violence. Surely my malignant stars had not made me the cause of her death; yet had I not rashly set in motion a machine over whose progress I had no control, and which experience had shown me was infinite in power? Every day might add to the catalogue of horrors of which this was the source. . . . I did appear—in the entry—did speak. The contrivance (speaking of biloquium) was mine, but—"[2]

---

1. Peacock, *The Fortunes of Elphin,* Chapters I, IX.
2. *Wieland,* 234, 239.

Like Prometheus, who was reputed to have been the creator of the human race, Frankenstein, a young student of physiology, constructed a monster mainly out of materials obtained from the churchyard and the dissecting room and gave it a sort of life. Rendered frantic by his unsatisfied human cravings, the monster commits atrocious crimes and inflicts most dreadful retribution on his creator. He finally rushes to the frozen regions of the North and destroys himself. The name Frankenstein has become synonymous for one destroyed by his own works and even for the name of the object constructed. The romance is a singular production. The author displays great power and imagination in her many terrifying incidents and withal in her depiction of the mental and emotional states of her chief actors.

In *The Last Man* (1826) is still more apparent the influence of Brown. Mrs. Shelley depopulates the whole earth within the years 2092 to 2100 by means of a plague very similar to the yellow fever which Brown had experienced and so accurately describes in *Ormond* and *Arthur Mervyn*. Her hero, Verney, who speaks in the first person as Arthur does, says:

"I had never before beheld one killed by pestilence. While every mind was full of dismay at the effects, a craving for excitement had led us to peruse DeFoe's account, and the masterly delineations of Arthur Mervyn. The pictures drawn in these books were so vivid, that we seemed to have experienced the results depicted by them. . . . Does the reader wish to hear of the pest-houses where death is the comforter—of the mournful passage of the death-cart—of the insensibility of the worthless, and the anguish of the loving heart—of harrowing shrieks and silence dire—of the variety of disease, desertion, famine, despair, and death. There are many books that can feed the appetite craving for these things; let them turn to the accounts of Boccaccio, DeFoe, and Browne (sic.)"[1]

"Mrs. Shelley in her novel, *The Last Man,* founds her whole description of an epidemic, which nearly destroys the human race, on 'the masterly delineations of Arthur Mervyn',"[2] said one critic. Many details by the two authors are similar. Quotations from Brown's two novels are given in Chapters III and VI.

1.   Shelley, Mrs. P. B., *The Last Man,* II, 208, 224-5.
2.   Higginson & Boynton, *A Reader's History of American Literature,* 71-2.

Giving the general effects of the plague upon London, Mrs. Shelley specifies:

"The symptoms of plague increased rapidly in London. It was deserted by all who possessed the power of removing. . . . The better sort of houses were shut up; the busy trade of the town palsied; there was an air of anxiety among the few passengers I (Verney) met. . . . I met several funerals; they were slenderly attended by mourners, and were regarded by the spectators as omens of direst import. Some gazed on these processions with wild eagerness—others fled timidly—some wept aloud. . . . The epidemic was gifted with a virulence before unfelt. . . . The green sward was strewn with corpses . . . with deathly exhalations. . . . It was called an epidemic. . . . No voice was heard telling us to *hold!* (a plain reference to Carwin's biloquial power in *Wieland*). . . . The vast cities in America . . . are menaced with utter ruin. . . . In the still uncultivated wilds of America . . . Plague should be numbered."[1]

A hospital scene described by Mrs. Shelley is in almost every respect a recasting of that in *Arthur Mervyn;* and she gives to the plague about the same symptoms as are given to yellow fever.

"O! Were you cruel enough to send me there. . . . The ward was filled with an effluvia that caused my heart to heave with painful qualms. The dead were carried out, and the sick brought in, with like indifference."[2]

The visitation of a plague separates people into two classes as Brown and Mrs. Shelley pointed out. The kind physician, Dr. Stevens, and his wife Eliza, Arthur, Medlicote and Estwick, in *Arthur Mervyn*, Thompson, Constantia and Sarah Baxter in *Ormond*, Adrian and Verney in *The Last Man*, who tenderly, unselfishly and wisely care for the sick, represent the helpful ones; and selfish persons, who pillage the unprotected estates of their neighbors and cast off or desert their ill friends and dependents, as Thetford, who had thrust out Wallace and a maid to live or die, in *Arthur Mervyn*, Ryland and the Methodist impostor in *The Last Man* represent the morally delinquent and heartless. Whiston in *Ormond*, who abandoned his dying sister, was carried from

"under the shelter of a hayrick . . . from this unwholesome spot to a barn . . . deserted by every human creature, burning with fever,

---

1. Shelley, Mrs. P. B., *The Last Man*, II, 186-7, 121, 165, 149, 151. (Cf. Arthur Mervyn, I, 139-41.)
2. *Ibid.*, II, 252.

tormented into madness by thirst, spent three miserable days in agony" and died.[1]   Mrs. Shelley says, "The poor wretch is deserted, dying succourless. . . . Deeds of heroism also occurred, whose very mention swells the heart and brings tears to the eyes. Such is human nature, that beauty and deformity are often closely linked. . . . Hope . . . was better than a doctor's prescription."[2]

Both authors tell of the abatement of fever when winter came on and of the re-opening of resorts of pleasure. "The theatres were open and thronged; dance and midnight festival were frequented."[3]

Comparisons other than the plague scenes might be made that no less prove Mrs. Shelley's debt to Brown's novels. Clara Wieland says, "still I live . . . with adders lodged in my bosom, and stinging me to madness."[4] Perdita threw herself on the floor. "The concentrated pride of her nature . . . awoke, and with its adder's sting pierced her heart."[5] The adder-viper complex was discussed in Chapter IV. Perdita's maid's name is Clara, who, like Constantia in the adverse circumstances of her father, made it "her perpetual study to relieve us from labour and to spread ease and every elegance over our altered mode of life."[6] There is a girl named Lucy; and Evadna has a delirium, like Clara Wieland. A few of Brown's peculiar words appear frequently—asperities, assiduities, aversion, prognostications, curiosity, transmigrated for transformed, impregnated, sedulously, circuitously.

Doesn't this sound like Brown's sort of investigation, as in the words of Jane Talbot, Chapter I? "I began, fold by fold, to unwind the many errors of my heart and to discover how brutish, savage and worthless I had hitherto been."[7]

Verney and Adrian and their families go to the Continent to escape other seasons of the plague; roving refugees accompany them; the deaths of many occur in France, Italy and Greece, leaving

---

1. *Ormond,* 40.
2. Shelley, Mrs. P. B., *The Last Man,* II, 224, 226, 234.
3. *Ibid.,* II, 237. (Cf. Ormond, 66, 215-6.)
4. *Wieland,* 247.
5. Shelley, Mrs. P. B., *The Last Man,* I, 293.
6. *Ibid.,* II, 320.
7. *Ibid.,* I, 47.

Verney, who bemoans himself:

"I remained alone of my race, . . . I was the LAST MAN." (He closes his career with some Brown-like ideas:) "O, worn and beating heart, may I dissect thy fibres, and tell how in each unmitigable misery, sadness dire, repinings, and despair existed. . . . I found writing materials on a table in an author's study. . . . I also will write a book . . . for whom to read?—to whom dedicated? . . . Behold the history of the last man. I will leave a monument of the existence of Verney the Last Man."[1]

Among Mrs. Shelley's *Tales and Stories* is "Transformation," evidently so titled from the alternate title of *Wieland*. Unlike Brown's natural transformations, the hero, through the supernatural, necromantic power of a dwarf, exchanges for gold and jewels his perfect body for that of the dwarf for three days; the dwarf overstays the time and the hero seeks him and fights him to intermingle their blood that the spell may be broken and he be transformed to his original self.

Borrowed names and other details appear in the stories, such as Helena, Constance for Constantia, Catherine, Clarice, Fanny, Henry, Bainbridge, a temple, a recess, a summer-house, "Serpents and adders were in my heart," "My brain and my heart seemed on fire."

As a youth Edward Bulwer-Lytton (Lytton, for short) read and enjoyed Brown's novels, which were in vogue in England a few years before he began to write his novels. Numerous minor details in the stories seem to reflect trifles from Brown's novels.

"In this work (Falkland, 1827), it has been my object to portray the progress of the passions; to chronicle a history rather by thoughts and feelings than by incidents and events, and to lay open the minutest and more subtle mazes and secrets of the human heart . . . I endeavor to perfect my knowledge of the human heart,"[2] which is reminiscent of Brown's words.

"All that day she (Emily) was silent and abstracted; the face haunted her like a dream. . . . The forehead, indeed, constituted the principal feature of his countenance, . . . all that night his soft low voice rung in her ear, like the music of an indistinct and half-remembered dream."[3]

---

1. Shelley, Mrs. P. B., *The Last Man*, III, 298, 342, 343.
2. Bulwer-Lytton, *Falkland*, 44, 26.
3. *Ibid.*, 33, 35.

One has but to recall Clara Wieland's sketch of Carwin after her first meeting him and hearing his thrilling tones,—her pondering his voice and features for a day and a night together and often thereafter.

Lady Flora in *The Disowned* (1828) had a small summer-house of stone similar to the Wielands,' situated in the most retired part of the grounds; and Devereux in his retirement in Italy dwelt near and often visited "a small *temple,* of the lightest architecture, . . . before the fountain," reminding one of the elder Wieland's temple.

"Hold! Hold!", which was Carwin's method of warning in *Wieland,* finds its echo in several of Lytton's stories, as also Brown's device of having concealed characters. In *The Disowned,* Glendower (Mordaunt) shouts, "Hold! hold! There will be no need of argument or refinement in this case; tell me at once your scheme and I at once will accept or reject it."[1]   In *Devereux* (1829) is the sentence: "Hold, Hold!" I cried; "do with me what you will; and I will act."[2]   In *Lucretia* (1846), Ardworth says to Percival: "Hold!—tempt me no more—do not lure me to loss of self-esteem!" "Hold, Hold!" he exclaimed then,—"hold, unhappy man!—it is your mother, whom you denounce!"—almost Carwin's words to prevent Wieland from murdering his sister. "Hold!" cried Lucretia tremulously. "Hold! and if he does, I shall owe his hate to you—to your lessons—to your deadly influence."[3]

Lytton has in mind transformation of character, though not as inherently as Brown does. Lucretia rages: "I will pluck out the weeds! I will transform myself." Of her it is said, she was "transformed at once into softness, meekness, even while racked with passion and despair," only to wield her own evil influence. "Hold, sir!" exclaimed Lucretia haughtily—but it passed quickly, and she added with fierce composure—"you are right, go on!"[4] Susan, Lucretia's half-sister, wept, amazed at Mainwaring's *transformation*—"No care now for new books—the music on the instrument goes

---

1. Bulwer-Lytton, *The Disowned,* 293.
2. Bulwer-Lytton, *Devereux,* 433.
3. Bulwer-Lytton, *Lucretia,* 337, 446, 33.
4. *Ibid.,* 33, 86, 322.

unheeded! Books, roses, music!—what are these trifles to a man thinking upon cent. per cent? Mainwaring's very countenance altered—it lost its frank affectionate beauty; sullen, abstracted, morose. It showed that some great care was at the core."[1]
In prefacing *Lucretia, or, The Children of the Night,* Lytton said, "Money the Arch-ruler of civilization insinuates itself into our thoughts and motives, our hearts and actions. . . . Labour and patience are the true school masters on earth."
Brown uses arch-foe, arch-deceiver and arch-villain.

Names may have significance. Following Brown, this author uses Conway, Talbot, a retired wealthy nobleman who discovers a great-nephew in the Disowned and makes him his heir, whose mother had been Miss Talbot, Clavering, Lucy, Susan, Gabriel, Mainwaring for Waring and Brown, a broker and salesman of second-hand goods, who is employed by one and then another to find missing persons, carry out errands and so on, a worldly-wise character. Lytton is fond of some of the same unusual words as Brown, which are not noticeable in his later novels, as aspersions, assiduously, interrogatories, ebullitions, nugatory, obsequious, prognosticated, sedulously, corroding (recollections), corrode (my tranquillity).

The story *Pelham* (1828), opens with a young man in a graveyard muttering and weeping over a grave. It is Granville who was accustomed to come to the grave of his sweetheart, seduced in his absence, becoming insane and dying. The behavior of Clithero in *Edgar Huntly* is similar. Nightly his sleep-walking habit was to come to a certain tree, dig up and rebury a box and weep bitterly at times. Granville sought to avenge his sweetheart's death upon Tyrrel. The latter was slain and a locket of Granville's, in which was a miniature of the girl, was found at the scene. He was accused of murder, which he did not commit, as Clithero had been accused. The locket was restored to him by his friend Pelham, to whom he makes a confession of his life, as Clithero did,—a mechanism, which is one of Brown's methods. In *Ormond* is a locket incident. Constantia had sold the locket, and her friend Sophia, whose miniature was in it, repossessed it and restored it

---

1. Bulwer-Lytton, *Lucretia,* 376.

to her.

How does Lytton parallel Brown's panther scenes in *Edgar Huntly?* Of Lucretia and her step-son Gabriel, who was constantly in her company, he says, "the whelp leopard sported fearlessly around the she panther." The author mentions American Indians and works out in specific detail an encounter of Gabriel with a poisonous snake.

"It glided by the sides of the oak, close to the very feet of the foe, and, emerging into the light, dragged its gray coils through the grass; but its hiss still betrayed it. Gabriel sprang through the fissure of the tree, which was hollow like a cavern, and struck at the craven, insulting it with a laugh of scorn as he struck. Suddenly it halted, suddenly reared its crest. The throat swelled with venom, the tongue darted out, and again, green as emeralds glared the spite of its eyes. No fear felt Gabriel Varney; his arm was averted; he gazed spelled and admiring with the eye of an artist. . . . Scarce a moment, however, had he for the gaze; the reptile sprang, and fell, baffled and bruized by the involuntary blow of its enemy. As it writhed in the grass, how its colours came out—how graceful were the movements of its pain. And still the boy gazed, till the eye was sated, and the cruelty returned."
Then Gabriel struck it till "its beauty was gone—shapeless and clotted with gore, that elegant head; mangled and disservered the airy spirals, that delicate shape. . . . The boy trampled the quivering relics into the sod with a fierce animal joy of conquest."[1]
Edgar concluded his killing of the panther to insure his safety; Gabriel not only kills a harmful reptile, but gloats over it and augments his own cruelty of disposition.

A Strange Story (1862) by Lytton reflects Brown's influence in certain details that cannot be called merely co-incidental. Like the whisper in Clara Wieland's ear, Dr. Fenwick says:
"Suddenly beside me I distinctly heard a sigh—a compassionate, mournful sigh. . . . I must have some morbid affection of the brain; I must be under an hallucination.—The phantom, yes—the trance, yes. . . . I heard distinctly a voice of warning and of anguish, that murmured, 'Hold.' I knew the voice, it was Lilian's."
Like Clara, Lilian has visions of a face. "Oh! that terrible face—those serpent eyes—the dead man's skull! Save me—Save me!"[2]

---

1. Bulwer-Lytton, *Lucretia*, 106.
2. Bulwer-Lytton, *A Strange Story*, 141, 235,205.

Margrave the necromancer (whose name may be imitative of Waldegrave) had lured Dr. Fenwick to a summer-house, used as an observatory—with a telescope—, in his sleep. Dr. Fenwick becomes a "sleep-walker . . . which, in your trance, or sleep-walking, made you the involuntary agent of my will," says Margrave, to which Dr. Fenwick replies: "Hold! Are you then, in truth, the murderer of Haroun, and your true name Louis Grayle?"[1] Assumed names are common, as in Brown' novels.

Within a few pages, the author groups many items that appear in *Edgar Huntly*:

"followed me into the cavern, down into the hollows of the cave. And then simultaneously arose all the choral songs of the wilderness; . . . impulsively I struck the block (of stone, for Dr. Fenwick was digging for gold among rocks and tree roots, like Clithero digging under a tree) with the hatchet, or tomahawk, I carried habitually about with me—into the torrent that raged below—the night was half gone. . . . When I had gained the familiar track—the swell of many winding creeks that now intersected the way obliged me often to retrace my steps, to find, sometimes, the bridge of a felled tree which had been providently left unremoved over the foaming current . . . where loose logs and torn trees went clattering and whirled: for I was in danger of life. A band of the savage natives were stealthily creeping on my track—the natives of those parts were not then so much awed by the white man as now. . . . a crowd of the savage natives had risen up as if from the earth . . . motionless, leaning on their clubs and spears," and he saw their eyes as of spirits round about, "who would shrink from a panther and laugh at a ghost."[2]

An old three-volumed novel that undeniably shows the influence of Brown's novels was published anonymously in London, 1829, thirty years after its particular predecessor, with the title—*Waldegrave, A Novel*. Now, Waldegrave was the special friend of Edgar Huntly. In the English novel, Edgar is the bosom friend of Waldegrave. After many disappointments and each suffering near-deaths, they marry with a double wedding the sisters, Edith and Constance Vivian, the latter being named from Brown's Constantia, perhaps. Waldegrave's fore-name is Henry, after Henry Pleyel in

---

1. Bulwer-Lytton, *A Strange Story*, 216-7, 272, 246.
2. *Ibid.*, 202-3, 236, 310.

Wieland. Sir Arthur, Louisa, Will, Watson, Julia, Fielding, the Wilmots and Cato (the dog) are Brown names.

Phrases and ideas seem inheritances: American plants, ebullitions, sedulously, interrogatories, arch-ruffian for arch-villain, "ductile childhood" like "ductile to her will," "I hardly knew you; my brain was on fire," says Waldegrave, recalling Wieland's "brain . . . scorched to cinders"; "a summer-house, built on a crag of jutting rock . . . the temple," similar to Wieland's "temple on a rock . . . the summer-house"; "I should be a serpent in the bosom of this family," like viper or adders in my bosom, of Brown.

Like Constantia and Sophia in *Ormond,* Constance and Edith often sing together: "Like nightingales! La Constanza has the finest voice, but La Edise has a sweetness that ravishes the soul."[1] "How gaily glides our bark along where Como's water glow" and "The breeze awakes, the bark prepares to waft me to a distant shore" are the beginnings of songs of the two pairs of singers. "Ravish the souls of those who study and reflect" are Brown's words in the prospectus of *Sky-Walk* (1798), quoted in the first chapter of this work.

The "Hold!", the apparition and the face in *Wieland* are reproduced in *Waldegrave.* Rathallan has raised his knife (like Clithero, a dagger) to kill Waldegrave. Edgar, thought drowned, appears just in time and warns,
"Hold! . . . put up your knife, or receive the contents of this (a gun). A simultaneous shriek burst from the combatants, whose veins and sinews stretched as if nigh to bursting. . . . They gazed on the spectre. . . . It was Edgar; as if suddenly arisen from the grave, wan, meagre, and shadowy; an unearthly light glared from his eyes, and the sound of his voice was strange and unnatural. . . . Rathallan's hair stood erect upon his head; his eye-balls were strained from their sockets; his lips muttered convulsively, and his limbs tottered."[2]

Lake Como, Italy and England give the author of *Waldegrave* an opportunity for descriptions of scenery for beauty and contrast, as in *Edgar Huntly.*

Spontaneous combustion, or self-combustion, is a pedigraic subject,

---

1. *Waldegrave,* I, 207.
2. *Ibid.,* III, 280, 281. (See Wieland, 166-7.)

which Brown seems to have started on its descent through subsequent novels. Captain Frederick Marryat's *Jacob Faithful* is one in the lineage. Jacob was born on a lighter, which freighted along the Thames River. He and his parents lived continuously on the freighter, except that once a month Jacob's father got off to buy supplies—gin for his wife, tobacco for himself, red herrings and decayed ship-biscuits for their food.

One night Jacob was thinking of the stars, as he slept on deck or in an abandoned dog-kennel when the weather was cold. He says,

"when a sudden I was interrupted in my reveries by a loud shriek, and perceived a strong smell of something burning. The shrieks were renewed again and again, and I had hardly time to get upon my legs when my father burst up from the cabin, rushed over the side of the lighter, and disappeared under the water. I caught a glimpse of his features as he passed me, and observed fright and intoxication blended together. . . . I was recalled to recollection by the smoke which encompassed me, and the shrieks of my mother. . . . I hastened to her assistance. A strong, empyreumatic thick smoke ascended from the hatchway of the cabin. . . . I attempted to go in, but . . . I found that was impossible; it would have suffocated me in half a minute. . . . The smoke had (now) disappeared, and all was silent. . . . I descended. . . . The lamp . . . was still alight. . . . Nothing was burning—not even the curtains of my mother's bed appeared to be singed. I was astonished—breathless with fear; with a trembling voice I again called out, 'Mother!' I . . . ventured to draw back the curtains of the bed—my mother was not there! but there appeared to be a black mass in the center of the bed. I put my hand fearfully upon it—it was a sort of unctuous, pitchy cinder. I screamed with horror."[1]

After a stupefied night of rest, Jacob steered the lighter back to the starting place and to its owner, Mr. Drummond.

"Cases of this kind do indeed present themselves but once in a century, but the occurrence of them is too well authenticated. She perished from what is termed *spontaneous combustion,* an inflammation of the gases generated from the spirits absorbed into the system. It is to be presumed that the flames issuing from my mother's body completely frightened out of his senses my father, who had been drinking freely; and thus did I lose both my parents, one by fire

---

1. Marryat, *Jacob Faithful,* 16-7.

and the other by water, at one and the same time. The propensity of my mother to ardent spirits (gin) had, as always is the case, greatly increased upon her, and her corpulence had increased in the same ratio. She was now a most unwieldly, bloated mountain of flesh. . . . She had seldom quitted her bed . . . indeed her obesity and habitual intoxication rendered her incapable."[1]

The care of the eleven-year-old orphan, Mr. Drummond undertook. Because so many people came to his warehouse to see Jacob and hear the reports of his parents' deaths, a collection plate was placed conveniently for visitors to drop their gifts in. By this method and by Jacob's sale of his mother's ashes and the bed curtains to a doctor for 20 L., he realized 41 L. in all. Jacob was placed in a school for orphans, whose master, Domine Dobbs, a notable teacher, trained him in Christian principles, in Latin and Greek and in love of learning. By one mean student, later expelled, Jacob was called Cinderella, because of the manner of his mother's death. At fourteen, Jacob was apprentised to one of Mr. Drummond's lighters. The story ends well with Jacob the recipient of a very large sum of money and the mansion of a Mr. Turnbull, an ex-whaler, whose life Jacob had saved when he had been carried by the current under the ice in the river; and Jacob married Sarah, Mr. Drummond's daughter.

There is strong probability that Brown influenced Charles Dickens. In *Bleak House* (1853), Dickens introduces spontaneous combustion, as Brown does in *Wieland*. The elder Wieland, who dies of the catastrophic disease, is the predecessor or antetype of Krook in *Bleak House*. Brown's influence in this instance may have been merely suggestive, as Dickens' authorities on the disease differ from those given by Brown, in so far as definite cases are cited.

The author observes, in the Preface,
"I do not willfully or negligently mislead my readers, and . . . before I wrote that description I took pains to investigate the subject. There are about thirty cases on record. I shall not abandon the facts until there shall have been a considerable Spontaneous Combustion of the testimony on which human occurrences are usually received."
Dickens lists certain examples here and then repeats them and gives

---

1. Marryat, *Jacob Faithful*, 17, 14.

additional ones in the text (Chapter XXXIII). Brown lists several cases in *Wieland,* Footnote, p. 39. Dickens' words about abandoning the facts sound very much like Brown's in his Advertisement of *Wieland,* September 3, 1798: "If history furnishes one parallel fact, it is sufficient vindication of the writer."

An almost conclusive evidence that Dickens had Brown's novel before him is the fact that in Chapter XXX, the second before the description of Krook's death by Spontaneous Combustion (Chapter XXXII), he mentions American Indians, which, of course, Brown does in *Wieland* and on only the fifth page before the record of the death of Wieland in a similar manner. Caddy Jellyby, in telling Esther of conditions in her home, the discouragement of her father and the ill care of her brothers and sisters, says:
"Then Pa began to cry again, and said the children were Indians." "Indians, Caddy?" asks Mrs. W. "Yes, Wild Indians," replies Caddy. "And Pa said . . . that he was sensible the best thing that could happen to them was, their being all tomahawked together."

Dickens' description of the effects of the disease is much more horrible, gruesome and disgusting than that of Brown. He tries to transfer the repulsive features of the case to his readers, to intensify their sensation of aversion. He tells of an investigation by the authorities, which makes quite an extended account altogether. He puns upon the words, "Spontaneous Combustion," a number of times, besides the one in the Preface, quoted above. Brown gives only the scientific phenomena attendant upon the disease:—Wieland's wakefulness, restlessness, alarm, hurried midnight exit from home to his temple of devotion, the sudden illumination, a loud report like the explosion of a mine, shrieks, groans, a wounded arm, clothes burned off and unconsciousness. He lived about two hours with partial insensibility, fever, delirium, mortification of the arm, insupportable exhalations, crawling putrefaction and final lethargic slumber into death. Only his caretakers were present.[1]

In *Bleak House* is the report of two men who investigate the dead man's chamber:—hateful with soot hanging about foul air,

---

1. *Wieland,* 34-8.

a thick, yellow liquor, offensive to touch, sight and smell, a stagnant, sickening oil, smouldering, suffocating vapor, dark greasy coating on walls, and ceiling, burnt ash,—all that was left of him. The black cat with tail bristled stands snarling at something on the floor. The men rush out and call, "Help, help, help!"

"Call the death by any name Your Highness will, attribute it to whom you will, or say it might have been prevented how you will, it is the same death eternally—inborn, inbred, engendered in the corrupted humors of the vicious body itself, and that only— Spontaneous Combustion, and none other of all the deaths that can be died."[1]

In the bare title of William Harrison Ainsworth's novel, *Mervyn Clitheroe,* is a clear give-away to Brown's influence over this English novelist. *Mervyn* is taken from the novel *Arthur Mervyn* and *Clitheroe,* from the character Clithero in *Edgar Huntly.* Many phases of the story show partiality for Brown's novels. The hero tells the story in the first person, as Arthur does, and favors him in his numerous adventures and escapes and in his generally benevolent and upright attributes.

Several names besides that of the hero and other Mervyns follow Brown's use of them:—The hero's mother is Clara and Jane is his nurse; Talbot is the name of the retriever belonging to the uncle in whose home he spent his vacations; and Tom, the white tom-cat, very vicious like the panther, is the pet of his aunt, whose death from shooting was cleverly laid to Mervyn by his cousin, Malpas Sale, to ingratiate himself into his uncle's favor that he might inherit the property, which is the object of contention between the two cousins. Two wills, the first against Mervyn because he was said to have killed the favorite cat, and the second, stolen for Malpas by Simon Pownall, an accomplice, make the main theme of the story.

Pownall in Ainsworth's novel is the Carwin of *Wieland.* He dresses as the ghost of Mervyn's uncle, now deceased, and as a phantom besets Mervyn and tries to frighten him by imitating the dead man's voice. He is an apothecary, necromancer and all-round villain. He imposes upon Mr. Hazelrigge (Old Hazy), who

---

1. Dickens, *Bleak House,* Chapter XXXII.

would become the dupe of any impostor who might choose to practice upon him, who read occult books and had dreams.

"Every nook and cranny of the old fellow's head is stuffed full of
tales of hobgoblins, spectres, wood-demons, gnomes, elves, and
fairies, and he reads nothing but books of necromancy, witchcraft,
and judicial astrology."[1]

To escape detection and be near his wealthy dupe, Pownall
(Dr. Hooker) secures a room in a farm building at the Grange,
where he sets up chemical apparatus and makes the bells ring
singly or together, at night, and where through a trap-door he
haunts a chamber, once when Mervyn occupied it, who is

"suddenly roused by an extraordinary knock—a dead, dull, but
distinct sound, as if caused by a heavy blow struck against the
inner side of a wall, just below the room. . . . The mysterious
sound was renewed—knock!—knock!—knock!"[2] from midnight
for two hours.

This reminds one of Carwin's entrance by trap-door into Clara's
house and room and his words—"Hold! Hold!" Mervyn detected
the rascal, who escaped through an underground runway. When he
reported next morning to Old Hazy, he was absolutely incredulous—
probably wilfully. He has an aged sister, who says: "His mania is
incurable, and must be tolerated—'tis well it's no worse. For my
part, I dislike your great bookworms."[3] Wieland became a maniac
from melancholy contemplation and reading.

A summer-house, "a pretty octagonal structure, situated . . .
on the top of a small mount, for a lookout," similar to the temple
of Wieland, built on a high hill, is the final meeting place of old
Hazy and Pownall, who, for much money, promises to hand over
certain relics. Mervyn, ascertaining the time and place of the
interview, by posting a ladder, like Carwin, at a window of the
house and listening, hides under a table covered with a heavy
drape and captures Pownall and recovers the rightful will; Pownall
says of Old Hazy, with a laugh, "he is the most credulous gull
I ever met with," to which the old gentleman cries, with an explosion of rage, "Oh! You prodigious villain! Oh! You arch

---

1. Ainsworth, *Mervyn Clitheroe*, 180.
2. *Ibid.*, 220.
3. *Ibid.*, 254.

deceiver! (Brown's words). I'll strangle you."[1]

Time and space will not permit details of likenesses. A number of Brown's words occur often: ruminate, prognostications, obsequiousness, sedulous, ebullition, capricious, aversion, asperity and tawny—uncleaned panes of windows, "yellow and almost tawny."

Mervyn says: "A hasty temper, indeed, was my failing" and Aphia's "temper frequently offered a wholesome check to my headlong impetuousity." Arthur Mervyn says: "Perhaps one of my grossest defects is a percipitate temper" and Achsa Fielding served to moderate and quell his tumults of untrained disposition. Mervyn's early schooling was attended with caning, as Arthur's, with feruling. Achsa and Aphia—are they allied?

The contrasting virtues of country and city life are given by Ainsworth as Brown had given them sixty years before in *Arthur Mervyn*. Seduction is not absent. Malpas is intrigued with the beauty and kindness of a gypsy girl and betrays her. Gypsies in Ainsworth's novel take the place of Brown's Indians, to give a local, primitive and predatory element. A terrible storm gives the author an occasion to produce a half-seen face, like Clara's glimpse of Carwin's. Mervyn says,

"I caught sight of something . . . namely, a haystack. . . . I was hastening thither when the sound of voices arrested me. Something seemed to whisper caution. . . . I peered cautiously round the corner, and a flash of lightning occurring at that moment, I beheld Simon Pownall conversing with Phaleg and Obed (gypsies). . . . I made a slight noise, which caught the quick ears of Obed."
"There's a man around the corner!" he said; "I saw him draw back his head."   "Phaleg swore lustily at his son, . . . but Obed stoutly maintained the contrary, declaring that he had seen a man's head as plainly as he now beheld his own father's."[2]
The gypsies inveigled Pownall to the rendesvous to try to get the true will to extort money out of both Malpas and Mervyn,—the will which Pownall had concealed somewhere.

In *Wieland*, Brown brings about a recognition by Major Stuart and his daughter Louisa, taken to America by her mother under an assumed name. Ainsworth employs the device of assumed names,

---

1. Ainsworth, *Mervyn Clitheroe*, 351.
2. *Ibid.*, 262.

also. Mervyn's father had gone to India, to war. The mother had died when the child was five years old. His father had married again and had other children. After his family had all died of plague, he returns to England, using the name Major Atherton, to conceal his identity from Mervyn until he established an estimate of his character. They happen to meet at the grave of the wife and mother. "My son! My dear son!" Major Atherton exclaimed. "My father! My dear father!" I rejoined, running into his embrace.[1]

The influence of Brown upon one more writer, George Meredith, will conclude this portion of the work. Constantia Dudley in *Ormond* had become almost a type character to succeeding writers. Brown made her express all that he would have a woman's education to mean. She was the original model of the new type of woman, independent, spirited, dependable (constant) and wise. Meredith utilized her in his character Constantia Durham in *The Egoist* (1879). His characters are distinct, extraordinary, but fully-developed, ready-made, static, as it were, including Constantia. She comes and remains only long enough and is mentioned only often enough to keep Willoughby in mind of the fact that he, the Perfect, has been the dupe of his ideal woman. The author does not sympathize with his characters or lose himself in them; they speak his thoughts; he created them synthetically of the elements he had previously chosen for them. They are little apart from the author.

Meredith might be linked definitely to Brown through the names of his characters. Constantia Durham and Clara Middleton are feminine types from Constantia Dudley and Clara Wieland and Clara Howard. Willoughby, the type man of egoism, talks to Clara of being all in all to each other, but is in love only with himself. Pleyel is true to Clara Wieland, talks little, and really honors her above himself. It is not from genuine passion that Willoughby proposes to Constantia or Clara. One critic said:

"His women are as they would be if emancipated, verging into women as they are, faultily educated, and hemmed in by historic conventions."[2]

---

1. Ainsworth, *Mervyn Clitheroe*, 362.
2. Cross, *The Development of the English Novel*, 262.

This novel by Meredith may reach perfection in expressing realistically and psychologically the author's purpose and meaning, but his characters seldom speak naturally. They pack a whole thought into a single epithet or exclamation, making his style obscure and difficult and limiting the reading of his novels to the student.

With further investigation one might trace the influence of Brown's novels more extensively; and so find the definition of a biography a true one in Brown's case, that in part, and perhaps the greater part, it consists of "what and how produced was his effect on society."

CHAPTER VI

CONTRIBUTIONS TO THE STOREHOUSE OF LITERATURE

The intent is now to segregate from Brown's novels, chiefly *Wieland, Ormond, Arthur Mervyn,* and *Edgar Huntly,* what may be called contributions to the storehouse of literature, from which all who will may read and borrow, omitting previous quotations.

Autobiographical Notes

The first section will give quotations that reveal Brown's character, it would seem. From them, one may judge that Arthur Mervyn is most nearly the author's prototype.

"His constitution was feeble, and he loved to stroll in the woods more than to plough or sow. This idleness was much against his father's inclination and judgment; and, indeed, it was the foundation of all his vices. . . . I hated school. . . . I loved to leap, to run, to swim, to climb trees, to clamber up rocks, . . . to obey the impulse of the moment, and to prate or be silent, just as my humour prompted me. . . . I hated to be classed, cribbed, rebuked, and feruled at the pleasure of one who, as it seemed to me, knew no guide in his rewards but caprice, and no prompter in his punishments but passion. . . . I preferred to ramble in the forest and loiter on the hill; perpetually to change the scene; to scrutinize the endless variety of objects; to compare one leaf and pebble with another; to pursue those trains of thought which their resemblances and differences suggested; to inquire what it was that gave them this place, structure, and form, were more agreeable employments than ploughing and threshing. . . . I sought not the society of persons of my own age, not from sullen or unsociable habits, but merely because those around me were totally unlike myself. Their tastes and occupations were incompatible with mine. In my few books, in my pen, in the vegetable and animal existences around me, I found companions who adapted their visits and intercourse to my convenience and caprice, and with whom I was never tired of communing. . . . I always loved literature, but never,

301

till of late, had I a mind enough at ease to read with advantage.
. . . Education and nature had qualified me for a different scene.
. . . I did not come into the world without my scruples and suspicions. I was more apt to impute kindnesses to sinister and hidden
than to obvious and laudable motives. . . . I was eager after knowledge, and was disposed to profit by every opportunity to survey
the interior of dwellings and converse with their inhabitants. I
scanned the walls, the furniture, the pictures. . . . It (a book)
came attended by recollections respecting a volume which I filled,
when a youth, with extracts from the Roman and Greek poets. . . .
Falsehoods were easily invented, and might lead her far away
from my true condition; but I was wholly unused to equivocation.
Never yet had a lie polluted my lips. . . . This intercourse was
strangely fascinating. My heart was buoyed up by a kind of intoxication. I now found myself exalted to my genial element, and began
to taste the delights of existence. In the intercourse of ingenuous
and sympathetic minds, I found a pleasure which I had not
previously conceived. . . . I did not forget the friends whom I had
left behind, but maintained a punctual correspondence with Stevens,
to whom I imparted all occurrences. . . . With all these my
correspondence was frequent and unreserved, but chiefly with
the latter. . . . I have often reflected with surprise on the nature
of my own mind. . . . That I am still alive, with so many causes
of death, and with such a slow-consuming malady, is surely to be
wondered at. I believe the worst foes of man, at least of men in
grief, are solitude and idleness. The same eternally-occurring round
of objects feeds his disease, and the effects of mere vacancy and
uniformity are sometimes mistaken for those of grief. . . . I reflected
that the source of all energy, and even of life, is seated in thought;
that nothing is arduous to human efforts; that the external frame
will seldom languish, while actuated by an unconquerable soul.
. . . My limbs were scarcely less weak, but my resolutions were
much more strenuous than his (Wallace's). . . . My thoughts have
ever hovered over the images of wife and children with more delight
than over any other images. My fancy was always active on this
theme, and its reveries sufficiently ecstatic and glowing. . . . The
vigour of his days had been spent in acquiring a slender capital;
his diligence and honesty had succeeded, and he had lately thought
his situation such as to justify marriage with an excellent woman,
to whom he had for years been betrothed, but from whom his

poverty had hitherto compelled him to live separate."[1]

"I likewise acquiesced in the proposal to go to Europe; not that I ever expected to arrive there, but because, since my principles forbade me to assail my own life, change had some tendency to make supportable the few days which disease should spare to me."[2] Brown's friends became importunate that he make a voyage to Europe. He was not able and died soon. His own marriage was put off to age thirty-three. (See Edgar Huntly, 162.) Biographers may search his works for tip-offs for the revelation of his character. He is his own best commentator.

Philosophy

By quoting some of Brown's philosophical sayings—How many there are of them!—one might build a survey of his mind.

"I looked forward to a speedy termination of my life with the fullest confidence. . . . I was not only enamoured of death, but conceived, from the condition of my frame, that to shun it was impossible. . . . Such is man. Time will obliterate the deepest impressions. Grief the most vehement and hopeless will gradually decay and wear itself out. . . . Courage is no definite or steadfast principle."[3] "How sudden and enormous the transition from uncertainty to knowledge! . . . Change is precious for its own sake."[4]

"It is one thing barely to comply with the urgencies of the case, and to do that which in necessitous circumstances is best. But to conform with grace and cheerfulness, to yield no place to fruitless recriminations and repinings, to contract the evils into as small a compass as possible, and extract from our condition all possible good, is a task of a different kind. . . . Every thing is progressive in the human mind. When there is leisure to reflect, ideas will succeed each other in a long train, before the ultimate point is gained. The attention must shift from one side to the other of a given question many times before it settles. . . . How bewildered is that man who never thinks for himself! who rejects a principle merely because the arguments brought in support of it are insufficient. I must not reject the truth because another has unjustifiably adopted it. . . . Justice and compassion are the fruit of knowl-

---

1. *Arthur Mervyn*, II, 17, 125, 129, 209; I, 72, 32-3, 65, 198, 67-8; II, 173, 178, 208-9; I, 169, 177; II, 75, 11.
2. *Wieland*, 208.
3. *Ibid.*, 253, 165.
4. *Edgar Huntly*, 2, 90.

edge. The misery that overspreads so large a part of mankind exists chiefly because those who are able to relieve it do not know that it exists. . . . happiness is only attendant on the performance of our duty."[1]   "Which is the most unerring touchstone of merit,—poverty or riches? Ingeniously to supply the place or gracefully to endure the want of riches is the privilege of great minds. To retain humility and probity in spite of riches, and to effect the highest good of ourselves and others by the use of them, is the privilege of minds still greater."[2]

"To be tranquil and steadfast, in the midst of the usual causes of impetuosity and agony, is either the prerogative of wisdom that sublimes itself above all selfish considerations, or the badge of giddy and unfeeling folly. . . . I choose my path suddenly, and pursue it with impetuous expedition. . . . To these considerations was added a sort of charm, not easily explained, and by no means justifiable, produced by the very temerity and hazardness accompanying this attempt. I thought, with scornful emotions, on the bars and hinderances which pride, and caprice, and delusive maxims of decorum, raise in the way of human intercourse. I spurned at these semblances and substitutes of honesty, and delighted to shake such fetters into air and trample such impediments to dust. . . . Methought that, as anger was the food of anger, it must unavoidably subside in a contest with equability. This opinion was intuitive, rather than the product of experience, and perhaps I gave no proof of my sagacity in hazarding my safety on its truth. . . . Blessed be the dispensers of law! . . . It was just, perhaps, to conjure up the demon avarice to fight with the demon anger. Reason alone would, in such a contest, be powerless, . . . 'A man of your bone need not fear a pigmy like me.' . . . Nothing was more a topic of surprise to himself than his forbearance. He knew not how it was. He had never been treated so before. He was not proof against entreaty and submission; but I had neither supplicated nor submitted. The stuff that I was made of was at once damnably tough and devilishly pliant. . . . It may by no means be uncommon for men to *fashion* their conclusions in opposition to evidence and *probability,* and so as to feed their malice and subvert their happiness. . . . Let me gain, from the contemplation of thy misery, new motives to sincerity and rectitude. . . . this man's (Welbeck's) coffers were supplied by the despair of honest men and the stratagems of rogues. . . . I

---

1. *Ormond,* 21, 121, 132, 203, 26.
2. *Clara Howard,* 360.

(Arthur) saw the emptiness of fame and luxury, when put in the balance against the recompense of virtue. Never would I purchase the blandishments of adulation and the glare of opulence at the price of my honesty. . . . I know full well how inexpiably stupid or wicked my act will appear to you, but I will not prevaricate or lie."[1]

"The incapacity of sound sleep denotes a mind sorely wounded. . . . Intense dark is always the parent of fears. . . . Every man, not himself the victim of irretrievable disasters, perceives the folly of ruminating on the past, and of fostering a grief which cannot reverse or recall the decrees of an immutable necessity; but every man who suffers is unavoidably shackled by the errors which he censures in his neighbour, and his efforts to relieve himself are as fruitless as those with which he attempted the relief of others. . . . Disastrous and humiliating is the state of man! By his own hands is constructed the mass of misery and error in which his steps are forever involved. . . . How little cognizance have men over the actions and motives of each other! How total is our blindness with regard to our own performances!"[2]

Pen and Books

What the personal re-actions of Brown were on the subject of writing and books may be known from remarks gathered from his novels.

Carlton was imprisoned for debt. Mrs. Stevens and Arthur visit his sister, and Arthur, casting an eye upon her parchment says: "How now? . . . this is strange employment for a lady. I knew that my friend pursued this trade, and lived by binding fast the bargains which others made; but I knew not that the pen was ever usurped by his sister," who replies, "The usurpation was prompted by necessity. . . . The pen was irksome and toilsome at first, but use has make it easy, and far more eligible than the needle, which was formerly my only tool." . . . "In conjunction with his sister, he once more assumed the pen, and, being no longer burdened with debts, he resumed, together with his pen, his cheerfulness. . . . By their mutual industry they might hope to amass sufficient to discharge the debt at no very remote period."[3]

In Arthur's dealings with Eliza, he ponders:

1. *Arthur Mervyn*, II, 66, 55, 101, 91, 92; I, 77; II, 118, 11; I, 72; II, 43.
2. *Edgar Huntly*, 10, 103, 115, 293-4.
3. *Arthur Mervyn*, II, 45, 173-4, 47.

"This destiny (a medical course) would not hinder punctual correspondence and occasional visits to Eliza. Her pen might be called into action, and her mind awakened by books"; and she asks: "What art so busy about, Arthur? Always at thy pen of late. Come, I must know the fruit of all *this* toil and all this meditation. . . . But, first, what is all this writing about? . . . Your pen cannot teach me like your tongue."[1]

Arthur replies to Eliza and then continues with his life story: "Mrs. Wentworth has put upon me a strange task, . . . She wants a written narrative (of my adventures), . . . Luckily, my friend Stevens has saved me more than half the trouble. He has done me the favour to compile much of my history with his own hand. . . . but he says that adventures and a destiny so singular as mine ought not to be abandoned to forgetfulness. . . . I am glad, however, that the task was performed. It has saved me a world of writing. . . . Mrs. Wentworth requested me to write not as if it were designed for her perusal, but for those who have no previous knowledge of her or of me." . . . (To Dr. Stevens Arthur writes) "I am glad, my friend, thy nimble pen has got so far upon its journey. What remains of my story may be despatched in a trice. . . . You might as well look for silver platters or marble tables in his (my father's) house, as for a book or a pen. . . . It occurred to me that the city might afford me an asylum. . . . I was qualified for no employment, compatible with a town life, but that of the pen. This, indeed, had ever been a favourite tool with me; and, though it may appear somewhat strange, it is no less true that I had had nearly as much practice at the quill as at the mattock. But the sum of my skill lay in tracing distinct characters. I had used it merely to transcribe what others had written, or to give form to my own conceptions. Whether the city would afford me employment, as a mere copyist, sufficiently lucrative, was a point on which I possessed no means of information. . . . He (Welbeck) asked me to give him a specimen of my penmanship. I told him that I had bestowed very great attention upon this art. Implements were brought, . . . and I wrote, 'My poverty, but not my will, consents'."[2]

Arthur had fallen in love with Achsa and thus apostrophizes his pen, perhaps in the manner of Godwin's talk to *paper* in *St. Leon*, published about the same time as *Arthur Mervyn*:

---

1. *Arthur Mervyn*, II, 96, 194, 182.
2. *Ibid.*, II, 194, 195, 137, 18; I, 21-2, 50-1.

"Move on, my quill! wait not for my guidance. Re-animated with thy master's spirit, all airy light! A heyday rapture! A mounting pulse sways him: lifts him from the earth. I must, cost what it will, rein in this upward-pulling, forward-going—what shall I call it? . . . The pen is a pacifier. It checks the mind's career; it circumscribes her wanderings. It traces out and compels us to adhere to one path. It ever was my friend. Often it has blunted my vexations; hushed my stormy passions; turned my peevishness to soothing; my fierce revenge to heart-dissolving pity. Perhaps it will befriend me now. It may temper my impetuous wishes; lull my intoxication; and render my happiness supportable; and, indeed, it has produced partly this effect already. . . . My thoughts range themselves in less disorder. . . . I must continue at the pen, or shall immediately relapse."[1]
Is the first part of this passage humorous? Or sentimental? The second part is pathetic. Was not the pen a "pacifier" and an outlet to Brown's surcharged creative mind and anxious heart?

"Books are cold, jejune, vexatious in their sparingness of information at one time and their impertinent loquacity at another."[2]
            "Books are too often insipid. In reading, the senses are inert and sluggish, or they are solicited by foreign objects. . . . It is only on extraordinary occasions that this faculty (attention) is at once sober and vigorous, active and obedient."[3]

Sentiment

To illustrate Brown's alliance with the sentimental writers a few passages will suffice.

"There is no book in which I read with more pleasure than the face of woman. *That* is generally more full of meaning, and of better meaning too, than the hard and inflexible lineaments of man; and *this* woman's (Achsa's) face has no parallel."[4]

One will remember a previous discussion of Achsa, how Arthur called her *Mamma*. After the burial of Susan, Arthur meditates:

"It seems as if I acted with too much precipitation; as if insensibility, and not reason, had occasioned that clearness of conceptions, and bestowed that firmness of muscles, which I then experienced. . . . If reason acquires strength only by the diminution of sensibility, perhaps it is just for sensibility to be diminished. . . . Ordinary

---

1. *Arthur Mervyn*, II, 196, 197.
2. *Ibid.*, II, 211.
3. Brown, "Alciun," in Dunlap, *op. cit.*, I, 72.
4. *Arthur Mervyn*, II, 185.

rules were so totally overlooked in my behaviour, that it seemed impossible for any one who knew me to adhere to them. . .. I was not conscious of this singularity. The internal and undiscovered character of another weighed nothing with me in the question whether they should be treated with frankness or reserve. . . . Any one who could listen found me willing to talk. Every talker found me willing to listen. Every one had my sympathy and kindness, *without* claiming it; but I *claimed* the kindness and sympathy of every one. . . . Minute details, respecting our own concerns, are apt to weary all but the narrator himself."[1]

"In this mood, her fancy was thronged with recollections of scenes in which her friend (Sophia) had sustained a part. . . . They were transitory but not infrequent, and were pregnant with such agonizing tenderness, such heart-breaking sighs, and a flow of such bitter yet delicious tears, that it were not easily decided whether the pleasure or the pain surmounted. When symptoms of their coming were felt, she hastened into solitude, that the progress of her feelings might endure no restraint."[2]

Thus at times the restrained Constantia became the natural sentimental young lady.

"Thou wilt shudder with my foreboding and dissolve with my tears. . . . Thus I," sobs Edgar Huntly, "who had escaped the deaths that had previously assailed me in so many forms, should have been reserved to solemnize a scene like this by—*dying for joy!*"[3]

Transformation

The alternate title of *Wieland* is *the Transformation*. Brown seems not only to have in mind the changing mental conditions of Wieland from a meditative, religious, kind-spirited man to a killer-maniac; but, regarding other characters, he speaks of transformation or transition, as though his underlying purpose in general was the process of changing individuals. In this attitude toward his characters he set a precedent for all time to true, careful novel writers. The following sentence gives concisely the idea of the devoluting transformation.

"The process by which the sympathies of nature are extinguished in our hearts, by which evil is made our good, and by which we are made susceptible of no activity but in the infliction and no joy but

---

1. *Arthur Mervyn,* II, 65, 179; I, 62.
2. *Ormond,* 155.
3. *Edgar Huntly,* 2, 253.

in the spectacle of woes, is an obvious process."[1]

This process of transformation will be illustrated by applying it to specific individuals—to those in *Wieland* first. As Clara tells the story, she reveals several transformed persons.

After the elder Wieland had read the exposition of the doctrine of the Camisards and the Bible,
"His progress towards the formation of his creed was rapid. . . . He imagined himself beset by the snares of a spiritual foe, and that his security lay in ceaseless watchfulness and prayer. His morals, which had never been loose, were now modelled by a stricter standard. The empire of religious duty extended itself to his looks, gestures, and phrases. All levities of speech, and negligence of behaviour, were proscribed. His air was mournful and contemplative. He laboured to keep alive a sentiment of fear, and a belief of the awe-creating presence of the Deity. Ideas foreign to this were sedulously excluded. To suffer their intrusion was a crime against the Divine Majesty, inexpiable but by days and weeks of the keenest agonies. No material variation had occurred in the lapse of two years. . . . (He built an edifice), the temple of his Deity. Twice in twenty-four hours he repaired hither, . . . Nothing but physical inability to move was allowed to obstruct or postpone this visit. . . . A sadness perpetually overspread his features, . . . His own belief of rectitude was the foundation of his happiness. . . . Suddenly the sadness that constantly attended him was deepened. . . . A command had been laid upon him, which he had delayed to perform. . . . At length he hinted to his wife that his end was near. . . . He was likewise haunted by the belief that the kind of death that awaited him was strange and terrible. His anticipations were thus far vague and indefinite; but they sufficed to poison every moment of his being and devote him to ceaseless anguish. . . . His silence and dejection were likewise in a more than ordinary degree conspicuous. . . . As the evening advanced, my father's inquietude increased. . . . in a tremulous and terrified tone, (he said) that his brain was scorched to cinders. He would then betray marks of insupportable anxiety. . . . At this hour his duty called him to the rock (temple)."[2]

A light was seen within the building, "a report like the explosion of a mine," was heard—piercing shrieks without intermission, a stroke on Wieland's arm and supposed spontaneous combustion

1. *Wieland,* 150-1.
2. *Ibid.,* 28, 29, 31-6.

took place.

The transformation of the son occupies most of the story.

"What a tale had thus been unfolded (Wieland's confession)! I was hunted to death, by one who deemed himself commissioned for this act by heaven; who regarded this career of horror as the last refinement of virtue; whose implacability was proportioned to the reverence and love which he felt for me, and who was inaccessible to the fear of punishment and ignominy". . . . (Wieland speaks) "Thou, Omnipotent and Holy! Thou knowest that my actions were conformable to thy will. I know not what is crime; what actions are evil in their ultimate and comprehensive tendency, or what are good. Thy knowledge, as thy power, is unlimited. I have taken thee for my guide, and cannot err. To the arms of thy protection I entrust my safety. In the awards of thy justice I confide for my recompense. . . . The peace of virtue, and the glory of obedience, will be my portion hereafter. . . . (Escaped from prison, Wieland, now mad, tries to kill Clara, after seemingly sane.) The cup is gone by, and its transient inebriation is succeeded by the soberness of truth. . . . Thinkest thou that thy death was sought to gratify malevolence? No. I am pure from all stain. I believed that my God was my mover! . . . I have done my duty; and surely there is merit in having sacrificed to that all that is dear to the heart of man. If a devil has deceived me, he came in the habit of an angel. If I erred, it was not my judgment that deceived me, but my senses. In thy sight, Being of beings! I am still pure. Still will I look for my reward in thy justice."[1]

Clara weighs his words:

"I wondered at the change which a moment had effected in my brother's condition. Now was I stupefied with tenfold wonder in contemplating myself. Was I not likewise transformed from rational and human into a creature of nameless and fearful attributes? . . . Did my ears truly report these sounds? If I did not err, my brother was restored to just perceptions. . . . all that was human in his face gave way to an expression supernatural and tremendous. . . . Trouble and dismay succeeded to the steadfastness that had lately been displayed in the looks of Wieland. . . . They implied doubt as to the nature of the impulse that hitherto had guided him, and questioned whether he had acted in consequence of insane perceptions. . . . Fallen from his lofty and heroic station; now, finally restored to the perception of truth; . . . Wieland was trans-

---

1. *Wieland*, 208, 195-6, 243.

formed at once into the *man of sorrows!* . . . He saw not that this discovery in no degree affected the integrity of his conduct; that his motives had lost none of their claims to the homage of mankind; that the preference of supreme good, and the boundless energy of duty, were undiminished in his bosom. It is not for me to pursue him through the ghastly changes of his countenance. . . . Thou who hast vied with the great Preacher of thy faith in sanctity of motives, and in elevation above sensual and selfish! Thou whom thy fate has changed into parricide and savage! . . . Speedily this train was broken. A beam appeared to be darted into his mind which gave a purpose to his efforts."[1]

Wieland closed his career by killing himself.

"I reflected," Clara says, "that this madness, if madness it were, had affected Pleyel and myself as well as Wieland."

Hearing a whisper at her ear one night as she lay abed, she says: "No other conclusion . . . but . . . that my imagination had transformed some casual noise into the voice of a human creature. . . . My heart began to palpitate with dread of some unknown danger. . . . I was habitually indifferent to all the causes of fear by which the majority are afflicted. . . . Slight movements and casual sounds were transformed into beckoning shadows and calling shapes. . . . The sound and the vision were present, and departed together at the same instant; but the cry was blown into my ear, while the face was many paces distant (apparition and biloquium of Carwin in Clara's house). . . . The state of my mind naturally introduced a train of reflections upon the dangers and cares which inevitably beset a human being. By no violent transition was I led to ponder on the turbulent life and mysterious end of my father. . . . I repeatedly perused this passage. The ideas which flowed in upon my mind affected me like an instant transition from death to life. . . . Carwin was detected. . . . I partook of Wieland's credulity, shook with his amazement, and panted with his awe. . . . My state was little different from that of my brother. I entered, as it were, into his thoughts. My heart was visited and rent by his pangs."[2]

Looking forward to her death, Clara determined to live in her isolated house, took to her bed and was rescued as the house burned to the ground. She says:

"It is true that I am now changed; but I have not the consolation to reflect that my change was owing to my fortitude or to my

---

1. *Wieland*, 198-9, 243, 247, 248, 249, 250.
2. *Ibid.*, 77, 75-6, 212, 167, 102, 148, 249, 250.

capacity for instruction. Better thoughts grew up in my mind imperceptibly. I cannot but congratulate myself on the change, though, perhaps, it merely argues a fickleness of temper and a defect of sensibility. . . . and a belief insensibly sprung up that tranquillity, if not happiness, was still within my reach."[1]

Clara is taken by her uncle to Europe. She writes letters to Pleyel. After his wife Theresa dies, they are married. Clara represents character transformation upward.

Carwin is one of Brown's transformed characters. He is an Englishman, who resided in Spain three years.

"His garb, aspect, and deportment were wholly Spanish. . . . He had embraced the Catholic religion. . . . On topics of religion and of his own history, previous to his *transformation* into a Spaniard, he was invariably silent."[2]

Such phrases as "conversion to the Catholic faith" and "a suspicion . . . that his belief was counterfeited" are found. A part of Carwin's confession to Clara reads:

"It (biloquium) enables me to mimic exactly the voice of another, and to modify the sound so that it shall appear to come from what quarter and be uttered at what distance, I please. . . . I shall not mention how diligently I cultivated this gift, which seemed capable of an unlimited improvement. . . . Having gained this interview, I purposed to seek some retreat in the wilderness, inaccessible to your inquiry and to the malice of my foe (Ludloe), where I might henceforth employ myself in composing a faithful narrative of my actions."   Clara discusses Carwin: "I ceased to upbraid or accuse. His guilt was a point to which I was indifferent. Ruffian or devil, black as hell or bright as angels, henceforth he is nothing to me. . . . Perhaps you are somewhat interested in the fate of Carwin. . . . So much affected was he by the catastrophe to which he was a witness, that he laid aside all regard to his own safety. He sought my uncle and confided to him the tale which he had just related to me. . . . It was easy for Carwin to elude the persecutions of Ludloe. It was merely requisite to hide himself in a remote district of Pennsylvania. This, when he parted from us, he determined to do. He is now probably engaged in the harmless pursuits of agriculture, and may come to think, without insupportable remorse, on the evils to which his fatal talents have given birth.

---

1. *Wieland*, 254-5, 256.
2. *Ibid.*, 87.

The innocence and usefulness of his future life may, in some degree, atone for the miseries so rashly and so thoughtlessly inflicted."[1]

"Clothes make the man," it is said. Leastwise Arthur Mervyn felt himself remade.

"You may imagine, if you can, the sensations which this instantaneous transformation produced. . . . Check shirt, buttoned at the neck, an awkward fustian coat, check trowsers and bare feet, were now supplanted by linen and muslin, nankeen coat striped with green, a white silk waistcoat elegantly needle-wrought, cassimere pantaloons, stockings of variegated silk, and shoes that in their softness, pliancy, and polished surface vied with satin."[2]

This passage illustrates Brown's realism in little things, as the subject of clothes.—a change from scanty, rustic garments to the finest of elaborate French attire,—to suit his underlying purpose of transforming Arthur's character.

"I have read of transitions effected by magic; I have read of palaces and deserts which were subject to the dominion of spells; poets may sport with their power, but I am certain that no transition was ever conceived more marvellous and more beyond the reach of foresight than that which I had just experienced. . . . I know that my emotions are in danger of being regarded as ludicrous by those who cannot figure to themselves the consequences of a limited and rustic education."[3]

From a green country youth to a philanthropist, the author transforms him.

Were one to pursue Brown's intention of transforming characters, he might go on and on with selections here and there to prove the author's pleasure in transformation. Of himself, Edgar Huntly says:

"My anguish was mingled with astonishment. In spite of the force and uniformity with which my senses were impressed by external objects, the transition I had undergone was so wild and inexplicable; all that I had performed, all that I had witnessed since my egress from the pit, were so contradictory to precedent events, that I still clung to the belief that my thoughts were confused by delirium. There is no standard by which time can be measured but the suc-

---

1. *Wieland,* 217, 218, 231, 251, 258.
2. *Arthur Mervyn,* I, 52.
3. *Ibid.,* I, 54-5.

cession of our thoughts and the changes that take place in the external world."[1]

Clithero, as a study in transformation of character, has been described in the discussion of the novel.

"His scanty and coarse garb had been nearly rent away by brambles and thorns; his arms, bosom, and cheeks were overgrown and half concealed by hair. There was somewhat in his attitude and looks denoting more than anarchy of thoughts and passions. His rueful, ghastly, and immovable eyes testified not only that his mind was ravaged by despair, but that he was pinched with famine. . . . His deeds were monstrous and infernal. His motives were sordid and flagitious. To display all their ugliness and infamy was not his province. No; he did not tell you that (Sarsefield says), . . . in recompense for every benefit (of Mrs. Lorimer), he stole upon her sleep and aimed a dagger at her breast." . . . "If she be alive," Clithero says, "then am I reserved for the performance of a new crime. My evil destiny will have it so. If she be dead, I shall make *thee* expiate."[2]

Clithero's change from incipient madness to the most distraught villainy is comparable to that of Wieland, despite the statement of one critic that there was "no apparent cause for his sudden madness." His madness was growing, deliberate, calculated, not sudden in the author's unraveling of it. Dunlap said: "The vacillation of his thoughts; the extremity of his perils; are described with the pen of a master."

Yellow Fever

Yellow fever is an American subject on which Brown exercised his realistic powers and provided material for future writers. His descriptions are consistent, detailed, personal, coming within his own cognizance. The spectacles which he saw and his sufferings impressed him so deeply that he resolved to transfer into writing his conceptions of the disease and such reflections as would impart to others some of the fruits of the melancholy lessons he had himself learned. He selected incidents which have a moral significance in line with his purpose to suggest methods of alleviation should epidemics recur and to contrast two classes of people acted upon by the same calamity.

---

1. *Edgar Huntly*, 204, 169.
2. *Ibid.*, 108, 276-7, 304.

In conformity with Dr. Miller's and Dr. Smith's acts of kindness, the fiction version has two similar cases. To honor these friends, Brown has Dr. Stevens care for Arthur in his home and has the hero, as one of his charitable enterprises, when on a trip to Baltimore, meet with a young Frenchman, who became ill after caring for a fever victim in his home.

"His malady was such as is known in the tropical islands (Guadaloupe) by the name of the yellow or malignant fever."[1]

Arthur cared for the young man till he died and then carried out his last wishes.

While living with the Hadwins, Arthur went to the city to look for Wallace, their nephew and Susan's lover:

"a rumour, which had gradually swelled to formidable dimensions . . reached us in our quiet retreats. The city . . . was involved in confusion and panic, for a pestilential disease had begun its destructive progress. Magistrates and citizens were flying to the country. The numbers of the sick multiplied beyond all example; . . . The malady was malignant and unsparing. The usual occupations and amusements of life were at an end. Terror had exterminated all the sentiments of nature. Wives were deserted by husbands, and children by parents. Some had shut themselves in their houses, . . . The consternation of others had destroyed their understanding, . . . Men were seized by this disease in the streets; passengers fled from them; . . . they perished in the public ways. The chambers of disease were deserted, and the sick left to die of negligence. None could be found to remove the lifeless bodies. Their remains, suffered to decay by piecemeal, filled the air with deadly exhalations and added tenfold to the devastation. Such was the tale. . . . Methought it was confuted by its own extravagance. . . . Every new day, however, added to the number of witnesses and the consistency of the tale, till, at length, it was not possible to withhold my faith. . . . Belding, Mr. Hadwin's next neighbour, though not uninfected by the general panic, persisted to visit the city daily with his *market-cart*. He set out by sunrise, and usually returned by noon. . . . These meditations did not enfeeble my resolution or slacken my pace. . . . From every mouth the tale of sorrow was repeated with new aggravations. Pictures of their own distress, or that of their neighbours, were exhibited in all the hues which imagination can annex to pestilence and poverty. . . . There was no difficulty or

---

1. *Arthur Mervyn*, I, 92-3.

reluctance in proceeding. . . . As I approached the door of which I was in search, a vapour, infectious and deadly, assailed my senses. It resembled nothing of which I had ever before been sensible. . . . I felt as if I had inhaled a poisonous and subtle fluid, whose power instantly bereft my stomach of all vigour. . . . The streets, as I passed, were desolate and silent. The largest computation made the number of fugitives two-thirds of the whole people; yet, judging by the universal desolation, it seemed as if the solitude were nearly absolute. . . . I wandered over the deserted mansion (Thetford's where Wallace lived). . . . Effluvia of a pestilential nature assailed me from every corner. . . . I imagined that I discovered vestiges of that catastrophe which the past night had produced. . . . The element which I breathed appeared to have stagnated into noxiousness and putrefaction. I was astonished at observing the enormous diminution of my strength. My brows were heavy, my intellects benumbed, my sinews enfeebled, and my sensations universally unquiet. These prognostics were easily interpreted."[1]   These were Brown's own symptoms. Soon after this, Dr. Stevens found Arthur ill.

One of Arthur's proposed philanthropies regarded the hospital. "To offer myself as a superintendent of the hospital was still my purpose. The languors of my frame might terminate in sickness, but this event it was useless to anticipate. The lofty site and pure air of Bush Hill might tend to dissipate my languors and restore me to health. . . . What qualities were requisite in the governor of such an institution? He must have zeal, diligence, and perseverance. He must act from lofty and pure motives. He must be mild and firm, intrepid and compliant. One perfectly qualified for the office it is desirable, but not impossible, to find. A dispassionate and honest zeal in the cause of duty and humanity may be of eminent utility. Am I not endowed with this zeal? Cannot my feeble efforts obviate some portion of this evil? No one has hitherto claimed this disgustful and perilous situation. My powers and discernment are small, but if they be honestly exerted they cannot fail to be somewhat beneficial."[2]

This is Brown's description of a hospital by Wallace, who survived his illness there.
"The atmosphere was loaded with mortal stenches. A vapour, suffocating and malignant, scarcely allowed me to breathe. . . . You

---

1. *Arthur Mervyn*, I, 129-30, 132, 139, 140, 144-5, 156, 165, 169.
2. *Ibid.*, I, 179, 176-7.

will scarcely believe that, in this scene of horrors, the sound of laughter should be overheard. While the upper rooms of this building are filled with the sick and the dying, the lower apartments are the scene of carousals and mirth. The wretches who are hired, at enormous wages, to tend the sick and convey away the dead, neglect their duty, and consume the cordials which are provided for the patients, in debauchery and riot. . . . Oh! how poor are the conceptions which are formed, by the fortunate few, of the sufferings to which millions of their fellow-beings are condemned. This misery was more frightful, because it was seen to flow from the depravity of the attendants. . . . A physician cast an eye upon my state. He gave some directions to the person who attended him. I did not comprehend them, they were never executed by the nurses. . . . Some inexplicable principle rendered harmless those potent enemies of human life. My fever subsided and vanished. My strength was revived. . . . The girl (at Thetford's) . . . entertained an unconquerable dread of the hospital. . . . In going to the hospital, she believed herself led to certain death, and to the sufferance of every evil which the known inhumanity of its attendants could inflict. This state of mind, added to exposure to a noonday sun, in an open vehicle, moving, for a mile, over a rugged pavement, was sufficient to destroy her. I was not surprised to hear that she died the next day. . . . These men will convey thee to the hospital at Bush Hill."[1]

Arthur contemplates his own case: "The mention of that contagious and abhorred receptacle inspired me with some degree of energy. . . . I knew in what manner patients were treated at the hospital, and removal thither was to the last degree abhorred. . . . Its facts were quickly supplanted in my thoughts by the disastrous picture he had drawn of the state of the hospital. I was confounded and shocked by the magnitude of this evil. The cause of it was obvious. The wretches whom money could purchase were, of course, licentious and unprincipled. Superintended and controlled, they might be useful instruments; but that superintendence could not be bought. . . . My new sensations assured me that my stomach had received this corrosive poison. Whether I should die or live was easily decided. The sickness which assiduous attendance and powerful prescriptions might remove would, by negligence and solitude, be rendered fatal; . . . My sickness being suspected, I should be dragged in a cart to the hospital; where I should, indeed,

---

1. *Arthur Mervyn*, I, 173, 174, 159, 149.

die, but not with the consolation of loneliness and silence. Dying groans were the only music, and livid corpses were the only spectacle, to which I should there be introduced."[1]

One wonders if Brown had investigated the hospital and if he had considered such a work or was advocating hospital reform only.

Prisons

The prison as a subject treated in literature was not a new thing when Brown wrote. From Biblical times, at least, to the present, dungeons have been used to hold prisoners and have been described in writings. It was said by Saintsbury that if Fielding had chosen he might have made the prison in *Amelia* as horribly realistic as the ship's hold in *Roderick Random* by Smollet. Imprisonment for debt was almost universal.

"A rascally attorney or a stony-hearted creditor might inflict great hardship under the laws affecting money: and a brutal or tyrannical squire might do the same under those affecting the tenure or the enjoyment of house and land," said the same writer.

English prison literature abounds in massy doors, resounding locks, gloomy passages and characteristic looks of keepers, accustomed to reject every petition and to steel their hearts against feelings of pity. It is indescribable the sort of squalidness and filth with which these prisons were distinguished. All kinds of felons were thrown together—horse thieves, sheep stealers, shop lifters, forgers, counterfeiters, highway robbers, burglars and debtors, young and old.

The prison scene into which Goldsmith has the vicar of Wakefield cast provides a familiar picture and the one with which Brown's prison for debtors tallies most exactly. In the common room were coarseness and vulgarity in conversation and stenches of beer drinking, smoking and dirty humanity. In 1786, when Brown was fifteen years old, Pennsylvania made the first effort at improvement of her prisons by the adoption of the solitary plan of discipline. Over one hundred years earlier, William Penn abolished all but two of the two hundred capital offenses recognized by English law,—murder and high treason. He had no imprisonment for expression of opinion or for debt. No doubt, Brown had in mind the reform of

---

1.   *Arthur Mervyn,* I, 149, 172, 176, 154-5.

prisons, both as a place of confinement for detention until cases could be tried and for actual punishment of some classes of offenders. He gives three views of American prisons of his time: a dungeon for the insane and apartments for debtors and criminals.

"Theodore Wieland, the prisoner at the bar, was now called upon for his defence. . . . You lead me hither manacled as a felon." When Clara proposed to her uncle to visit her brother, he says: "you will never more behold the face of this criminal, unless he is gifted with supernatural strength, and severs like threads the constraints of links and bolts." After Clara had read her brother's confession of his murders, she exclaims: "For this he was condemned to die; to die upon the gallows!" She determined to visit him, but asks, "the fetters which constrained his limbs, . . . how could I endure to behold?" Her uncle says, "You must not enter his dungeon; his eyes will no sooner be fixed upon you than . . . He will shake off his fetters in a moment and rush upon you." . . . "His chains, and the watchfulness of his guards, were redoubled; but again . . . he restored himself to liberty."[1] Wieland killed himself after threatening Clara. Thus is portrayed the treatment of a murderer and a maniac.

In this quotation is inferred the custom of imprisonment for debt:

"Dr. Stevens is requested to come immediately to the Debtors' Apartments in Prune Street." . . . (The doctor explains.) "One of my friends, by name Carlton, was embarrassed with debts. . . . I arrived at the prison. . . . The apartment was filled with pale faces and withered forms. The marks of negligence and poverty were visible in all; but few betrayed, in their features or gestures, any symptoms of concern on account of their condition. Ferocious gayety, or stupid indifference, seemed to sit upon every brow. The vapour from a heated stove, mingled with the fumes of beer and tallow that were spilled upon it, and with the tainted breath of so promiscuous a crowd, loaded the stagnant atmosphere. At my first transition from the cold and pure air without, to this noxious element, I found it most difficult to breathe. . . . Almost every mouth was furnished with a cigar, and every hand with a glass of porter. Conversation, carried on with much emphasis of tone and gesture, was not wanting. Sundry groups, in different corners, were beguiling the tedious hours at whist. Others, unemployed, were strolling to

---

1. *Wieland*, 183, 181-2, 196, 204, 207.

and fro, and testified their vacancy of thought and care by humming or whistling a tune. . . . He (Carlton) shrunk, with fastidious abhorrence, from the contact of the vulgar and the profligate. . . . He had no money wherewith to purchase food. . . . He had not provided a bed on which to lie."[1]

Some time after his visit to Clemenza, Arthur recollects: "Talked she not of Welbeck? Said she not that he was in prison and was sick? Poor wretch!" (So Arthur visits him in prison where he was taken for his crimes.) "Having inquired for Welbeck, I was conducted through a dark room, crowded with beds, to a staircase. Never before had I been in a prison. Never had I smelt so noisome an odour, or surveyed faces so begrimed with filth and misery. The walls and floors were alike squalid and detestable. It seemed that in this house existence would be bereaved of all its attractions; and yet those faces, which could be seen through the obscurity that encompassed them, were either void of care or distorted with mirth. . . . Here brawling and the shuffling of rude feet are eternal. The air is loaded with the exhalations of disease and the fumes of debauchery. . . . We reached a chamber in the second story. . . . The prisoner lay upon the bed, . . . his head upon the pillow."[2]

Virtue and Seduction

Virtue, like curiosity, is its own reward, is giving the reverse of the axiom set forth by Brown: "Curiosity, like virtue, is its own reward." This subject enters into most of his novels incidentally, except in *Ormond,*—virtue versus seduction. One critic, in particular, condemned Brown for introducing it into his fiction, as if he were only copying from the writings from abroad. In a recent number of *The Reader's Digest,* February, 1943, in the article "Paul Revere" by Esther Forbes, are the words:

"The English troops arrived. . . . You cannot quarter troops on a resentful town (Boston) and not have fracases. There were nightly tavern brawls. Redcoats were accidentally jostled off bridges and wharves into water. . . . According to Sam Adams, the British regulars spent most of their leisure beating up small boys, violating the Sabbath and worse yet the women of Boston. The 'lobsters' answered that female virtue was so easy in this stronghold of Puritanism that 'the Yankey war contrary to all others will produce

---

1. *Arthur Mervyn,* II, 37, 38-9.
2. *Ibid.,* II, 116, 118, 119.

more births than burials'."

Brown began writing novels fifteen years after the close of the Revolutionary War. As he thought and wrote on all moral questions, there can be no doubt that he had examples of real cases in mind as well as the method of telling of them in the novels he had read.

Not only does Brown consider virtue its own reward, but that virtue is capable of its own safety, as specifically expounded in *Wieland*. Carwin speaks:

"With succour like this at hand you may safely defy me. He is my eternal foe; . . . Twice have you been saved by his accursed interposition. But for him I should long ere now have borne away the spoils of your honour. . . . I was impelled by a sentiment that does you honour; a sentiment that would sanctify my deed; but, whatever it be, you are safe. Be this chimera still worshipped; I will do nothing to pollute it. . . . Fear me not: . . . I cannot lift a finger to hurt you. Easier would it be to stop the moon in her course than to injure you. The power that protects you would crumble my sinews and reduce me to a heap of ashes in a moment, if I were to harbour a thought hostile to your safety. . . . Environed by the arms of this protection, all artifices will be frustrated and all malice repelled. . . . Your principles teach you to abhor a voluptuous temper; but, with whatever reluctance, I acknowledge this temper to be mine. You imagine your servant Judith to be innocent as well as beautiful; but you took her from a family, where hypocrisy, as well as licentiousness, was wrought into a system. My attention was captivated by her charms, and her principles were easily seen to be flexible. . . . she was taught that the best use of her charms consists in the sale of them. . . . Deem me not capable of the iniquity of seduction."[1]

Clara Wieland meditates upon the subject: "I used to suppose that certain evils could never befall a being in possession of a sound mind; that true virtue supplies us with energy which vice can never resist; that it was always in our power to obstruct, by his own death, the designs of an enemy who aimed at less than our life. . . . Whoever has pointed steel is not without arms; yet what must have been the state of my mind when I could meditate, without shuddering, on the use of a murderous weapon, and believe myself secure merely because I was capable of being made so by

---

1. *Wieland*, 109, 110, 111, 220.

the death of another! . . . A penknife lay open upon my table. . . . It will be immediately supposed that I meant it for my last refuge, and that, if all other means should fail, I should plunge it into the heart of my ravisher. . . . I drew forth from my pocket, and opened, a penknife. 'This be my safeguard and avenger. The assailant shall perish, or myself shall fall.' . . . Reputation and life might be wrested from me by another, but my rectitude and honour were in my own keeping, and were safe. . . . I knew how to find way to the recesses of life. I could use a lancet with some skill, and could distinguish between vein and artery. By piercing deep into the latter, I should shun the evils which the future had in store for me, and take refuge from my woes in quiet death. . . . (When accused by Pleyel, she says) The gulf that separates man from insects is not wider than that which severs the polluted from the chaste among women. . . . My integrity was tarnished and withered in his eyes. I was the colleague of a murderer and the paramour of a thief!"[1]

Regarding the case of Mrs. Stuart, Clara reasons:

"The lady's affections were withdrawn from her husband and transferred to him. . . . Since a legal marriage was impossible, no doubt his views were flagitious. . . . That virtue should become the victim of treachery is, no doubt, a mournful consideration; but it will not escape your notice, that the evils of which Carwin and Maxwell were the authors owed their existence to the errors of the sufferers."[2]

Several such cases are exposed in *Arthur Mervyn*. Arthur says:

"The depravity of Welbeck was inferred from it. The charms of this angelic woman (Clemenza) were tarnished and withered. I had formerly surveyed her as a precious and perfect monument, but now it was a scene of ruin and blast. This had been a source of sufficient anguish; but this was not all. . . . the claims of a parent had been urged. . . . they heightened the iniquity of Welbeck into the blackest and most stupendous of all crimes."[3]

Welbeck had placed Clemenza with Mrs. Villars and her three daughters, a disreputable houeshold, among them Lucy Villars whom Welbeck was misleading. Arthur, as one of his acts of benevolence, rescues Clemenza.

In Welbeck's confession, he tells of the sister of his absent

---

1. *Wieland*, 109-10, 163, 116, 165, 213, 132.
2. *Ibid.*, 260, 262, 263.
3. *Arthur Mervyn*, I, 77.

friend Watson:

"She imagined she had found in me a friend worthy to partake in all her sympathies and forward all her wishes. We were mutually deceived. She was the victim of self-delusion; but I must charge myself with practising deceit upon both myself and her. I reflect with astonishment and horror on the steps which led to her degradation and to my calamity. . . . She was the dupe of the most audacious sophistry and the grossest delusion. I was the slave of sensual impulses and voluntary blindness. . . . Shame and remorse had no power over my life. . . . Am I known to be a seducer and assassin?"[1] he asks Arthur.

The woman died of anguish and a broken heart. Arthur says: "I . . . encountered a thousand dangers to my virtue under the disastrous influence of Welbeck."[2]

The attitude of the author on the subject is clearly revealed in the attitudes of Helena, who yielded to Ormond, and of Constantia, who defied him. Of Helena, it is said:

"To continue in her present situation was not to be endured. Disgrace was a demon that would blast every hope of happiness. She was excluded from all society but that of the depraved. Her situation was eminently critical. It depended, perhaps, on the resolution she should now form whether she should be enrolled among the worst of mankind. Infamy is the worst of evils. It creates innumerable obstructions to the path of virtue. It manacles the hand and entangles the feet that are active only to good. To the weak it is an evil of much greater magnitude. It determines their destiny, and they hasten to merit that reproach which at first it may be, they did not deserve. . . . (Helena) shrunk aghast from her own reproaches and the contumelies of the world."

She withered when Ormond told her roughly that he no longer loved her after he had met Constantia. He called on her later and

"He shrunk from the spectacle that presented itself. . . . Her visage was serene, but sunken and pale. Death was in every line of it." . . . "Thou hast done my work for me. Thou hast saved thyself and me from a thousand evils. . . . You say (reading from a letter she had written) you love her. . . . It is this that sweetens the cup I am going to drink. Never did I go to sleep with more good will than I now go to death."[3]

---

1. *Arthur Mervyn*, I, 88, 89; II, 43.
2. *Ibid.*, II, 116.
3. *Ormond*, 116, 103, 141, 142.

She takes laudanum, the method which Fanny Imlay, Godwin's protege, used later to take her life.

Constantia, locked in and cornered by Ormond, considers her situation:

"to inflict death was no iniquitous exertion of self-defence, and that the penknife which she held in her hand was capable of this service. She had used it to remove any lurking obstruction in the wards of her key. . . . The truth in this respect unveiled itself with the rapidity and brightness of an electrical flash. . . . Death, untimely and violent, was better than the loss of honor . . . 'Ormond! Beware! Know that my unalterable resolution is to die uninjured. I have the means in my power. Stop where you are; one step more, and I plunge this knife into my heart.' . . . She looked at those lineaments of Ormond which evinced his disdain of supplication and inexorable passions. . . . All appeals to his compassion and benevolence would counteract her purpose, since, in the unexampled conformation of this man's mind, these principles were made subservient to his most flagitious designs. . . . To find safety for her honor, even in the blood of an assailant, was the prescription of duty."[1]

In Ormond's reply, he jeers: "Die with the guilt of suicide and the brand of cowardice upon thy memory, or live with thy claims of felicity and approbation undiminished."[2]
Sophia arrives and peeks through the keyhole and hears Constantia gasp: "Shall I never be released? . . . I am imprisoned!"[3] Sophia brings aid; they break the door in and find Craig and Ormond dead and Constantia apparently dead. Later Constantia says:
"My deed was scarcely the fruit of intention. . . . My stroke was desperate and at random. . . . His heart was pierced, and he sunk, as if struck by lightning, at my feet."[4]

Murder and Suicide

Closely related to the foregoing subject, seduction, are those of suicide and murder, as just illustrated and heretofore touched upon. Clara Wieland considers suicide because of Carwin and, as above stated, explains how she would do it, with a lancet.
"At that moment my despair suddenly became vigorous. . . . My

---

1. *Ormond*, 233-4.
2. *Ibid.*, 235.
3. *Ibid.*, 238.
4. *Ibid.*, 240.

bosom swelled with a sudden energy, and the conviction darted through my mind, that to end my torments was, at once, practicable and wise"; and, when her mad brother threatened her, she says: "I grasped it (the knife) with force. . . . Even now I hesitated to strike. . . . Why not . . .? Hurry to the verge of the precipice, and cast myself forever beyond remembrance and beyond hope? . . . Still I live; . . . Have I not resolved? I will die, . . . he seized it with the quickness of thought. I shrieked aloud, but it was too late. He plunged it to the hilt in his neck; . . . He was stretched at my feet."[1]

Arthur Mervyn had an intimate knowledge of a case of seduction ending in suicide.

"Three years ago, a man, by name Colvill, came . . . readily obtained the station . . . of a schoolmaster. . . . A daughter of one of his patrons, young, artless, and beautiful, appeared to have fallen a prey to the arts of some detestable seducer. . . . Colvill was the arch-villain. . . . she whose ruin was first detected, was—*my sister.* This unhappy girl escaped from the upbraidings of her parents, from the comtumelies of the world, from the goadings of remorse, and the anguish flowing from the perfidy and desertion of Colvill, in a voluntary death."[2]

In *The Antiquary* (XXXIV), Scott summarizes in a sentence a like set of circumstances: "Her despair had found a dreadful remedy for all the ills of life."

Arthur himself was the prey of inducements: "I scarcely know how to repel the charge of illicit conduct, . . . There was no point at which it was possible for her (Betty) to get possession of my fancy. I watched her while she practised all her tricks and blandishments."[3]

Brown continues on the subject of decorum, further intrigue and temptation by Betty, in vain. In the same novel, Achsa Fielding relates the story of her life to Arthur and tells of the death of her father-in-law:

"A shocking tale it was! . . . The *kind* of death— . . . It was horrible. . . . (He) had still determined not to survive the day that should reduce him to indigence. The desperate act was thus preconcerted—thus deliberate."[4]

---

1. *Wieland,* 213, 247, 250.
2. *Arthur Mervyn,* I, 187, 188. (See II, 127.)
3. *Ibid.,* II, 129.
4. *Ibid.,* II, 201.

Other murders are recorded, some of which were mentioned in the treatment of the novels individually. Wieland confesses to the murder of his wife Catharine, their four children and Louisa: "It is true, they were slain by me; they all perished by my hand. The task of vindication is ignoble." In the supplementary chapter of *Wieland* is discussed a proposed duel between Stuart and Maxwell. Before it could come off the next morning, as Stuart was returning home in the evening, a swarthy and malignant figure started from behind a column and plunged a stiletto into his body.

Brown in no way condones murder except as the last chance to save one's own life and makes many recorded murders the result of the insanity of the murderers. Edgar Huntly ponders every possibility of escape before taking the life of an Indian and then delays almost too late. Brown no doubt thought on suicide as a way out of suffering.

"By escaping from life, I should be delivered from this scene, but should only rush into a world of retribution, and be immersed in new agonies. . . . They have saved me from murdering myself, a guilt more inexpiable than any which it was in my power to commit. . . . Henceforth I determined to live, . . . and wait till my God should summon me to retribution. To anticipate his call is only to redouble our guilt."[1]

Description

"We know not where could be found such striking and grand descriptions of American forests, wildernesses and caverns. Nature had feeling to rejoice in the strength of men and sorrow with their sorrow. It was a being, not dead, but a frightful, beautiful, powerful, mystifying might. Not the delusive, longed-for belier of mankind of the later romanticists,"
commented the editor in the Introduction of *Edgar Huntley*, London, 1831.

The descriptions of nature in this romance are of scenes through which the author wandered as a youth. In the wild scenery of New York and Pennsylvania and especially in the wilderness at the Forks of the Delaware and Schuylkill rivers he was as much at home as in his native city. His love of beautiful scenery resulted from his ramblings, usually on foot, recommended by his preceptor as a re-

---

1. *Edgar Huntly*, 88, 284, 285.

laxation from the close confinement to his studies, for his health's sake,—a practice he never relinquished. From his store he has given pictures of the land and people, conditions and events, with exact and minute details, showing closeness of observation of particulars. In his portrayals, he selects the details that most nearly tally with a chosen mood. In speaking of moods, he usually includes something of the gloominess and impenetrability of the primeval forest and its solitude.

"I (Arthur) shrouded myself in the gloom of the neighbouring forest, or lost myself in the maze of rocks and dells. . . . Never, in the depth of caverns or forests, was I equally conscious of loneliness. I was surrounded by the habitations of men; but I was destitute of associate or friend."[1]　　　"There was a desolate and solitary grandeur in the scene, . . . A sort of sanctity and awe environed it, owing to the consciousness of absolute and utter loneliness. It was probable that human feet had never before gained this recess, that human eyes had never been fixed upon these gushing waters."[2]

Some one may fairly ask whether Brown was directed to the use of scenery by Mrs. Radcliffe. Yet there seems to be no description of scenery for scenery's sake, just as the author used no art for art's sake, which one has firm ground for saying of Mrs. Radcliffe. His scenes are mostly here a little and there a little, incidentally, as it were, to accord with the mood and circumstances of the story being related.

It is interesting to make a running account of picturesque sentences and phrases.

"The path to the mansion was planted by a double row of walnuts."　　　"I saw nothing but a vista of catalpas, leafless, loaded with icicles."　　　In connection with the burial of Susan, Arthur enumerates: "The tallest tree . . . its sequestered situation, its luxuriant verdure, and profound quiet. On one side was a potato-field, on the other a *melon-patch;* and before me, in rows, some hundreds of apple-trees."　　　"How almost palpable was this dark! . . . The storm passed away, and a radiant moon succeeded. . . . The moonlight was once more universal and brilliant."　　　"the effulgence was meteorus . . . the tangible obscurity to which it succeeded rendered it conspicuous as an electrical flash."

---

1. *Arthur Mervyn,* I, 135, 142.
2. *Edgar Huntly,* 107.

"darksome hours,"   "the blandness of the air and the brightness of the verdure,"   "sudden gust of rain falling,"   "a neighboring quarry,"   "smooth turf,"   "dropping with dew and glistening with the moon's rays,"   "a row of poplars,"   "the effluvia of gunpowder was perceptible,"   "the eastern sky began to brighten with the dawn of morning,"   "sapless stalks and rugged masses were covered with hoarfrost,"   "*limestone;* a substance that eminently abounds in rifts and cavities,"   "hillocks and steeps and pits and brooks . . . slippery and tremulous verge of the dizziest precipices,"   "the reverberations of the torrents and the whistling of the blasts."

"The channel, however, was encumbered with asperities over which the river fretted and foamed with thundering impetuosity. . . . the late storm had purified the air, and the radiance of a full moon was universal and dazzling."

Extensive descriptions are found also, as that of Norwalk, copied in the discussion of *Edgar Huntly,* and this of the contrast of the Delaware and the Schuylkill:

"He (Pleyel) was become the prey of a gloomy and unsociable grief. His walks were limited to the bank of the Delaware. This bank is an artificial one. . . . Reeds and the river are on one side, and a watery marsh on the other, in that part which bounded his lands, and which extended from the mouth of Hollander's Creek to that of Schuylkill. No scene can be imagined less enticing to a lover of the picturesque than this. The shore is deformed with mud and encumbered with a forest of reeds. The fields, in most seasons, are mire; but, when they afford a firm footing, the ditches, by which they are bounded and intersected are mantled with stagnating green, and emit the most noxious exhalations. . . . The scenes which environed our dwellings at Mettingen (home of the Wielands) constituted the reverse of this. Schuylkill was here a pure and translucid current broken into wild and ceaseless music by rocky points, murmuring on a sandy margin, and reflecting on its surface banks of all varieties of heights and degrees of declivity. These banks were checkered by patches of dark verdure and shapeless masses of white marble, and crowned by copses of cedar, or by the regular magnificence of orchards, which, at this season, were in blossom, and were prodigal of odours. The ground which receded from the river was scooped into valleys and dales. Its beauties were enhanced by the horticultural skill of my brother, who bedecked this exquisite assemblage of slopes and risings with every species of vegetable ornament, from the giant arms of the oak to the clustering tendrils of the honeysuckle. . . . In all my rambles I (Carwin) never found a spot in which so many picturesque beauties and rural delights were assembled as at Mettingen. No corner of your little domain unites fragrance and secrecy in so perfect a degree as the recess in the bank. The odour of the leaves, the coolness of the shade, and the music of its waterfall, had early attracted my attention."[1]

If a person reads Brown's descriptions, noting, one by one, the impressions gained from the re-actions of his senses, he realizes that they must have been very keen,—sights, sounds, odors, feelings, rhythm. Yes, rhythm. On almost every page is revealed a sense of rhythmic form. He was constantly alert to the most elusive of sights and sounds, from the shadows made by leaves to the undertones of waters and the changes of seasons and weather.

"The wind was in that direction in which, aided by the deathlike repose of nature, it brought to me the murmur of the waterfall. This was mingled with that solemn and enchanting sound which a breeze produces among the leaves of pines. . . . Next day arose in darkness and storm. Torrents of rain fell during the whole day, attended by incessant thunder, which reverberated in stunning echoes from the opposite declivity. . . . Night at length returned, and the storm ceased. The air was once more clear and calm, and bore an affecting contrast to that uproar of the elements by which it had been preceded."[2]   "Since my departure, winter had visited the world, and the aspect of nature was desolate and dreary. . . . The contrast between these appearances and those which I had noticed on my first approach to it, when the ground and the trees were decked with the luxuriance and vivacity of summer, was mournful and seemed to foretoken ill."[3]

The question might be asked,—Was Brown afraid of water? Of the sea? Several times the thought is expressed.
"He must undergo the perils and discomforts of the ocean; . . . I ridiculed his dread of the sea, and his attachment to home. . . . (He was rescued) from the hazards and fatigues of a fruitless voyage, . . . his absence, in that instance, had been occasioned by his falling from a boat into the river, in consequence of which he had run the most imminent hazard of being drowned. . . . Experience had taught me the insecurity of a canoe, . . . I was, likewise,

---

1. *Wieland*, 66-7, 222.
2. *Ibid.*, 103, 73-4.
3. *Arthur Mervyn*, II, 55-6.

actuated by an hereditary dread of water."[1]
The following is an impression of seeing the ocean for the first
time:

"It was flood-tide and the sandy margin formed a pretty steep
shelf. The billows, therefore, rose to a considerable height, and
broke with great fury against it; and my soul was suspended for
half an hour, with an awe, a rapture which I never felt before."
Of another aspect of the ocean he wrote:

"The scene without was extremely dreary, and the vicinity of the
sea, not being a quarter of a mile distant, gave us very distinctly
the music of his multitudinous waves."[2]

Was Scott reminded of the first description when he wrote of the
cliff of Cornwall in *Guy Mannering?*

The descriptive powers of Brown are graphically displayed in
his telling of Clara's delirium dream, in his portraiture of several
types of persons and the contrasts in two of them.

"Sometimes I was swallowed up by whirlpools, or caught up
in the air by half-seen and gigantic forms, and thrown upon pointed
rocks or cast up among the billows. Sometimes gleams of light
were shot into a dark abyss, on the verge of which I was standing,
and enabled me to discover, for a moment, its enormous depth and
hideous precipices. . . . I was conscious, even during my dream,
of my real situation. . . . and I continued to suffer these abortive
creations till a loud voice at my bedside, and some one shaking me
with violence, put an end to my reverie."[3]

Mr. Melbourne says to Ormond:

"I should like to have heard your opinion of a face that has just
left us. . . . Complexion and hair and eyebrows may be painted,
but these are of no great value in the present case. It is in the
putting them together that nature has here shown her skill, and
not in the structure of each of the parts individually considered."[4]

"But then she is unsightly as a *night-hag,* tawny as a Moor, the
eye of a gypsy, low in stature, contemptibly diminutive, scarcely
bulk enough to cast a shadow as she walks, less luxuriance than
a charred log, fewer elasticities than a sheet pebble."
"Hush! hush! blasphemer! . . . have I not told you that in mind,

---

1. *Wieland*, 59, 63, 66, 101.
2. Brown, Letter concerning his visit to Rockaway, in Dunlap,
op. cit., I, 63, 62.
3. *Wieland*, 255.
4. *Ormond*, 90.

person, and condition, she is the type after which my enamoured fancy has modelled my wife? . . . Never saw I one to whom the term *lovely* more truly belonged. And yet in stature she is too low; in complexion dark and almost sallow; and her eyes, though black and of piercing lustre, have a cast which I cannot explain. It lessens without destroying their lustre and their force of charm; but all personal defects are outweighed by her heart and her intellect. There is the secret of her power to entrance the soul of the listener and beholder. . . . It is not only when the occasion is urgent and the topic momentous that her eloquence is rich and flowing. They are always so."[1]

The first delineation was by Dr. Stevens of Achsa Fielding in pleasantry and the reply by Arthur who loved her.

Edgar Huntly gives a two-way description of himself:
"The sleek locks, neat apparel, pacific guise, sobriety and gentleness of aspect by which I was customarily distinguished, would in vain be sought in the apparition which would now present itself before them. My legs, neck, and bosom were bare, and their native hue was exchanged for the livid marks of bruises and scarifications. A horrid scar upon my cheek, and my uncombed locks, hollow eyes, made ghastly by abstinence and cold, and the ruthless passions of which my mind had been the theatre, . . . would prepossess them with the notion of a maniac or ruffian."[2]

The three following quotations show with how few words Brown can depict uncouth persons.
"Seated on a bench at the door (of the residence of a tailor) was a young man, with coarse uncombed locks, breeches knee-unbuttoned, stockings ungartered, shoes slipshod and unbuckled, and a face unwashed, gazing stupidly from hollow eyes."[3]
"His (Carwin's) pace was a careless and lingering one, . . . His gait was rustic and awkward. His form was ungainly and disproportioned. Shoulders broad and square, breast sunken, his head drooping, his body of uniform breadth, supported by long and lank legs, were the ingredients of his frame. His garb was not ill adapted to such a figure. A slouched hat, tarnished by the weather, a coat of thick gray cloth, cut and wrought, as it seemed, by a country tailor, blue worsted stockings, and shoes fastened by thongs and deeply discoloured by dust, which brush had never

---

1. *Arthur Mervyn*, II, 216-7, 197. (See also II, 218.)
2. *Edgar Huntly*, 248.
3. *Arthur Mervyn*, I, 60.

disturbed, constituted his dress."[1]

"No one was there but an old man, squatted in the chimney-corner. His face, though wrinkled, denoted undecayed health and an unbending spirit. A homespun coat, leathern breeches wrinkled with age, and blue yarn hose, were well suited to his lean and shrivelled form. On his right knee was a wooden bowl, which he had just replenished from a pipkin of hasty pudding still smoking on the coals; and in his left hand a spoon, which he had, at that moment, plunged into a bottle of molasses that stood beside him."[2]

This statement made by John Neal, Brown's contemporary and countryman, rings true:

"You feel, after he has described a thing . . . not as if you had been reading about it; but, as if you, yourself had seen it; or, at least,—as if you had just parted with a man who *had* seen it—a man whose word had never been doubted."[3]

Indians

From childhood Brown had heard stories of the Indians—their forays, depredations, kidnapings, stealings and murderings,—mostly in retaliation for the treatment rendered generally first by the Whites. Tales of the wars between the English and Indians were matters of common talk to Brown as a boy, for the wars had been concluded but eight years before his birth. Cruel adventures were perpetrated by both Reds and Whites in the hostility between the European settlers in the states and the Indian tribes.

In 1794 were published Timothy Dwight's *The Burning of Fairfield* and *The Destruction of the Pequods,* both concerning events occurring about one hundred fifty years before, the latter a terrible massacre and burning of the wigwams of the Indians by the white settlers of Connecticut. The Pequods had been a terror to the colonists of Connecticut and Massachusetts and to Indian tribes friendly to the colonists. These poems, two of the seven parts of the long poem, *Greenfield Hill,* were well known to Brown, doubtless. He had traversed Connecticut and parts of Pennsylvania, which abound with magnificent scenery; and, as he dealt with the wild, rugged life of nature, he fitted into the solitude and grandeur

---

1. *Wieland*, 70.
2. *Arthur Mervyn*, II, 56.
3. Neal, in *Blackwood's Magazine*, XVI, 305, Sept., 1824.

the natural inhabitants, Indians and cougars. If Charles and his three brothers were like boys of today, they probably played being Indians times without number, imitating their outdoor feats of courage, endurance, observation, resourcefulness, which they had heard of from their elders, about the early times when the Indians were a daily and nightly menace as marauders.

In his descriptions of Indians in *Edgar Huntly,* Brown brings into prominence their rudeness, uncouthness, cruelty, cunning, craftiness and unmitigated ferocity, though very likely he was acquainted only with Indians who made their appearance in the settlements surrounding Philadelphia, seen occasionally and then for trade or pillage. According to Brown's wonderfully lively way of telling it, however, he makes the hero's brush with the Indians a melodramatic procedure,—sleep-walking into a pit, with a weapon close at hand, ascending into a cavern, by-passing four sleeping Indians without waking them, killing an Indian sentry outside the cave, returning to the cave to rescue a white girl kidnaped and bound, meeting the Indians the next day and killing them.

This is not the first account of Indians by Brown. He was brought up a Quaker and, no doubt, knew perfectly well of William Penn's treaty with the Indians and the friendly treatment of the Indians by that colony. His mind did not naturally hate the Indians, as evidenced by Huntly's reluctance to kill them. He gives actual facts as he knew them. In *Wieland,* he thus speaks of the elder Wieland. The book he read contained an exposition of the doctrine of the Camisards. After that he secured a Bible and ardently entered on the study of it. When his apprenticeship was concluded and residence in England became almost impossible on account of his religious tenets, there was another motive of the most imperious and irresistible necessity.

"He had imbibed an opinion that it was his duty to disseminate the truths of the gospel among the unbelieving nations. He was terrified at first by the perils and hardships to which the life of a missionary is exposed. . . . The North American Indians naturally presented themselves as the first objects for this species of benevolence. . . . he . . . embarked for Philadelphia. Here his fears were revived, and a nearer survey of savage manners once more shook his resolution."

For fourteen years he worked, married and gained leisure. Then through the reading of the Scriptures,

"His ancient belief relative to the conversion of the savage tribes was revived with uncommon energy. To the former obstacles were now added the pleadings of parental and conjugal love. . . . His efforts were attended with no permanent success. His exhortations had sometimes a temporary power, but more frequently were repelled with insult and derision. In pursuit of this object he encountered the most imminent perils, and underwent incredible fatigues, hunger, sickness, and solitude. The license of savage passion, and the artifices of his depraved countrymen, all opposed themselves to his progress. His courage did not forsake him till there appeared no reasonable ground to hope for success . . . till his heart was relieved from the supposed obligation to persevere."[1]

It might be surmised that Brown had thought of such a mission for himself and relates personal trials.

Clara Wieland, telling the story, says:

"The Indians were repulsed on the one side, and Canada was conquered on the other. . . . I live not in a community of savages: yet . . . I am in perpetual danger of perishing; of perishing under the grasp of a brother. . . . It was worthy of savages trained to murder and exulting in agonies."[2]

An interesting view is presented by Volney, a Frenchman, visitor in the United States, whose work on America Brown translated:

"The Quakers are missionaries on a new plan, since their object is not to influence the religious faith of the Indians, but merely to convert them into husbandmen, carpenters, smiths, and weavers. The true problem is not why the Indian cannot be changed into a shopkeeper or mechanic, but why he cannot . . . add to the enjoyment of his native woods, to hunting and fishing, the keeping of a cow or a few sheep, and the occasional culture of a cornfield or a potatoe patch. This is all that the welfare of the United States, and their own happiness and dignity require of them. . . . Their (the Indians') condition would doubtless be improved, if they abjured everything new and European. They would profit, on the whole, if they got rid of spirits and the small-pox, together with every beneficial acquisition."[3]

---

1. *Wieland,* 29-30, 30-1.
2. *Ibid.,* 46, 208, 193.
3. Brown, *Volney's A View of the Soil and Climate of the United States of America,* 370, 377, 385, note.

This sounds a bit sarcastic, doesn't it?

Negroes

The negro, like the Indian, began his career as a notable figure in American fiction in the novels of Brown, who introduced both Indians and negroes as types of persons distinctly native and suitable to incite curiosity. He was followed by Marryat and Irving, in whose stories negroes appear, and by Mrs. Stowe, whose *Uncle Tom's Cabin* was written half a century after Brown's novels.

In *Memoirs of Stephen Calvert*, one of Brown's earliest, unfinished romances, appear the scenery, negro problem and figures which form a precedent to Mrs. Stowe's famous novel, which championed the cause of American negroes and helped much in bringing about the Civil War and their freedom. Brown's introduction of negroes into his stories as actors makes them the logical forerunners of Mrs. Stowe's book and of the negro romance. Harriet Elizabeth Beecher, born, June 14, 1811, in the year following Brown's death, no doubt, read his romances, as the most popular fiction during her girlhood. She may even have named her character Eliza from his double use of the name in *Arthur Mervyn*.

Earlier tales than these had introduced the negro. In England (1668) was published *The Isle of Pines,* by Henry Neville, the story of a shipwreck and colony, including a negro girl. Prior to this was published *Parthenissa* (1654) by Roger Boyle, an Oriental tale of an Arabian prince, who travelled through the country attended by twenty-four negroes as pages. The word *tawny* applied by Brown to a Jewess, "tawny as a Moor," and to an Indian (Edgar Huntly, 201) raises a question—Did he borrow the word? In 1688, over a hundred years before the date of *Arthur Mervyn,* in which the word first occurs (II, 216), came out in England the humanitarian tale *Oroonoko, or, The Royal Slave* by Aphra Behn, who Saintsbury said, "was a woman of very great ability, with a suspicion of genius." When romantic fiction was at its height, she wrote many novels of a picaresque type, seeking new regions abroad for some of her material, as *Oroonoko,* the story of a negro, mistreated by Whites. He was a love-lorn and magnanimous hero of "very little religion," but "admirable morals," who meets a tragic death. He was an African prince, a "tawny boy," gentle and faithful, kidnaped and carried away as a slave and put to death at

Surinam, South America. Mrs. Behn had been in Guiana and probably saw unusual characters, which she fit into her heroic adventure romances. Credit should be given her for using real life in
a novel.

Negroes are mentioned quite frequently by Brown, who thus
brings into his novels another American institution. He treats
them incidentally, usually in the capacity of servants, not as a social
problem or the issue of slavery. The general attitude toward
slavery in both the North and South at this time may be inferred
from the words said of Wieland by Clara:
"The cheapness of land, and the service of African slaves, which
were then in general use, gave him, who was poor in Europe,
all the advantages of wealth."[1]
The servants of Clara's sister-in-law are spoken of, but it is in
Arthur Mervyn that references to negroes occur most often. In the
North, negroes were employed chiefly as house servants.
Mrs. Wentworth "sent a messenger to Welbeck with a request to
see him. Gabriel, the black servant, informed the messenger that
his master had gone into the country for a week."[2]
When Arthur had transformed himself from the appearance of a
beggar to a stylish French gentleman, at the invitation of Welbeck,
he says, "I was roused from these doubts by a summons to breakfast,
obsequiously delivered by a black servant."[3]

In merely copying the references to negroes, one gathers the
different phases of their lives.
". . . the elder Lodi had flattered one of his slaves with the prospect
of his freedom, but had, nevertheless, included this slave in the
sale he had made of his estate. Actuated by revenge, the slave
assassinated Lodi in the open street, and resigned himself, without
a struggle, to the punishment which the law had provided for
such a deed."[4]

A trader's vessel was sailing for Europe and would be forfeited
if contraband were discovered on it.
"Two French mulattoes had, after much solicitation, and the most
solemn promises to carry with them no articles which the laws of

---

1. *Wieland*, 30.
2. *Arthur Mervyn*, I, 122.
3. *Ibid.*, I, 52.
4. *Ibid.*, I, 93.

war decree to be contraband, obtained a passage in the vessel."[1]

During the yellow fever plague, negroes were regularly employed to remove the dead, which meant also the near dead, because it was a disagreeable, menial job and negroes were practically immune against the disease.

"Presently a coffin, borne by two men, issued from the house. The driver was a negro; but his companions were white."[2]

"Instead of summoning a physician, . . . he called a negro and his cart."[3]   "two men, negroes, . . . (one a) wood-carter . . . had betaken himself, like many others of his color and rank, to the conveyance and burial of the dead,"[4] to make money.

While carrying out his self-imposed enterprises, Arthur sees typical negro servants. He called on Mrs. Watson in Baltimore to deliver a packet from her deceased husband. Looking in at a window, he saw a

"cherub of a boy, tossing something to a black girl who sat opposite, . . . The black girl . . . in order to reach the ball which was thrown at her, unluckily caught a glance of my figure through the glass. In a tone of half surprise and half terror, she cried out, 'Oh! see dare! a man!' "

Arthur knocked and was bidden to enter. Mrs. Watson put the child she was rocking, "not yet awakened, into the arms of the black, who kissed it and rocked it in her arms with great satisfaction."[5]

Next Arthur calls on the Maurices to deliver some money, due them by Watson. As he pulled the door-bell, "A negro came, of a very unpropitious aspect, and, opening the door, looked at me in silence." A voice within, Madam's, said: "Come in, Cato, and shut the door." This injunction was obeyed by Cato without ceremony. Arthur knocks again and Mrs. Maurice's daughter called Cato and Bob: "By this time, Bob and Cato, two sturdy blacks entered the room." When she ordered them to evict Arthur, they looked one upon the other and hesitated.

" 'Villains! why don't you do as I bid you?' . . . The blacks looked

1. *Arthur Mervyn*, I, 102-3.
2. *Ibid.*, I, 141.
3. *Ibid.*, I, 158.
4. *Ormond*, 44.
5. *Arthur Mervyn*, II, 155, 156.

upon each other, as if waiting for an example. Their habitual deference for every thing *white,* held their hands from what they regarded as a profanation. At last Bob said, in a whining, beseeching
tone, 'Why, missee, massa buckra wanna go for doo, dan he winna
go fo' wee'." Arthur finally sees the elderly Mrs. Maurice, who
being faint on receiving the money, calls, " 'Oh, I am sick; sick unto
death. Put me on the bed.' . . . Some of the domestics, of both
colours, entered, and gazed at me with surprise."[1]

"His religious duty compelled him to seek his livelihood by
teaching a school of blacks. . . . He was teacher of the negro free-
school when he died,"[2] said of Waldegrave.

The quotation which follows gives an inside picture of a stagecoach and a portrayal by Brown of two female blacks, stagecoach
travelling companions:

"I mounted the stage-coach at daybreak the next day, in company
with a sallow Frenchman from St. Domingo, his fiddle-case, an ape,
and two female blacks. The Frenchman, after passing the suburbs,
took out his violin and amused himself with humming to his own
tweedle-tweedle. The monkey now and then munched an apple,
which was given to him from a basket by the blacks, who gazed
with stupid wonder, and an exclamatory *La! La!* upon the passing
scenery, or chattered to each other in a sort of open-mouthed,
half-articulate, monotonous, singsong jargon. The man . . . spoke
only to rebuke the frolics of the monkey. . . . As to me, my thought
was busy in a thousand ways. I sometimes gazed at the faces of my
four companions, and endeavoured to discern the differences and
samenesses between them. I took an exact account of the features,
proportions, looks, and gestures of the monkey, the Congolese, and
the Creole Gaul. I compared them together, and examined them
apart. I looked at them in a thousand different points of view,
and pursued, untired and unsatiated, those trains of reflections
which began at each change of tone, feature, and attitude."[3]

Here one gets an insight into the author's habit of observation
and contemplation, which complements a statement in the Rockaway
letter quoted below: "I, for the most part, was mute, as I usually am,
in a stagecoach and among strangers." May not Brown have had
in mind the meaning of the Hebrew word in the title of Psalm 56—

---

1. *Arthur Mervyn,* II, 160-1, 163.
2. *Edgar Huntly,* 148.
3. *Arthur Mervyn,* II, 153.

Jonath-elem-rechokim, one of whose alleged meanings is "mute dove among strangers"; perhaps, alluding to David as the uncomplaining meek dove, driven from his native home to wander in exile. Brown liked to read a natural history of the human mind as he did of natural objects.

Travel

Methods of travel and its difficulties in the time of Brown may be pieced together from realistic descriptions of it in his novels. According to his biographer Dunlap, Brown disclaimed any abiiity to make trivial things interesting:
"What possible amusement can you expect from *my* recital of a jaunt to Rockaway? I cannot dignify trifles or give to vulgar sights a novelty, by making them pass through my fancy. . . . having left society in New York, the loss of which all the pleasures of Rockaway would poorly compensate."[1]
Yet this traveller through his characters does specify certain details of his travels. Modes of travel were chiefly by ferry, stageboat and stagecoach. There are numerous references to travel by stagecoach over roads almost impassable part of the year.

"I set out, on Tuesday morning, for Baltimore," writes Philip Stanley, from Wilmington. "The usual flood of this season having carried away the bridge on the Schuylkill, we prepared to pass it in a boat. The horses which drew the stage, being unaccustomed to this mode of conveyance, and being startled by the whirlpools and eddies, took fright when the boat had gained the middle of the river, and suddenly rushed out at the farther end into the stream. . . . The coach and horses instantly sunk."
All the passengers but two girls had dismounted from the carriage into the boat. Stanley rescued one, bringing on his illness; the father trying to save the other daughter was drowned with her.
"It is said that the late storms have overflowed the rivers, swept away the bridges, and flooded the roads. . . . The wind and rain! how will you endure them in your crazy vehicle, thumping over rocks and sinking into hollows? . . . and this river,—to cross it at any time is full of danger,—what must it be at night, and in a storm? But well know I the dangers and toils of a midnight journey, in a stage-coach, in America. The roads are knee-deep in

---

1. Brown, Letter concerning a visit to Rockaway, in Dunlap, *op. cit.,* I, 58, 60.

mire, winding through crags and pits, while the wheels groan and totter, and the curtains and roof admit the wet at a thousand seams,"[1] replies Clara Howard from New York to Stanley when he is planning to return home.

Several times Arthur Mervyn takes the stages on his good-will missions: from Philadelphia to Baltimore to interview Mrs. Watson and Mrs. Maurice and to learn of his father at Newtown. He says:

"My way led past the inn (in New York) where one of the stages from Baltimore was accustomed to stop." Of a journey to Baltimore, he writes:

"I marked the country as it successively arose before me, and found endless employment in examining the shape and substance of the fence, the barn, and the cottage, the aspect of earth and of heaven. How great are the pleasures of health and mental activity! . . . My chief occupation, however, related to the scenes into which I was about to enter. My imaginations were, of course, crude and inadequate; and I found an uncommon gratification in comparing realities, as they successively occurred, with the pictures which my wayward fancy had depicted."[2]

In contrast to Brown's occupation within a stagecoach, he here gives a panoramic view of the landscape, looking out a stage window.

The hardships of a journey from New York to Constantia's home in Jersey are related by Sophia:

"A stage-boat, accustomed twice a day to cross New York Bay to Staten Island, was prevailed upon, by liberal offers, to set out upon the voyage at the dawn of day. . . . The wind, suddenly becoming tempestuous and adverse, rendered the voyage at once tedious and full of peril. A voyage of nine miles was not effected in less than eight hours and without imminent and hairbreadth danger of being drowned. Fifteen miles of the journey remained to be performed by land. A carriage . . . was procured, but lank horses and a crazy vehicle were but little in unison with my impatience. We reached not Amboy ferry till some hours after nightfall. I was rowed across the Sound, and proceeded to accomplish the remainder of my journey—about three miles—on foot."[3]

---

1. *Clara Howard,* 407-8.
2. *Arthur Mervyn,* II, 153-4.
3. *Ormond,* 237.

Music

At his death, Brown left unfinished *Two Dialogues,* on Music and on Painting, respectively, each as a female accomplishment or mode of giving subsistence and fortune. Before considering music as a theme for a treatise to encourage young women to study music for pleasure or train them for an occupation, Brown must have studied music and have enjoyed it, from his oft mention of it in his novels. If one gleans circumspectly through the pages, he might make an outline for the treatise and recover much of its content from the references to music directly and to music as a symbol. Snatches about music infiltrate all his novels, just as flashes of scenery do, barring *Edgar Huntly,* which majors in scenery. Brown may have been influenced by Mrs. Radcliffe, whose passion for music and ability to waken wonder and awe by means of it, as in *The Mysteries of Udolpho,* probably fascinated him. As a journalist, writing on numerous subjects, suggested by his reading and by the needs of his countrymen and having previously written *The Rights of Women,* Brown contemplated the studies suitable for young ladies and began the two treatises.

To drive away corroding care, Clara Wieland utilizes the music of her grandfather: "For some time I indulged myself . . . in these gloomy thoughts; . . . I endeavoured to dissipate it with music. I had all my grandfather's melody and poetry by rote"; she says of her mother, "she was punctual . . . in the performance of hymns to her Saviour"; and of her childhood years: "Our tasks, our walks, our music, were seldom performed but in each other's company," and of later years, "Opposite to this (in the temple) was a harpsichord, sheltered by a temporary roof from the weather. . . . Here we sung, and talked, and read, and occasionally banqueted," which, with the following, may reveal Brown's own home life or of meetings of the Friendly Club: "Pleyel, like his friends (the Wielands), was fond of music and poetry. Henceforth our concerts consisted of two violins, a harpsichord, and three voices. . . . My brother's voice and Pleyel's were musical and energetic. . . . The voice (of Carwin) was not only mellifluent and clear, but the emphasis was so just, and the modulation so impassioned, that it seemed as if a heart of stone could not fail of being moved by it."[1]

---

1. *Wieland,* 75, 32, 41, 43, 44, 45, 71, 72.

The lute is the favorite instrument of Mr. Dudley, Constantia's father, who whiled away many hours of his blindness by playing it: "it was a powerful, because the only, solace of his melancholy." Brown himself played the lute and, no doubt, introduced it to show his appreciation of its "notes of peculiar sweetness."[1]

In *Arthur Mervyn,* one recognizes that Brown is most surely revealing himself; and in that novel he has much to say about music. Clemenza Lodi seems to embody best the spirit of music: "the lady . . . sat down to a piano-forte. . . . I was not wholly destitute of musical practice and musical taste. . . . which enabled me to estimate the transcendent skill of this performer. . . . I found after some time that the lawless jarrings of the keys were chastened by her more liquid notes. . . . a soft voice said, 'who is there?' The accents were as musical as those of Clemenza."[2]

Speaking of the Hadwin sisters, Arthur says,

"They (Susan and Eliza) thought and acted in different but not discordant keys. . . . this diversity was productive not of jarring, but of harmony";
and comparing the tinkling-cymbal sounds of Eliza with the refined music of Achsa Fielding, he says of the former:
"to hold her in my arms, and listen to her prattle, always musically voluble, always sweetly tender, or artlessly intelligent—and this you will say is the dearest privilege of marriage; . . . a sweet and melodious voice vibrated in my ear" . . . (Eliza replies) "I will be as good a housewife and dairywoman, stir about as briskly, and sing as merrily"; and of the latter: "The best solace on these occasions was the company of Mrs. Fielding; her music, her discourse, or some book which she set me to rehearsing to her. . . . My friend noticed my discomposure." . . . (Achsa replies) "What, Arthur! thou art quite the 'penseroso' tonight. Come, let me cheer thee with a song. Thou shalt have thy favorite ditty." . . . "She stepped to the instrument, and, with more than airy lightness, touched and sung:

> 'Now knit hands and beat the ground
> In a light, fantastic round,
> Till the telltale sun descry
> Our conceal'd solemnity.'

1. *Ormond,* 154, 152.
2. *Arthur Mervyn,* I, 54; II, 101.

Her music, though blithesome and aerial, was not sufficient for the end. . . . It is not only when she sings that her utterance is musical. . . . Music she loved, but never sought it in places of public resort, or from the skill of mercenary performers; and books were not the least of her pleasures. . . . Sweet sounds that she once loved, and especially when her darling child was the warbler, were heard no longer,"[1] Achsa says of her mother.

A variety of music phrases suggests a variety of uses of music. Wieland, about to kill his wife, says: "Eternal fire, and the bickerings of hell, compared with what I felt, were music and a bed of roses." Arthur, exhausted by yellow fever, "hummed a cheerful and favourite air." "There were others in the same apartment (in a tavern), lounging, or whistling, or singing." In the Villars' questionable house were, "a harpsichord, uncovered, one end loaded with *scores*, tumbled together in a heap, and the other with volumes of novels and plays." "Her (Mrs. Watson's) eyes were now fixed upon the fire . . . while she sung, in low and scarcely-audible strains, an artless lullaby." "some catch of melting music she had lately breathed, stole incessantly upon my fancy," Clithero says of Clarice. "No music was ever more thrilling than the tones of Clara (Howard). . . . May thy smiles, my beloved Clara," writes Stanley to her, "and thy voice, musical and thrilling as it used to be, disperse every disquiet!"

Brown makes Helena a most skilful player and Constantia his ideal singer, as did Shelley after him: "If ever human tones were qualified to convey the whole soul, they were those of Constantia when she sung." Constantia recognizes her friend Sophia on her return from Europe to America by her singing to the harpsichord their favorite ditty:

"Ah! far beyond this world of woes
We meet to part—to part no more."[2]

---

1. *Arthur Mervyn*, I, 125; II, 189, 181, 180, 185, 212, 202.
2. *Ormond* 155, 184. (See p. 107.)

CHAPTER VII

BROWN'S PLACE IN AMERICAN LITERATURE

The novels of Brown exhibit a transitional state between romance and realism, a transition from the novel of sentiment, the uncouth Gothic romance and the almost pure didactic novels of the School of Theory. He eliminated much of the gushy sentimental, modified the Gothic by ridding his novels of the very artificial ingredients of their style and moderated the drastic teachings of the novel of purpose. He did not deal only with "things as they are" or with sensations for sensation's sake, but rather with ideas and ideals.

Brown combined with these elements an American historical and scientific and scenic background. Until the first work of Cooper in 1820, Brown stood for twenty years almost alone as the representative American novelist; and his novels were best sellers for a longer time than is covered by most best sellers today. Whatever of importance the Gothic, the idealistic romantic, the autobiographical, the historical and the revolutionary or purposeful had in American fiction, it was concentered in Brown's novels. Among the "20 leading Books of the 1790's," Pattee listed Brown's *Alcuin* (1798) and *Wieland* (1798) and among the "26 in any way notable, from 1800-1815," books of prose and poetry, he listed *Edgar Huntley* (1801) and *The Life of Charles Brockden Brown,* (Allen and) Dunlap (1815).

Brown shows peculiar ingenuity in making natural causes produce the semblance of supernatural effects and in the way abnormal effects are given logical explanations. His phenomena border on the supernatural; yet the limits of possibility are never transgressed. If anyone considers Brown unduly influenced by the elaborate, sensational romances of his predecessors with their extravagant emotions and that his novels express a sentiment not in accord with romanticism as it is thought of today, he had some excuse when

344

most of the writers of Germany and many of England had burst out in peculiar ways from the illiberalism of Classicism. He aimed at realistic portraiture. His adventures are noteworthy for vividness, circumstantiality and originality; and the description of his scenes shows the minuteness of careful observation. Although many of his scenes and incidents are somber, they are not altogether unreal. They partake of the immensity, tenebrosity and fearsomeness of the unfamiliar wilderness and the strange acts committed there.

In mere power of conception, Brown's novels rank very high among the products of imagination. They have much of thrilling interest that engages the reader's attention even today. Notwithstanding the imperfections in style and irregularity in plot construction, they reveal the unmistakable skill of their author and have a lasting intrinsic value in life and literature.

The plot actions of the novels take place in American settings and show a beginning of that divergence of type from English literature that has gradually formed American literature, distinctive in thought and feeling and expressive of the youthful spirit of the New World. Brown made a serious, meritorious commencement of American fiction, of which the nation may wisely be proud.

Brown himself was in transition. He was an immature, many-sided genius, untrained by long years of apprenticeship in writing and in growth from one achievement to another. His first published work was *Alcuin: The Rights of Women* (1797), a conversational dialogue, which demonstrates his absorption of the writings of Mrs. Wollstonecraft and others on the same subject. A romance came next, a correspondence between two feigned characters, Julia and Jessy, the rich girl and the poor girl,—unfinished. Unfinished also were two fragments, parts of plans of extensive works of imagination in which social and historical facts are mingled and the air of history imitated. The first, *Sketches of a History of Carsol,* is an experiment to be conducted on the Island Carsol in the Mediterranean, where all the inhabitants are free and share alike in everything—property, printing, selling, government, religion, the judiciary and war. In the second, *Sketches of the History of the Carrils and Ormes,* a system of government and manners was developed and castles and abbeys built. Then followed the destroyed romance *Sky-Walk,* the six published novels, the journalistic writings and a few more fiction fragments, some of which show improvement over his novels in structure and in a more simple, fluent style and suggest the probability that, had Brown lived, he might have become a superior writer of historical fiction with a romantic appeal.

From Dunlap have been gathered many of the preceding statements. He quoted from the Preface of *The Life* of Brown:
"It was supposed that by combining these (Selections from Brown's works) the reader would be able to conceive with more accuracy the power which the writer possessed in so eminent a degree, of changing his topic when the one which he handled became irksome. He is thus made in a measure to speak his own biography, and to supersede the necessity of further comment."

A significant phrase as to what ailed Brown was given by Dunlap —"excess of his genius." He was too full for orderly, deliberate utterance. One feels in pursuing the study of the man and in reading his novels and parts of his other works that he was panting for the expression of the ideas jostling in his brain and the possibility of their transference to his fellowmen for their pleasure and enlightenment, by one method or another—poetry, essays, political pamphlets, novels, journalism—in season and out of season.

Genius has been defined by Fielding. How well Brown measured up to the intent of the definition, only selections from which are quoted, readers will be left to decide.
"There are but two ways by which men become possessed of this excellent quality (caution). The one is from long experience and the other is from nature, which last, I presume, is often meant by genius, or great natural parts; and it is infinitely the better of the two, not only as we are masters of it much earlier in life, but as it is much more infallible and conclusive. . . . By genius I would understand that power or rather those powers of the mind, which are capable of penetrating into all things within our reach and knowledge, and of distinguishing their essential differences. These are no other than invention and judgment; . . . they are not sufficient for our purpose, without a good share of learning. . . . Again, there is another sort of knowledge, beyond the power of learning to bestow, and this is to be had by conversation. . . . The true practical system can be learnt only in the world. . . . Nor will all the qualities I have hitherto given my historian avail him, unless he have what is generally meant by a good heart,

and be capable of feeling."[1]

Many circumstances tended to keep Brown's mind in turmoil—his journalistic training with early contributions of that class, the uncertainty of the place of fiction in the scheme of letters, especially because of British criticism, puritanism and his fragile health. His very versatility of powers kept him and his works in a continual transformation,—which is, of course, what one would wisn in a long-lived writer.

Although Brown's position in literature today rests on his novels, yet it has been observed of him, said his biographer Dunlap, that, "whether he lets himself loose in the region of argumentative speculation or ranges the field of fancy, he is in either case perfectly at home"; that from a long train of subtile and metaphysical reasoning he would fly to fancy (fiction-writing) for recreation. "The author considered all his fanciful works as mere matters of recreation and amusement. As long as his imagination was prolific in blossoms, he scattered them with the same prodigal profusion." But that when this light employment was accomplished, he never returned to them to beautify the work; after interest for himself was lost in them, he turned to something else. Such were the precise ideas which he author formed of his works of this character.[2]

Naturally a journalist, Brown, like most early American public-spirited writers, wrote much on many matters of national interest before and after the writing of his novels, convincing in style rather than artistic. He might have become an eminent publicist. He was a man of indisputable genius and a true scholar, notable for copiousness of information, liberality of views, independence from foreign prejudices, loyal and heart-felt patriotism and exemption from the bitterness of party spirit. He had indefatigable application, diligence and enterprise.

In his novels, Brown's richness of invention is seen in the large number of admirable situations and mysterious adventures presented, though not all are fully developed and many show lack of thoroughness. One no more than experiences one catastrophe before

---

1. Fielding, *Tom Jones*, I, 404, 463-4, 466.
2. Dunlap, *op. cit.*, I, 259, 261.

he is on the brink of another. If he had confined his attempts to single episodes;—that is, if he had had originality enough to have invented the short story, he might have done work comparable with that of Irving, Poe and Hawthorne. Since his time the romantic short story, whose motive is mystery, has proved itself the most characteristic phase of American fiction.

His novels are evidences of what they might have been if their author had judged his purposes in writing fiction more far-sightedly, if he had taken time, before having them published serially, to weave the varied threads of their narratives into preconceived patterns, if he had correlated the various incidents into a consistent whole, if he had perfected each one as he wrote, if he had thought more seriously of style and if he had lived to mature years. They plainly show the character of his mind. It was undisciplined genius that prevented him from excelling. There is no lack of agreement among critics as to his capacity to have excelled in this department of letters.

As it is, Brown's stories stand chronologically at the beginning of the type and illustrate what were to be the qualities of the American novel,—in some respects of all American literature. The seriousness of life is exhibited in the subsequent romances and novels in this country; his intention to be of service to the community,—to explore life and distribute moral ideas for the public good, which was the motive of most of the prose and verse of his time—has been projected into the best novels in America to this day, like those of Hawthorne, Mrs. Stowe, Louisa May Alcott, Edward Everett Hale, Brander Matthews, Lew Wallace, Edward Eggleston, Samuel L. Clemens, Helen Hunt Jackson,— to mention a few of the type preceding the twentieth century.

Conceiving such a variety of scenes and inventing such extraordinary incidents as Brown did proclaim that he had a daring imagination. He describes abnormal and fantastic happenings, but was no imitator of his predecessors in the Gothic lineage, though some critics flippantly call him a Gothic romancer. He presents his situations and depictions distinctly and vividly to the mind. His defects are chiefly due to haste in composition and from crowding too many incidents into short spaces of time. So electrified was he by his first success and by the whirlwind speed with which he wrote that he was unaware of whether all of the mysteries were elucidated and unsure where or when the whole story would end. He uses the word *curiosity* frequently and proceeds from one surprising adventure to another to play upon the curiosity of his readers,—perhaps, to feed his own curiosity, also.

Many defects of Brown's novels are of the same general nature as the defects of contemporaneous literature; yet his genius is everywhere visible on the pages of his books. It is seen in the skill with which he is able to pique curiosity or call forth the sympathies of his readers, in the strong fictive power which shows itself in the fullness, variety and spontaneity of his scenes and incidents and their effective presentation and in the ability of describing weird scenes and morbid psychological conditions that produce a sense of genuine, not conventional, horror. If one would do justice to Brown, he must look to the elements, not the form, of his genius, as has been tersely said.

The characters are led by the author to the highest point of excitement and fearful expectation, by many real perils, as by the yellow fever scourge and in the natural wilds. He analyzes the feelings of his characters with remarkable subtlety and enters into their contemplations and gives their sensitive re-actions to external impressions with accuracy. In a few potent words he may disclose his insight into a character; as for instance, Welbeck, who hesitates to reveal his purpose: "When he spoke there was hesitation in his manner and circuity in his expressions" and "His own tale had shown him to be versed in frauds, and flexible to evil."[1] The author's Quaker upbringing, involving a placid temperament and intellectual demeanor, combined with his wide reading and aloofness, make it appear simple for him to analyze character, as if he were only making a self-analysis.

All of Brown's novels are studies in psychology, with usually problems in morals or religion as a background. The story was never the principal thing. He may be considered the precursor of the modern scientific novelist, for the development of each of his principal characters, in the first four novels at least, is based upon the effects upon the human mind, of some phenomenal truth of

---

1. *Arthur Mervyn*, I, 71, 192.

science. He treated his scientific material in a scientific manner. He chose little-understood facts of science, since he realized that they are always a source of wonder and superstition. He had a true appreciation of the way mystery and terror affect the mind and freely invented extraordinary and unlikely situations that he might observe the action of the passions and feelings under those conditions. Dr. Richard Burton made this assertion:

"It is instructive to find a writer and thinker thus early making use of psychologic marvels in fiction, yet treating them as did Poe after him in the temper of the scientific investigator."[1]

The modern scientific spirit in its fullness did not develop till about the middle of the nineteenth century, fifty years after the death of Brown. From the raw, experimental display of science in *Frankenstein* (1818) by Mrs. Shelley to the highly-wrought scientific treatment of the facts of life in the *Egoist* (1879) by George Meredith is a long step in the development of the scientific method. Yet Brown nearly a century earlier attempted to use the same modern spirit of scientific investigation that is used today, whether he was treating of his scientific facts or of his other material.

Great literary men, no less than great scientists, have made the search for truth their chief endeavor. The present demand upon any literature is that it be true to the life or to the facts which it represents; besides that it must have a definite moral purpose or lesson for humanity. Even though a work may deal with only fanciful or imaginative situations and incidents, it must be true to the truths of life; it must present an ideal. This age is spoken of as practical and materialistic; therefore the type of literature is realistic; this literature reflects the practical problems and interests of mankind and is a powerful instrument of human progress. Brown is in these respects a man of the present age. He conscientiously meant to picture American conditions as he saw them and to teach his countrymen lessons in morals and in social life. With absolute sincerity, so it seems, he tried to reveal his inmost thoughts and, with desperate earnestness, strove to convince his readers for their benefit. His works are a literature of wholesome pleasure and of true refinement, so that one feels uplifted and

---

1. Burton, *Literary Leaders of America,* 11.

edified from reading them.

"Art can engage in no better pursuit than to stimulate noble and healthful thought on all matters of human concern, and thereby clear the prejudiced mind and raise the average of human happiness."[1]

Three tests will now be applied to Brown's novels. Are they literature? Are they novels or romances? To which period of the art of fiction do they belong?

"No definition of it (literature) ever yet given has surpassed that magnificent Latin sentence of Bacon's . . .:—'It (literature) hath something divine in it, because it raises the mind and hurries it into sublimity, by conforming the show of things to the desires of the soul, instead of subjecting the soul to external things, as reason and history do' (De Augmentis, Book II). It is only literature then, in Bacon's definition, which truly 'raises the mind and hurries it into sublimity.' All else is reason (or reasoning) and history (or narrative)."[2]

The same critics continue: "Its (literature's) foundation is thought, but it goes farther. . . . Thought, emotion, the instinct toward expression—the whole personality of the man and his skill as an artist—must work together in perfect adjustment, in order to gain this end. Very few men are both strong and skillful enough for this; and that is why, out of the great mass of written and printed matter which the world produces, so little is worth preserving in the treasury of pure literature."[3]

Brown has been given a substantial place in this work and in American literature by these joint-authors, which is testimony that he, in a positive way, fulfils the conditions of these statements,—potentially, at least.

"Literature is, as Wordsworth said of poetry in particular, not science, but 'the antithesis of science.' If there be an intellectual world outside of science, where is the boundary-line of that world? We pass this line, it would seem, whenever we enter the realm usually called intuitive or inspirational; a realm whose characteristic it is that it is not subject to processes or measurable by tests. The yield of this outer world may be as real as that of the scientific

---

1. Boyesen, "The American Novelist and His Public," in *Literary and Social Silhouettes*, 57.
2. Higginson and Boynton, *A Reader's History of American Literature*, 5.
3. *Ibid.*, 6-7.

world, but its methods are not traceable, nor are its achievements capable of being duplicated by the mere force of patient will. . . . Such manifestations of genius are necessarily rare, and are, in the long run, the outcome, even more than the impelling force, of a firm and wholesome way of life."[1]

In a measure Brown was a "double minded man"; and the conclusion of that verse, "unstable in all his ways," is also to some degree true. He was born into the intuitive or inspirational realm. After wavering over the study of law, superimposed over his genius, he gave that up for literature. The shaky condition of novel-writing as a manly-man's life work unstabilized him in his mind as to whether to continue to write novels to serve his purposes or whether to take up journalism as the stronger, better course, which he had pursued earlier in contributing to the magazines of others. Now, he gave up fiction writing and established magazines on his own initiative. Science he introduced in his novels, but he treated it in the intuitive manner. By choosing American incidents and characters, he emancipated himself in subject matter; but the conventions that hampered all literature served partly to curb his genius, and that, together with precarious health from the cradle to his early grave, prevented the instability of his youth being righted sufficiently for him to write pure unadulterated literature.

The second test this author would apply to Brown's novels is from the discussion of the novel and romance by Clayton Hamilton. Consider that the three-fold process of fiction-making—scientific discovery, philosophic understanding and artistic expression of the truths of human life—are common to realists and to romantics alike. The true distinction is one of method, not of material. In setting forth his view of life, the realist follows the inductive method of presentment and the romantic follows the deductive method. The difference between the two systems is based upon the *direction* of the train of thought. In the inductive, we reason from the particular to the general; in the deductive, from the general to the particular. Scientists and ethical philosophers have in-

---

1. Higginson and Boynton, *A Reader's History of American Literature,* 278-9, 281.

ductive minds; preachers, deductive. The realist leads us through a series of imagined facts as similar as possible to the details of actual life, which he has studied to arrive at his general conception. The romantic leads in the contrary direction;—from his general conception, not showing how he arrived at it, his care is to convey his general idea effectively by giving it a specific illustrative embodiment. Realism, like inductive science, is a strictly modern product and usually attempted by mature writers. The facts of the realist both illustrate and support the truth to be developed. The imagined facts of the romantic are related merely to illustrate the truth he wishes to convey.[1]

Which was Brown—a realist or a romantic? It can confidently be said that he was a romantic, at least, in the statements of his general concepts. In *Wieland,* on the first page, he says,

"it will inculcate the duty of avoiding deceit. It will exemplify the force of early impressions, and show the immeasurable evils that flow from an erroneous or imperfect discipline."

In the author's Preface to *Arthur Mervyn,* he says,

"It is every one's duty to profit by all opportunities of inculcating on mankind the lessons of justice and humanity."

The general truth is easily found stated for each romance; and one may take a hint from the alternate titles. Brown lacked the maturity needful to treat a series of imagined facts. However, in his outspoken truthfulness in regard to his chosen material, he foreshadowed the modern realist. He was verily a combination of the romantic and of the realist.

As to the three-fold process, Brown was true to scientific discovery, limiting his field to the unusual, was true pre-eminently in the realm of psychology and sane in philosophy, but was lacking somewhat in artistry. He had the narrative sense, in that he relates his series of events to his purpose in time order, but he lacked the dramatic sense which sees the end of the story from the beginning and prosecutes a vigorous movement toward that end. He failed in *Arthur Mervyn,*—perhaps, to some extent in all his romances,—in the conventional parts of plot construction.

The third test—To what period of the art of fiction do Brown's

---

1. Hamilton, *A Manual of the Art of Fiction,* 80 ff.

novels belong?—is taken from Brander Matthews' *Aspects of Fiction*. The interchange between the writings of England and America was natural and frequent because of the same language; but, as we can clearly see Americans differentiated from Englishmen, so differences in our literature are undeniable and understandable from springing from other natural scenes and social conditions. Literature will continue to flourish as naturally as ever after the parent stem has been parted into its branches. If writers make use of the English language, they are contributing to English literature, though the divisions follow the names of the various peoples, as American, Canadian, Australian.

Literature is a criticism of life and is only valuable in proportion as it is truthful. The life that is most needful to us Americans to have criticized is our own life. It is only in our own literature that we can learn the truth about ourselves. Considering the American branch of English literature, the growth of a healthy feeling in regard to it has been hindered by two unfortunate destructive failings—provincialism and colonialism. Provincialism is local pride unduly inflated. Colonialism is a timid deference toward foreign opinion and unquestioning acceptance of the foreign estimate upon our own writers. The former can be remedied by the study of other languages and letters to give us a standard and methods of comparison. The latter can be obviated by a manly self-respect, a wholesome self-reliance, a determination to independent thinking and a resolve to survey our life with our own eyes.

Brown had mastered Latin, Greek and French and had read voraciously of all sorts of writings, of which there is evidence in his novels. But his mass of knowledge was in a kind of melting-pot stage. Only half of a normal life gave him little time to refine his methods and standards by the best that he had read. Six novels in four years does not give much time for comparison. Cooper lives today, having written his romances during a period of thirty years, the first at age thirty-one, older by a year than Brown was when he had completed his. In his novels, not at all, or little,—in his journalistic work, somewhat,—he was hindered by colonialism, lacking thus in the two respects mentioned above, probably due rather to his immaturity than to any fault in his ability or intention.

There is a department of literature in which we can define

four chronological periods, stated Mr. Matthews—the art of fiction. The four stages are the *Impossible,* in which fiction deals with wonders, mystery and the supernatural; the *Improbable,* adventures that might befall anybody, but in quantity more than would be likely to happen to any one person, as the hero; the *Probable,* events that might happen to anyone; the *Inevitable,* foregone conclusions that must follow a certain series of events. Each succeeding step is superior to the preceding one in the scale of fiction progress. Not that all the people can be led to arrive at class four, the inevitable character re-action to the circumstances outlined. Many people prefer the stories of wonder and excitement that take them into fairyland or at least out of themselves. Many want merely to be amused by swift-moving events in which they feel that they might have participated. Another class of readers will read nothing joyfully unless they feel that the writer is sincere and is telling only what he knows to be the truth—truth in events and truth in sentiment. The fourth class of readers seek novels in which the subtle, underlying Inevitable must result from the characters, events and environment presented.[1]

Now, where does novelist Brown belong? Certainly not in class one, where the supernatural holds sway, and not consistently in class four. He dwells upon the idea of transformation, in his principal characters, resulting from the events and environments of their lives, as has been explained. He sought to "amuse and instruct." His material is unusual, yet of the real, making him fit into classes two and three. All classes of people in America and in England read his novels for diversion; some profited by the instruction in them. A few will continue to read them for their intermediary position between the Impossible and Inevitable stages in the development of the novel.

Mr. Matthews continued:—There is no common standing-ground anywhere for those who hold fiction to be primarily an amusement and those who believe that it ought to be chiefly a criticism of life. The extreme romanticist considers fiction as an art, and as an art only; while the extreme realist is inclined to look

---

1. Matthews, *Aspects of Fiction,* 63-75.

upon it almost as a branch of science.[1]

Where does Brown stand in this distinction? He is neither an extreme romanticist nor an extreme realist. He treated his material in two ways—the improbable remnants of the Gothic element and the rarer facts of science, in the manner of the romanticists; and the probable and real in his descriptions of scenery, of yellow fever details, of the Indians, of the dilemmas into which the beneficence of Arthur led him and of the multitude of minor facts of American living, in the manner of the realists.

The principle of the literary art requires that a man should write spontaneously and simply about those things he is fullest of and best understands. "Literature," Matthews defined, "consists not so much in the mere making up of stories as in the frank telling of the truth." This seems to limit literature to realism. The story-teller must have the gift of story-telling; that is, a "native faculty of narrative which the writer of fiction must needs have as a condition precedent to the practice of his craft, and without some small portion of which the conscious art of the most highly trained novelist is of no avail. This gift of story-telling can exist independent of any other faculty. It may be all that the possessor has"; that is, the writer may lack education, intelligence, knowledge of the world and of society, insight into character, style, even grammar: "all these deficiencies are as nothing if only he have the gift of story-telling";[2] that is, the narrative sense.

Had Brown this gift of story-telling? This writer believes that he had, though restricted in a degree by his own self-distrust, by the virulent criticisms of some English critics and by the fashions in fiction. Besides the gift, he had learning, acquired chiefly by his private study and reading, an adequate family life and some years of social life in the form of memberships in a Law Society, the Belles-Lettres Club and the Friendly Club. Brown was the most popularly-read novelist in America for twenty years, even at the expense of Irving; and all his novels were published in England and read avidly before Scott had begun to write his romances.

Four years after his novel writing had ceased, Brown had this

---

1. Matthews, *Aspects of Fiction,* 110-1.
2. *Ibid.,* 142-3.

to say

"concerning the art of fiction-writing, a rule that may be framed as the first American word concerning short-story art: 'Much has been written to explain and to teach the art of story-telling; but no science is more difficult to attain, nor can it be taught by any settled rules. If the teller can but contrive to keep the attention of his audience awake to the end of his tale, he has certainly gained a great point, let the method be what it will; and if he can add to their attention some emotions of pleasure, or of surprise, he may justly be deemed a good story-teller'."[1]

Commentators have been solicitous to fit Brown into the history of American literature. It might be of service to think how wide and deep would be the "chasm" if he had not written at all. Inventors who follow new paths have need of forerunners. Although the literature of a new country receives all other literature as a precious heritage, yet new conditions call for a new type of literary leaders. The reverse is also true,—a new literary genius may start an individualistic type of literature and lead others in the paths he has broken open. Suppose an interim of fifteen years (1795-1810), Brown's writing period, were dropped out.

Suppose:—No one had pictured as a background ˙American scenery with its mountains, streams, rivers, lakes, limestone caverns and forests, visited by roving Indians and inhabited by fierce panther cats.

Suppose:—No one had presented the life and customs of New York, Philadelphia and the surrounding country from which one may restore with truth features and conditions of a time long past, of more interest today than they could have been at the time they were written—recurring epidemics of yellow fever with suggested measures for its treatment, hospitals and prisons with need of reform, city houses with "repose and splendour, pictured walls, glossy hangings, gilded sofas, mirrors . . . from ceiling to floor, carpets of Tauris, spotless and transcendent brilliancy of coverlets and napkins," suburban summer country villas, recently made clearings with clay-plastered cabins, the well-pole, worm-fence and hayrick, difficulties of stagecoach travel over almost impassible

---

1. Brown, Literary Magazine and American Register, in Pattee, *The First Century of American Literature,* 1770-1870, 192-3.

roads, stagecoaches carried across rivers on flatboats in times of flood, a stageboat accustomed twice a day to cross New York Bay to Staten Island, then on by stagecoach and ferry to Perth Amboy in New Jersey, mail service and travel between America and Europe, English, German, French, Italian, Irish, Greek immigrants arriving with their Old World prejudices and their continued attachment to their friends and estates in Europe, "ten thousand French in this city (Philadelphia), fugitives from Marat and from St. Domingo," negroes in their Northern occupations, "A British packet would shortly sail from New York," "Zehel Hackney was master . . . of a fishing smack, and voyaged sometimes to New York" from Portsmouth in New Hampshire, "At Cape Francois we found a ship which transported us . . . to Richmond in Virginia," "Our scheme was, for the most part, a patriarchal one. Each farmer was surrounded by his sons and kinsmen."

Suppose:—No one had regarded the mysterious happenings and reports puzzling his countrymen, such as religious hallucinations, mania, spontaneous combustion, ventriloquism, good and evil spirits, demons and genii, sleep-walking and dreams.

Suppose:—No one had written treatises on scores of cultural themes, like music, painting, the value of the pen and books, learning a language, geography, general knowledge and the United States Government.

Suppose:—No one had showed the way to the full-orbed historical tales of Cooper, Scott, Prescott, who wrote the *Conquest of Mexico* and the *Conquest of Peru,* and Parkman, who wrote *France and England in North America,* both surely having in mind or in hand Brown's "sketched plans of three distinct epic poems, one on the discovery of America, another on Pizarro's conquest of Peru, and a third on Cortez's expedition to Mexico" (Dunlap).

Suppose:—No one had illustrated the transformation of mind and character before Irving, Poe and Hawthorne.

Suppose:—No one had upheld the rights of women in this country, treading the path before the following: Catharine Maria Sedgewick (1789-1867) who conducted a school for girls for fifty years and wrote many stories, among them, *A New England Tale* (1822), her first book of fiction, *Redwood* (1824) and *The Poor Rich Man and the Rich Poor Man* (1826), which takes over the idea of Brown's unfinished story of the rich girl and the poor girl; and Lydia Maria Child (1802-1880), who, among her numerous books, wrote the *History of the Condition of Women in All Ages and Nations* (1835).

Suppose:—No one had travelled Indian-file, almost alone, before those early writers on Indian affairs, among whom were Lydia Maria Child, mentioned above, who wrote *Hobomok* (1824), an Indian story; and Lydia Huntly Sigourney (1791-1865), who, among her fifty-three volumes, wrote *Traits of the Aborigines of America, Pocahontas and other Poems* (1841) and *Letters to Young Ladies* (1833).

Suppose:—No one had elevated magazine editorship, type of contributors and criticism, when few writers did or would write above a mediocre average, except Dennie with his *Port Folio*. From 1799 until his death, with but slight intermissions, Brown edited his own magazines and wrote much of the material in them himself. They were an American review, a literary journal and general depository of history, politics and science of the young Republic. Brown paved the way for the great editors a few years later, among whom were Alexander and Edward Everett, Richard Henry Dana, Bryant, Poe, Whittier, Lowell, Edward F. Tyrrel and William Henry Channing, and for the best magazines, among which were (or are) *The North American Review,* established five years after his death, *Harper's Magazine* (1817), *The Mercury* (1822), *The Dial* (1840), organ of the Transcendentalists, Emerson, Alcott, Thoreau, Parker, Fuller, of which Margaret Fuller Ossoli (1810-1850) was the first editor, which was, perhaps, the most like Brown's magazines. She wrote *Art, Literature, and the Drama, Papers on Literature and Art* (1846), in which she mentions Brown, quoted heretofore, and *Woman in the Nineteenth Century* (1845). Also, *The Nineteenth Century,* which had a survey of his works in its first issue, January, 1848, and *The Atlantic* (1857). On the centenary of Brown's death, 1910, *The Dial* published an article comparing Brown and Irving. Magazines of this type which later gave estimates of Brown and his works are—*The North American Review* (1819), *Fortnightly Review* (1878), *The Century* (1883), *The Atlantic Monthly* (1888), *Cornhill Magazine* (1902), *The Critic* (1905), *The*

Bookman (1907), *The Sewanee Review* (1910), *The Mentor Magazine* (1916).

Suppose:—No one in America had dared to write as a profession, setting standards for creative literature and urging a national literature separate from England's. Following in Brown's footsteps, William Ellery Channing recommended an original literature: "Remarks on a National Literature" in his *Discourses* (1834).

For all these accomplishments and many others, Brown suffered the opposition usual to inventors and innovators and has since been too much considered but an ordinary short link in a literary chain. He was a prolific writer in various fields of literature and noteworthy in most of them and ought not be misesteemed.

When one reflects that Brown wrote all his novels before his thirtieth year, with self-impelled rapidity and without the aid of critical advice, he can understand something of the personality of the man who pursued a literary profession in spite of censure and sacrifices, laid the foundations for a national fiction, stimulated in his countrymen the love of purposeful literature and encouraged some of the new generation to adopt it as a profession. Cut off when he began to gauge his own powers and to control his almost unbridled imagination, Brown left a sure indication of the possible achievements of which he was capable. He was not permitted to attain the heights which seemed accessible to such uncommon talents, such restless energy and such powerful inspiration and aspiration. Not even Hawthorne or Cooper shows so great latent original genius. He was the herald of those whose works received world-wide recognition. American literature began with Charles Brockden Brown.

Two explicit, almost contradictory, estimates of Brown were made by Scott and his biographer Lockhart. It is gratifying, to say the least, to learn what Scott thought of one from whom he had benefited. Samuel G. Goodrich, the notable editor, publisher and author, while visiting in Edinburgh, in 1824, fourteen years after Brown's death, was invited by Lockhart to a dinner attended by Scott, his wife, his son Charles, Blackwood, Robinson and a few others, Miss Edgeworth coming in opportunely to call. After some discussion of authors, the conversation came upon Cooper's *Pioneers,* and Lockhart said,

"Mr. Cooper is a man of genius: no one can deny that; but it seems to me that Brockden Brown was the most remarkable writer of fiction that America has produced. There is a similarity in his style to that of the Radcliffe school, and in the tone of mind of Godwin's *Caleb Williams;* but in his machinery, he is highly original. In his display of the darker passions, he surpasses all his models."[1]

To which Sir Walter answered: "That may be true, but it is neither a wholesome nor a popular species of literature. It is almost wholly ideal; it is not in nature; it is in fact contrary to it. Its scenes, incidents, characters, do not represent life: they are alien to common experience. They do not appeal to a wide circle of sympathy in the hearts of mankind. The chief emotion that it excites is terror or wonder. The suggestive manner of treating every subject, aims at keeping the mind constantly on the rock of uncertainty. This trick of art was long ago exhausted. Brown had wonderful powers, as many of his descriptions show; but I think he was led astray by falling under the influence of bad examples, prevalent at his time. Had he written his own thoughts, he would have been, perhaps, immortal: in writing those of others, his fame was of course ephemeral."[2]

This judgment, viewed in retrospect one hundred twenty years after it was spoken, seems fairly accurate. Scott was born the same year as Brown, 1771. He wrote his first novel in 1814, at age forty-three, when fiction was well established and after he had several renowned predecessors in the field, with whom he might compare, including Brown, either to avoid errors or to follow excellencies. Brown wrote when fiction was dubiously thought of as a kind of writing and completed his six novels between his twenty-eight and thirty-first years, with no good example to whom to look for guidance. It is to be deplored that he died so young in the midst of his powers. Scott's criticism was made at age fifty-three, having written about a score of novels himself, associating with many writers and benefiting from literary criticism both in the Edinburgh and the London magazines.

"To Mr. Brown his country is indebted both for the quantity and quality of his literary productions. It is said that his published

1. Goodrich, *Recollections of a Lifetime,* II, 203.
2. *Ibid.,* II, 204.

writings would amount to twenty-four volumes."[1]

"In passion, in the ugly realism of powerful scenes, in speculative pathology, in pictures of Indian life, and in analysis of motives that stir men's souls, Brown made a distinctive contribution to American literature. . . . His struggle for American literary independence was notably successful. And the essential quality of his genius will endure."[2]

Emphatically is it true, as was pointed out by E. P. Whipple many years ago, that—

"With all his faults, Brown does not deserve to be the victim of the bitterest irony of criticism, that, namely, of not being considered worth the trouble of a critical examination. His writings . . . have that vitality which comes from the presence of genius, and a little stirring of the ashes under which they are buried would reveal sparks of genuine fire."[3]

"We see we have omitted honoured names in this essay. We have not spoken of Brown, as a novelist by far our first in point of genius and instruction as to the soul of things. . . . 'Brown, man of the brooding eye, the teeming brain, the deep and fervent heart; if thy country prize thee not and hast almost lost thee out of sight, it is that her heart is made shallow and cold, her eye dim, by the pomp of circumstance, the love of gross outward gain. . . . As there is more soul thou wilt be more sought, and many will sit down with thy Constantia to the meal and water on which she sustained her full and thoughtful existence.' . . . Brown's high standard of the delights of intellectual communion and friendship correspond with the fondest hopes of early days. But in the relations of real life, at present, there is rarely more than one of the parties ready for such intercourse as he describes,"[4] wrote Mrs. Ossoli.

The closing paragraph of this work will relate the words of Nathaniel Hawthorne, a contemporary of Brown for the last six years of his short life, who probably read Brown's novels with zest as the most outstanding fiction, during his boyhood years.

"In niches and on pedestals around about the hall stood the statues or busts of men who in every age have been rulers and demigods in the realms of imagination and its kindred regions."

1. Simpson, *The Lives of Eminent Philadelphians*, 152.
2. Clark, Introduction to *Edgar Huntly*, XX, XXII.
3. Whipple, *American Literature*, 29.
4. Ossoli, *Literature and Art*, Part II, 142, 149-50.

Thus began Hawthorne in describing the literary section in "The Hall of Fantasy."[1] He lists Homer, Aesop, Dante, Ariosto, Rabelais, Cervantes, Shakespeare, Spenser, Milton, and Bunyan, that chiefly attracted his eye, and then concludes with the two sentences following.

"Fielding, Richardson, and Scott occupied conspicuous pedestals. In an obscure and shadowy niche was deposited the bust of our countryman, the author of Arthur Mervyn."

Among what a glorious company of rulers and demigods in the realm of imaginative writings does Hawthorne associate Charles Brockden Brown!

---

1. Hawthorne, "The Hall of Fantasy," in *Mosses from an Old Manse,* 196-211.

Bibliography

OF THE WORKS OF

CHARLES BROCKDEN BROWN

The Rhapsodist. A series of essays in "The Columbian Magazine" of Mathew Carey. Philadelphia, April, 1789.

Alcuin: a Dialogue on the Rights of Women. 16 mo. T. and J. Swords, No. 99 Pearl Street, New York, 1798 (1797, Foley). The Advertisement was signed by E. H. Smith. This work was slightly revised and reprinted in "The Weekly Magazine" of Philadelphia (March 17-April 7, 1798) as *The Rights of Women.* The *Alcuin* quoted by Dunlap (1815) must have been from the Philadelphia Dialogue, as was the London edition of the work as *The Paradise of Women* (1822).

Alcuin; a dialogue . . . a type-facsimile reprint of the first edition, printed in 1798; with an introduction by LeRoy Elwood Kimball and photogravure reproductions of portraits of Charles Brockden Brown and Elihu Hubbard Smith. New Haven, Carl & Margaret Rollins, 1935. 250 copies printed. (L. C.)

The Man at Home, in "The Weekly Magazine of Original Essays, Fugitive Pieces, and Interesting Intelligence," conducted by James Watters of Willing's Alley, 1798-9. *The Man at Home* ran through thirteen numbers (February 3-April 28, 1798). Volume I, p. 288, contained the first three pages of *Sky-Walk* and on p. 318 was explained the title; in Volume II, June 16, 1798, appeared Chapter I of *Arthur Mervyn* and in Volume III, August, 1798-April, 1799, *Arthur Mervyn* was continued.

Wieland; or, the transformation. An American tale. (Four lines of poetry.) Copy-right secured. (Device.) New York. Printed by T. and J. Swords, for H. Caritat, 1798. 2 p. 1., 298 p. 17½ cm. "Advertisement" signed "C. B. B." (3 vols.) Reprinted in London, 1811. 12°. (L. C. and Wegelin.)

Wieland; or, the Transformation. An American tale. (By C. B. B., i. e. C. Brockden Brown.) New York. 1798. 12°. (Brit. Mus. Cat.)

Wieland; or, the Transformation: a romance. 3 vols. 12 mo. 15s. Colburn, Nov. 10 (1810). (Eng. Cat. of Books.)

Wieland; or, The transformation. By C. B. Brown. Boston, S. G. Goodrich, 1827. XXIV, IV, (5) - 227 p. 19 cm. On title page: The novels of C. B. B., (v. I) Wieland . . . with a memoir of the author. (L. C.)

Wieland; or, The Transformation. By C. B. Brown. New York, Philadelphia (etc.). W. Taylor and co., 1846. 2 p. 1., 124 p. 23½ cm. Library of Standard Romance, no. 1. (L. C.)

Wieland; or, The transformation. By C. B. Brown . . . With a memoir of the author. Philadelphia, M. Polock, 1857. 251 p. 19 cm. (L. C)

Wieland; or, The Transformation. By Charles Brockden Brown. Philadelphia: David McKay, Publisher, 23 South Ninth Street, 1889. American Classic Series.

Brown, Charles Brockden, *Wieland;* or, The Transformation, Together with Memoirs of Carwin the Biloquist. A Fragment . . . edited with an Introduction by Fred Lewis Pattee. New York, Harcourt, Brace and Company, c 1926. American Authors Series.

Ormond; or the Secret Witness. By the author of Wieland; or The Transformation. New York: Printed by G. Forman, for H. Caritat.—1799.—(Facsimile of title page of first edition, in *Ormond,* American Book Company.)

Ormond; or, the Secret Witness. 3 vols. 12 mo., 15s. Colburn, Nov. 10 (1810). (Eng. Cat. of Books.)

Ormond; or, The secret witness. By C. B. Brown. (Uniform ed.) New York, Philadelphia (etc.). W. Taylor & co., 1846. 144 p. 23½ cm. Library of Standard Romance, no. 2. (L. C.)

Ormond; or, The secret witness. By C. B. Brown. Philadelphia, M. Polock, 1857. 270 p. 19 cm. (L. C.)

Ormond or The Secret Witness—Clara Howard or the Enthusiasm of Love. Being volume VI of Charles Brockden Brown's novels. Philadelphia, David McKay, Publisher, 1887. (Ormond, p. 284; Clara Howard, p. 285-410.)

Ormond By Charles Brockden Brown. Edited, With Introduction, Chronology, And Bibliography by Ernest Marchand, Stanford University. American Book Company, New York (etc.), c 1937. American Fiction Series.

Arthur Mervyn; or, Memoirs of the year 1793, by the author of Wieland and Ormond; or the secret witness. Philadelphia, H. Maxwell, 1799. 2 v. 18 cm. Vol. 2, imprint: New York, Printed and sold by G. F. Hopkins, 1800. Preface signed C. B. B. (L. C.)

Arthur Mervyn: a tale. 3 vols., 12 mo. 12s. Nov. '02. New ed., 3 vols., 12 mo. 16s. 6d. Newman, June, '21. (London, 1803, Vols. I & II.) (Eng. Cat. of Books.)

Arthur Mervyn; or, Memoirs of the year 1793. . . . Philadelphia, M. Polock, 1857. 2 v. 19 cm. (L. C.)

Arthur Mervyn; or, Memoirs of the Year 1793. By Charles Brockden Brown. (Quotation from Hawthorne.) Philadelphia: David McKay, Publisher, 1022 Market Street. (n.d.) American Classic Series. (1889).

Edgar Huntly; or, Memoirs of a Sleep-Walker. By the Author of Arthur Mervyn, Wieland, Ormond, etc. . . . Philadelphia: Printed by H. Maxwell, No. 3 Lititia Court, and sold by Thomas Dobson, Asbury Dickins, and the Principal Booksellers. 1799. 3 vols., 8 vo, pp. 250-252-193. At the end of Volume III is "Death of Cicero, a Fragment," pp. 48, probably written by Brown. Introduction signed C. B. B. (Wegelin.) The Henry E. Huntington Library and Art Museum, San Marino, California, has this first edition copy: Philadelphia, 1799, 3 vols. of Charles Brockden Brown's Edgar Huntly, and the Philadelphia 1801 ed. 3v.

Edgar Huntley; or, Memoirs of a sleepwalker: a novel. 3 vols., 12 mo. 10 s. 6 d. Nov. '02. (Eng. Cat. of Books.)

Edgar Huntley; or, The Sleep Walker. By Charles Brockden Brown. London: Henry Colburn and Richard Bentley. New Burlington Street; Bell and Bradfute, Edinburgh; Cumming, Dublin; and Galinani, Paris. 1831. London: Printed by A. & R. Spottswoode, New-Street-Square. XVI, 258 p. 17½ cm. (L. C.)

Edgar Huntley; or, The Sleep Walker. By C. B. Brown. London, R. Bentley, 1842. 1 p. 1., (V) - XVI, 258 p. 17 cm. Standard Novels, no. 10. (L. C.)

Edgar Huntley; or, the Sleep-Walker, and Schiller's Ghost Seer. 1 vol., 2 s. 6 d. 1831, etc. 8°. (R. Bentley's Standard novels and romances.) (Another edition.) The Parlour Library. Vol. 157, 1847, etc. 8°. (Eng. Cat. of Books.)

Edgar Huntley; or, the Sleep walker, a Tale. 12 mo., n. e., 2 s. 6 d. 1849; 1s. T. Hodgson, 1857. (Eng. Cat. of Books.)

Edgar Huntley; or, Memoirs of a sleepwalker. By C. B. Brown. Philadelphia, M. Pollock, 1857. 263 p. 19 cm. (L. C.)

Edgar Huntly or Memoirs of a Sleep-Walker By Charles Brockden Brown, edited with an introduction by David Lee Clark. The Macmillan Company, New York, 1928. The Modern Readers' Series.

Clara Howard, in a Series of Letters. Philadelphia, A. Dickins, 1801. 16 mo. pp. IV, 5-268. (Wegelin.)

Clara Howard; or, the Enthusiasm of Love. Philadelphia, 1801. London, 1806.

Philip Stanley; or, The Enthusiasm of Love. A novel. 2 vol. Lane, Newman & Co., London, 1807. 12° (Brit. Mus. Cat.) A republication of *Clara Howard.*

Clara Howard; or, the enthusiasm of love. By C. B. Brown. Philadelphia, M. Polock, 1857. 126 p. 19 cm. (L. C.)

Jane Talbot, A Novel. By the author of Arthur Mervyn, Wieland, Ormond, Edgar Huntly, and Clara Howard. Philadelphia, 1801. 12 mo, pp. 346. (Plate by Seymour.)

Jane Talbot: a novel. Plate. 16 mo. New York and Philadelphia, 1804. (Foley.)

Jane Talbot: a novel. 2 vols. 12 mo. 8 s. Lane, April, 1804. (London.) (Eng. Cat. of Books.)

Jane Talbot. By C. B. Brown. Philadelphia, M. Polock, 1857. 237 p. 19 cm. (L. C.)

Jane Talbot by Charles Brockden Brown. Being volume V of Charles Brockden Brown's Novels. Philadelphia, David McKay, Publisher. 1887. (p. 237.)

Novels of Brown reprinted by S. G. Goodrich, Boston, 1827, in uniform edition, with a memoir of the author. 7 vols in 6 books. 19 cm. (Brit. Mus. Cat.) The Bibliotheca Americana states that *Arthur Mervyn* sold for $2.00 and each of the other novels for $1.00 each.

Standard Novels. (Published by Colburn and Bentley and afterwards by R. Bentley.) 129 vols. London. 1831-1856. 8°. Imperfect; wanting vol. 34, 56. (Brown's first four novels are included among Bentley's Standard Novels.) (Brit. Mus. Cat.)

The Parlour Library. (Another edition of Standard Novels.) Vol. 1-208, 210-231, 233-247, 269, 274, 275. London, 1847— (63). 8°. Brit. Mus. Supplement, 1900.

Novels of Charles Brockden Brown, with memoir of author, complete and revised edition published by M. Polock, Philadelphia, No. 406 Commerce Street, 1857. 6 v. 19 cm. ea. $1. (Bibliotheca Americana gives prices—Arthur Mervyn, $1.50, ea. of the others $.75.)

Complete Edition of the Novels and Fragments of C. B. Brown. Edited and published by David McKay, 1022 Market Street, Philadelphia, 1887. 6 vols. 8 mo. hf. vel. $18.00. Edition limited to 500 sets. With a memoir of the author. American

Classic Series. (The last two paragraphs are from Dunlap's
Life. . . . The American Catalogue of Books lists the same.
My copy of *Wieland* has the date 1889.)

Charles Brockden Brown's Novels. (With a memoir of the author.)
6 vol. D. McKay, Philadelphia, 1887. 8°. (Brit. Mus. Cat.)

Works of C. B. Brown, complete in 6 vols. 8 vo. 94 s. 6 d. (Sold
only in sets.) Philadelphia, 1887. (Eng. Cat of Books)

Carwin, the biloquist, and other American tales and pieces. By
C. B. Brown, author of Wieland, Ormond, Arthur Mervyn,
&c., &c. London, H. Colburn and co., 1822. 3 v. 18 cm.
Contents:—v.1, Carwin, the biloquist. Stephen Calvert.—v.2,
Stephen Calvert.—v.3, Stephen Calvert. Jessica. The scribbler.
(L. C.)

Carwin, the biloquist, and other American tales and pieces. 3 vol.
London, 1822. 12° (Brit. Mus. Cat.)

Carwin, the Biloquist, and other American Tales and Pieces. By
C. B. Brown, . . . London, H. Colburn and co., 1822. 12 mo.
(Foley.)

(See also Wieland, Primary Sources.)

*An address to the government of the United States, on the cession
of Louisiana to the French;* and on the late breach of treaty
by the Spaniards; including the translation of a memorial, on
the war of St. Domingo, and cession of the Mississippi to
France, drawn up by a French counsellor of state. (Brown.)
Philadelphia, J. Conrad & co.; Baltimore, M. and J. Conrad &
co., (etc., etc.) 1803. 8 vo. 1 p. 1., 92 p. 23½ cm. (Anon.)
(L. C.)

(Same as Above.) A new edition, revised, corrected and improved.
. . . Philadelphia, J. Conrad & Co.; Baltimore, M. and J.
Conrad & co.; (etc., etc.). 1803. 1 p. 1., 56 p. 22 cm.

A view of the soil and climate of the United States of America;
with supplementary remarks upon Florida, on the French
Colonies of the Mississippi and Ohio, and on Canada, and on
the Aboriginal Tribes of America, by the Comte de Volney
(1803). Translated with occasional remarks, by C. B. Brown.
With maps and plates. Philadelphia, published by J. Conrad &
co.; Baltimore, M. and J. Conrad & co., (etc., etc.,) Printed by
T. and G. Palmer, 1804. XXVIII, 446p. 2 fold.pl., 2 fold.maps
(incl. front.) 21½ cm. Supplement (p. (265)-439). (Foley
omitted "with occasional—(1803)" and gave "12 mo., Phila.,
1804.")

The Monthly magazine, and American review. . . . v. 1-3; Apr.
1799-Dec. 1800. New York, printed by T. and J. Swords,

1800. 3 v. 21½ cm. C. B. Brown, editor. Continued as the American review, and literary journal. (L. C.) It contained E. Huntly, A Fragment; Thessalonica, A Roman Story; Memoirs of Stephen Calvert; a series of six original letters taken from what Paul Allen in the Allen-Dunlap biography called Brown's first romance; A Lesson in Concealment, or Memoirs of Mary Selwyn; The Trials of Arden; and two of the Dialogues of the Living.

The American review, and literary journal, for 1801-1802 . . . v. 1-2. New York, printed by T. and J. Swords, 1801-02. 2 v. 23 cm. quarterly. Edited by C. B. Brown and others. 8 issues. No more published. (L. C.)

The Literary magazine, and American register. . . . v. 1-8; Oct. 1803-Dec. 1807. Philadelphia, J. Conrad & Co.; (etc., etc.) 1804-08. 8 v. 22 cm. monthly. C. B. Brown, editor, (who was also the principal contributor—Foley). No more published. (L. C.) Vol. 2, Sept. 1805, p. 554, contained "A Sketch of the Life and Character of John Blair Linn," who had died Aug., 1804; also, an elegy "Philadelphia," written during the prevalence of the yellow fever 1797, both written by Brown. "Carwin, the Biloquist" ran as a serial from November, 1803, monthly till May, 1804. Then three other installments appeared irregularly,—in July, 1804, February and March, 1805,— "To be continued," but was not. Foley said, "8 volumes, 8 vo. Philadelphia, 1803-1807."

The American register, or general repository of history, politics and science. v. 1-7; 1806/7-1810. Philadelphia, C. & A. Conrad & co.; Baltimore, Conrad, Lucas & co.; (etc., etc.) 1807-11. 7 v. 23 cm. Editors: v.1-5, C. B. Brown—v.6-7, R. Walsh. No more published. (L. C.)

The British treaty of Commerce and navigation, concluded Dec. 31, 1806. (Philadelphia? 1807?) 86 p. 21½ cm. (C. B. Brown, 1771-1810, supposed author.) (L. C.) The pamphlet berates Thomas Jefferson on his attitude toward the treaty.

The British treaty with America; with an Appendix of State Papers which are now first published. 8 vo. London, 1808. (Signed C. B. B., i.e. C. Brockden Brown.—Foley.)

An Address to the Congress of the United States, on the utility and justice of restrictions upon Foreign Commerce, with reflections on Foreign Trade in general and the future prospects of America. 8 vo. Philadelphia, 1809. (Pamphlet.) (Signed C. B. B., i.e. C. Brockden Brown.—Foley.)

Valerian, a Narrative Poem . . By John Blair Linn. With a sketch of the life and character of the author (by C. B. Brown.—Foley). Brown also wrote a biographical sketch of J. B. Linn for Dennie's *Port Folio* in 1809. Foley says, "With a memoir of the author by C. B. Brown, 4°. Philadelphia, 1805."

Beauties of Tom Brown, by C. H. Wilson. Edited, with a biography of the author, by C. B. Brown. 12 mo. London, 1810. (Foley.)

A Compleat System of Geography; containing a Topographical, Statistical, and Descriptive Survey of the Earth. A prospectus of the two volumes was actually issued shortly before Brown's death. (Philadelphia, 1809?) Paul Allen was hired to finish it. The volumes and manuscript are lost or in hiding.

History of American Painting. By Samuel Isham. N. Y. 1805. Contributions by C. B. Brown, pp. 11, 17-24, 43-9, 72-9, 186-9.

A Treatise on Rome During the Age of the Antonines was left uncompleted at Brown's death in 1810.

Manuscript Letters in the Historical Society of Pennsylvania and in the Library of Congress. Letters to and from Thomas Jefferson, copied in Chapter I, are in the Library of Congress.

Other Writings by Brown, included in William Dunlap's Life of Brown . . . Selections from the rarest of his printed works, from his original letters and from his manuscripts before unpublished—are the following:
Volume I.
2-18   Title, Preface, Biography of Brown.
18-20   The Relations, Dependence, and Connection of the several parts of knowledge: from Brown's Journal.
21-31   Address on the Objects of the Institution of the Belles Lettres Club, and address on Language.
31-39   Decisions of Cases by Brown as President of the Law Society.
40-58   Biography of Brown.
58-70   Brown's Letter to "Dear R.," concerning his visit to Rockaway.
71-107   Part of Alcuin.
108-169   Romance of Sophia and Jessy: unfinished.
170-258   Sketches of a History of Carsol: unfinished.
258-261   Biography of Brown.
262-396   Sketches of the History of the Carrils and Ormes: unfinished.
Volume II.
3-68   Biography of Brown, Letters to his Brothers con-

cerning yellow fever and comments on his novels: from his Journal.
68-85 Treatises to the United States Government.
85-90 Brown's Death.
91-122 A Few Letters from C. B. Brown to his Friends.
122-139 Two Dialogues: the first on Music, the second on Painting, as a female accomplishment, or mode of giving subsistence and fortune: both unfinished.
140-169 Segnior Adini: a fragment.
170-199 Thessalonica, A Roman Story: a fragment.
200-263 Memoirs of Carwin, the Biloquist: a fragment.
264-273 The Scribbler: a fragment.
274-472 Memoirs of Stephen Calvert: a fragment.

BIBLIOGRAPHY

Primary Sources

Brown, Charles Brockden, *Wieland; or, The Transformation.* David McKay, Philadelphia, 1889.

Brown, Charles Brockden, *Wieland, or The Transformation* together with Memoirs of Carwin the Biloquist . . . edited by Fred Lewis Pattee. Harcourt, Brace and Company, N. Y., c 1926.

Brown, Charles Brockden, *Ormond.* Edited . . . by Ernest Marchand. American Book Company, N. Y., c 1937.

Brown, Charles Brockden, *Arthur Mervyn;* or, *Memoirs of the Year* 1793. David McKay, Philadelphia, n.d. (1889).

Brown, Charles Brockden, *Edgar Huntly or Memoirs of a Sleep-Walker.* Edited . . . by David Lee Clark, The Macmillan Company, N. Y., 1928.

Brown, Charles Brockden, *Clara Howard; or, The Enthusiasm of Love.* Bound with Ormond, p. 285-409. David McKay, Philadelphia, 1887.

Brown, Charles Brockden, *Jane Talbot.* M. Polock, Philadelphia, 1857.

Selected List of Secondary Sources

Ainsworth, William Harrison, *Life and Adventures of Mervyn Clitheroe.* George Routledge and Sons, London, (1858).

Allibone, S. Austin, *Critical Dictionary of British and American Authors* (1854). 5 vols. Lippincott, Phila., 1902.

Angoff, Charles, *A Literary History of the American People.* Alfred A. Knopf, N. Y., 1931.

Appleton's Cyclopaedia of American Biography. Appleton, N. Y., 1898-1899.

Atlantic Monthly 61:710-714, May, 1888. "Charles Brockden Brown."

Austen, Jane, *Sense and Sensibility.* Nelson & Sons, n.p., n.d.

Bates, Katherine Lee, *American Literature.* Macmillan, N. Y., 1898.

Beers, Henry Augustin, *Century of American Literature, 1776-1876.* Henry Holt & Co., N. Y., 1901.

Beers, Henry Augustin, *Initial Studies in American Letters.* The Chautauqua Press, N. Y., 1891.

Beers, Henry Augustin, *Studies in American Literature.* Jacobs, Phila., 1900.

Birkhead, Edith, *The Tale of Terror: A Study of the Gothic Romance.* Constable & Company, London, 1921.

Blackwood's Magazine 6: 554-561, Feb. 1820. "Of the Writings of Charles Brockden Brown and Washington Irving."

Blackwood's Magazine XVI: 305+, Sept. 1824. "American Writers I"; XVI: 421-426, Oct., 1824. "American Writers II." (Signed X. Y. Z.)

Bleecker, Ann Eliza, *The Posthumous Works of Ann Eliza Bleecker, in Prose and Verse. . . .* T. and J. Swords, N. Y., 1793.

Bookman 12: 379, 1900. "First Books of P. B. Shelley" by Luther S. Livingston.

Bookman 25: 3-5, Mar., 1907. "Charles Brockden Brown—First American Novelist."

Boyesen, Hjalmar Hjorth, *Literary and Social Silhouettes.* Harper & Bros., N. Y., 1894.

Brandes, Georg Morris Cohen, *Main Literary Currents in the Nineteenth Century Literature.* "German Romanticism." Macmillan, N. Y., 1906.

Bronson, Walter C., *A Short History of American Literature.* D. C. Heath & Co., N. Y., 1900.

Brooke, Stopford A., *English Literature with Chapters on American Literature by George R. Carpenter.* Macmillan, N. Y., 1900.

Burney, Frances, *Evelina: The History of a Young Lady's Entrance into the World.* A. L. Burt Co., N. Y., n.d.

Burton, Richard, *Forces in Fiction.* Bobbs Merrill, Indianapolis, Ind., 1902.

Burton, Richard, *Literary Leaders of America.* Chautauqua Press, N. Y., 1903.

Cairns, William B., *Selections from American Authors, 1607-1800.*

Macmillan, N. Y., 1909.

Carpenter, George Race, *American Prose*. Macmillan, N. Y., 1898.

Century 26: 289, 1883. "The Native Element in American Fiction" by James Herbert Morse.

Chambers, Robert, *Cyclopaedia of English Literature*. New ed. by David Patrick. 3 vols. Lippincott, n.p., n.d.

Clark, David Lee, *Brockden Brown and the Rights of Women*. University of Texas Bulletin No. 2212. Austin, Texas, 1922.

Clark, David Lee, *Charles Brockden Brown: A Critical Biography*. Columbia University Press, (N. Y., 1923).

Cleveland, Charles Dexter, *A Compendium of American Literature*. Barnes, N. Y., 1859.

Cooper, James Fenimore, *The Pioneers; or, The Sources of the Susquehanna*. Macrae Smith Co., Phila., n.d.

Cornhill Magazine 86: 494, 1902. "Alms for Oblivion" and "Minor Writings of Charles Brockden Brown" by Richard Garnett.

Critic 47: 228-231, 1905. "Criticism with Portrait of Charles Brockden Brown."

Cross, Wilbur L., *The Development of the English Novel*. Macmillan, N. Y., 1923.

Dana, Richard Henry Sr., *Poems and Prose Writings*. Russell, Odiorne, and Co., Boston, 1833.

Dana, Richard Henry Sr., *Poems and Prose Writings*. 2 vols. Baker and Scribner, N. Y., 1850.

Day, Thomas, *The History of Sandford and Merton*. Harper, N. Y., 1856.

Dial 48: 109-110, Feb. 16, 1910. "The Centenary of America's First Novelist" by Annie Russell Marble.

Dickens, Charles, *Bleak House*. Complete illustrated ed. Getz and Buck, Phila., 1854.

Dunlap, William, *Memoirs of Charles Brockden Brown, the American Novelist*. Henry Colburn & Co., London, 1822.

Dunlap, William, *The Life of Charles Brockden Brown; together with Selections from the Rarest of his printed works. . . .* 2 vols. James P. Parke, Phila., 1815.

Duyckinck, Everet A. and George L., *Cyclopaedia of American Literature* (1855). 2 vols. C. H. Davis, Phila., 1875.

Edgeworth, Maria, *Ormond, A Tale* (1817). Macmillan, N. Y., 1903.

Erskine, John, *Leading American Novelists*. Holt, N. Y., 1910.

Fielding, Henry, *The History of Tom Jones: A Foundling* (1749). 2 vols. G. Bell and Sons, London, 1925.

Foley, Patrick Kevin, *American Authors, 1795-1895. A bibliography.* P. K. Foley & Co., Boston, 1897.

Fortnightly Review 30: 399-421, Sept., 1878. "Brockden Brown" by George Barnett Smith.

Gates, Lewis Edwards, *Studies and Appreciations.* Macmillan, N. Y., 1900.

Gentleman's Magazine 81: 364, April, 1811.

Godwin, William, *An Enquiry Concerning Political Justice . . .* (1793). Edited by Raymond A. Preston. 2 vols. Knopf, N. Y., 1926.

Godwin, William, *Caleb Williams; or, Things As They Are* (1794). Routledge, London, 1903.

Godwin, William, *Fleetwood; or, The New Man of Feeling.* Richard Bentley, London, 1832.

Godwin, William, *Mandeville; A Tale of the Seventeenth Century in England.* 3 vols. Longman, Hurst, Rees, Orme, and Brown, London, 1817.

Godwin, William, *St. Leon: A Tale of the Sixteenth Century.* Henry Colburn and Richard Bentley, London, 1831.

Goodrich, Samuel Griswold, *A Pictorial History of the United States.* J. H. Butler & Co., Phila., 1877.

Goodrich, Samuel Griswold, *Recollections of a Lifetime, or Men and Things I Have Seen.* 2 vols. Miller, Orton and Mulligan, N. Y., 1857.

Griswold, Rufus Wilmot, *The Prose Writers of America* (1846). Parry & Macmillan, Phila., 1856.

Halleck, Reuben Post, *History of American Literature.* American Book, Chic., 1911.

Hamilton, Clayton, *A Manual of the Art of Fiction.* Reprint . . of "Materials and Methods of Fiction" (1908). Doubleday, Doran, Garden City, 1930.

Hart, John Seely, *Manual of American Literature.* Eldredge, Phila., 1872.

Hawthorne, Julian, and Others, *The Masterpieces and the History of Literature.* 10 vols. E. R. DuMont, N. Y., 1903.

Hawthorne, Nathaniel, *Mosses from an Old Manse.* Houghton, Mifflin, Boston, c 1882.

Hawthorne, Nathaniel, *The House of the Seven Gables.* Houghton, N. Y., n.d.

Hawthorne, Nathaniel, *The Marble Faun, or, The Romance of Monte Beni.* Ticknor & Fields, Boston, 1860.

Hawthorne, Nathaniel, *The Scarlet Letter.* Houghton, N. Y., n.d.

Hemstreet, Charles, *Literary New York.* G. P. Putnam's Sons,

N. Y., 1903.

Herringshaw, Thomas William, *Encyclopedia of American Biography*. American Publishing Association, Chic., 1898.

Higginson, Thomas Wentworth, *Carlyle's Laugh and Other Surprises*. "Charles Brockden Brown." Houghton, Mifflin, Boston, 1908.

Higginson, Thomas Wentworth, and Boynton, Henry Walcott, *A Reader's History of American Literature*. Houghton, Mifflin, N. Y., c 1903.

Holliday, Carl, *English Fiction from the fifth to the twentieth century*. Century, N. Y., 1912.

Irving, Washington, *Tales of a Traveller*, by Geoffrey Crayon, Gent. Putnam's Sons, N. Y., 1868.

Just, Walter, *Die Romantische Bewegung in der Amerikanischen Literatur: Brown, Poe, Hawthorne*. Mayer and Muller, Berlin, 1910.

King, Moses, *Philadelphia and Notable Philadelphians*. Moses King, N. Y., 1901.

Lanier, Sidney, *The English Novel: A Study in the Development in Personality*. Charles Scribner's Sons, N. Y., 1897.

Lewis, Matthew Gregory, *The Monk* (1794). Edited by E. A. Baker. E. P. Dutton & Co., N. Y., 1907.

Lewisohn, Ludwig, *Expression in America*. Harper, N. Y., 1932.

Lockhart, John Gibson, *Life of Sir Walter Scott*. Thomas Y. Crowell, Boston, n.d.

Long, William J., *English Literature*. Ginn & Co., Boston, 1909.

Loshe, Lillie Deming, *The Early American Novel*. Columbia University Press, 1907.

Lossing, Benson John, *Eminent Americans*. Hurst, N. Y., 1883.

Lytton, Edward Bulwer, *A Strange Story* (1862) and *The Haunted and the Haunters*. Lippincott, Phila., 1891.

Lytton, Edward Bulwer, *Devereux* (1829) and *The Disowned* (1828). Caxton Edition. Vol. 2. Routledge, London, 1895.

Lytton, Edward Bulwer, *Falkland* (1827) and *Zicca*. Caxton Edition, Routledge, London, 1895.

Lytton, Edward Bulwer, *Pelham* (1828) and *Eugene Aram*. Edition deluxe. The O. C. Brainard Pub. Co., Boston, n.d.

Lytton, Edward Bulwer, *Pelham* (1828) and *Lucretia* (1846). Caxton Edition. Routledge, London, 1853.

Lytton, Edward Bulwer, *Zanoni* (1842). Little, Brown, Boston, 1930.

Marble, Annie Russell, *Heralds of American Literature*. "Charles Brockden Brown and Pioneers in Fiction." University of

Chicago Press, Chic., 1907.

Marryat, Captain (Frederick), *Jacob Faithful*. Peter Fenelon Collier, N. Y., n.d.

Matthews, Brander, *American Literature*. Scribner, N. Y., n.d.

Matthews, Brander, *An Introduction to the Study of American Literature*. American Book, Chic., 1911.

Matthews, Brander, *Aspects of Fiction and Other Ventures in Criticism*. Harper, N. Y., 1896.

Maturin, Charles Robert, *The Fatal Revenge; or, The Family of Montorio. A Romance.* J. Clements, London, for the Romancist and Novelist's Library, 1840.

Maurois, André, *Ariel, The Life of Shelley*. Appleton-Century, N. Y., 1939.

Melville, Herman, *Pierre or the Ambiguities* (1852). Knopf, N. Y., 1930.

Melville, Herman, *Redburn: His First Voyage* (1849). The St. Botolph Society, Boston, c 1924.

Mentor Magazine. Serial No. 106, Vol. 4, No. 6, May 1, 1916. "American Pioneer Prose Writers: Charles Brockden Brown."

Mitchell, Donald Grant, *American Lands and Letters*. 2 vols. Scribner's Sons, N. Y., 1901.

Mitchell, S. Weir, *The Red City, A Novel of the Second Administration of President Washington*. Century, N. Y., 1909.

Modern Language Association of America, Publications of, XLV, December, 1930. "Shelley and Charles Brockden Brown" by Eleanor Sichels.

Modern Language Notes, XLV, 18-20. "Scott on Cooper and Brockden Brown" by Tremaine McDowell. The University of Minnesota, January, 1930.

More, Paul Elmer, *The Drift of Romanticism*. Shelburne Essays, VIII. Houghton, Mifflin, N. Y., 1913.

Moulton, Charles Wells, *Library of Literary Criticism of English and American Authors*. 8 vols. H. Watkin, N. Y., 1901.

Nation 99: 577-578, November 12, 1914. "Early American Realism" by Carl Van Doren.

Newcomer, Alphonso Gerald, *American Literature*. Scott, Foresman, N. Y., 1901.

Nichol, John, *American Literature: A Historical Sketch, 1820-1880*, in Encyclopaedia Britannica; also, published separately, by Adam and Charles Black, Edinburgh, 1882.

Nineteenth Century 1: 290-1, January, 1848. "The Heart Broken" by George Lippard.

North American Review 9: 58-77, June, 1819. "The Life of Charles

Brockden Brown . . . By William Dunlap. Reviewed by Giulian C. Verplank.

Oberholtzer, Ellis Paxton, *Literary History of Philadelphia.* Jacobs, Phila., 1906.

Ossoli, S. Margaret Fuller, *Papers on Literature and Art.* Two Parts, in One Volume. Fowlers and Wells, N. Y., 1852.

Painter, Franklin Vergelius Newton, *Introduction to American Literature.* Sibley & Co., Boston, 1903.

Pancoast, Henry Spackman, *Introduction to American Literature.* Holt., N. Y. 1898.

Parrington, Vernon Louis, *The Romantic Revolution in America,* 1801-1860. Vol. 2., Main Currents in American Thought. Harcourt, Brace, N. Y., c 1927.

Pattee, Fred Lewis, *American Writers: A Series of Papers Contributed to Blackwood's Magazine,* 1824-1825. By John Neal. Edited with Notes and Bibliography. Duke University Press, Durham, N. C., 1937.

Pattee, Fred Lewis, *History of American Literature.* Silver, Burdette & Co., N. Y., 1909.

Pattee, Fred Lewis, *The First Century of American Literature,* 1770-1870. Appleton-Century, N. Y., 1935.

Peacock, Thomas Love, *Crotchet Castle, The Misfortunes of Elphin, Gryll Grange.* "The Tale of a Shadow" in Gryll Grange. Chapter XXXIV. Routledge, London, n.d.

Peacock, Thomas Love, *Peacock's Memoirs of Shelley.* Edited by H. F. B. Brett-Smith. Henry Frowde, London, 1909.

Perry, Bliss, *The American Mind.* Houghton, Mifflin, Boston, 1912.

Poe, Edgar Allen, *Prose Tales.* Century, N. Y. 1901.

Poe, Edgar Allan, *The Complete Poetical Works of Poe, including essays on poetry.* Burt, N. Y., 1904.

Prescott, Frederick C., and Nelson, John H., *Prose and Poetry of the Revolution: The Establishment of the Nation,* 1765-1789. Crowell, N. Y., c 1925.

Prescott, William Hickling, *Miscellaneous Essays: Biographical and Critical.* "Memoir of C. B. Brown, the American Novelist," originally in Spark's Library of American Biography. Lippincott, Phila., 1875.

Radcliffe, Mrs. Ann, *The Mysteries of Udolpho*s *A Romance.* Routledge, London, n.d.

Railo, Eino, *The Haunted Castle.* Routledge, London, 1927.

Raleigh, Walter, *The English Novel from the earliest time to Waverley.* Scribner's Sons, N. Y., 1894.

Ransome, Arthur, *History of Storytelling.* "Poe and the New Technique." "William Godwin." Stokes, N. Y., 1910.

Reeve, Clara, *The Old English Baron*. Cassell's Nat'l Library, London, 1888.

Repplier, Agnes, *Philadelphia: the Place and the People*. Macmillan, N. Y., 1907.

Richardson, Charles Francis, *American Literature, 1607-1885*. Putnam's Sons, N. Y., 1887-1888.

Ridpath, John Clark, *The Ridpath Library of Universal Literature*. 25 vols. Fifth Avenue Library Society, N. Y., 1906.

Saintsbury, George Edward Bateman, *The English Novel*. J. M. Dent, London, 1913.

Scharf, John Thomas, and Westcott, Thompson, *History of Philadelphia, 1609-1884*. 3 vols. L. H. Everts & Co., Phila., 1884.

Schiller, Johann Christoph Friedrich von, *Gesämliche Werke*. Sechster Band. Der Geisterseher. Zeite 395-532. Hempel, Berlin, 1868-1874.

Schiller, Johann Christoph Friedrich von, *The Ghost-Seer; or, Apparitionist*. Bell, London, 1912.

Scott, Sir Walter, *Waverley* (1814); *Guy Mannering* (1815); *The Antiquary* (1816); *Old Mortality* (1816); *Rob Roy* (1817). Edition of 1829. Collier, N. Y., n.d.

Sears, Lorenzo, *American Literature in the Colonial and National Periods*. Little, Boston, 1902.

Sedgewick, Catharine Maria, *A New England Tale and Miscellanies*. J. C. Derby, N. Y., 1854.

Shelley, Mary Godwin (Mrs. P. B.), *Frankenstein; or, The Modern Prometheus*. Dutton, N. Y., n.d.

Shelley, Mary Godwin (Mrs. P. B.), *Shelley Memorials*. Smith, Elder and Co., London, 1857.

Shelley, Mary Godwin (Mrs. P. B.), *Tales and Stories*. Now First Collected with an Introduction by Richard Garnett. Paterson's Treasure-House of Tales. Paterson, London, 1891.

Shelley, Mary Godwin (Mrs. P. B.), *The Last Man*. 3 vols. Colburn, London, 1826.

Shelley, Percy Bysshe, *The Complete Poetical Works of P. B. Shelley*. Edited by Wm. M. Rossetti. Scribner, N. Y., 1910.

Shelley, Percy Bysshe, *The Prose Works of P. B. Shelley from the Original*. Vol. I, Vol. II editions . . . by Richard Herne Shepherd. 2 vols. Vol. I, "Zastrozzi," "St. Irvyne," etc. Chatto and Windus, London, 1888.

Simms, William Gilmore, *Martin Faber; The Story of a Criminal*. J. & J. Harper, N. Y., 1833.

Simonds, William Edward, *Student's History of American Litera-*

ture. Houghton, Mifflin, N. Y., 1909.

Simpson, Henry, *The Lives of Eminent Philadelphians now deceased*. William Brotherhead, Phila., 1859.

Smiley, James Brady, *Manual of American Literature*. American Book, Chic., 1905.

Smyth, Albert H., *Philadelphia Magazines and Their Contributors, 1741-1850*. Robert M. Lindsay, Phila., 1892.

Sparks, Jared, *Library of American Biography* (1834-1838). 10 vols. "Charles Brockden Brown" by Wm. H. Prescott. Harper, N. Y., 1902.

Stedman, Edmund Clarence, and Hutchinson, E. M., *A Library of American Literature*. 11 vols. Webster, N. Y., 1888-1890.

Stephen, Leslie, *English Literature and Society in the Eighteenth Century*. Putnam's Sons, N. Y., 1904.

Stephen, Leslie, *The History of English Thought in the Eighteenth Century*. 2 vols. Putnam's Sons, N. Y., 1902.

Sterne, Laurence, *A Sentimental Journey through France and Italy*. Cornell Series. Burt, N. Y., n. d.

Symonds, John Addington, *History of English Literature*. "Romantic Movement." Houghton, Mifflin, N. Y., 1902.

Tappan, Eva March, *Short History of England's and America's Literature*. Houghton, Mifflin, N. Y., 1906.

Taylor, George Robert Stirling, *Mary Wollstonecraft: a Study in Economics and Romance*. Lane, N. Y., 1911.

The Chautauquan 64: 99-102, September, 1911. "Charles Brockden Brown" and extracts from *Wieland*.

The Fred Newton Scott Anniversary Papers: Contributed by former Students and Colleagues . . . 1888-1926. "Mad Shelley" by Ernest Sutherland Bates, p. 117-140; "Shelley and the Novels of Brown" by Melvin T. Solve, p. 141-156. The University of Chicago Press, Chicago, Illinois, c 1929.

The Sewanee Review, XVIII, 431-443. "Brockden Brown and the Novel" by Warren Barton Blake. Longmans, Green and Co., N. Y., October, 1910.

Trent, William Peterfield, *History of American Literature, 1607-1865*. Appleton, N. Y., 1903.

Trent, William Peterfield, and Erskine, John, *Great American Writers*. Holt, N. Y., c. 1912.

Trent, William Peterfield, and Wells, Benjamin Willis, *Colonial Prose and Poetry*. 3 vols. Crowell, N. Y., 1901.

Tuckerman, Henry T., *Essays: Biographical and Critical; or, Studies of Character* (1856). Phillips, Sampson & Co., Boston, 1857.

Tyler, Moses Coit, *History of American Literature*. 2 vols. Putnam's

Sons, N. Y., 1904.

Vilas, Martin Samuel, *Charles Brockden Brown*: *A Study of Early American Fiction*. Free Press Association, Burlington, Vermont, 1904.

Volney, C. F., *A View of the Soil and Climate of the United States of America.* Translated . . . by C. B. Brown. J. Conrad & Co., Phila., 1804.

Waldegrave, A Novel. (Anon.) 3 vols. Colburn, London, 1829.

Walpole, Horace, *The Castle of Otranto.* Edited by Prof. I. Gollancz. Chatto and Windus, London, 1907.

Warner, Charles Dudley, *Library of World's Best Literature.* 46 vols. J. A. Hill & Co., N. Y., 1896.

Warner, Charles Dudley, *Washington Irving.* "Preliminary." Houghton, Mifflin, Boston, 1881.

Wegelin, Oscar, *Early American Fiction,* 1774-1830, being a compilation of the titles of American novels, written by writers born or residing in America, and published previous to 1831. Wegelin, Stamford, Conn., 1902.

Wendell, Barrett, *A Literary History of America.* Scribner, N. Y., 1901.

Wendell, Barrett, and Greenough, Chester Noyes, *History of Literature in America.* Scribner, N. Y., 1904.

Westminster Review 157: 687-691, 1902. "St. Leon—a forgotten novel" by W. B. Wallace.

Whipple, Edwin Percy, *American Literature.* Houghton, Mifflin, N. Y., 1903.

Whittier, John Greenleaf, *The Conflict with Slavery, Politics and Reform, The Inner Life Criticism*: "Fanaticism." Houghton, Mifflin, Boston, 1889.

Wieland, Christoph Martin, *The Adventures of Don Sylvio de Rosalva* (1764). Introduction by Ernest A. Baker. Routledge, London, n.d.

Wilkins, Frederic H., *Early Influence of German Literature in America.* Vol. III, No. 2, p. 137-9, 170, 171. Americana Germanica, 1899.

Wilson, Margaret Oliphant, *Literary History of England in End of Eighteenth and Beginning of Nineteenth Century.* 3 vols. "William Godwin." Macmillan, N. Y., 1902.

Wollstonecraft, Mary, *A Vindication of the Rights of Woman.* Edited by Mrs. Henry Fawcett. New ed. T. Fisher Unwin, London, 1891.

Woodberry, George Edward, *America in Literature.* Harper, N. Y., 1903.

Woodberry, George Edward, *Literary Memoirs of the Nineteenth Century.* "Charles Brockden Brown," reprinted from the Atlantic Monthly, May, 1888. Harcourt, N. Y., 1921.

Woodberry, George Edward, *Makers of Literature.* Macmillan, N. Y., 1900.

Index

psychoanalyst, 30, 44; marriage, 32; unhealth, 33; suicide
thoughts, 34; death, 34-35; character, 36-37; literary profession,
39-40; novels, 43, 59, 79-80, 171; letter to Thomas Jefferson
and his reply, 45-46; first American novelist, 52-53; Gothecisms,
80-82; German influence, 83-84; fiction-writing, 357; place in
American literature, 344-363
Bulwer-Lytton, Edward, 287-291
Burney, Frances, 55, 66-67
Burton, Richard, 53, 350

Characters in Brown's novels, 194-198
Clara Howard, 116, 172-176, 200
Clark, David L., 132, 190, 362
Cooper, James F., 208, 215-217
Cross, Wilbur L., 227, 299

Dana Sr., Richard H., 9, 11, 208, 217-222, 227
Davis, John, 210-211
Day, Thomas, 87, 135
Defoe, Daniel, 27, 55, 68-70, 134-135
De la Fayette, Madame, 60-61
Dennie, Joseph, 21, 47
Description, 326-332
Dickens, Charles, 56, 294-296
Dunlap, William, 8-9, 17, 20, 24, 36, 38-39, 41, 121, 154, 170-171,
188, 191-192, 346, 347

Edgar Huntly, 24, 40, 44, 52, 109, 116, 117, 120, 155-171, 175,
193, 199, 202, 209, 210, 231, 233-234, 235
Edgeworth, Maria, 56, 270-272
Erskine, John, 104

Fielding, Henry, 42-43, 50-51, 56, 57, 61-63, 136, 146, 346-347
Franklin, Benjamin, 1, 4, 27, 91
Freneau, Philip, 5, 213-214

Gates, Lewis E., 102
Godwin, William, 56, 57, 58, 87, 89, 114, 120, 146, 147, 149,
164, 243-252
Goethe, Johann W., 40
Goldsmith, Oliver, 55, 65-66
Goodrich, Samuel G., 49, 154, 360-361
Griswold, Rufus W., 110, 190

21314